FOCALITY AND EXTENSION IN KINSHIP
ESSAYS IN MEMORY OF HAROLD W. SCHEFFLER

FOCALITY AND EXTENSION IN KINSHIP
ESSAYS IN MEMORY OF HAROLD W. SCHEFFLER

EDITED BY WARREN SHAPIRO

PRESS

Published by ANU Press
The Australian National University
Acton ACT 2601, Australia
Email: anupress@anu.edu.au
This title is also available online at press.anu.edu.au

 A catalogue record for this book is available from the National Library of Australia

ISBN(s): 9781760461812 (print)
          9781760461829 (eBook)

This title is published under a Creative Commons Attribution-NonCommercial-NoDerivatives 4.0 International (CC BY-NC-ND 4.0).

The full licence terms are available at creativecommons.org/licenses/by-nc-nd/4.0/legalcode

Cover design and layout by ANU Press. Cover photograph of Hal Scheffler by Ray Kelly.

This edition © 2018 ANU Press

To the memory of Harold Walter Scheffler,
a compassionate man of the highest scholarly standards

Contents

List of Figures and Tables ix
Acknowledgements xiii
Contributors xv

Part I.

Introduction: Hal Scheffler's Extensionism in Historical Perspective and its Relevance to Current Controversies 3
Warren Shapiro and Dwight Read

Part II. The Battle Joined

1. Hal Scheffler Versus David Schneider and His Admirers, in the Light of What We Now Know About Trobriand Kinship 31
   Warren Shapiro

2. Extension Problem: Resolution Through an Unexpected Source . . 59
   Dwight Read

Part III. Ethnographic Explorations of Extensionist Theory

3. Action, Metaphor and Extensions in Kinship 119
   Andrew Strathern and Pamela J. Stewart

4. Should I Stay or Should I Go? Hunter-Gatherer Networking Through Bilateral Kin 133
   Russell D. Greaves and Karen L. Kramer

5. Properties of Kinship Structure: Transformational Dynamics of Suckling, Adoption and Incest 177
   Fadwa El Guindi

6. Of Mothers, Adoption and Orphans: The Significance of Relatedness in a Remote Aboriginal Community 203
   Victoria Katherine Burbank

Part IV. Extensionist Theory and Culture History

7. Enhancing the Kinship Anthropology of Scheffler with Diachronic Linguistics and Centricity 227
   Patrick McConvell

Part V. Questioning Extensionist Theory

8. Why Do Societies Abandon Cross-Cousin Marriage? 263
   Robert Parkin

9. Toward Reinvigorating an Ethnolinguistic Approach to the Study of 'Kin Terms': A View from Nascent-based Zuni Relational Terminology 303
   Linda K. Watts

Part VI. Extensionist Theory and Human Biology

10. Creeping Plants and Winding Belts: Cognition, Kinship, and Metaphor 327
    Bojka Milicic

11. Kinship in Mind: Three Approaches 343
    Doug Jones

12. Do Women Really Desire Casual Sex? Analysis of a Popular Adult Online Dating/Liaison Site........................369
    Michelle Escasa-Dorne and William Jankowiak

Index 395

List of Figures and Tables

Figure 1. Kin-term product of L (aunt) and K (daughter) is M (cousin) 76

Figure 2a. Structure of the American/English kinship terminology... 81

Figure 2b. Structure of the Shipibo kinship terminology 81

Figure 3. Minimal graph of the positions, indicated by boxes, making up a Family Space 84

Figure 4. Graph of the Family Space with a self position for reference.. 88

Figure 5. Kin-term product of *parent* with itself generates a new kin-term relation, *parent* o *parent*, given the name *grandparent*... 90

Figure 6. Primary kin terms and structural equations for generating the American/English terminology........................ 97

Table 1. Pumé sample description 149

Figure 7. Pumé postmarital dispersal patterns from natal village for first marriage 149

Figure 8. Pumé postmarital residence patterns 150

Figure 9. Postmarital residential stability for Pumé residents....... 151

Figure 10. Reassessment of hunter-gatherer postmarital patterns from Marlowe (2004: 280)............................. 153

Figure 11. Schematic model of a married hunter-gatherer's relationship to bilateral kin under two common residential patterns 159

Figure 12. Brothering matrilateral parallel cousins 183

Figure 13. Template 1 and Hypothetical Case 1, employed
in UREP project as a kinship elicitation method 187

Figure 14. Ethnographic interview conducted by Raneen,
student researcher on the project 187

Figure 15. Depiction of mother–son and text illustrating incest
and avoidance 189

Figure 16. Depiction by author representing kin positions
in the *sura* to demonstrate prohibitions 190

Figure 17. Somebody's mother's sister is equivalent to that
somebody's mother, and reciprocally, some woman's sister's
descendant is equivalent to that woman's own descendant 229

Figure 18. Somebody's father's brother is equivalent to that
somebody's father, and reciprocally, some man's brother's
descendant is equivalent to that man's own descendant 229

Figure 19. Somebody's mother's brother's child is equivalent
to that somebody's own brother's child, and reciprocally,
somebody's father's sister's child is equivalent to that
somebody's father's sibling 230

Table 2. Common equations and paths of semantic change
in Australian kinship terms 231

Figure 20. Transitional polysemy 232

Figure 21. Extension in change: Whistler on Wintun 233

Figure 22. Murdock on Wintun kinship system reconstruction 234

Figure 23. Whistler vs. Murdock on Wintun kinship system
reconstruction 234

Figure 24. A diachronic sequence of Omaha skewing in Australia . . 239

Figure 25. *Kaala* MB > Cross-cousin/spouse. 240

Figure 26. *tyuwa+: Woman's child > FZC > Sister-in-law 241

Figure 27. Aluridja grandparents 243

Figure 28. *tyamu MF > MF + FF in Western Desert. 244

Figure 29. *Kami* and *Kaparli* 244

Figure 30. Kariera to Aluridja. 245

Figure 31. *Katya* brother > son 248

Figure 32. The change brother > son 250

Figure 33. Zuni household-group roles. 311

Figure 34. Image schema of the domain of plants and the domain of clothing 335

Figure 35. The mind as a chapel 337

Table 3. Descriptives of the sample. 375

Table 4. Type of encounter sought by males and females 379

Table 5. Sexual content of profiles 381

Table 6. Females' motives listed by sexual orientation. 382

Acknowledgements

First and foremost, I must acknowledge the hard work of my fellow contributors, and their tolerance in putting up with my multitudinous editorial remarks. Here, Dwight Read deserves special mention for directing my focus, especially in the Introduction. Peter Wood of the National Association of Scholars provided encouragement, and helped pay for the cost of copyediting. Ray Kelly sent me the cover photo for this book. Jan Simpson, Hal's widow, supplied additional encouragement, as did Mary Smith, her secretary. Christine Huber of the ANU Press Humanities and Arts Editorial Board was especially helpful and supportive during the early stages in the preparation of this volume. Finally, Carolyn Brewer did an outstanding job of copyediting.

Warren Shapiro
Brooklyn, New York
July 2017

Contributors

Victoria Katherine Burbank is Professor Emerita of Anthropology at the University of Western Australia. She is currently engaged in a cooperative research project on the sociocultural context in which Aboriginal adolescents make or do not make decisions about their sexuality. Her publications include *An Ethnography of Stress: The Social Determinants of Health in Aboriginal Australia*; *Fighting Women: Anger and Aggression in Aboriginal Australia*; and *Aboriginal Adolescence: Maidenhood in an Australian Community*.

Michelle Escasa-Dorne is Assistant Professor of Anthropology at the University of Colorado, Colorado Springs. She received her PhD in anthropology from the University of Nevada, Las Vegas in 2012. Her areas of research interest are human behavioural ecology, human reproduction and sexuality, maternal health, and evolutionary medicine. Corresponding areas of geographical interest include the United States, Ecuador and the Philippines.

Russell D. Greaves is a Research Associate with the Peabody Museum of Archaeology and Ethnology at Harvard University, a Consulting Scholar with the American Section of the University of Pennsylvania Museum of Archaeology and Anthropology, and an Adjunct Associate Professor in the Department of Anthropology at the University of Utah. His archaeological background focuses on hunter-gatherer adaptations to varied and changing environments, primarily in the American West, as well as geoarchaeology and taphonomic research. He has carried out ethnographic and ethnoarchaeological fieldwork with hunter-gatherers in Venezuela, comparative studies with related horticulturalists, as well as with Maya agriculturalists in the Yucatan Peninsula of Mexico.

Fadwa El Guindi is currently Retiree Anthropologist at the University of California, Los Angeles. She was formerly Distinguished Professor and Head of the Department of Anthropology at Qatar University. She has carried out ethnographic research in Nubia, Qatar, and among the Valley Zapotec in Mexico. She is the author of *Veil: Modesty, Privacy and Resistance*; *By Noon Prayer: The Rhythm of Islam*; *Visual Anthropology: Essential Method and Theory*; and *The Myth of Ritual: A Native's Ethnography of Zapotec Life-Crisis Rituals*, among other books, as well as dozens of articles and book chapters on these and related topics. She has also produced several award-winning visual ethnographies. She was recently elected as a Fellow of the World Academy of Art and Science.

William Jankowiak has authored over 115 academic and professional publications. He is the author of *Sex, Death, and Hierarchy in a Chinese City: An Anthropological Account* and a 2016 book-length overview (with Robert Moore) on the Chinese family (Polity Press). He is also editor of *Romantic Passion: A Universal Experience?*, *Intimacies: Love and Sex Across Cultures*, and (with Dan Bradburd) *Stimulating Trade: Drugs, Labor and Colonial Expansion*. In addition, he has edited two special journal volumes: *Well Being, Family Affections, and Ethical Nationalism in Urban China* (*Journal of Urban Anthropology*), and (with Jiemin Bao) *Polygynous Society: Ethnographic Overviews from Five Cultures* (*Ethnology*). His current writing projects include completing *City Days, City Nights: The Individual and Social Life in a Chinese City*. Presently, he is completing an ethnography of a Mormon Fundamentalist polygamous community.

Doug Jones is Associate Professor of Anthropology at the University of Utah, Salt Lake City, Utah. He is the author of *Sexual Attractiveness and the Theory Of Sexual Selection* (1996), co-editor (with Bojka Milicic) of *Kinship, Language, and Prehistory: Per Hage and the Renaissance in Kinship Studies* (2011), and author of articles on kinship, language, cognition, and evolutionary theory (among other topics). His work on kinship aims to revise our understanding of the evolved psychology of kinship to accommodate what's uniquely human about human kinship.

Karen L. Kramer is Professor of Anthropology at the University of Utah. She is a behavioural ecologist with research interests in the evolution of human sociality, life history, childhood and cooperative breeding. She has worked with a group of Amazonian foragers, as well as the Yucatec Maya of Mexico, for the past 25 years.

CONTRIBUTORS

Patrick McConvell holds adjunct positions at The Australian National University and Western Sydney University. He is a linguistic anthropologist who has worked mainly among northern Aboriginal people. With Helen Gardner he co-authored *Southern Anthropology – a History of Fison and Howitt's Kamilaroi and Kurnai*, a volume dealing with the collaborative work of A.W. Howitt and Lorimer Fison on Aboriginal people in the last two decades of the nineteenth century. He has been involved in regional language centre development and land and native title claims of Aboriginal people, as well as a chief investigator in the AustKin project, whose aim is to compile an online database on kinship and social category terms in Aboriginal languages. A volume he co-edited with several other scholars, *Skin, Kin and Clan: The Dynamics of Social Categories in Indigenous Australia*, is shortly to be published by ANU Press.

Bojka Milicic is Associate Professor/Lecturer of Anthropology at the University of Utah. She has carried out fieldwork in her native Croatia, as well as in India and the Peruvian Andes. She has published widely in anthropological journals in such areas as kinship, symbolism and the origin of language and is co-editor (with Doug Jones) of *Kinship, Language, and Prehistory: Per Hage and the Renaissance in Kinship Studies*.

Robert Parkin is Departmental Lecturer in Social Anthropology in the School of Anthropology and Museum Ethnography at the University of Oxford. He has carried out fieldwork in India. He is the author of *The Munda of Central India: An Account of Their Social Organization*; *Kinship: An Introduction to the Basic Concepts*; *The Dark Side of Humanity: The Work of Robert Hertz and its Legacy*; and *Louis Dumont and Hierarchical Opposition*. More recently he has carried out fieldwork on local politics, religion and identity in western Poland.

Dwight Read is Distinguished Emeritus Professor of Anthropology at the University of California, Los Angeles. His PhD, from the same university, is in mathematics. He has carried out ethnographic research among the Ju'hoansi (formerly known as !Kung San) in Botswana. He is the author of *Artifact Classification: A Conceptual and Methodological Approach*, *How Culture Makes Us Human: Primate Social Evolution and the Formation of Human Societies*, and dozens of articles on kinship, mathematical formalisation of cultural constructs, classification and quantitative methods in archaeology, and human evolution, as well as co-author (with Murray Leaf) of *Human Thought and Social Organization: Anthropology on a New Plane*.

Warren Shapiro is Emeritus Professor of Anthropology at Rutgers University. He has carried out fieldwork among Aboriginal people in northeast and central Arnhem Land. He is the author of *Social Organization in Aboriginal Australia*; *Miwuyt Marriage: The Cultural Anthropology of Affinity in Northeast Arnhem Land*; *Partible Paternity and Anthropological Theory: The Construction of an Ethnographic Fantasy*; and dozens of articles on kinship and the history of anthropology. This is his second 'go' at editing a *Festschrift*, having compiled *On the Generation and Maintenance of Person: Essays in Honour of John Barnes*, as a Special Issue of *The Australian Journal of Anthropology* in 1990. He also co-edited (with Uli Linke) *Denying Biology: Essays on Gender and Pseudo-Procreation*. He is a recent recipient of the Albert Nelson Marquis Lifetime Achievement Award.

Pamela J. Stewart (Strathern) and **Andrew Strathern** are a wife-and-husband research team at the University of Pittsburgh and codirectors of the Cromie Burn Research Unit there. They have published over 50 books and hundreds of articles and book chapters on their research. Their most recent co-authored books include *Witchcraft, Sorcery, Rumors, and Gossip*, *Kinship in Action: Self and Group*; *Peace-Making and the Imagination: Papua New Guinean Perspectives*; *Ritual: Key Concepts in Religion*; *Working in the Field: Anthropological Experiences across the World*; and *Breaking the Frames: Anthropological Conundrums*. They are also the series editors of the Palgrave Studies in Disaster Anthropology.

Linda K. Watts is Associate Professor of Anthropology at the University of Colorado, Colorado Springs. She is the author of *The Social Semiotics of Relational Terminology at Zuni Pueblo*, as well as various journal articles offering an ethnolinguistic approach to Zuni relational terminology—all based on her extensive research in the American Southwest.

Part I.

Introduction: Hal Scheffler's Extensionism in Historical Perspective and its Relevance to Current Controversies

Warren Shapiro and Dwight Read

Hal Scheffler was one of the world's great anthropologists and, without question, its foremost authority on human kinship. These considerations in themselves would be quite enough to merit a collection of essays in his memory, but his work also touches upon certain larger issues in our appreciation of the human condition, as well as current social controversies.

It was for his *extensionist* position on *kinship terminologies*—what he liked to call 'systems of kin classification'—that he was best known. In a nutshell, Scheffler would come to raise two questions: (1) What is the primary meaning—what he called the *focus*—of kinship terms like English 'mother', 'father', 'brother', 'sister' etc.? (2) By what procedures do people *extend* these meanings from their foci to others? His answers, based upon meticulous analyses of kinship terminologies in various parts of the world, were that focal membership is supplied mostly by nuclear family relationships, from which relationships it is *extended* to people—even to things—outside the nuclear family; and that these extensions are accomplished by ordered sets of rules that have considerable generality cross-culturally.

The man himself[1]

Harold Walter Scheffler was born in St Louis, Missouri, United States, on 24 October 1932, to working-class parents, William C. Scheffler, an office clerk, and Dorothy C. Scheffler (née Briggs), a housewife. He registered at Southeast Missouri State College in 1952, moving to the University of Missouri the following year. Hal's quest for his first degree was interrupted by service in the United States Army (1954–55) but, after an honourable discharge, he returned to his studies, receiving a BA in anthropology and sociology in 1956. He went on to postgraduate study at the University of Chicago, from which he received an MA in anthropology in 1957. Remaining at Chicago in pursuit of a doctorate, and with support from the Carnegie Corporation and the Fulbright Foundation, he carried out 18 months of fieldwork on the island of Choiseul in what was then the British Solomon Islands, 1960–61. This research was the basis of his PhD dissertation (1963), under the joint supervision of Fred Eggan and David Schneider. A revision of this work was published by the University of California Press two years later as *Choiseul Island Social Structure* (see below). In the interim Hal taught anthropology at the University of Connecticut and Bryn Mawr College before moving to Yale University the year he received his doctorate. He remained at Yale for four and a half decades, before retiring in 2008. Two years later he began to suffer from Parkinson's disease; he passed away from the associated dementia on 24 July 2015, survived by his wife Jan Simpson, his daughter Mary Lindholm, and a sister, Joan Wiesehan.

Choiseul Island kinship

Scheffler's first publication on kinship, based upon his doctoral dissertation, was his book-length treatment of sociality on Choiseul Island (Scheffler 1965), now part of the independent Solomon Islands. Two things deserve special emphasis in Scheffler's Choiseul analysis. First, there are rich data on distinctions *made by the Choiseulese themselves*. Second, Choiseulese ideas about kinship are not so different from our own.

---

1 We are especially indebted for this personal information from Jan Simpson, Hal's widow, her secretary Mary Smith and Ray Kelly, his Yale colleague.

With regard to the first point, even though more distant kin are superficially classed with one's parents, siblings, children, and other close kin, these latter are said, in native parlance, to be the 'true' members of their respective kin classes (Scheffler 1965: 75, 81). The singling out of focal membership by words translatable as 'true' (or 'real') is typical of a very large number of kinship terminologies throughout the world—a point Hal Scheffler would repeatedly make in subsequent analyses (e.g. Scheffler 1972b: 354; Scheffler 1973: 766; Scheffler and Lounsbury 1971: 43) and which probably supplies the most frequently encountered evidence in the ethnographic literature for the extensionist position (Shapiro 2016, 2017). With regard to the second point, Scheffler notes an expression in the Choiseul language that he translates as 'kin', which implies that they idiomise kinship in ways that are entirely familiar to English speakers.

Towards a general theory of human kinship

A year after the publication of his Choiseul analysis, Hal Scheffler put forward nothing less than a general statement on human kinship. In this important but neglected essay Scheffler lays the groundwork for his general position on human kinship, to wit:

> [D]ifferent societies perceive 'the facts of procreation' differently … but they differ within certain clear limits and have … the same formal organization. All such theories provide for the existence of a 'genitor' and a 'genetrix' (parents), their offspring, who are related to one another (as 'siblings'), and … for the existence of what may be called genealogical connections [among] such persons … Kinship as a cultural phenomenon has to do first and foremost with any particular person's … relationships with other persons as these are … conceived to result from what his culture takes to be 'the facts of procreation.' From the point of view of any particular [person], he, his mother, and her brother do *not* constitute a procreatively or socially self-sufficient unit. [Instead h]is father … is as necessary to his existence as is his mother … so … *it is the triad self-genitor-genetrix that should be considered to be the 'atom' of kinship. For it is that unit which 'generates' the elements 'brother' and 'sister' … Clearly, then, the elementary relations of a kinship system are parent/child, husband/wife, and sibling/sibling … These are of course the constituent relationships of the nuclear family* [emphasis added] (Scheffler 1966: 83–84).

The competing position to which Scheffler alludes is that of Claude Lévi-Strauss (1963: 31–54), who maintained that the irreducible elements in human kinship are those between two men, one of whom has married the other's sister, and the son of the first man. While Lévi-Strauss's schema has been challenged statistically (Ryder and Blackman 1970), Scheffler's formulation fits virtually all the data at our command.

Adoption in the New Hebrides

Scheffler's concern with kinship semantics, especially his emphasis on the distinction between focal and nonfocal members of a kin class, is developed in his article on adoption in the northern New Hebrides (Scheffler 1970b). Much earlier, based on his own fieldwork, William H.R. Rivers (1915) had argued that among some of the peoples of the New Hebrides:

> the relationship of parent and child does not come into existence by the facts of procreation and parturition, but [rather] it is such acts as the payment of the midwife, the first feeding of the child, or the planting of a tree on the occasion of a birth that determine who are to be the parents of the child (Rivers 1915: 700).

Scheffler provides a counterargument based on earlier ethnographic literature on the area. He notes that in the pertinent languages one's procreative parents are distinguished from others in their kin classes by a lexical marker translatable as 'the real (or main) thing', 'very', and 'undoubted' (Scheffler 1970b: 373)—in short, they enjoy focal status in these classes. He further notes that only the 'real' parents must undergo various taboos, lest harm come to their child. 'Such beliefs and customs,' he adds, 'are virtually incomprehensible unless [the people] presume some sort of substantial and inalienable ... connection between the child and his [or her] genitor and genetrix' (ibid.: 374). Thus, by the end of 1970, Hal Scheffler had presented a general theory of human kinship and illustrated it with detailed analysis of particular ethnographic cases (see also Scheffler 1970a).

INTRODUCTION

The Scheffler/Lounsbury collaboration

The move to Yale played a vital role in the development of Scheffler's thought and hence his career. The anthropology department there had been influenced by eminent linguists such as Edward Sapir, Leonard Bloomfield and George Trager, and linguistics was widely seen to have a rigour that was lacking in much earlier ethnography circa 1950. This move led to Hal Scheffler's collaboration with his senior colleague Floyd Lounsbury consequent upon his—Scheffler's—move to Yale in 1963. At the time Lounsbury was in the process of establishing himself as an important linguist (see especially Lounsbury 1963), and a year later he published the first two of his analyses of a system of kin classification (Lounsbury 1964a, 1964b), followed in the next year by another (Lounsbury 1965). His concern in this latter group of articles was with what he called a 'formal analysis' of the pertinent kinship terminologies—more especially, with stipulating a focal member for each lexically labelled but unmarked kin class and then, by appealing to sets of genealogically based and ordered rules, showing that these rules could account for the allotment of kin terms to particular genealogical positions, including distant ones, as these had been recorded in, or inferred from, the pertinent ethnography. In this sense his argument was *extensionist*, though it was much less attuned to native distinctions than the extensionist position that Hal Scheffler was developing.

The collaboration between Scheffler and Lounsbury led to their jointly authored volume *A Study in Structural Semantics: The Siriono Kinship System* (1971). The Siriono are a group of nomadic hunter-gatherers in the Bolivian Amazon, known to the anthropological world primarily through a monograph by Allan Holmberg (1969). The goal of the Scheffler and Lounsbury project was to provide a formal semantic analysis of a particular kinship terminology, in the sense noted in the preceding paragraph. At the same time they were concerned with wider matters. A key point they noted is that kin terms are *polysemic*, that is that each term has several significata, or meanings, and these significata are semantically related. They provided the English kin term *uncle* as an example of such polysemy. *Uncle* has as one of its meanings 'my parent's brother', but it may also mean 'my aunt's husband', or even 'my grandparent's brother', that is my *great-uncle*. The first meaning can also be expressed, using genealogical dimensions, by the statement 'male consanguineal relative of the first ascending (i.e. the parental) generation and the first degree of collaterality', whereas the third definition excludes the criterion 'first ascending generation' and the second excludes the criterion 'consanguineal'. Hence the second and third meanings are, in this sense, extended versions of the meaning provided in the first definition. Nonetheless, all three meanings have to do with 'uncleness', hence the kin term *uncle* in English is polysemic, that is its several meanings are semantically related.

Because several critics (e.g. D'Andrade 1970; Tyler 1966; Wallace 1965) have argued that this sort of analytical procedure is more reflective of the heads of Scheffler and Lounsbury than those of 'the natives', it is well worth noting here that the latter two take considerable pains to relate their principles to Siriono understandings (Scheffler and Lounsbury 1971: 40–47). Because this concern with native conceptualisation occurs regularly in Scheffler's other writings but not in Lounsbury's, we believe its occurrence in what Hal Scheffler liked to call 'the Siriono book' reflects *his* influence upon his senior colleague, and probably explains why *his* name occurs first in their joint production.

'Social paternity'

Hal Scheffler's analysis of New Hebridean adoption was part of his project to dispel the idea that in certain communities paternity is established not by procreation but by 'social' or performative criteria, an argument put forward not only by Rivers but, as well, by more recent scholars, most notably David Schneider (1984). The most exhaustive treatment of the ubiquity of locally posited notions of biological paternity and the *secondary* status of 'social paternity' can be found in an encyclopedic article in which Scheffler (1973: 749–51) pointed out that the claims for an 'ignorance of physiological paternity' in the Trobriands and among Aboriginal people are without merit. Instead, the reported entry into the mother by a spirit-being is *not* held to *cause* conception, as the 'ignorance' theory holds, but rather is posited to occur at foetal quickening: it thus appears to be a native theory of *vivification* of the foetus.

INTRODUCTION

Baniata kin classification

In his work subsequent to the collaboration with Lounsbury, Hal Scheffler combined his senior colleague's concern with formal analysis with his own emphasis upon explicit native theory. This can be seen in two articles he published in 1972. One of these, based upon his own fieldwork among the Baniata of the Solomon Islands (Scheffler 1972b), is, from the standpoint of anthropological debate, his most important publication. In his Introduction to this analysis he tells us that '[t]he principal aim of this study is to demonstrate the ethnographic [i.e. the psychological] validity, in this instance and others, of positing [rules] of [kin] terminological extension' (ibid.: 350). Scheffler further observes that kin-term product statements (see Read Chapter 2) 'may be used … to specify extended ranges of terms. For example, the people say "the *dare* of my *ae* is my *ae* also," i.e. "my father's brother is my 'father' also…"' (Scheffler 1972b: 350). In other words, the kin-term product of the kin term *dare* ('brother') and the kin term *ae* ('father') is the kin term *ae* ('father'), according to informants, and the extension of the kin term *ae* to the genealogical position occupied by the father's brother is through the kin-term product stipulating that 'the *dare* of my *ae* is my *ae*'. It should be emphasised that *it is the kin-term product rule that determines the application of a kin term to a particular genealogical position beyond primary kin*, not *vice versa*, as conventional genealogical diagrams suggest (Read 2007). Analogous considerations apply to the 'mother' and 'child' terms.

Aboriginal kinship terminologies

Scheffler's other 1972 article was an Afterword to the publication of a manuscript left by Donald Thomson, based upon that anthropologist's fieldwork on the Cape York Peninsula (Scheffler 1972a), and Scheffler's own interviews with Lauriston Sharp, who also worked on Cape York. Both of these ventures culminated in his seminal *Australian Kin Classification* (Scheffler 1978), one of whose chief goals was to counter 'social category' views of Aboriginal sociality. Such views had been common in Victorian theory (e.g. Fison and Howitt 1880; Lubbock 1912: 84 et seq.; Morgan 1877: 50–60), but were subsequently challenged by early twentieth-century scholars, pointing to the apparent ubiquity of the nuclear family among Aboriginal people and the unsustainability of Victorian claims of communal social regimes (e.g. Lang 1905; Malinowski 1913; N. Thomas 1906). But none of the latter had much sophistication in semantic theory.[2]

Australian Kin Classification, we believe, is best viewed as the culmination of the more empirically grounded studies of Aboriginal sociality that appeared in the previous decade.[3] The book begins with a statement of various theories of Aboriginal kinship, including the procreatively based one sometimes espoused by A.R. Radcliffe-Brown (e.g. 1913) as well as various 'social category' perspectives. In order to lay the basis for his chief argument that Aboriginal sociality is indeed kinship based, Hal Scheffler here repeats his 1973 thesis against claims of 'ignorance of physiological paternity' among Aboriginal people. Aboriginal notions of fatherhood, he concludes, are founded upon native appreciations of the reproductive process, though augmented by a spiritual experience at foetal quickening, usually though not always undergone by the presumed genitor.[4] From here he proceeds to a comprehensive and meticulous analysis of the pertinent ethnographic literature that forms the core of the book. His conclusion from all this is that:

> kin-class statuses are the elementary structures of Australian [Aboriginal] social life. Originating in nuclear families and in the genealogical relations [within] them, these statuses are extended to encompass … virtually all social relations within human communities … Beyond this they are extended metaphorically to encompass … social relations between human communities and the community of the Dreamtime [i.e. the mythical] beings. In this way, Australian [Aboriginal] cultures establish a moral community that embraces the cosmos … In postulating a morally ordered universe and in attempting to comprehend it metaphorically, by analogy with the forms of their own social life, [Aboriginal] Australians demonstrate … their intellectual kinship with the rest of [hu]man kind … Dissent from the opinion that 'kinship' is a misnomer for … [Aboriginal] Australian culture is likely now, no less than in the past, to encounter charges of ethnocentrism … and of imposing alien forms on social and cultural categories that it is our first responsibility as anthropologists to comprehend … As it happens, however, some of the concepts by which

---

2   For partial exceptions, see Howitt (1891) and Lang (1905: 49).
3   This is not to say that subsequent work has been without value. But none has the theoretical sweep and scholarly detail of Hal Scheffler's great work.
4   In some areas a distinction is made between the 'finder' and the genitor (Goodale 1971: 137–38; Stanner 1960: 254). For a theorisation of this arrangement, including Christian baptism and other non-Aboriginal examples, see Bloch and Guggenheim (1981) and Shapiro (1988).

[Aboriginal] Australians order their social lives – indeed ... the most fundamental concepts – are not at all alien to us or to the rest of [hu]man kind. Clothed in their own linguistic forms ... [and] elaborated upon in somewhat unusual ways, concepts of kinship are as basic as they are pervasive in [Aboriginal] Australian social life (Scheffler 1978: 530–31).

Wider implications of Hal Scheffler's thought

This last quote is key. Current kinship studies as we write are dominated by what Lounsbury (1969) called 'complete relativism', largely because of the publications and personal influence of David Schneider (e.g. 1968, 1972, 1984), who did indeed argue that kinship, at least outside the West, is a misnomer. As Scheffler lucidly points out (see below), this is disrespectful of our common humanity. In his review of Schneider's 1968 book, Scheffler (1976) was highly critical of Schneider's use of the term 'symbol', upon which Schneider's critique of kinship studies depends. Thus he—Scheffler—refers to 'Schneider's ... casual and unanalyzed use of the word [symbol] in its many ordinary, everyday senses' (ibid.: 85). More generally, Schneider's 'method' was entirely intuitive, unchecked by a concern for intellectual discipline (Fogelson 2001: 41, 53). Consider the following bit of rambling, meant to pass for 'analysis':

> Sexual intercourse is love and stands as a sign of love, and love stands for sexual intercourse and is a sign of it. The two different kinds of love ... are nevertheless both symbols for unity, identity, oneness, togetherness, belonging. Love symbolizes loyalty, faith, support, help, and so forth (Schneider 1968: 52).

We alluded above to another implication of Hal Scheffler's scholarship— one which we consider most important from an intellectual standpoint. We are referring here to his emphasis upon what was once called 'the psychic unity of humankind'. Here special emphasis, we think, should be placed upon his insistence—supported by an enormous mass of evidence— that, apparently everywhere, systems of kin classification are ordered into classes which contain focal and nonfocal members, and that *the focal membership of these classes is constant,* or very nearly so. More particularly, it embraces an individual's mother, father, siblings and children. These people thus everywhere constitute a conceptual unit and in most cases a residential unit as well, at least when the children are young. And in most of those few cases in which such residential unity is absent and the mother resides with her dependent children in the absence of a mate, sometimes augmented by one or more of her siblings, there is nonetheless not only a recognition of fatherhood but, as well, the (presumed) genitor has a special and locally recognised relationship with his children (Gough 1961: 364; Sobo 1993: 147; Stacey 2009: 247). For Scheffler, contrary to the claims of Schneider and his followers, 'the facts of procreation' viewed cross-culturally 'differ only within certain clear limits … What all these [latter] enterprises', he observed, 'have in common is that they would deprive us of any dimensions of human, cross-cultural similarity, other than our symbol-creating capacity, by reference to which cross-cultural differences may be ordered' (Scheffler 1991: 375).

Hal Scheffler and gender studies

Hal Scheffler's work on kinship in itself is a major intellectual accomplishment—surely enough to count him among the most important anthropologists who have ever lived. But his scholarship was not confined to kinship studies. The analysis most pertinent here has to do with gender classification, which he tackled in his 1991 contribution to feminism. Several scholars (e.g. Herdt 1994; Roscoe 1994; W. Thomas 1997) have accepted at face value claims of a 'third sex' in certain nonwestern societies. But here is Scheffler's response:

> Consider [the] claim that in some North American Indian societies 'gender role' rather than genital anatomy determined … classification as a male or a female … [This] argument is intended to liberate gender from any biological basis … [and] to show that a system of two genders is by no means inevitable. [Such scholars] acknowledge, however, that 'gender role' is definable only as … behavior normative for a member of one or the other genital-sex class … and that assignment to one or the other sex class is typically at birth and *not* dependent on any … behavior on the part of the person being classified. Because, logically, categories must be defined … by criteria independent of the normative implications of inclusion in those categories, certain forms of conduct cannot be both criteria for and normative implications of inclusion in … the same category. It must be that [we] are dealing with situations in which some men (less often women) are permitted to act, in some degree, as *though* they were women (or men), and may be spoken of as though they were women (or men), or as an anomalous 'he-she' or 'she-he.' … It is only to be expected that [one] cannot … produce any linguistic data to demonstrate that [members of the alleged 'third sex'] are treated in any language as a genuine third gender [emphasis in original] (Scheffler 1991: 377–78).

In short, Scheffler argues that the focal gender classes in these societies are 'male' and 'female', with the 'third gender' labels *derived from* these foci, just as a *godfather* is a specialised kind of 'father'. And the defining characteristics of these foci are genital anatomy: pertinent behaviour, Scheffler argues (e.g. 1972c: 312, 1973: 766; Scheffler and Lounsbury 1971: 39), is not logically prior but logically *subsequent*—just as how a father should behave is logically subsequent to those criteria that define being a father in the first place. We think it a matter of considerable intellectual importance to underscore the similarities between Scheffler's analyses of gender and his findings on kinship.

Shortcoming of Scheffler's analyses

Despite the great respect we have for Hal Scheffler's scholarship, we do not consider it beyond criticism. Recall that in his 1966 general statement on human kinship he maintained that 'it is the triad self-genitor-genetrix that should be considered to be the "atom" of kinship—that is that unit which generates the elements "brother" and "sister", and that this "formal organization" is universal'. This is a prescient statement of what Dwight Read (Chapter 2; see also Read, Fischer and Lehman 2014) has called the Family Space concept. We believe this to be a necessary construct if we are to take account—as we must—of those situations in which a marriage occurs but the couple does not co-reside, those in which extramarital genitorship is recognised even in the absence of coresidence, those in which neither condition applies but the presumed genitor is nonetheless recognised, and those based upon adoption, fosterage, or the remarriage of one of the natal parents. In all of these situations genealogies may be constructed that are *not*—not necessarily, anyway—based upon the 'facts of procreation' that Scheffler emphasised. But although the concept was put forward while he was still active, Hal Scheffler never took note of it, nor of the pertinent ethnographic materials that made its development necessary.

The essays

Warren Shapiro's essay (Chapter 1) grounds Hal Scheffler's ideas in the classic ethnographic case of the Trobriand Islanders east of Papua New Guinea. He shows that the extensionist position is hardly new, and that 'the natives' themselves, quite contrary to the arguments of the performativists, *really are* extensionists; which is to say that, contrary to Schneider and his admirers, extensionism is *not* a Eurocentric imposition upon nonwestern peoples. The essay carries the implication that kin ties established through procreation are *everywhere* basic, as Hal Scheffler contended. By contrast, other principles upon which kinship is reckoned are *everywhere* logically dependent upon local procreative notions.

Dwight Read's essay (Chapter 2) considers Scheffler's extensionist argument in view of the immense ethnographic corpus on what he calls 'kin-term products'. The essay continues a project he began more than three decades ago (Read et al. 1984; see also Leaf and Read 2012; Read 2001, 2007). He demonstrates how a kinship terminology can be generated from the terms designating the relations making up a conceptual nuclear family—what he calls the Family Space (see Figure 4 in Chapter 2). The concept is rooted in mathematical theory, which will be unfamiliar to most readers, but it is empirically necessary, for reasons we have already noted.[5] Using the kin-term product concept, he proceeds to work out a sort of 'grammar' for the kinship terminology. From here he shows how the genealogical employment of kin terms is derived from the 'grammar', rather than the reverse. His essay is not easy reading, so the reader should prepare, but it provides vital insights into kinship cognition. Specifically, it demonstrates how the extensionism that forms a centrepiece of Hal Scheffler's scholarship derives from the internal logic of a kinship terminology, much as we understand how the structure of English sentences derives from the (mostly unconscious) rules of English grammar.

Extensionist theory is first and foremost meant to provide richer ethnographic description. This is just what is in evidence in the essay by Andrew Strathern and Pamela Steward (Chapter 3). Their chief concern is the practical employment of kin terms among the Melpa of the Papua New Guinea Highlands. Yet at the same time they provide rich ethnographic

---

5   We might note here the marriage of two women among the Nuer of South Sudan (Evans-Pritchard 1951: 108–09) and elsewhere in Africa (e.g. Cadigan 1998; Krige 1974; Oboler 1980). But in all of these cases, so far as we can see, such marriages constitute only a minority of conjugal unions and in *no* instance is the actual genitor denied all rights with regard to the children he has sired. The commune movement in the United States in the nineteenth century and, more recently, the *kibbutz* movement in Israel might be thought to constitute a class of exceptions to our generalisation, but nothing is clearer in the relevant literature than the problems these arrangements have encountered in attempting to suppress the pair-bond, parents' interest in their own children, and other forms of favouritism towards close kin (e.g. Brumann 2003: 409 et seq.; Kanter 1972: 91, 158; Spiro 2004: 562).

support for the extensionist position. Thus they report that adoptive kinship is here lexically marked relative to its procreative analogue, much like the English *adoptive mother* and *adopted child* in relation to *mother* and *child*, respectively. As we understand them, they invoke a more comprehensive notion of meaning which includes both procreative and performative significance, but at the same time they acknowledge that the latter builds upon the former. To boot, they are concerned with kinship metaphor—something with which, as we shall see, another essay deals.

In his superb summary, noted above, of what we know about human kinship, Hal Scheffler (1973: 758) stressed that kinship everywhere is reckoned through both parents—that is *bilaterally*. In many societies, Scheffler (ibid.: 756–65) went on to point out, this essential bilaterality is augmented by notions which are based not upon the reckoner but rather upon ancestral figures—which are, in Goodenough's terms, not 'ego-oriented' but rather 'ancestor-oriented' (Goodenough 1961). The latter are usually associated with real or posited collectivities, often involved in the control of productive property. We have known since at least 1920 that hunter-gatherers usually lack such categories (Lowie 1920: 148 et seq.). Most Amazonian societies—even the Siriono—practise some horticulture, but Rusty Greaves and Karen Kramer (Chapter 4) worked with one group that subsists exclusively by foraging. The 'patrilocal band' model of hunter-gatherer sociality espoused by Service (1971: 46–98) does not fit here, nor are there any ancestor-oriented social categories. The sole modes of social differentiation are locality, age, sex and ego-oriented kinship. This last, Greaves and Kramer point out, dovetails nicely with Hal Scheffler's ideas on focality and extension.

Any general theory of human kinship must take account of attachment in early childhood (Cassidy and Shaver 2008), which is just what the essays by Fadwa El Guindi (Chapter 5) and Vicky Burbank (Chapter 6) do. Analysing her ethnographic materials on Qatari Arabs, El Guindi shows that both suckling and procreation are held to establish kinship, as does marriage. She notes a distinction between wet-nursing, which is often a paid service and which antedates Islam, and suckling. It is only the latter that has kinship connotations. Even so, kinship through suckling—usually called 'milk kinship' in the pertinent literature—is, among Qatari Arabs, *locally construed* to be *logically derived* from procreative kinship, which perforce enjoys focal status—as indeed it does, apparently, throughout the Islamic World and parts of Europe (e.g. Chapman 2012; Khatib-Chahidi 1992; Parkes 2006). Adoption, for its part, is unrecognised.

But this is not the case amongst the Aboriginal people of Numbulwar, southeast Arnhem Land, whose sociality is the subject of Vicky Burbank's essay (Chapter 6). Here adoption *is* recognised as a means by which kinship is created. Now it might be thought that adoption poses problems for a theory of kinship based upon procreation, because it results in the transfer of attachment mechanisms to people other than the natal parents, or, more commonly, the sharing of these mechanisms with those parents (Silk 1987). Warren Shapiro, however, has shown that adoption seems usually *not* to affect this theory, that is that natal parents retain focal status in the local 'parent' categories (Shapiro 2016). Burbank presents a partly contrary case. At Numbulwar both adoptive and procreative kin are said to be 'close family' in the local creole, but the latter are said to be 'closer' than the former. This suggests a 'layered' focality, something which Hal Scheffler noted in his Choiseul analysis (Scheffler 1965: 74) and which Shapiro found in his research among the Aboriginal people of northeast Arnhem Land (Shapiro 1981: 38–40). Moreover, the 'close' status of adoptive kin at Numbulwar suggests a *rapprochement* between extensionists and performativists.

Just as Hal Scheffler's ideas have relevance for more searching ethnographic analyses, so they shed light on historical process. Thus Pat McConvell (Chapter 7) considers the extensive research done by Scheffler on Aboriginal kinship terminologies as a basis for enquiry into historical change in these terminologies, as well as for the reconstruction of their ancient predecessors. He shows that these reconstructions fit well with extensionist theory, particularly in the ways in which this theory illuminates their semantic properties. But, like Strathern and Stewart, he thinks that extensionism needs to be augmented by a consideration of the pragmatic usage of kin terms. McConvell further points out that not all semantic change in the pertinent terminologies fits what might be predicted from Scheffler's seminal analysis of such systems (Scheffler 1978): some, for example, disrespect gender and generational classes.

So, however valuable they are, we ought not to regard Hal Scheffler's ideas as Received Truth. In fact, Warren Shapiro, in his role as editor, made a point of inviting scholars with a track record of contesting Scheffler's thought to participate in this *Festschrift*. Thus Scheffler was critical of the idea that an 'alliance' relationship is foundational to human kinship (e.g. Scheffler 1970b, 1973: 780–86, 1977). It needs to be added here that, after his initial formulation of what would come to be called 'alliance theory', noted above, Lévi-Strauss (1949) would develop his scheme into one emphasising societies with paternally (or, less often, maternally) based groups that regularly intermarry, as opposed to those in which such groups exist but prefer to scatter their marriages among a large number of equivalent groups, and those that have no such groups. In the former class of societies, he maintained, kinship terms are *not* polysemic: rather, each has a single meaning, and this meaning refers *primarily* to intergroup relations and only incidentally to close kin. This might be considered a variety of the 'social categories' position. Bob Parkin (Chapter 8), the only 'alliance theorist' who has taken serious account of the extensionist position, is here concerned with the disappearance of regular intermarriage between groups. He points out that this disappearance stems from nonmarital factors which prevent group interaction. Otherwise he maintains the 'alliance theory' position on kin terms. His essay, however, does not counter Hal Scheffler's viewpoint that kin terms in societies with intermarrying groups are like kin terms everywhere else: their foci are close procreative kin, from which they are *extended to* others, including those related by marriage.

The 'performativist' view of kinship is taken up in Linda K. Watts's essay (Chapter 9). Previously, Watts had authored two exceptional analyses of the kinship terminology of the Zuni of New Mexico (Watts 1997, 2000) in which she seriously engaged the extensionist position. For her, the expression 'kinship terminology' is a misnomer: she prefers 'relational terminology', because, she has argued, the foci of the terms in question are provided by people with whom one is especially close emotionally, who may or may not be close procreative kin. The argument is pursued further in this volume. Her essay is without question the most passionate and erudite defence to date of the performativist position. As such, it invites a rethinking of the extensionist theory, though not, we think, an abandonment of it.

Watts also stresses the necessity for richer linguistic analysis in kinship studies, which we fully endorse. She draws attention to the fact that such an analysis of a 'relational terminology' would be more encompassing than one concerned solely with terms of reference, which have received by far the most attention in kinship studies: here her position is similar to those taken in several of the other essays in this volume, particularly those of Strathern and Stewart, Burbank, and McConvell. Watts's advocacy would, she notes, lead to a fuller appreciation of the range of relations an individual has with others. Thus the native terms that anthropologists translate as 'mother' and 'father' do indeed, we think, have primary reference to procreation, but this does not preclude extensive connotative meaning.

This links up with Bojka Milicic's essay (Chapter 10). But while Watts's chapter is concerned with synchronic ethnographic studies, Milicic pursues the role of metaphor in human thought more generally, including its possible origin as one of the ways by which kinship is conceptualised. Kinship and metaphor, she points out, are both fundamentally relational: kinship involves the relation of individuals to one another, metaphor the relation of one semantic domain to another through analogy, as when her Croatian informants liken their kinship networks to winding clusters of plants. Milicic suggests that, in the course of human evolution, thinking about kinship is what led to metaphorical thought. Her essay thus deals with an area noted but insufficiently explored by Hal Scheffler, but, like his concern with focality in nonmetaphorical kinship, she roots it in our species' heritage.

Doug Jones's essay (Chapter 11), like McConvell's, is concerned with historical change in kinship terminologies, but, like Milicic's, it focuses upon more general properties of human thought. More specifically, his focus is on how these properties impose internal constraints on change in systems of kin classification. Such systems, he suggests, display a degree of cross-cultural regularity suggestive of a common structural foundation, and this foundation transcends variation in local theories of procreation. The suggestion, then, is that Hal Scheffler's ideas, relying as they do on such theories, need to be supplemented. In the same vein, Jones expands the extensionist argument by calling attention to certain constraints on kin-term usage not considered by Scheffler.

An even more unabashedly innatist position is taken in the essay by Michelle Escasa-Dorne and Bill Jankowiak (Chapter 12), whose argument dovetails nicely with Hal Scheffler's interest in gender. Just as Scheffler's analysis provides no support for modish claims about gender classification, so the findings of Escasa-Dorne and Jankowiak square not at all with current arguments concerning gender equality in sexual behaviour. More specifically, these two scholars studied partner-preferences as indicated on Internet dating sites; since one can be largely anonymous on such sites, it might be expected that women would be more inclined to shake off what could be called 'conservative' social views, and more inclined consequently to approximate men in this area. But, it turns out, this is anything but the case: even on the Internet men evidence significantly more interest in casual sex with multiple partners than women do, whereas when it comes to committed relationships the reverse is true. We should perhaps emphasise here, especially given the political climate in academia these days, that the tendencies discovered by Escasa-Dorne and Jankowiak are *just that—tendencies*. Their research found that some men prefer committed relationships, some women casual sex with multiple partners. Biology is *not* destiny: it is *likelihood*. All of the chapters in this *Festschrift*, in fact, should be read with this in mind.

Conclusion

Even an Introduction should have one. We believe we now have a general theory of human kinship that is consistent with all the data at our command: kinship is primarily about locally posited procreative ties, thence extended to other social relationships, as well as to construed relationships with the phenomena of nature and of people's imagination. Moreover, the relation of all this to the nuclear family, though not absolute, is strongly tendential. These are truly monumental conclusions, and we have Hal Scheffler most of all to thank for them. We hope that the essays that follow are worthy of this remarkable scholar.

Acknowledgements

We are grateful to Tom Parides for reading earlier versions of this Introduction. It remains, nonetheless, our own responsibility.

References

Basso, Keith H. and Henry A. Selby (eds). 1976. *Meaning in Anthropology*. Albuquerque: University of New Mexico Press.

Bloch, Maurice and Stephen Guggenheim. 1981. 'Compadrazgo, baptism and the symbolism of a second birth'. *Man* (n.s.) 16(3): 376–86. doi.org/10.2307/2801290

Brumann, Christoph. 2003. '"All the flesh kindred that ever I see": A reconsideration of family and kinship in utopian communes'. *Comparative Studies in Society and History* 45(2): 395–421. doi.org/10.1017/S0010417503000197

Cadigan, R. Jean. 1998. 'Woman-to-woman marriage: Practices and benefits in Sub-Saharan Africa'. *Journal of Comparative Family Studies* 29(1): 89–98.

Carroll, Vern (ed.). 1970. *Adoption in Eastern Oceania*. Association for Social Anthropologists in Oceania Monograph 1. Honolulu: University of Hawaii Press.

Cassidy, Jude and Phillip R. Shaver (eds). 2008. *Handbook of Attachment: Theory, Research, and Clinical Applications*. 2nd edition. New York: The Guilford Press.

Chapman, Cynthia R. 2012. '"Oh that you were like a brother to me, one who had nursed at my mother's breasts": Breast-milk as a kinship-forging substance'. *Journal of Hebrew Scriptures* 12: 1–41. doi.org/10.5508/jhs.2012.v12.a7

D'Andrade, Roy G. 1970. 'Structure and syntax in the semantic analysis of kinship terminologies'. In *Cognition: A Multiple View*, edited by Paul L. Garvin, 87–114. New York: Spartan Books.

di Leonardo, Micaela (ed.). 1991. *Gender at the Crossroads of Knowledge: Feminist Anthropology in the Postmodern Era*. Berkeley, CA: University of California Press.

Evans-Pritchard, E.E. 1951. *Kinship and Marriage among the Nuer*. Oxford: Clarendon Press.

Feinberg, Richard and Martin Ottenheimer (eds). 2001. *The Cultural Analysis of Kinship: The Legacy of David M. Schneider*. Urbana, IL: University of Illinois Press.

Fison, Lorimer and A.W. Howitt. 1880. *Kamilaroi and Kurnai*. Melbourne: G. Robertson.

Fogelson, Raymond D. 2001. 'Schneider confronts componential analysis.' In *The Cultural Analysis of Kinship: The Legacy of David M. Schneider*, edited by Richard Feinberg and Martin Ottenheimer, 33–45. Urbana, IL: University of Illinois Press.

Garvin, Paul L. (ed.). 1970. *Cognition: A Multiple View*. New York: Spartan Books.

Goodale, Jane C. 1971. *Tiwi Wives: A Study of the Women of Melville Island, North Australia*. American Ethnological Society Monograph 51. Seattle: University of Washington Press.

Goodenough, Ward H. 1961. 'Comments on cultural evolution'. *Daedalus* 90: 521–28.

Gough, E. Kathleen. 1961. 'Nayar: Central Kerala'. In *Matrilineal Kinship*, edited by David M. Schneider and Kathleen E. Gough, 298–384. Berkeley, CA: University of California Press.

Hammel, Eugene A. (ed.). 1965. *Formal Semantic Analysis*. American Anthropologist Special Publications. Menasga, WI: American Anthropological Association.

Herdt, Gilbert. 1994. 'Preface'. In *Third Sex, Third Gender: Beyond Sexual Dimorphism in Culture and History*, edited by Gilbert Herdt, 11–20. New York: Zone Books.

Herdt, Gilbert (ed.). 1994. *Third Sex, Third Gender: Beyond Sexual Dimorphism in Culture and History*. New York: Zone Books.

Holmberg, Allan R. 1969. *Nomads of the Long Bow: The Siriono of Eastern Bolivia*. Garden City, NY: Natural History Press.

Honigmann, John J. (ed.). 1973. *Handbook of Social and Cultural Anthropology*. Chicago: Rand McNally.

Hook, Sidney (ed.). 1969. *Language and Philosophy*. New York: New York University Press.

Howitt, A.W. 1891. 'The Dieri and other kindred tribes of central Australia'. *Journal of the Royal Anthropological Institute of Great Britain and Ireland* 20: 30–104. doi.org/10.2307/2842347

Jacobs, Sue-Ellen, Wesley Thomas and Sabine Lang (eds). 1997. *Two-spirit People: Native American Gender Identity, Sexuality, and Spirituality*. Urbana, IL: University of Illinois Press.

Kanter, Rosabeth M. 1972. *Commitment and Community: Communes and Utopias in Sociological Perspective*. Cambridge: Harvard University Press.

Khatib-Chahidi, Jane. 1992. 'Milk kinship in Shi'ite Islamic Iran'. In *The Anthropology of Breast-Feeding: Natural Law or Social Construct*, edited by Vanessa Maher, 109–32. Oxford: Berg.

Krige, Eileen J. 1974. 'Woman-marriage, with special reference to the Louedu. Its significance for the definition of marriage'. *Africa: Journal of the International African Institute* 44(1):11–37. doi.org/10.2307/1158564

Lang, Andrew. 1905. *The Secret of the Totem*. New York: Longmans, Green & Co.

Leaf, Murray J. and Dwight Read. 2012. *The Conceptual Foundation of Human Society and Thought: Anthropology on a New Plane*. Lanham, MD: Lexington Books.

Lévi-Strauss, Claude. 1949. Les structures élémentaires de la parenté. Paris: Presses Universitaires Françaises; rev. and trans. James Harle Bell and John Richard von Sturmer, ed. Rodney Needham as *The Elementary Structures of Kinship*. Boston: Beacon Press, 1969 (page citations are to the translated edition).

——. 1963. *Structural Anthropology*. New York: Basic Books.

Lounsbury, Floyd G. 1963. 'Linguistics and psychology'. In *Psychology: A Study of a Science*, edited by Sigmund Koch, 552–82. New York: McGraw-Hill. doi.org/10.1037/10590-010

——. 1964a. 'A formal account of the Crow- and Omaha-type kinship terminologies'. In *Explorations in Cultural Anthropology: Essays in Honor of George Peter Murdock*, edited by Ward H. Goodenough, 351–93. New York: McGraw-Hill.

——. 1964b. 'The structural analysis of kinship semantics'. In *Proceedings of the Ninth International Congress of Linguistics*, edited by H.G. Lunt, 1073–93. The Hague: Mouton.

———. 1965. 'Another view of the Trobriand kinship categories'. In *Formal Semantic Analysis*, edited by Eugene A. Hammel. Special issue of *American Anthropologist* (n.s.) 67(5) Part 2: 142–85. doi.org/10.1525/aa.1965.67.5.02a00770

———. 1969. 'Language and culture'. In *Language and Philosophy: A Symposium*, edited by Sidney Hook, 3–29. New York: New York University Press.

Lowie, Robert H. 1920. *Primitive Society*. New York: Boni and Liveright.

Lubbock, John. 1912. *The Origin of Civilisation and the Primitive Condition of Man: Mental and Social Condition of Savages*. London: Longmans, Green and Co.

Lunt, H.G. (ed.). 1964. *Proceedings of the Ninth International Congress of Linguistics*. The Hague: Mouton.

Maher, Vanessa (ed.). 1992. *The Anthropology of Breast-Feeding: Natural Law or Social Construct*. Oxford: Berg.

Malinowski, Bronisław. 1913. *The Family among the Australian Aborigines: A Sociological Study*. London: University of London Press.

Morgan, Lewis H. 1877. *Ancient Society; or Researches in the Lines of Human Progress from Savagery, through Barbarism to Civilization*. New York: Henry Holt.

Oboler, Regine S. 1980. 'Is the female husband a man? Woman/woman marriage among the Nandi of Kenya'. *Ethnology* 19(1): 69–88. doi.org/10.2307/3773320

Parkes, Peter. 2006. 'Celtic fosterage: Adoptive kinship and clientage in northwest Europe'. *Comparative Studies in Society and History* 48(2): 359–95. doi.org/10.1017/S0010417506000144

Radcliffe-Brown, A.R. (Alfred Reginald). 1913. 'Three tribes of Western Australia'. *Journal of the Royal Anthropological Institute* 43: 143–94. doi.org/10.2307/2843166

Read, Dwight W. 2001. 'What is kinship?' In *The Cultural Analysis of Kinship: The Legacy of David M. Schneider*, edited by Richard Feinberg and Martin Ottenheimer, 78–117. Urbana, IL: University of Illinois Press.

———. 2007. 'Kinship theory: A paradigm shift'. *Ethnology* 46(4): 329–64.

Read, Dwight, John Atkins, Ira R. Buchler … William D. Wilder. 1984. 'An algebraic account of the American kinship terminology'. *Current Anthropology* 25(4): 417–40. doi.org/10.1086/203160

Read, Dwight, Michael D. Fischer, Kris Lehman (Chit Hlaing). 2014. 'The cultural grounding of kinship: A paradigm shift'. *L'Homme* 210(2): 63–89. doi.org/10.4000/lhomme.23550

Reining, Priscilla (ed.). 1972. *Kinship Studies in the Morgan Centennial Year*. Washington: The Anthropological Society of Washington.

Rivers, William H.R. 1915. 'Kin, kinship'. In *Encyclopedia of Religion and Ethics*, vol. 7, 700–07.

Roscoe, Will. 1994. 'How to become a berdache: Toward a unified analysis of gender diversity'. In *Third Sex, Third Gender: Beyond Sexual Dimorphism in Culture and History*, edited by Gilbert Herdt, 32–72. New York: Zone Books.

Ryder, James W. and Margaret B. Blackman. 1970. 'The avunculate: A cross-cultural critique of Claude Lévi-Strauss'. *Cross-Cultural Research* 5(2): 97–115. doi.org/10.1177/106939717000500202

Scheffler, Harold W. 1965. *Choiseul Island Social Structure*. Berkeley: University of California Press.

———. 1966. 'Structuralism in anthropology'. *Yale French Studies* 36–37: 66–88. doi.org/10.2307/2930400

———. 1970a. 'Kinship and adoption in the northern New Hebrides'. In *Adoption in Eastern Oceania*, edited by Vern Carroll, 369–89. Association for Social Anthropologists in Oceania Monograph 1. Honolulu: University of Hawaii Press.

———. 1970b. '*The Elementary Structures of Kinship*, by Claude Lévi-Strauss: A review article'. *American Anthropologist* 72: 251–68. doi.org/10.1525/aa.1970.72.2.02a00020

———. 1972a. 'Afterword'. In *Kinship and Behaviour in North Queensland: A Preliminary Account of Kinship and Social Organisation on Cape York Peninsula*, by Donald Thomson, 37–52. Australian Aboriginal Studies No. 51. Canberra: Australian Institute of Aboriginal Studies.

———. 1972b. 'Baniata kin classification: The case for extensions'. *Southwestern Journal of Anthropology* 28(4): 350–81. doi.org/10.1086/soutjanth.28.4.3629317

———. 1972c. 'Kinship semantics'. *Annual Review of Anthropology* 1: 309–28. doi.org/10.1146/annurev.an.01.100172.001521

———. 1973. 'Kinship, descent, and alliance'. In *Handbook of Social and Cultural Anthropology*, edited by John J. Honigmann, 747–93. Chicago: Rand McNally.

———. 1976. 'The "meaning" of kinship in American culture: another view'. In *Meaning in Anthropology*, edited by Keith H. Basso and Henry A. Selby, 57–91. Albuquerque: University of New Mexico Press.

———. 1977. 'Review: Kinship and alliance in South India and Australia'. *American Anthropologist* 79(4): 869–82. doi.org/10.1525/aa.1977.79.4.02a00060

———. 1978. *Australian Kin Classification*. Cambridge Studies in Social Anthropology No. 23. Cambridge: Cambridge University Press. doi.org/10.1017/CBO9780511557590

———. 1991. 'Sexism and naturalism in the study of kinship'. In *Gender at the Crossroads of Knowledge: Feminist Anthropology in the Postmodern Era*, edited by Micaela di Leonardo, 361–82. Berkeley, CA: University of California Press.

Scheffler, Harold W. and Floyd G. Lounsbury. 1971. *A Study in Structural Semantics: The Siriono Kinship System*. Englewood Cliffs, NJ: Prentice Hall.

Schneider, David M. 1968. *American Kinship: A Cultural Account*. Englewood Cliffs, NJ: Prentice Hall.

———. 1972. 'What is kinship all about?' In *Kinship Studies in the Morgan Centennial Year*, edited by Priscilla Reining, 32–63. Washington: Anthropological Society of Washington.

———. 1984. *A Critique of the Study of Kinship*. Ann Arbor, MI: The University of Michigan Press. doi.org/10.3998/mpub.7203

Schneider, David M. and Kathleen Gough (eds). 1961. *Matrilineal Kinship*. Berkeley, CA: University of California Press.

Service, Elman R. 1971. *Primitive Social Organization: An Evolutionary Perspective*. New York: Random House.

Shapiro, Warren. 1981. *Miwuyt Marriage: The Cultural Anthropology of Affinity in Northeast Arnhem Land*. Philadelphia: Institute for the Study of Human Issues.

———. 1988. 'Ritual kinship, ritual incorporation, and the denial of death'. *Man* (n.s.) 23(2): 275–97. doi.org/10.2307/2802806

———. 2016. 'Why Schneiderian kinship studies have it all wrong: With special reference to adoptive kinship'. *Structure and Dynamics* 9(2): 218–39. Online: escholarship.org/uc/item/1vp7c25g (accessed 31 May 2017).

———. 2017. 'Toward a post-Schneiderian perspective on kinship'. *Journal of Anthropological Research* 73(2): 238–61. doi.org/10.1086/692004

Silk, Joan B. 1987. 'Adoption and fosterage in human societies: Adaptations or enigmas?' *Cultural Anthropology* 2(1): 39–49. doi.org/10.1525/can.1987.2.1.02a00050

Sobo, Elisa J. 1993. *One Blood: The Jamaican Body*. Albany: State University of New York Press.

Spiro, Melford E. 2004. 'Utopia and its discontents: The kibbutz and its historical vicissitudes'. *American Anthropologist* 106(3): 556–68. doi.org/10.1525/aa.2004.106.3.556

Stacey, Judith. 2009. 'Unhitching the horse from the carriage: Love and marriage among the Mosuo'. *Utah Law Review* 11: 287–321.

Stanner, William E.H. 1960. 'On Aboriginal religion. II: Sacramentalism, rite and myth'. *Oceania* 30(4): 245–78. doi.org/10.1002/j.1834-4461.1960.tb00226.x

Thomas, Northcote W. 1906. *Kinship Organisations and Group Marriage in Australia*. Cambridge: Cambridge University Press.

Thomas, Wesley. 1997. 'Navajo cultural constructions of gender and sexuality'. In *Two-spirit People: Native American Gender Identity, Sexuality, and Spirituality*, edited by Sue-Ellen Jacobs, Wesley Thomas and Sabine Lang, 156–73. Urbana, IL: University of Illinois Press.

Tyler, Stephen A. 1966. 'Whose kinship reckoning? Comments on Buchler'. *American Anthropologist* 68(2): 513–16. doi.org/10.1525/aa.1966.68.2.02a00240

Wallace, Anthony F.C. 1965. 'The problem of the psychological validity of componential analysis'. In *Formal Semantic Analysis*, edited by Eugene A. Hammel, 229–48. American Anthropologist Special Publication. Menasha, WI: American Anthropological Association.

Watts, Linda K. 1997. 'Zuni family ties and household group values: a revisionist cultural model of Zuni social organization'. *Journal of Anthropological Research* 53(1): 17–29.

———. 2000. *The Social Semiotics of Relational Terminology at Zuni Pueblo*. Lewiston, NY: Edward Mellen Press.

Part II. The Battle Joined

1

Hal Scheffler Versus David Schneider and His Admirers, in the Light of What We Now Know About Trobriand Kinship

Warren Shapiro

[T]he anti-kinship views of ... David Schneider have been influential ... out of proportion to their good sense ... I have often wondered how or why it is that such logically and empirically shoddy claims got to be so widely accepted ... Many anthropological lemmings, infatuated with radical cultural constructionism ... have blindly followed [him] over a cliff. Paying no attention to or even denying the validity of a distinction between the literal and the metaphoric, they have enabled themselves to create numerous esoteric 'others' whose 'relationship systems' are for the most part nothing more than clones of Schneider's interpretation of 'American kinship' ... They would thereby open the way for virtually endless commodity differentiation unconstrained by even the most minimal standards of intellectual or social value (Scheffler 2003: 341–43).

[I]t is important to remember, as bearing upon the status of the family, that in many primitive tribes the terms used for the immediate members of the family are either distinguished from the same terms in the extended sense by the addition of some particle, or terms corresponding to 'own' are used ... Family is family, whatever the system of relationship (Goldenweiser 1937: 301).

FOCALITY AND EXTENSION IN KINSHIP

My goal in this chapter is to further Hal Scheffler's critique of the so-called 'new kinship studies' (see my first epigraph), using a strictly ethnographic/analytical basis. Following his lead—he began this critique years earlier (Scheffler 1976)—I have argued in quite a few places (Shapiro 2008, 2009, 2010, 2011b, 2012, 2013, 2014, 2015, 2016) that these studies, indebted mostly to David Schneider's publications, especially his *A Critique of the Study of Kinship* (Schneider 1984), are empirically and analytically badly flawed. Here I provide further evidence of these flaws. I forewarn the reader that he/she will have regularly to refer back to the presentation of Scheffler's ideas in the Introduction to this volume.

I need first to say something about the new kinship studies. As shown in the Introduction, Hal Scheffler has made a strong case that kin-reckoning throughout the world is based upon native notions of procreation. Schneider, by contrast, argued that an emphasis upon procreative kinship derives not from the ethnography itself but, rather, from the cultural background of the western ethnographer, emphasising as it does procreation in kin-reckoning: he took Hal Scheffler, among others, to task on this very matter (Schneider 1984: 113–26).[1] The new kinship studies, then, emphasise nonprocreative or *performative* means of establishing kinship connexion, like commensality (e.g. Carsten 1997); name-sharing (e.g. Sahlins 2013: 68–73), or just saying that two or more people are kin (e.g. Weston 1991). This in itself is fine, but in so doing these scholars fail to appreciate an obvious but nonetheless salient fact, noted in the Introduction but well worth repeating: whenever two people are recognised as kin to each other, by either procreative or performative means, they ipso facto are recognised as members of reciprocal kin classes. These classes, moreover, have an internal structure, to which an enormous literature is testament. If one chooses *not* to deal with this literature, which is what the performativists mostly do (see below), he or she is unable to raise (let alone answer) the question of *focality*, of the semantic relationships of the various forms of kin-reckoning within a community. To take Janet Carsten's highly celebrated example: it is misleading to imply that, among Malays, both commensality and

---

1   Actually, Schneider argued that the primacy of procreative notions does not hold even in American kinship, and that it was projected onto ethnographic data by anthropologists committed to a genealogical model of kinship. Hence he could argue that American kinship has two 'distinctive features' that are on a logical par with each other—'biogenetic relationship' and 'code for ... conduct'—the latter having nothing to do with procreation (Schneider 1968: 101). Scheffler (1976) has criticised this argument—and, indeed, Schneider's entire analysis of his data from Chicago and environs.

procreation are equally means of establishing kinship. For the fact is that there is overwhelming evidence, completely ignored by Carsten, that for these people commensality and other forms of performative kinship are *derived from*, are *modelled upon*, procreative ones (Shapiro 2011b)—just as Hal Scheffler would have predicted.

I offer as my first piece of evidence my second epigraph, taken from the second edition of Alexander Goldenweiser's introductory text. Now I know that Goldenweiser is not a household name, even in anthropological households.[2] But his anticipation some of Hal Scheffler's ideas is remarkable, and if he and Scheffler are even half right about what were once openly called *kinship terminologies*, then we need seriously to question whether Schneider and his admirers have anything resembling an argument. Could it be, rather, that the assumption of the primacy of procreative kinship was *not* an assumption, that the heads of the practitioners of (what might be dubbed by default) the old kinship studies, however influenced by their personal experience, were also influenced by what they indeed found in the field?

Goldenweiser was surely generalising from the ethnographic data available at the time he wrote. Indeed, there are examples aplenty in the early literature on both sides of The Pond (e.g. Freire-Marreco 1914; Lowie 1912; Rivers 1914; Speck 1918; Walker 1914), but they have achieved the semioblivion that attaches, however undeservingly, to Goldenweiser. For my part I would argue that anyone claiming expertise in human kinship should be aware of at least some of this scholarship, but I am prepared, for present purposes, to be lenient. My example, therefore, is drawn from what is the best-known ethnographic corpus we have, a corpus with which, it seems fair to presume, all kinship specialists are at least partly familiar. I deal mostly with data which are directly pertinent to extensionist theory. But, following Hal Scheffler's emphasis on the link between that theory and the importance of the nuclear family (again see the Introduction), I begin my analysis of each case with the ethnographers' report of domestic life.

---

2   Goldenweiser is not a voice in the wilderness. Comparable statements on focality and extension can be found in Kroeber (1917: 73), Firth (1936: 261), Keesing (1990: 163–64), and, most recently, Goodenough (2001: 217). The last named makes the vital point that procreative kinship provides a *model* for other forms of kin-reckoning (ibid.: 210–11) and thus anticipates one of my arguments here. Goodenough's essay should be required reading for anyone who believes that Schneider had anything resembling an argument. In the present context, the following remark is especially significant: 'I agree with Harold Scheffler that all systems of social relationship recognized by anthropologists cross-culturally as kin relationships are rooted in parturition' (ibid.: 217).

Trobriand kinship

Early in *The Sexual Life of Savages* Bronisław Malinowski calls our attention to 'the groups of people sitting in front of their dwellings', informing us that 'each group consists of one family only – man, wife, and children' (1929: 17). Other ethnographers of the Trobriands echo him. Thus Harry A. Powell notes that '[a] man and a woman united by the marriage contract are responsible for one or more dependent children, whom they bring up as members of a single household' (1956: 137). Susan P. Montague tells us that 'people prefer to live in nuclear family units, one to a house' (1974: 33). Mark Mosko observes that during certain ceremonies men 'sleep and socialize' in a special edifice because these rituals 'forbid cohabitation with wives and children' (2013: 493). And elsewhere Mosko, citing information from Katherine Lepani, another scholar who has recently worked in the Trobriands, tells us:

> that it is only when a couple agree to create a publicly affirmed domestic relationship that they initiate sexual relations with one another and also lie and sleep together, sit and eat as a couple ... and so on (2005: 58).

To turn to wider circles of sociality: Malinowski tells us that *only* people of one's own local matrilineal[3] group are lexically marked as 'real kinsmen' (*veyola mokita*), in contradistinction to *kakaveyola,* which he translates as 'pseudokindred' and 'spurious kinsmen', that is members of a more inclusive matrilineal category but not of one's own local group (Malinowski 1929: 495–96, 513, 527; see also Powell 1956: 191). 'Real kinsmen', by contrast, may also be rendered simply as *veyola*—that is, without the lexical marker (see also Malinowski 1926: 113; Powell 1969b: 602–03; Weiner 1976: 53–54, 1983: 695)—much as when I refer to *my mother* I virtually never say *my real mother:* I assume that the expression *my mother* is taken by my listener to mean the focal member of her kin class and not, say, my Cub Scout *denmother* when I was a boy. This example apparently has Trobriand counterparts. Thus Bernard Baldwin reports an expression

---

3   I use the label 'matrilineal' here because it has become standard in kinship studies. In truth there is only scant evidence that Trobrianders make much of extended genealogical chains. Malinowski (1929: 498, 527) and Powell (1956: 97 et seq.) are quite explicit on this point (see also Sider 1967: 96). It is probably more accurate to render these groupings as *matrifilial,* insofar as membership is dependent upon that of one's mother and is identical with it. Compare Keen (1994), who, to my mind rightly, refers to Yuulngu groupings as *patrifilial* rather than 'patrilineal'. This is a more appropriate label in most of Aboriginal Australia, as well as in both halves of Native America (Murphy 1979; Tooker 1971; see also Shapiro 1979: 13–14).

that he translates as 'she who begot me' and 'the real one', 'which is used sometimes in speech to specify the actual mother as apart from the crowd of maternal aunts and foster mothers' (1945: 228). Montague even notes that nonfocal members of the Trobriand 'mother' (*ina*) class can be said to be 'not *ina*' (2001: 175–76)—in other words, not the focus of the *ina* class, though still, apparently, called *ina*. But she maintains that focal *ina* status is based on nurturance rather than procreation—specifically on who feeds (especially, apparently, *breast*-feeds) the individual in question (ibid.; see also Baldwin 1945: 224; Crain, Darrah and Digm'Rina 2003: 12; Powell, cited in Sider 1967: 96; Powell 1969a: 192–94, 1969b: 603). But Annette B. Weiner tells us that in cases of adoption 'everyone knows the child's true genealogy', and that 'adoption does not effect a severance between the child and its true parents' (1976: 124). Still, I found Montague's statement curious, so I ran it by Gunter Senft, an anthropological linguist who has worked in the Trobriands and written extensively on their ideology and sociality (Senft 1985, 1991, 1995, 1996, 1998, 2009, 2011). In an email communication Senft tells me that small children single out the people who nurture them as 'real' members of both the 'mother' and the 'father' classes but then, where pertinent, they are corrected by their elders, who nominate their procreative parents (8 October 2013). We ought certainly to attend to children's models of the world, here and elsewhere, but for comparative purposes we need to rely on adult models (Scheffler and Lounsbury 1971: 9). I conclude, therefore, that despite Trobriand lack of concern with extended genealogies (see footnote 3), the procreative mother is the focal member of her kin class; and, moreover, that close maternal kin provide one focus for general Trobriand ideas about kinship. But this latter conclusion, though true de facto, needs to be modified, for the pertinent criterion is locality rather than genealogy; and, this being so, it provides some support for the performative position.[4]

---

4   With the exception of this last conclusion my remarks will be seen to jibe with Lounsbury's well-known analysis of Trobriand kin classification (Lounsbury 1965), but is less tied to extended genealogies and more to native distinctions. Many of these distinctions appeared in the ethnographic record after he wrote but Malinowski was far from oblivious to them (see main text). This being so, I can only wonder why Lounsbury failed to take account of them. Dwight Read and I consider this matter in the Introduction.

In his initial publication on the Trobriands, Malinowski tells us:

> the state of knowledge ... is just at the point where there is a vague idea as to some *nexus* between sexual connection and pregnancy, whereas there is no idea whatever concerning the man's contribution towards the new life which is being formed in the mother's body (1916: 407).

Trobriand Islanders, Malinowski would have us believe, are, according to the established expression, 'ignorant of physiological paternity': conception occurs, in native theory, when a spirit-child (*baloma*) enters a woman, her husband only 'opening the way' through repeated copulations (ibid.: 412–13; see also Malinowski 1927a: 89)—this presumably is the 'vague idea' to which Malinowski alludes. It would extend this essay very considerably if I were to consider the intellectual background to this 'finding', as well as its influence on subsequent scholarship.[5] Suffice it to say, for present purposes, and regarding the latter concern only, that Marshall Sahlins accepts the 'finding' uncritically, as part of his argument that human kinship is or can be independent of biological considerations (1976: 37–39); and that, more recently, Sarah Franklin in a supposedly comprehensive view of human conception ideologies inspired by David Schneider, does much the same (1997: 33–43), as does Janet Carsten (2000: 8).

In point of fact, there is contrary evidence even in Malinowski's initial presentation. Thus he describes a ritual bath undergone by a woman, which occurs 'four to five months after the first symptoms of pregnancy' (1916: 404). The ceremony, he tells us, 'is connected with incarnation of the spirit children' (ibid.: 405), and he further notes:

> The view taken by one of my informants was that during the first stage of pregnancy the [spirit-child] has not really entered the woman's body ... Then, during the ceremonial bathing, the spirit-child enters the body of the woman (ibid.).

Other informants, Malinowski continues, disagreed. In *The Sexual Life of Savages*, these data are repeated (1929: 225), but we also learn that:

---

5 It is well worth noting here that Hal Scheffler pointed this out some time ago, citing also remarkably similar findings for Aboriginal people, the other locus classicus for claims of 'ignorance of physiological paternity' (Scheffler 1973: 749–51, 1978: 5–13; see also Shapiro 1996, 2014: 25–33). I deal with these matters more comprehensively in an essay on Trobriand kinship currently in preparation.

1. HAL SCHEFFLER VERSUS DAVID SCHNEIDER AND HIS ADMIRERS

> Pregnancy is first diagnosed by the swelling of the breasts and the darkening of the nipples. At *this* time a woman may dream that the spirit of one of her kinsmen brings her the child from the outer world to be reincarnated [emphasis added] (ibid.: 211).

This is to say that the woman is already pregnant when entered by the spirit-child. This is made plainer by Carveth Read (1918): writing only two years after Malinowski's initial formulation, he states expressly that spirit-entry occurs at *foetal quickening*. Subsequently, Leo Austen reported this as well (1934: 103). Thus he tells us that a woman encounters the spirit-child in a dream *when she is already pregnant,* which state is held to result from 'the blood filling up the uterus … intermix[ing] with some water-like fluid from the woman's body. Where the fluid comes from is unknown' (ibid.: 108; see also Mosko 2005: 58). We shall see in a moment that there is reason to believe that it is anything but unknown. The thing to note now is that what we are dealing with is *not* a *conception* ideology at all: *it is a doctrine about the generation of the spiritual aspect of the person,* and, as such, is comparable to baptism in Christianity, as well as to other metaphysical ideas to which Göran Aijmer (1992) has given the label *animation*.

There is considerable evidence that water, either in ritual bathing or swimming in the sea, is in native ideology a semen surrogate. I shall present only some of this evidence here. As noted, Malinowski reports that a woman's husband is supposed to 'open the way' for the spirit-child by repeated sexual intercourse. In Trobriand mythology a comparable 'opening' is caused by rain—or, especially noteworthy, this—by stalactites, whose dripping 'water' does the 'opening' (Malinowski 1916: 411–13; 1927a: 89; 1927b: 50–51; 1929: 182–83, 426; 1960: 89). In case there is any doubt about the entailed symbolism, we have the direct statement from Alex C. Rentoul (1932: 275) that the stalactite in question 'is looked upon as a phallic symbol' (see also Barton 1917: 109; Malinowski 1929: 182–83; Senft 2011: 18). Malinowski (1916: 404) also notes that a woman swimming in the sea announces her pregnancy by saying 'A fish has bitten me!'—erotic biting, he elsewhere notes, being a common practice in coitus (1929: 333–34). There is, in this connection, considerable evidence that fish represent spirit-children in Trobriand symbolism and, less certainly, the 'water'—that is, semen-surrounded phalluses from which the spirit-children are implicitly held to emanate (see especially Crain, Darrah and Digm'Rina 2003: 15; Glass 1986: 54, 58; Malinowski 1929: 172–76; Senft 2011: 31). Patrick Glass's research based on Malinowski's unpublished fieldnotes as well as his publications, and his—Glass's—own examination of Trobriand art in various museums, echoes and expands upon this (Glass 1986, 1988). Glass notes that a particular shoreline in the Trobriand area is called *momola*—an expression which, following Malinowski (1929: 167, 339), he translates as both 'semen' and 'female sexual discharge'. '[I]t was generally by bathing in the *momola*', Glass tells us, 'that women announced that they had become pregnant' (1988: 63–64). Malinowski insists that that '[t]he spermatic fluid ... serves merely the purposes of pleasure and lubrication' (1916: 408–09; see also Malinowski 1929: 167). But this conclusion is gainsaid by Glass's 1986 analysis of the artwork on Trobriand war shields. These shields contain more or less explicit images of phalluses, the female reproductive tract, coitus, semen and human embryos. Thus Glass is led to the following conclusion: 'What is overtly negated on land (male fertility) takes place on the seashore, *momala* (semen ...), through water and fish ... which [are] linked to the phallus' (1986: 58). Glass even has an explanation for the covert nature of this symbolism: 'The Trobrianders,' he tells us, 'were very guarded about articulating their knowledge of paternity *for fear of offending "the ears of the spirits"* [emphasis added]' (ibid.: 60; see also Glass 1988: 60–61; Senft 1996: 386–87, 2011: 29–30). In other words, one does not talk about sex, or talks about it only circumspectly, in connection with the sacred—something which is hardly confined to the Trobriands.

Now Malinowski seems to have worked almost exclusively with *men* (Malinowski 1916: 362; Senft 2009: 221), but Alex Rentoul, a resident colonial magistrate, was less limited. Not long after Malinowski's report, Rentoul noted a decided concern among Trobriand women with native measures '*to expel the male seed* [emphasis in original]' after coitus in an attempt to abort pregnancy (Rentoul 1931: 153; see also Powell 1980: 701; Senft 2009: 221–22, 2011: 33–34).[6] Some of Rentoul's further remarks are worth pursuing:

> [T]ogether with this practical knowledge of physiological paternity, there has always existed the magico-religious explanation ... [T]his is the Story of Birth, as it is believed by intelligent Trobrianders as thoroughly as a modern [western religious] congregation would believe the curate's shy announcement that during the night the angels had brought him a little son ... Presently the [spirit-child] will visit the woman and place

---

6   Malinowski, by contrast, says that he 'can say with complete confidence [that] no preventive means of any description are known, nor the slightest idea of them entertained' (1929: 197; see also Malinowski 1927b: 75–76). It seems fair to suggest that his assuredness on the matter was grossly misplaced.

upon her forehead a miniature babe … The babe descending the body of the mother will visit each breast for nourishment, then descending further will enter the womb, where it will remain until the day of its birth. In this process the father's part is simply 'to keep open the way' by sexual intercourse (1931: 153).

Note the apt comparison with western religious notions connected with conception, presaging Sir Edmund Leach's well-known conclusion (Leach 1966). Note, too, that the spirit-child is held to enter the mother nonvaginally—through the forehead—suggesting that it is seen as antithetical to carnal generation (see footnote 10). Thus Malinowski tells us that the heads of chiefs are sacred (1926: 92; 1929: 34), but in an email communication to me Mark Mosko notes that the heads of everyone are 'regarded as in some sense *bomaboma* ("sacred")' (1 May 2014). Moreover, according to Rentoul, entrance occurs 'presently'—that is *after* conception: we now know that this is at (or, probably, deemed to be the cause of) foetal quickening. A final consideration in Rentoul's remarks is that the 'physiological theory' was most plainly held by Trobriand *women*: this is in fact a recurrent theme in subsequent ethnographic and theoretical literature on the area (Austen 1934: 104, 113; Hocart 1954: 99; Mosko 1985: 211; Powell, cited in Montague 1971: 359; Senft 2011: 33–34; Sider 1967: 95–96, 105; Young 2004: 431). Why, then, should Trobriand *men* be so concerned with the spiritual contribution to the fetus?

Here, I think, we need to recall that the local matrilineal group is construed to be part of one of the four clans that, in native theory, have always existed, and that emerged from the Underworld at the Beginning of Things (Eyde 1983: 67–68; Malinowski 1926: 113; 1929: 494; Montague 1971: 354). It is thus much like Aboriginal Australian patrifilial groups, which William E.H. Stanner aptly calls 'sacramental corporations of a perennial order' (1960: 253). Malinowski himself noted that the 'ignorance' theory 'gives a good theoretical foundation for matriliny: for the whole process of introducing new life into a community lies between the spirit world and the female' (1929: 179). This 'new life', he further tells us, is held to be a reincarnation of an old one, which merely housed its spirit, and that this spirit has always existed and will continue to do so, going to yet another individual after the demise of its present host. He notes further that the spirit is specific to a particular local matrilineal group, from which it cannot be alienated (Malinowski 1926: 113; 1929: 182; but see

Malinowski 1916: 406). From this perspective, then, *each local matrilineal group is self-generating through a process in which sexual intercourse has no place,* given the incest barrier within each such group (see Moore 1964).

Moreover, the ongoing social and spiritual life of each such group seems to be a *male* concern. Men of the group own its gardens and have a virtual monopoly on garden and other magic, as well as local political leadership and *kula* trading (Brindley 1984: 93–94; Glass 1986: 50; Malinowski 1929: 41, 43; Montague 1971: 362; Mosko 1995: 774 et seq., 2013: 493; Weiner 1977: 67). By contrast, Montague (1983: 38–39) tells us that in Trobriand theory women are construed as animal-like, as not quite the real human beings that men are held to be (see also Crain, Darrah and Digm'Rina 2003: 9). This is especially remarkable in view of the fact that even those Trobriand men who insisted on the 'magico-religious explanation' with Malinowski were entirely explicit on the 'physiological explanation' in accounting for animal reproduction (Malinowki 1916: 411, 413; see also Rentoul 1931: 153; but see Malinowski 1927b: 64–67).[7] So it makes sense that men, being human beings par excellence, and, as such, leaders of enduring corporations, should wish to sustain the fiction that *their* reproduction is noncarnal, especially in public encounters with anthropologist and other foreigners (see Austen 1934: 103–04, 113; Montague 1971: 359; Mosko 1985: 211, 226, 2013: 492–96; Powell 1969b: 652; Rentoul 1932: 275; Senft 1995: 216; Sider 1967: 95–96, 105; Weiner 1976: 122).[8]

From this perspective we can understand the unkind reception Malinowski got when he expressly raised the 'physiological theory' with informants. Thus he tells us that 'as a means of testing the firmness of their belief [in spirit-entry], I sometimes made myself ... aggressively an advocate of the ... physiological doctrine of procreation' (1929: 185). When he did this, he goes on, 'I was sometimes astonished at *the fierce opposition evoked by my advocacy of physiological paternity* [emphasis added]' (ibid.: 186).

---

7   Later Malinowski claimed that this conclusion is incorrect (1927b: 62–67, 1929: 192). But he appears not to have inquired deeply into Trobriand theories of animal reproduction. Moreover, he concludes that 'animals are not subject ... to the same causal relationships as man' (ibid.).

8   Senft deals with several modes of speech recognised by Trobrianders (1985, 1991). He notes that although sexual talk is normally prohibited, in one of these modes it can occur: it is said to be 'only playing' (1991: 238–39; see also Weiner 1983). Malinowski (1929: 467, 486, 1960: 87) was aware of 'bad talk', but it seems never to have occurred to him that the avoidance of such discourse was one of the factors that led him to conclude that Trobrianders are 'ignorant of physiological paternity'. Senft speculates that Malinowski 'became the victim of the Trobriand Islanders' love to make fun of people – with their ... lying or joking or indirect language ... and they really took him for a ride' (2011: 35).

Further evidence of such a 'fierce opposition' is provided in Reo Fortune's account of the neighboring Dobuans (Fortune 1934). Since there is considerable mixing between the two peoples:

> The Dobuans know the Trobriand belief that procreation is from the reincarnation of spirits of the dead, not from the biological father. They say bluntly that the Trobrianders lie. The subject is not brought up between Trobrianders and Dobuans as it has been the subject of anger and quarrel too often in the past. My Dobuan friends warned me not to mention the matter in the Trobriands before I went there. Once I was there I deliberately made the experiment. The Trobrianders asserted the spiritual belief, just as Dr. Malinowski had published it. But the head of every Dobuan in the room immediately was turned away from me towards the wall. They affected not to hear the conversation; but afterwards when they had me alone they were furious with me (ibid.: 239).

In other words, Trobriand *men*—it is *men* who deal with outsiders (Brindley 1984: 94)—*pretend* that coitus and procreation are unrelated, while Dobuan men *pretend* that they are unaware of the 'fierce opposition' of Trobriand men to the 'physiological theory'. I cannot explain why Trobrianders and Dobuans, who share much the same ideology and sociality, differ so starkly in what they are willing to talk about in public, but it is surely clear that, on the Trobriand side, something more is at stake than a knowledge of the real facts of life—something Edmund Leach recognised in his famous article on 'Virgin Birth' (Leach 1966). Jerry Leach seems to have hit the nail on the head:

> Trobrianders believe in spirits of the dead who reincarnate themselves [within] their ... matrilineal group[s]. The formal belief seems to deny males any role in reproduction, and the Trobrianders convinced Malinowski that their religious belief was a true statement of their actual knowledge ... [H]owever, males are recognized as part of the reproductive process ... *The public denial of this seems intended for the ears of the spirits[,] who jealously guard their pre-eminent role in the formation of new human beings,* but it has led the world to believe that the Trobrianders do not associate intercourse with [conception] [emphasis added] (quoted in Glass 1986: 47).[9]

---

9   This is part of a more general denigration of sexual reproduction in the Trobriands, a subject that is beyond the scope of the present essay (for details see Mosko 2013: 495, 500). A subsequent essay by Mosko (2014) provides a remarkable statement of Trobriand pseudoprocreative thought (see also Brindley 1984: 17 et seq.; Tambiah 1968: 197). There are two ironies in all this. One is that, thanks mostly to Malinowski, these people have been portrayed, both in anthropological and popular circles, as inhabitants of 'islands of love' (Senft 1998). The other, with the same indebtedness, is that alleged 'ignorance of physiological paternity' in the Trobriands is part of this thought: it has absolutely nothing to do with real-world knowledge.

Indeed, as Gunter Senft put it in an email communication to me, 'all the discussions about virgin birth in the Trobriands were simply void from the very beginning' (8 May 2015).

It is also plain, it is worth noting, that in Trobriand thought spiritual generation is *modelled on* carnal generation, just as it is in baptism (see especially Gudeman 1972) and many other rituals which, following Hiatt (1971), are aptly dubbed *pseudoprocreative*.[10]

The same phenomenon is reflected in Malinowski's report that the father is said to be 'a stranger' or an 'outsider' (*tomakava*) (1927a: 39; 1927b: 14, 1929: 5, 1960: 39). Once again Sahlins sees in this evidence of a radical disconnect between the facts of biology and native representations of these facts, and once again he is wrong (1976: 38). Weiner's rendition of *tomakava* as referring to 'nonclanspeople' (1976: 53–54) is probably closer to the truth. But the term is also applied to people in mourning regardless of matrilineal group affiliation (Seligman 1910: 720), so, whatever its focal significance, its widest application would seem to be something like 'anyone who is outside the sphere of normal social relations in the situation at hand' (see also Montague 2001: 181–82). Comparable considerations apply to the Trobriand father. Here is Weiner on the matter:

> Malinowski ... placed great emphasis on the classification of [one's] father as *tomakava* ... 'stranger,' rather than own kinsman (*veyola tatola*). My informants [however] said that no one would ever call their father

---

10   Schneider (1989) has objected to my use of this label (Shapiro 1988), presumably on the grounds that it assumes the logical priority of (what he takes to be) only western ideas about kinship. This is not so. In all the Aboriginal ceremonies mentioned in Hiatt's classic analysis, there is abundant evidence that ritual generation is *modelled on* native appreciations of the processes of carnal reproduction. This is also true of those rituals, like Easter celebrations, that commemorate an *antithesis* between (what we might call) women's ability to give life and men's ability to give death, regarding the latter as ontologically superior to the former. On this see Jay (1985, 1992) and Rosaldo and Atkinson (1975). Thus Jesus is said never to have participated in carnal generation, to have been born of a woman who was similarly a nonparticipant, and who was impregnated nonvaginally—through the ear. Compare the Trobriand doctrine that spirit entry occurs in the mother's head (Malinowski 1927b: 34–35, 47, 61, 1929: 175, 188; Mosko 2005: 58; Rentoul 1931: 153), remarkably similar notions in Aboriginal Australia (Shapiro 2014: 25–33), and the propositions that the Buddha was born through his mother's sexual *abstinence* and entered her in prefoetal form through her *side*. Malinowski also mentions spirit entry through the vagina and the abdomen for the Trobriands, but he says that the former proposition is 'decidedly less authoritative' than the one that ascribes entry via the head (1929: 176, 181). I suspect this means that he was told this by younger male informants. In any case, Senft's male informants mentioned vaginal entry as well as entry through the head (Senft 2011: 31–32), but the former mode, apparently, only occurs if the woman 'swims somewhat carelessly' (ibid.: 31). Jay Crain, Allan Darrah and Linus Digm'Rina note that, to avoid another pregnancy during lactation, a Trobriand woman covers her loins with a skirt and then covers her head—the latter to prevent spirit-entry, 'which would spoil her milk' (2003: 16). We are, alas, not told what prevents her husband from lifting the skirt.

tomakava. They said [instead] that he was the most important kinsman (*veyola*) they had. *It was only in conversations or debates concerning ... rights of a [local matrilineal group] where a man as father would be referred to as* tomakava [emphasis added] (1976: 124; see also Powell 1969a: 178; Sider 1967: 103–06).

In an email communication Gunter Senft confirms Weiner on this last matter, but he points out that none of his informants held that the father was *veyola* to his children (13 September 2012). Apparently, the term is reserved for maternal kin (see also Lepani 2012: 70). Nevertheless, I think it reasonable to conclude that Trobriand notions of fatherhood are based on native appreciations of the reproductive process—as is probably the case everywhere else. Even Malinowski would eventually hedge on his initial formulation (Pulman 2004–05). A key point in this regard is the conceptual unity of husband and wife, quite apart from matrilineal group affiliation. Thus in an email communication Kathy Lepani informs me of a word—*kalitouna*—'meaning the man and woman who gave life to you' (8 June 2012).[11] She adds—apropos Montague's analysis of Trobriand kin terms (see above)—that the word 'generally isn't used to refer to adoptive parents, although children might well choose to refer to their adoptive parents' in this manner 'as an expression of endearment, respect, and gratitude' (ibid.). In a later email Dr Lepani notes that the word *tounai*, apparently cognate to *kalitouna*, means 'true parent', as does *toula unai'I*, 'where *toula* means "true" or "genuine"' (23 September 2012). In the same vein, Mark Mosko, in an email communication to me notes a Trobriand expression *toil una'I*, which can be used to refer to one's mother *and* one's father as a couple. He further notes that *una'I* means 'to *conceive*'! (13 August 2012).

We have already seen that *ina*, the Trobriand 'mother' term, has the primary significance of 'genetrix'. Is there evidence, therefore, that *tama*, the 'father' term, *primarily* denotes one's genitor? Trobrianders have a Crow-type kinship terminology: all members of one's father's matriline are designated by a single term, or two terms depending on sex. Even this rendition of Crow-type logic suggests that one's father is the focal member of his kin class, for he provides the conceptual focus for its terminological isolation: the class is defined in the first place by reference to him (see Introduction). Moreover, Malinowski expressly notes that '[t]he primary

---

11   This is apparently the same word that Weiner (1976: 123) renders as *kalitonai* and that she translates as 'true father'.

meaning of *tabu* [the term for females of the father's matriline] is "father's sister"',[12] and that both this term and the 'father' term (*tama*) are applied more widely, to any local matrilineal group other than one's own (1929: 502, 515). Presumably this means that the father's sister is rendered as *tabu makita*; in any case, as noted in the Introduction, we know from other Crow-type systems that this relative is separated by subclassification from other members of her kin class, who are lexically unmarked or else rendered by a lexical marker meaning 'false' or some such. In any case, reverting to the Trobriands, what we seem to have here is a native extension rule that says, in effect, 'Let any female member of *any* local matrilineal group *other than my own* be terminologically equated with my father's sister'.

It would be most unusual if analogous considerations did not apply to the 'father' term: indeed, I know of no ethnographic instance in which this is the case. So we should not be surprised to find, in a recent essay by Mark Mosko (2014) on Trobriand magic, that a magical spell that a man utters is said to be 'his child'—that is something that *emanates from* him.[13] The entailed notion—that a man can give birth—or otherwise create—through his head or mouth—has numerous ethnographic parallels. In the Old Testament, God creates by *naming*; in the New Testament, Jesus is regularly referred to as The Word: hence the Holy Spirit's entry into Mary's *ear*. Aboriginal fathers 'find' the spirits of their children *in utero* in *dreams*, which occur, as in the Trobriands, at foetal quickening (Malinowski 1929: 197, 1927b: 75–76). A Piaroa man in the Venezuelan rainforests may refer to his child as 'my thought' (Overing 1985: 167). In Greek mythology Athena springs from the head of Zeus, just as this

---

12   Elsewhere, in *The Sexual Life of Savages*, Malinowski says that the father's sister's daughter is the 'true' member of her kin class (1929: 101). It may be that both are subclassified in this way.

13   I must note that this analysis is my own. I have for some time maintained an email correspondence with Professor Mosko, and after reading his latest article I wrote to him about my conclusions. In the main, he seems *not* to agree with them. Thus, in a communication dated 15 March 2015, he maintains that 'everything anyone produces from their labors of all kinds, including the production of magical spells, is a *gwadi*, i.e. a child' with respect to the producer, and that he finds no reason to grant 'privileged' status to the procreative father/child relationship. Yet in the article just cited he says that magical spells are '*modeled on* ... the ordinary reproduction of offspring [emphasis added]' (2014: 33). And elsewhere he suggests, with regard to the gardening of yams, a series of metaphorical equations, to wit:

> The gardener is the yams' father (*tama*) and his wife their mother (*ina*). And like their human children, their yams are gendered. Capable of reproducing, yam seeds are like daughters. As agents of exchange and feeding other humans, subsistence yams are likened to human sons ... Even the manner of sowing yam seeds is suggestive of these parental relations. During ... planting, the gardener turns the soil with his digging stick ... Nearby he inserts a vertical yam stick. My interlocutor ... likened the soil to a womb and the stick to an erect penis (Mosko 2009: 686).

essay is my *brainchild*. In the working-class Brooklyn precincts in which I was raised, an older man might say to a younger one, 'I knew you when you were just a gleam in your father's eye'. The 'gleam' carries at least two connotations—lust (which could never be expressed more directly in regard to one's mother) and illumination—both connected with semen. Thus a *seminar* is a gathering in which *illumination* is supposed to take place. Alas, the symbolism of light in the Judaeo–Christian tradition is far too complex a matter to be considered here. Finally, among Janet Carsten's very many errors of omission in her analyses of Malay sociality is the absence of a detailed account of the male role in reproduction—something that, happily, Carol Laderman has corrected. Consider this doozy:

> before conception takes place in the mother's womb, the father has been pregnant for forty days. Indeed, people remember *ex post facto* male food cravings preceding the wife's pregnancy. The baby begins life not as a creation within the mother's belly, but in a more elevated sphere: his father's brain (Laderman 1982; see also Laderman 1983: 75).

More prosaic evidence for the Trobriand father being considered kin to his children comes from the classification of patrilateral parallel cousins with siblings and matrilateral parallel cousins (Sider 1967: 105). Since the last two are unquestionably one's kin, it would be most unusual if someone of the same kin class *and* the same degree of genealogical proximity were not so regarded: certainly I know of no such case in the ethnographic record.

In sum, Trobriand kinship, like kinship probably everywhere else, is founded on local appreciations of the reproductive process within the nuclear family, from which it is *extended to* other people and things.[14] The performative interpretation of it is quite mistaken. The focal members of kin classes are close procreative kin, and there are *native* extension rules. Finally, *pace* Sahlins, there is indeed a 'third party' posited in Trobriand generative ideology, but it has nothing to do, in native theory, with conception: not only is it *not* posited to occur at conception, but, as well, it is seen as *antithetical to* it (Shapiro 2013).

---

14   This is *not* the same as Malinowski's conclusions about extension (Malinowski 1962: 138), which deal with the ontogenic processes whereby children acquire and employ kinship terms, although the correlation between the two senses of 'extension' is probably very high (Scheffler and Lounsbury 1971: 61–62).

Conclusion

All of these conclusions are part of Hal Scheffler's legacy. In the Introduction Dwight Read and I referred to his pointing out the near-ubiquity of the nuclear family. His concern with kinship terminologies is what he is best known for, but his demonstration that performative kinship notions are derived from procreative ones runs a close second. A concern with cross-cultural regularities is entailed by these conclusions.

All this being so, I conclude that Hal Scheffler was very nearly right on the mark when it comes to discerning what human kinship is primarily about. By contrast, although performative criteria clearly have a role in kin-reckoning, it is a logically and empirically subordinate one, and so Schneider and his admirers are well off that mark. Hence the conclusion seems reasonable that Hal Scheffler was the single most important figure in the history of kinship studies.

Acknowledgements

I am especially grateful to Herb Damsky, Tom Parides, Dwight Read and Gunter Senft for encouragement, and for their comments on earlier versions of this essay. Thanks are also due to the last-named, as well as to Ira Bashkow, Kathy Lepani and Mark Mosko for pertinent information supplied to me via email. Bashkow notes that both Alex Rentoul and F.E. Williams:

> preferred, in treating the issue of [Trobriand] paternity, to insist that the Trobrianders had a pragmatic, common sense level of reproductive knowledge. Williams ... was willing to grant that the Trobrianders might in certain contexts hold an elaborate 'magico-religious theory' of conception. But [he] insisted that they also had 'a common sense theory' (1996: 11).

Both views could in fact be 'held ... by the same individuals, who diplomatically cited one or the other depending on context'. He is quoting from an unpublished letter from Williams to Leo Austen. Although Williams is well known among Melanesianists for his fieldwork elsewhere in Papua New Guinea (e.g. Williams 1936), both Bashkow and I incline to the view that he never visited the Trobriands.

References

Aijmer, Göran. 1992. 'Introduction: Coming into existence'. In *Coming into Existence: Birth and Metaphors of Birth*, edited by Göran Aijmer, pp. 1–19. Gothenburg, Sweden: Institute for Advanced Studies in Social Anthropology.

Atkinson, Clarissa W., Constance H. Buchanan and Margaret R. Miles (eds). 1985. *Immaculate and Powerful: The Female in Sacred Image and Social Reality*. Boston: Beacon Press.

Austen, Leo. 1934. 'Procreation among the Trobriand Islanders'. *Oceania* 5(1): 102–13. doi.org/10.1002/j.1834-4461.1934.tb00133.x

Baldwin, Bernard. 1945. 'Usituma! Song of heaven'. *Oceania* 15(3): 201–38. doi.org/10.1002/j.1834-4461.1945.tb00425.x

Barton, F.R. 1917. 'The spirits of the dead in the Trobriand Islands'. *Man* 17:109–10. doi.org/10.2307/2788966

Bashkow, Ira. 1996. '"To be his witness if that was ever necessary": Raphael Brudo on Malinowski's fieldwork and Trobriand ideas of conception'. *History of Anthropology Newsletter* 23(1): 3–11.

Basso, Keith H. and Henry A. Selby (eds). 1976. *Meaning in Anthropology*. Albuquerque: University of New Mexico Press.

Brindley, Marianne. 1984. *The Symbolic Role of Women in Trobriand Gardening*. Pretoria: University of South Africa.

Carsten, Janet. 1997. *The Heat of the Hearth: The Process of Kinship in a Malay Fishing Community*. Oxford: Clarendon Press.

———. 2000. 'Introduction: Cultures of relatedness'. In *Cultures of Relatedness: New Approaches to the Study of Kinship*, edited by Janet Carsten, 1–36. Cambridge: Cambridge University Press.

Crain, Jay, Allan Darrah and Linus Digm'Rina. 2003. 'Trobriand health and the cosmetics of cyclical ontology'. *Trobriand Islands Digital Ethnography Project*. Online: trobriandsindepth.com/Trobriand%20health.html (accessed 3 June 2017).

Eyde, David B. 1983. 'Sexuality and garden ritual in the Trobriands and Tikopia: Tudava meets the Itua I Kafika'. In *Concepts of Conception: Procreation Ideologies in Papua New Guinea*, edited by Dan Jorgensen. Special issue of *Mankind* 14: 66–74. doi.org/10.1111/j.1835-9310.1983.tb01252.x

Feinberg, Richard and Martin Ottenheimer (eds). 2001. *The Cultural Analysis of Kinship: The Legacy of David M. Schneider*. Urbana, IL: University of Illinois Press.

Firth, Raymond. 1936. *We, the Tikopia: A Sociological Study of Kinship in Primitive Polynesia*. London: George Allen & Unwin.

Fortune, Reo F. 1934. *Sorcerers of Dobu: The Social Anthropology of the Dobu Islanders of the Western Pacific*. New York: E.P. Dutton & Co.

Franklin, Sarah. 1997. *Embodied Progress: A Cultural Account of Assisted Conception*. London: Routledge. doi.org/10.4324/9780203414965

Freire-Marreco, Barbara. 1914. 'Tewa kinship terms from the pueblo of Hano, Arizona'. *American Anthropologist* 16(2): 269–87. doi.org/10.1525/aa.1914.16.2.02a00070

Glass, Patrick. 1986. 'The Trobriand code: An interpretation of Trobriand war shield designs'. *Anthropos* 81(1–3): 47–63.

———. 1988. 'Trobriand symbolic geography'. *Man* (n.s.) 23(1): 56–76. doi.org/10.2307/2803033

Goldenweiser, Alexander A. 1937. *Anthropology: An Introduction to Primitive Culture*. New York: Crofts.

Goodenough, Ward H. 2001. 'Conclusion: Muddles in Schneider's model'. In *The Cultural Analysis of Kinship: The Legacy of David M. Schneider*, edited by Richard Feinberg and Martin Ottenheimer, 205–18. Urbana, IL: University of Illinois Press.

Gudeman, Stephen. 1972. 'The *compadrazgo* as a reflection of the natural and spiritual person'. *Proceedings of the Royal Anthropological Institute of Great Britain and Ireland* 1971: 4, 45–71. doi.org/10.2307/3031761

Hammel, Eugene A. (ed.). 1965. *Formal Semantic Analysis*. Special issue of *American Anthropologist* (n.s.) 67(5).

Hiatt, Lester R. 1971. 'Secret pseudo-procreation rites among the Australian Aborigines'. In *Anthropology in Oceania: Essays Presented to Ian Hogbin*, edited by Lester R. Hiatt and Chandra Jayawardena, 77–88. San Francisco: Chandler Publishing Company.

Hiatt, Lester R. and Chandra Jayawardena (eds). 1971. *Anthropology in Oceania: Essays Presented to Ian Hogbin*. San Francisco: Chandler Publishing Company.

Hocart, Arthur M. 1954. *Social Origins*. London: Watts.

Jay, Nancy. 1985. 'Sacrifice as remedy for having been born of woman'. In *Immaculate and Powerful: The Female in Sacred Image and Social Reality*, edited by Clarrisa W. Atkinson, Constance H. Buchanan and Margaret R. Miles, 283–309. Boston: Beacon Press.

——. 1992. *Throughout Your Generations Forever: Sacrifice, Religion, and Paternity*. Chicago: University of Chicago Press.

Jones, Doug and Bojka Milicic (eds). 2011. *Kinship, Language, and Prehistory: Per Hage and the Renaissance in Kinship Studies*. Salt Lake City: University of Utah Press.

Jorgensen, Dan (ed.). 1983. *Concepts of Conception: Procreation Ideologies in Papua New Guinea*. Special issue of *Mankind* 14(1).

Keen, Ian. 1994. *Knowledge and Secrecy in an Aboriginal Religion: Yolngu of North-East Arnhem Land*. Oxford: Clarendon Press.

Keesing, Roger M. 1990. 'Kinship, bonding, and categorization'. In *On the Generation and Maintenance of Person: Essays in Honour of John Barnes*, edited by Warren Shapiro. Special issue of *The Australian Journal of Anthropology (TAJA)* 1(2–3): 159–67. doi.org/10.1111/j.1757-6547.1990.tb00380.x

Kroeber, Alfred L. 1917. 'Zuni kin and clan'. *American Museum of Natural History*, Paper 18: 41–204. New York: American Museum of Natural History.

Laderman, Carol. 1982. 'Putting Malay Women in Their Place'. *Women of Southeast Asia*, edited by Penny Van Esterik, 79–99. De Kalb, Ill.: Northern Illinois University, Center for Southeast Asian Studies.

———. 1983. *Wives and Midwives: Childbirth and Nutrition in Rural Malaysia*. Berkeley: University of California Press.

Leach, Edmund R. 1966. 'Virgin birth'. *Proceedings of the Royal Anthropological Institute of Great Britain and Ireland* (1966): 39–49. doi.org/10.2307/3031713

Lepani, Katherine. 2012. *Islands of Love, Islands of Risk: Culture and HIV in the Trobriands*. Nashville: Vanderbilt University Press.

Lounsbury, Floyd G. 1965. 'Another view of the Trobriand kinship categories'. In *Formal Semantic Analysis*, edited by Eugene A. Hammel. Special issue of *American Anthropologist* (n.s.) 67(5) Part 2: 142–85. doi.org/10.1525/aa.1965.67.5.02a00770

Lowie, Robert H. 1912. 'Social life of the Crow Indians'. *Anthropological Papers of the American Museum of Natural History* 9(2): 181–248.

Lyons, Harriet, Ann Chowning, Claudia Gross and Dorothy Ayers Counts (eds). 2005. *A Polymath Anthropologist: Essays in Honour of Ann Chowning*. Research in Anthropology and Linguistics Monograph 6. Department of Anthropology, University of Auckland

Malinowski, Bronisław. 1916. 'Baloma: The spirits of the dead in the Trobriand Islands'. *Journal of the Royal Anthropological Institute of Great Britain and Ireland* 46: 353–430. doi.org/10.2307/2843398

———. 1926. *Crime and Custom in Savage Society*. London: Routledge and Kegan Paul.

———. 1927a. *Sex and Repression in Savage Society*. Kegan Paul, Trench, Trubner and Co. Ltd; reprint 1960, Oxford: Routledge & Kegan Paul (page references are to the reprint edition).

———. 1927b. *The Father in Primitive Psychology*. New York: W.W. Norton and Company.

———. 1929. *The Sexual Life of Savages in North-Western Melanesia: An Ethnographic Account of Courtship, Marriage, and Family Life among the Natives of the Trobriand Islands, British New Guinea*. London: Routledge.

———. 1962. *Sex, Culture and Myth*. New York: Harcourt, Brace & World, Inc.

Margolis, Maxine L. and William E. Carter (eds). 1979. *Brazil: Anthropological Perspectives: Essays in Honor of Charles Wagley*. New York: Columbia University Press.

Montague, Susan P. 1971. 'Trobriand kinship and the Virgin Birth controversy'. *Man* (n.s.) 6(3): 353–68. doi.org/10.2307/2799026

———. 1974. 'The Trobriand society'. PhD dissertation, Department of Anthropology, University of Chicago.

———. 1983. 'Trobriand gender identity'. In *Concepts of Conception: Procreation Ideologies in Papua New Guinea*, edited by Dan Jorgensen. Special issue of *Mankind* 14(1): 33–45. doi.org/10.1111/j.1835-9310.1983.tb01249.x

———. 2001. 'The Trobriand kinship classification and Schneider's cultural relativism'. In *The Cultural Analysis of Kinship: The Legacy of David M. Schneider*, edited by Richard Feinberg and Martin Ottenheimer, 168–86. Urbana, IL: University of Illinois Press.

Moore, Sally F. 1964. 'Descent and symbolic filiation'. *American Anthropologist* 66(6) Part 1: 1308–20. doi.org/10.1525/aa.1964.66.6.02a00060

Mosko, Mark. 1985. *Quadripartite Structures: Categories, Relations, and Homologies in Bush Mekeo Culture*. Cambridge: Cambridge University Press. doi.org/10.1017/CBO9780511753084

———. 1995. 'Rethinking Trobriand chieftainship'. *Journal of the Royal Anthropological Institute* 1(4): 763–85. doi.org/10.2307/3034960

———. 2005. 'Sex, procreation, and menstruation: North Mekeo and the Trobriands'. In *A Polymath Anthropologist: Essays in Honour of Ann Chowning*, edited by Harriet Lyons, Ann Chowning, Claudia Gross and Dorothy Ayers Counts, 55–61. Research in Anthropology and Linguistics Monograph 6. Department of Anthropology, University of Auckland.

———. 2009. 'The fractal yam: Botanical imagery and human agency in the Trobriands'. *Journal of the Royal Anthropological Institute* 15(4): 679–700. doi.org/10.1111/j.1467-9655.2009.01579.x

———. 2013. 'Omarakana revisited, or "do dual organizations exist?" in the Trobriands'. *Journal of the Royal Anthropological Institute* 19(3): 482–509. doi.org/10.1111/1467-9655.12046

———. 2014. 'Malinowski's magical puzzles: Toward a new theory of magic and procreation in Trobriand society'. *HAU: Journal of Ethnographic Theory* 4(1): 1–47. doi.org/10.14318/hau4.1.001

Murphy, Robert F. 1979. 'Lineage and lineality in lowland South America'. In *Brazil: Anthropological Perspectives: Essays in Honor of Charles Wagley*, edited by Maxine L. Margolis and William E. Carter, 217–24. New York: Columbia University Press.

Overing, Joanna. 1985. 'Today I shall call him "Mummy": Multiple worlds and classificatory confusion'. In *Reason and Morality*, edited by Joanna Overing, 152–79. Association of Social Anthropologists Monograph 24. London: Tavistock Publications.

Overing, Joanna (ed.). 1985. *Reason and Morality*. Association of Social Anthropologists Monograph 24. London: Tavistock Publications.

Powell, Harry A. 1956. 'An analysis of present day social structure in the Trobriand Islands'. PhD thesis, University of London.

———. 1969a. 'Genealogy, residence and kinship in Kiriwina'. *Man* (n.s.) 4(2): 177–202. doi.org/10.2307/2799567

———. 1969b. 'Territory, hierarchy and kinship in Kiriwina'. *Man* (n.s.) 4(4): 580–604. doi.org/10.2307/2798197

———. 1980. 'Review of Annette B. Weiner, *Women of Value, Men Of Renown: New Perspectives on Trobriand Exchange*'. *American Anthropologist* 82(3): 700–702. doi.org/10.1525/aa.1980.82.3.02a01180

Pulman, Bertrand. 2004–05. 'Malinowski and ignorance of physiological paternity'. *Revue francaise de sociologie* 45: 121–42. doi.org/10.3917/rfs.455.0121

Read, Carveth. 1918. 'No paternity'. *Journal of the Royal Anthropological Institute of Great Britin and Ireland* 48: 146–54. doi.org/10.2307/2843507

Rentoul, Alex C. 1931. 'Physiological paternity and the Trobrianders'. *Man* 31: 152–54. doi.org/10.2307/2791374

——. 1932. 'Papuans, professors, and platitudes'. *Man* 32: 274–76. doi.org/10.2307/2789803

Rivers, William H.R. 1914. *The History of Melanesian Society*, vol. 1. Cambridge: Cambridge University Press.

Rosaldo, Michelle Z. and Jane M. Atkinson. 1975. 'Man the hunter and woman: Metaphors for the sexes in Ilongot magical spells'. In *The Interpretation of Symbolism,* edited by Roy Willis, 43–75. London: Malaby Press.

Sahlins, Marshall D. 1976. *The Use and Abuse of Biology: An Anthropological Critique of Sociobiology.* Ann Arbor, MI: The University of Michigan Press.

Sahlins, Marshall. 2013. *What Kinship Is – And Is Not.* Chicago: University of Chicago Press. doi.org/10.7208/chicago/9780226925134.001.0001

Scheffler, Harold W. 1973. 'Kinship, descent, and alliance'. In *Handbook of Social and Cultural Anthropology,* edited by John J. Honigmann, 747–93. Chicago: Rand McNally.

——. 1976. 'The "meaning" of kinship in American culture: another view'. In *Meaning in Anthropology,* edited by Keith H. Basso and Henry A. Selby, 57–91. Albuquerque: University of New Mexico Press.

——. 1978. *Australian Kin Classification.* Cambridge: Cambridge University Press.

——. 2003. 'Observations on *The Fall of Kinship*'. *Journal of Cognition and Culture* 3(4): 341–43. doi.org/10.1163/156853703771818091

Scheffler, Harold W. and Floyd G. Lounsbury. 1971. *A Study in Structural Semantics: The Sirionó Kinship System.* Englewood Cliffs, NJ: Prentice Hall.

Schneider, David M. 1968. *American Kinship: A Cultural Account.* Englewood Cliffs, NJ: Prentice Hall.

——. 1984. *A Critique of the Study of Kinship.* Ann Arbor: University of Michigan Press.

———. 1989. 'Australian Aboriginal kinship.' *Man* (n.s.) 24(1): 165–66.

Seligman, Charles G. 1910. *The Melanesians of British New Guinea*. Cambridge: Cambridge University Press.

Senft, Gunter. 1985. 'How to tell – and understand – a dirty joke in Kilivila'. *Journal of Pragmatics* 9(6): 815–34. doi.org/10.1016/0378-2166(85)90005-0

———. 1991. 'Prolegomena to the pragmatics of "situational-intentional" varieties in Kilivila language'. In *Levels of Linguistic Adaptation: Selected Papers from the International Pragmatics Conference, Antwerp, August 1987*, edited by Jef Verschueren, 235–48. Amsterdam: John Benjamins. doi.org/10.1075/pbns.6.2.15sen

———. 1995. 'Notes from the field: Ain't misbehavin'? Trobriand pragmatics and the field researcher's opportunity to put his (or her) foot in it'. *Oceanic Linguistics* 34(1): 211–26. doi.org/10.2307/3623120

———. 1996. 'Past is present – present is past: Time and the harvest rituals on the Trobriand Islands'. *Anthropos* 91(4–6): 381–89.

———. 1998. '"Noble savages" and the "islands of love": Trobriand Islanders in "popular publications"'. In *Pacific Answers to Western Hegemony: Cultural Practices of Identity Construction*, edited by Jürg Wassmann, 119–40. Oxford: Berg.

———. 2009. 'Bronislaw Kasper Malinowski'. In *Culture and Language Use*, edited by Gunter Senft, Jan-Ola Östman and Jef Verschueren, 210–25. Amsterdam: John Benjamins.

———. 2011. *The Tuma Underworld of Love: Erotic and Other Narrative Songs of the Trobriand Islanders and their Spirits of the Dead*. Amsterdam: John Benjamins. doi.org/10.1075/clu.5

Shapiro, Warren. 1979. *Social Organization in Aboriginal Australia*. Canberra: The Australian National University Press.

———. 1988. 'Ritual kinship, ritual incorporation, and the denial of death'. *Man* (n.s.) 23(2): 275–97. doi.org/10.2307/2802806

——. 1996. 'The Quest for Purity in Anthropological Inquiry'. *Denying Biology: Essays on Gender and Pseudo-Procreation*, edited by Warren Shapiro and Uli Linke, 167–189. Lanham, MD: University Press of America.

——. 2003. 'Review of Richard Feinberg and Martin Oppenheimer (eds) *The Cultural Analysis of Kinship: The Legacy of David M. Schneider*'. *American Anthropologist* 105: 375–77. doi.org/10.1525/aa.2003.105.2.375

——. 2005. 'Universal systems of kin categorization as primitivist projects'. *Anthropological Forum* 15(1): 45–59. doi.org/10.1080/0066467042000336706

——. 2008. 'What human kinship is primarily about: Toward a critique of the new kinship studies'. *Social Anthropology* 16(2): 137–53. doi.org/10.1111/j.1469-8676.2008.00038.x

——. 2009. 'A.L. Kroeber and the new kinship studies'. *Anthropological Forum* 19(1):1–20. doi.org/10.1080/00664670802695418

——. 2010. 'The old kinship studies confronts gay kinship: A critique of Kath Weston'. *Anthropological Forum* 20(1): 1–18. doi.org/10.1080/00664670903524178

——. 2011a. 'The nuclear family *versus* the men's house: A re-examination of Mundurucú sociality'. *Anthropological Forum* 21(1): 57–75. doi.org/10.1080/00664677.2011.549450

——. 2011b. 'What is Malay kinship primarily about? Or the new kinship studies and the fabrication of an ethnographic fantasy'. In *Kinship, Language, and Prehistory: Per Hage and the Renaissance in Kinship Studies*, edited by Doug Jones and Bojka Milicic, 141–51. Salt Lake City: University of Utah Press.

——. 2012. 'Anti-family fantasies in "cutting-edge" anthropological kinship studies'. *Academic Questions* 25(3): 394–402. doi.org/10.1007/s12129-012-9314-7

——. 2013. 'The nuclear family and its derivatives: *That's* what kinship is!' *Journal of the Anthropological Society of Oxford* 5(2): 171–93.

——. 2014. 'Contesting Marshall Sahlins on kinship'. *Oceania* 84(1): 19–37. doi.org/10.1002/ocea.5033

———. 2015. '*Not* "from the natives' point of view": Why the new kinship studies need the old kinship terminologies'. *Anthropos* 110: 1–13.

———. 2016. Why Schneiderian kinship studies have it all wrong: With special reference to adoptive kinship'. *Structure and Dynamics* 9(2): 218–39. Online: escholarship.org/uc/item/1vp7c25g (accessed 31 May 2017).

Shapiro, Warren (ed.). 1990. *On the Generation and Maintenance of Person: Essays in Honour of John Barnes*. Special issue of *The Australian Journal of Anthropology (TAJA)* 1(2–3).

Sider, Karen B. 1967. 'Affinity and the role of the father in the Trobriands'. *Southwestern Journal of Anthropology* 23(1): 90–109. doi.org/10.1086/soutjanth.23.1.3629296

Speck, Frank G. 1918. 'Kinship terms and the family band among the northeastern Algonkian'. *American Anthropologist* 20(2): 143–61. doi.org/10.1525/aa.1918.20.2.02a00010

Stanner, William E.H. 1960. 'On Aboriginal religion. II: Sacramentalism, rite and myth'. *Oceania* 30(4): 245–78. doi.org/10.1002/j.1834-4461.1960.tb00226.x

Tambiah, Stanley J. 1968. 'The magical power of words'. *Man* (n.s.) 3(2): 175–208. doi.org/10.2307/2798500

Tooker, Elizabeth. 1971. 'Clans and moieties in North America'. *Current Anthropology* 12(3): 357–76. doi.org/10.1086/201211

Verschueren, Jef (ed.). 1991. *Levels of Linguistic Adaptation: Selected Papers from the International Pragmatics Conference, Antwerp, August 1987*. Amsterdam: John Benjamins.

Walker, James R. 1914. 'Oglala kinship terms'. *American Anthropologist* 16(1): 96–109. doi.org/10.1525/aa.1914.16.1.02a00080

Wassmann, Jürg (ed.).1998. *Pacific Answers to Western Hegemony: Cultural Practices of Identity Construction*. Oxford: Berg.

Weiner, Annette B. 1976. *Women of Value, Men of Renown: New Perspectives on Trobriand Exchange*. Austin: University of Texas Press.

———. 1977. 'Trobriand descent: Female/male domains'. *Ethos* 5(1): 54–70. doi.org/10.1525/eth.1977.5.1.02a00050

———. 1983. 'From words to objects to magic: Hard words and the boundaries of social interaction'. *Man* (n.s.) 18(4): 690–709. doi.org/10.2307/2801903

Weston, Kath. 1991. *Families We Choose: Lesbians, Gays, Kinship*. New York: Columbia University Press.

Williams, F.E. 1936. *Papuans of the Trans-Fly*. Oxford: Clarendon Press.

Willis, Roy (ed.). 1975. *The Interpretation of Symbolism*. London: Malaby Press.

Young, Michael W. 2004. *Malinowski: Odyssey of an Anthropologist*. New Haven, CT: Yale University Press.

2

Extension Problem: Resolution Through an Unexpected Source

Dwight Read

> I said, indeed, that the science of colour was mathematical ... the absolute certainty of a science cannot exceed the certainty of its principles ... And if these principles be such that on them a mathematician may determine all the phenomena of colours ... the science of colour will be granted mathematical (Sir Isaac Newton 1782 [1672]: 342).[1]

Prologue

A long-standing issue in kinship theory stems from the presence of kinship terminologies with kin terms having genealogical referents crosscutting, rather than following, the pattern for genealogical relations. The notion that the genealogical referents should be in agreement with genealogical relations arises from the assumption, going back to Lewis Henry Morgan, that the kinship relations identified through a kinship terminology are based on procreation in conjunction with marriage. If both kin terms and genealogical relations are determined mainly through procreation, then, at first glance, it appears that they should be mutually consistent, but this is not the case for some terminologies. Despite attempts from Morgan onwards to account for this seeming anomaly, the issue still

---

1 I thank Burt Voorhees for bringing this quote to my attention.

remains unresolved. Much of the writing of Harold Scheffler, both alone and in conjunction with Floyd Lounsbury, was directed towards a possible resolution of the 'extension problem' of a terminology having kin terms with both close and distant genealogical referents. They proposed that a kin term has a primary meaning expressed through the genealogical referent(s) closest, in a culturally meaningful way, to speaker and a secondary meaning provided by the other referent(s). The primary meaning, they argued, derives from procreation and so the resolution task becomes, from their perspective, one of addressing the secondary meanings that do not derive from procreation in any obvious way. Their solution involved first relating the secondary referents to the primary ones and then accounting for why more distant genealogical referents should be so equated as genealogical referents of a kin term.

Their project was only partially successful. They implemented the first part of the project through formal equivalence rules that reduced the secondary referents to the primary ones, but the second part became mired in debates over whether the equivalence rules had cultural saliency or merely provided an elegant, formal descriptive account of a terminology. Though their project did not achieve all of its goals, it did establish that terminologies are not just a collection of terms with genealogical referents whose patterning is determined by external factors such as the group organisation of the society in question, as argued by Edmund Leach (1958) for the Trobrianders. Instead, their work implied that terminologies must have an internal logic, thereby contributing to our understanding of what is common across terminologies despite surface differences. It is here where Scheffler's work will leave an enduring mark.

In my contribution to this *Festschrift*, I begin, in effect, where the work of Scheffler and Lounsbury left off, namely by working out the internal logic of kinship terminologies and using this logic to resolve the extension problem. Another motivation for so doing, beyond its relevance to furthering our understanding of kinship systems by resolving the extension problem, relates to whether it is culturally reasonable to consider kinship terminologies as being mathematical in the manner expressed in the epigraph to this chapter when we replace the word 'colour' by the phrase 'kinship terminologies', hence amenable to formal analysis in a culturally salient manner using mathematical reasoning. A positive answer would confirm what W.H.R. Rivers foresaw as a possibility: 'the time will come when ... parts of the description of social systems of savage tribes will resemble a work on mathematics' (1914: 10).

Carrying out this enterprise in toto requires rethinking widespread assumptions such as 'kin categories are genealogically structured' and 'kinship space is built up recursively out of genealogical primitives' (Jones Chapter 11) that have led to an ontology going from procreation to genealogical relations to categories of genealogical relations to kin terms as labels for those categories and then replacing this ontology with a different one. The different ontology is based on tracing the implications of the cultural knowledge that culture bearers bring to bear when they compute kinship relations directly from kin terms without reference to the genealogical relations that supposedly are the underpinnings of those terms. Considering kinship terminologies from this perspective has been surprisingly fruitful and leads to resolution of the extension problem by showing that the extensions are the consequence of the generative logic giving structure to kinship terminologies.[2] To go from where Scheffler and Lounsbury left off to this resolution of the extension problem, though by a different route than the one they followed, is the primary goal of this chapter and is necessarily a long trip, but hopefully one worth taking, as it validates the basic ideas that Scheffler had about the extension of kinship terms, but by a different means than the one he used.

Introduction

The distinctions among, and organisation of, the terms making up a kinship terminology relate to various aspects of social systems through the kinship relations they represent. These kinship relations have generally been viewed, since the time of Lewis Henry Morgan (1871), from the perspective of being formed either through procreation or through marriage. Typically, analysis begins by working out the distribution of kin terms over genealogical positions in accordance with the genealogical method introduced by Rivers (1910, 1912; see also Warren Shapiro Chapter 1). In the genealogical method, informants are asked for the kin terms that would be used by speaker for persons in various genealogical positions with respect to speaker. The underlying presumption has been that the structural pattern of kin terms over genealogical positions should reflect the structural organisation of genealogical relations, though

---

2   In email correspondence, Warren Shapiro suggested to me the possibility that the generative logic underlying kinship terminology structure addresses the extensionist problem (2009). What I present here is my follow-up to his suggestion.

modified according to the way the social organisation of a society relates to, and is expressed through, the kinship relations corresponding to the kin terms. However, from the very start of Morgan's systematic study of kinship terminologies, terminologies like that of the Seneca (Iroquois) presented an anomaly by virtue of having kin terms with genealogical referents that crosscut the structural pattern of genealogical relations. In the Seneca terminology, the kin term *no-yeh'* ('mother') (and similarly *hä-nih'* ('father'), is used not only for mother, a lineal relation, but also for collaterally related females in her generation, meaning that the terminology does not systematically distinguish lineal from collateral genealogical relations.[3] Morgan, through his background as a lawyer, was familiar with the importance of this genealogical distinction for English family law regarding inheritance. Accordingly, he divided terminologies into those that consistently keep lineal genealogical relations separate from collateral relations and those that do not. He referred to the former as descriptive terminologies and to the latter as classificatory terminologies. In his scheme, the English terminology is descriptive and the Seneca terminology is classificatory.[4]

With regard to the occurrence in some societies of the classificatory terminologies, Morgan asked: Why should a term used for individuals with a close, lineal relation to speaker also be extended to speaker's distant collateral relatives? In particular, why should there be kin terms such as *no-yeh'* and *hä-nih'* that refer to mother and father, respectively, as well as to persons in collateral positions of the same generation and sex as mother and father? This disjunction between the pattern of genealogical relations corresponding to kin terms in what he called the classificatory terminologies and the pattern of genealogical distinctions derived through procreation has come to be known as the *extension problem*. For what reason are there terminologies in which genealogical referents of a kin term are extended from close, lineal genealogical relations consistent with procreation to more distant, collateral genealogical relations for some of the kin terms?

---

3   Because an English word such as mother can either refer to a genealogical relation or to a kin term, I will use italics when the word refers to a kin term. The English kin-term translation for a non-English kin term will be given in single quotes.
4   The classificatory part of Morgan's two-part typology has subsequently been divided into *bifurcate merging terminologies* in which the lineal terms merge together both lineal and collateral genealogical relations as their referents and the lineal line of kin terms are bifurcated into terms that distinguish between matrilateral and patrilateral relations, and *generational terminologies* that primarily distinguish between sex and generation of the kin-term referents.

Morgan's answer to this question derives from his assumption that kinship relations are determined either through procreation or marriage. If the pattern for the genealogical referents of a kin term does not derive from procreation, as was evident for the Seneca terminology, then it must derive from marriage or a combination of procreation and marriage. Accordingly, Morgan hypothesised an earlier practice of group brother-sister marriage as a way to account for terminologies with kin terms that include both lineal and collateral genealogical referents. This, however, was subsequently dismissed as empirically unfounded (but see Knight 2011 for an alternative viewpoint), leaving the extension problem unresolved.

The solution to the extension problem that will be presented here requires reconsidering the widespread assumption that kin terms are primarily names for already established categories of genealogical relations. This leads me to ask whether the kinship relations labelled by the kin terms making up a kinship terminology are derived directly from primary relations, such as the relations linking family members. The (positive) answer to this question leads me to the discovery that kinship relations identified through kin terms can be derived directly from the family relations through a computational logic based on the way culture bearers determine kinship relations directly from kin-term usage. Once this logic has been worked out, I can then show how the extension problem is resolved by reference to an unexpected source for a solution, namely whether siblings are culturally understood as those persons who share the same parents as oneself rather than as the children of one's parents other than oneself. These two ways of conceptualising siblings are biologically equivalent, but differ according to whether parents are viewed from the sibling's perspective as having commonly shared ascendants or from the parent's perspective as their descendants. As we will see, the first way for conceptualising siblings both underscores extension of the referents of kin terms from lineal to collateral genealogical relations and accounts for Morgan's distinction between descriptive and classificatory terminologies. This makes the distinction between these two kinds of terminologies, and the presence of terms in the classificatory terminologies that include both collateral and lineal genealogical referents, a consequence of properties internal, rather than external, to the kinship system.

Previous attempts to solve the extension problem

Like Morgan's proposed solution, possible answers to the extension problem offered subsequent to him have also been problematic. Some have used a semantic/linguistic approach to resolve or even dismiss the problem (Buchler and Selby 1968). Notably, Alfred Kroeber (1909) attempted to dismiss the problem by asserting that Morgan had erred in making a distinction between descriptive and classificatory terminologies in the first place since, in his view, all terminologies have kin terms that are classificatory in their scope, but his argument rests upon a misreading of Morgan's classificatory/descriptive distinction. Morgan's distinction is not based on whether *kin terms* are descriptive or classificatory (Kroeber's misreading), but whether the terminology structurally and consistently distinguishes between lineal and collateral *genealogical relations*. Morgan was fully aware that English terms such as English *uncle* or *aunt* are classificatory in Kroeber's sense, yet the English terminology is descriptive in his schema since the kin terms with lineal genealogical referents do not include collateral referents.[5]

Subsequent to Kroeber, Arthur Maurice Hocart (1937) and Joseph Daniel Unwin (1929) also dismissed the extension problem. They each considered the problem to be an artefact of how the problem was defined in the first place. Hocart considered that assigning a primary and an extended meaning to a kin term reflected more the way kin terms were elicited and learned by the ethnographer than the cultural reality of the primary/extended distinction. Thus, he argued, the term *tama* in Melanesian terminologies ought to be translated as 'all males of the previous generation on the father's side' (Hocart 1937: 546) in an undifferentiated sense, rather than as *tama* meaning, first of all, father, and then, by extension, 'father's brother, father's father's brother's sons and so on' (ibid.: 545). However, whether a term such as *tama* should be considered polysemic (Scheffler's position, discussed below) or monosemic (Hocart's and Unwin's position) does not resolve the problem identified

---

5   See, for example, Morgan's (1871) comment regarding the English terminology: 'the second [collateral line], *uncle, cousin, cousin's son,* and *cousin's grandson* … **reveal[s] a tendency to avoid the full descriptive phrases**. It is evident from the present structure and past history of the English system … [that] an uncle was described as *father's brother*, or *mother's brother* [italics in the original, bold added]' (32, 33).

by Morgan regarding the discordance between the genealogical referents of the term and the structural pattern of genealogical relations. Instead, viewing kin terms monosemically mainly changes what a resolution to the problem needs to address.

Others, such as Edward Evan Evans-Pritchard (1929, 1932), Brenda Seligman (1929), and Bronisław Malinowski (1927a, 1930) used a social learning approach to account for the presumed kin-term extensions going from primary to extended meanings (Buchler and Selby 1968). In this approach, the extensions are considered to be psychological phenomena reflecting how behaviour patterns are learned by a growing child, initially in accordance with a child's close, genealogical relations and subsequently extended to more distant genealogical relations. Evans-Pritchard (1929), for example, argued for the extension of the emotions and sentiments expressed within the family to individuals outside of the family as the source for kin-term extensions. For Malinowski, more was involved than the extension of sentiments within the family to those outside of the family. Malinowski considered the so-called classificatory terms to result from a gradual substitution process through which the child undergoes vicarious parent substitutions involving close kin relations in which 'the substitute parent resembles in certain respects the original one and ... the naming [of kin terms] expresses this partial assimilation' (1962: 73). As others have pointed out, though, Malinowski incorrectly equates the learning process of a child with the evolutionary origin of the kin terms whose meanings are being learned by the child. In addition, no criterion is provided for when the substitution process should occur and when it should not, hence the argument becomes circular when used to resolve the extension problem.

Other scholars such as A.R. Radcliffe-Brown, though accepting the assumptions made by Morgan, included properties in addition to those of reproduction and marriage as a way to account for the extensions. Radcliffe-Brown (1950) hypothesised, as a solution to the extension problem, what he dubbed 'the equivalence of siblings', meaning that a term used for one sibling would be used in the same manner for all other siblings. According to this hypothesis, if speaker refers to genealogical father by the kin term 'father', then speaker would extend that kin term to speaker's father's brother. However, Radcliffe-Brown did not provide a criterion for when the hypothesis is applicable (Murdock 1949); hence every terminology should be classificatory according to his hypothesis if it applies at all. Also problematic, his hypothesis did not address features common to classificatory (but not descriptive) terminologies such as an older/younger distinction in the referents of the sibling kin terms.[6]

A formal attempt to resolve the extension problem

Primary versus secondary meaning of kin terms

The extension problem has also been addressed formally, first by Floyd Lounsbury (1964, 1965) with regard to the logic of kinship terminologies, then with Harold Scheffler (especially Scheffler and Lounsbury 1971), and subsequently by Scheffler alone (see in particular, Scheffler 1978) with regard to the semantics of kinship terminologies. They, too, assumed that kinship relations are engendered through procreation, but avoided turning to marriage as the basis for the extension of the genealogical referents of kin terms. They accomplished this by separating the category of genealogical referents into two parts: (1) primary (or kernel) referents consisting of close genealogical relations and (2) secondary referents consisting of the more remote genealogical relations (Lounsbury 1965: 149). For the classificatory terminologies, the primary referents of a kin term are its lineal referents and the collateral referents its secondary referents. For a descriptive terminology, such as the English terminology, the primary referents include most, if not all, of the genealogical referents of a kin term; for example, the primary referents of English *uncle* are father's brother and mother's brother. After determining the primary referents, they constructed *equivalence rules* that formally relate the secondary meanings to the primary meanings.

---

6   The matter is more complex, though, than just not addressing the older/younger distinction. The term translated as 'older brother' or 'older sister' is, in some classificatory terminologies, also used for a reference person younger than speaker. In the Tongan terminology, a male speaker refers to the son of the older brother of father as *ta'okete* ('older same-sex sibling') regardless of their relative ages, even though the terminology makes no distinction between father and father's brother, with both of these males referred to as *ta'mai* ('father') (Biersack 1982: 184). From an ascending/descending perspective (discussed below), *ta'okete* would be 'ascending same-sex sibling.' Since *ta'mai* is an ascending primary term, 'son' of *ta'mai* can be considered to be part of the ascending kin-term structure and so referring to 'son' of *ta'mai* as *ta'okete* for the older brother of father, regardless of the relative ages of speaker and alter, is structurally consistent.

Their methodology of equivalence rules has played a central role in our understanding of the semantics of kinship terms (McConvell Chapter 7) and was utilised extensively by David Kronenfeld (2009) as part of his analyses of the kinship terminology of the Fanti in Ghana, Africa, from a behavioural perspective. Since others have already discussed the widely appreciated ground-breaking character of Lounsbury's work in detail, there is no need to review it further here. In addition, the importance of Scheffler's contribution to this work is also well established, as discussed in the Introduction and in the chapter by Patrick McConvell, hence also needs no further elaboration. Instead, the thread I take up in this chapter relates to the reasons, despite the important contribution that equivalence rules have made to our understanding of the logic of kinship terminologies, that these rules do not resolve the extension problem. Then I show that, *in lieu* of considering kin terms formally as a means for the categorisation of genealogical relations, if we trace out, instead, the implications of the logic by which culture bearers compute kinship relations directly through the kin terms making up their kinship terminology (which may be done without reference to genealogical relations), we now find a solution to the extension problem.[7]

The underlying problem with the equivalence rules as explanation for kin-term extensions is that they leave unanswered the reasons why terminologies like the classificatory terminologies deviate so widely in both their semantic and their syntactical form from the genealogical framework generally assumed to be the basis for the systems of kinship relations expressed through kinship terminologies. More specifically, Lounsbury and Scheffler's proposed resolution of the extension problem through equivalence rules has three critical problems (discussed below) that limit their role to one of identifying clues leading to answers, rather than providing the answers, with regard to questions about intersystem differences in the structure and organisation of kinship terminologies.[8]

---

7   Other formalism accounts include the book by the mathematician Sydney Gould (2000) aimed at improving on the equivalence rules and the book by Pin-Hsiung Liu (1986) aimed at formally showing how the genealogical space is structured by a kinship terminology. With regard to Gould's book, Scheffler (2002: 295) comments that his attempt to improve on the formalism of equivalence rules 'has to be reckoned a complete failure'. Anna Wierzbicka (2016: 409 n1) criticises Gould for the lack of natural language evidence justifying his assumption, made for formal reasons, that 'father's child' and 'mother's child' are primary relations.
8   The limitations apply equally to the work of Gould (2000). These limitations also include the circularity that enters in when the equivalence rules are read as being explanatory of the extension problem, since delineation of the rules requires already knowing both the structural organisation of kin terms as a kinship terminology and the genealogical definitions of kin terms.

Another major concern is the issue raised virtually a half-century ago by Kris Lehman—perhaps the foremost scholar in the area of integrating mathematical reasoning with anthropological theorising. Lehman recognised that the equivalence rule analysis relied upon a formally naïve (in a mathematical sense) notion of genealogy that leads to a genealogical space infinite in size, hence exceeding the capacity of the human mind to consider all possible genealogical relations making up a genealogical space in a holistic sense (Lehman 2011). This implied, he pointed out, that a kinship terminology system, supposedly derivative from a genealogical space (see Jones Chapter 11), cannot provide the kind of holistic analysis presumed by the methodology of equivalence rules. Instead, he argued, rather than relying on an intuitively understood genealogical space expressed through the notational system of kin types, the methodology of equivalence rules needs a well-formulated mathematical representation of the genealogical space before one can adequately define, in a conceptually closed manner (see Leaf and Read 2012; Jones Chapter 11), what would formally constitute an adequate extension-based analysis of kinship terminologies. Accordingly, Lehman developed a mathematical representation of the genealogical space that he referred to as the Primary Genealogical Space (PGS) (see Lehman and Witz 1974). From this perspective, a formal system should, for example, encompass Kronenfeld's (2009) formal representation of the Fanti kinship terminology.

Subsequently, and building on the arguments of Read, Lehman came to realise that the entire equivalence rule enterprise was inadequate and could not achieve its goals:

> Lounsbury's rewrite system said nothing about the organization of the genealogical space itself ... [and] there is no evidence to suggest that ... compacting of PGS [through rewrite rules] generates the actual structure of any KTS [Kin Term Space] (2011: 260, 262).

That is, the rewrite rules leave unexplained precisely what we want to understand, namely the basis upon which one kinship terminology differs structurally from another kinship terminology. As Lehman notes:

> Read and his colleagues (Behrens and Read 1993; Read and Behrens 1990; Read 2001, 2007, 2010a, 2010b; Bennardo and Read 2005, 2007) have shown persuasively that a KTS has a distinct algebraic structure that is not all that much like PGS, and that is altogether unlikely to be generated by the compacting of PGS (2011: 264).

2. EXTENSION PROBLEM

Where, by 'compacting', Lehman means the equivalence rule mapping of genealogical relations expressed through kin-type notation to the extended meaning of the kin terms making up a kinship terminology. It is precisely an analytical foundation suitable for explicating the structure of a kinship terminology that is lacking in the formalism developed by Lounsbury and Scheffler, a lack that stems from the following three problems with their equivalence rules paradigm.

Problem 1: Description versus explanation

By itself, the distinction between primary and secondary referents only describes, but does not explain, the structural difference between descriptive and classificatory terminologies, as Lounsbury (1965: 175–81) recognised. Scheffler and Lounsbury attempted to build explanation into the primary/secondary distinction through the equivalence rules, but the rules are open ended (Chomsky 1963); that is, there is no restriction on what can be an equivalence rule. Thus it is always possible to make the extended, genealogical referent of a kin term equivalent to a primary referent with a rule such as: 'Rewrite the non-primary genealogical referents for a kin term as a primary genealogical referent for that kin term', with one rule per term, along with the stipulation that the rule applies only to that term. Consequently, just being able to formally reduce the extended genealogical referents of kin terms to primary referents through equivalence rules only describes how the extended referents of a kin term can be related to its primary referents (Keen 1985), not *why* the extensions occurred in the first place (Read 2000).

Problem 2: Equivalence rules provide a window only partially opening onto the structural logic of kinship terminologies

Though equivalence rules, by themselves, are not explanatory, nonetheless the rules indicate that there is an underlying logic to kinship terminologies since many of the rules are not terminology specific. As Roy D'Andrade has commented: 'it is reassuring that most analyses [of kinship terminologies] can be accomplished with only a few rules' (1970: 112–13). The parsimony of the rules used to formally connect the primary and secondary referents of a kin term suggests that there is a structural logic by which the kin terms form a coherent whole, but they do not make that logic evident. As Keen has put it, the equivalence rules 'may be said to capture "underlying principles" *in some sense* [emphasis added]' (1985: 82). It is through making the logic of those underlying principles complete, and not the equivalence rules, *per se*, that provides, as we will see, the means to effect a culturally salient resolution to the extension problem.

Problem 3: Cultural saliency

Scheffler and Lounsbury (1971) recognised that the equivalence rules do not provide an explanatory account unless they are meaningful to the users of the terminology. Though Lounsbury sketched out a possible sociological justification for the equivalence rules he had adduced for the Trobriand terminology, he also considered his sketch to only be 'a suggestion as to the kinds of data in which we might expect to find some answers' (1965: 180). Yet with regard to the kinship terminology of the Fanti, instead of finding ethnographic support for equivalence rules, Kronenfeld (2009) discovered that the rules were not meaningful to the Fanti. Kronenfeld had analysed their terminology in two ways: first, through an equivalence rules account based on the formalism of Lounsbury (1964, 1965) that he referred to as an 'L analysis', and second, through the way the Fanti determined the kinship relation between two individuals directly from kin terms without reference to genealogical relations using what Kronenfeld referred to as the relative products of kin terms (actually, kin-term products, as discussed below).[9] Kronenfeld referred to the latter as an 'F analysis' and commented that the Fanti *explained or justified* their terminological assignment of kinsmen [emphasis added]' (2009: 60) through the 'logic contained in the relative products'. He observed that:

> The F analysis seems closer to the way Fanti define their own kin terms than does the L analysis. It is based on the categories that the Fanti use, and it performs the operations on these categories that Fanti informants were observed to use … the F analysis is psychologically real in the sense that it very directly represents what my informants did in their heads when they themselves calculated correct kinship relations (ibid.: 67).

For the Fanti, it is the 'F analysis', based on products of kin terms, and not the 'L analysis', based on equivalence rules, that is culturally salient. Kris Lehman makes much the same point with regard to the Lai (Haka) Chin among whom he did fieldwork:

---

9   As noted by Lehman (2011: 264–65), 'kin term products … are algebraically not the same thing as the relative products of kin type strings.'

Any speaker simply knows that, for example, C[*fa*] of B [u-*naau*] = C [*fu*], whilst C of Z [*far*] = grandchild [*tu*]. One can more or less indirectly deduce such equations from the logic of the PGS > KTS morphism map [i.e. from the equivalence rules], but that is demonstrably *not what native speakers do*; it is not how they represent or talk about such knowledge [emphasis added] (2011: 264).

Despite recognising its cultural saliency, Kronenfeld rejected the F analysis for comparative purposes since the Fanti categories and relations among them are not universal, whereas, he argued, the units for the L analysis are derived from a genealogical space that is universally applicable: '[T]he categories and operations of [the F] analysis are too peculiar to the Fanti to make them a good basis for comparing the Fanti system with others' (Kronenfeld 2009: 70). Kronenfeld reconciled the two kinds of analysis by viewing them as having different purposes, hence different criteria for analytic validity: criteria relating, he asserts, to psychological reality in the case of the F analysis and to the requirements of intersystem comparison for the L analysis (ibid.: 70; see also Keen 1985).[10] The value of the L analysis, he says, lies in 'how well it facilitates comparison of the given system with other similar ones' (Kronenfeld 2009: 69), and the L analysis, he argues, unlike the K analysis, identifies 'the different means by which different kinds of social facts can affect a terminology' (ibid.), which presumes that social facts are the driver of terminological distinctions, a proposition found wanting in previous attempts to resolve the extension problem through, for example, marriage rules.

While Kronenfeld observes correctly that some of the specific properties of the Fanti terminology are not universal, his conclusion that this obviates intersystem comparison through what he calls an F analysis is not correct unless one were to limit comparison to using the units and kin-term products of the Fanti terminology. Obviously, units specific to the Fanti terminology cannot be treated as universal units upon which intersystem comparison of structural differences among kinship terminologies should be based. What Kronenfeld did not recognise, though, is that the principles leading to the generation of a kinship terminology from primary kin terms—the latter being the kin terms specifying family relations

---

10 This dichotomy is rejected by Anna Wierzbicka (2016) on the grounds that one and the same analysis can both elucidate the cognitive/psychological operations employed by the users of a terminology and enable a cross-cultural comparison of terminologies.

(Read, Fischer and Lehman 2014)—leads universally to computational systems enabling culture bearers to determine kinship relations (Read 2007; Leaf and Read 2012; Read, Fischer and Lehman 2014), and these computational systems can be the basis for comparison.[11] It is the structure generated from the units of a kinship terminology, not the units themselves, through which intersystem structural comparison should be made.

What is common across kinship terminologies is a conceptually bounded set of kin terms (Leaf 2006; Leaf and Read 2012), the kin-term product (technically, a binary product) as the means for working out the structural relations among those kin terms, and culturally salient, structural equations giving a terminology structure its particular form. By recognising that intersystem comparison may be made at the level of these elements, Lehman (2011) draws the opposite conclusion as does Kronenfeld from the ethnographic facts establishing the cultural saliency of computing kin relations using kin terms and the kin-term product. Whereas Kronenfeld sees noncomparable units, Lehman perspicaciously observes:

> It seems to me that one of the most significant facts ... is something that I have never been able to handle effectively from the standpoint of PGS, namely, that Read's algebraic structures are in large measure based upon the kin knowledge speakers have of the proper way to 'navigate' the KTS system ... the KTS structure is indeed independently motivated [from PGS] and ... *products in KTS become a symbolic computational system* [emphasis added] (2011: 264).

We can compare computational systems of kin terms with regard to their structural properties even when each is built out of different units since a structure is determined by the relations holding among units, not by the individual properties of the units, hence comparison may be made with regard to those relations rather than the properties of the units connected through those relations (see Read 2011 for examples of this kind of structural comparison across otherwise unrelated domains). For

---

11   Were his argument applied to the comparison of the grammars of different languages, analysis could not be made unless each language was first expressed using a universal vocabulary. Kronenfeld does not take into account the fact that structural forms are analytically comparable even when each is generated from different units and structural equations. The basis for structural differences among terminologies needs to be made evident, not simply described through translating them into a common framework such as genealogical relations organised in the form of the genealogical grid. Even here, though, the supposed universality is problematic with terminologies that have sibling kin terms differentiated by criteria in addition to sex since sibling kin types typically only incorporate sex as a distinguishing feature.

kinship systems, we may make comparison through the product relations structurally connecting kin terms to one another, rather than through the properties of the kin terms, per se, such as their genealogical definitions. It is the logic of making kinship relation computations using primary kin terms, then, that leads, as we will see, to a resolution of the extension problem.

Kin-term calculations and cultural saliency

The kind of kin-term calculations made by the Fanti or the Lai (Haka) Chin without reference to genealogical relations is widespread and has been commented upon by numerous ethnographers (Keen 1985 and references therein), thus showing the widespread, if not universal, cultural saliency of emic calculations like this. For instance, in reference to the Kariera, a huntergatherer group in Western Australia, Radcliffe-Brown wrote:

> The method of determining the relationship of two individuals is extremely simple. Let us suppose ... that two men, A and B, meet each other for the first time. The man A has relative C who is his mama. At the same time, C is the kaga of B. It immediately follows that A and B are kumbali to each other (1913: 150–51).

Similarly, Marshall Sahlins comments for the Moala Fijians:

> [Kin] terms permit comparative strangers to fix kinship rapidly without the necessity of elaborate genealogical reckoning—reckoning that typically would be impossible. With mutual relationship terms all that is required is the discovery of one common relative. Thus, if A is related to B as child to mother, veitanani, while C is related to B as veitacini, sibling of the same sex, then it follows that A is related to C as child to mother although they never before met or knew it. Kin terms are predicable. If two people are each related to a third, then they are related to each other (1962: 155).

In reference to the Kondaiyankottai Maravar, a Dravidian language group in southern India, Anthony Good writes:

> If ego knows what term to use for alter A, and also knows what term A uses for alter B, he can easily work out what term he himself should use for B (1981: 113).

With regard to the Shipibo, a horticulture group in Amazonian Peru, Clifford Behrens observes that:

> Kin terms are elicited from informants without their recourse to genealogical relationships; rather, terms of reference are assigned to individuals by tracing only through the terms themselves ... Two women used the kin terms they applied to a third individual in order to determine the kin relation between their offspring and that person (1984: 146).

In the same vein, Stephen Levinson notes with respect to those living on Rossel Island in New Guinea:

> Kinship reckoning on Rossel does not rely on knowledge of kin-type strings ... What is essential in order to apply a kin term to an individual X, is to know how someone else, of a determinate kinship type to oneself, refers to X. From that knowledge alone, a correct appellation can be deduced. For example, suppose someone I call a tîdê 'sister' calls X a tp:ee 'my child', then I can call X a chênê 'my nephew', without having the faintest idea of my genealogical connection to X (2006: 18).

Laurent Dousset also makes it evident that reckoning kinship relations between individuals in this manner applies not only to the two persons in question, but also to everyone in the community:

> When two foreigners can both trace their classificatory relationships towards a third person, the remaining relationships among *all other members of the community* can be deduced from this set [emphasis added] (2005: 22).

Others have also commented on the way kin relations can be determined directly from kin terms, such as Rusiate Nayacakalou (1955) for the TokaToka villagers in Fiji, Martin Silverman (1971) for the Banaban Islanders in Polynesia, Raymond Case Kelly (1977: 69) for the Etoro of Papua New Guinea, Masri Singarimbun (1975: 147) for the Karo Batak of North Sumatra, Joanna Overing Kaplan (1975: 181) for the Piaroa of the Orinoco Basin, Lorna Marshall (1976) for the !Kung san of Botswana, Richard Feinberg (1981: 106) for the Anuta of Polynesia, Peter Gow (1991: 193–94) for the Piro of the Peruvian Amazonia, Aparecida Vilaça (2002: 352) for the Wari' of Brazil, and Alan Barnard (2010: 252) for the Naro of southern Africa, among others.

Kin-term products

These observations imply that if two persons know their respective kin-term relationship to a third person, then they may compute the kinship relation they have to each other through their cultural knowledge regarding how the kin terms making up their kinship terminology are interrelated. They do the computations without reference to the genealogical relations subsumed under the kin terms. I will refer to computing a kin term from a pair of kin terms in this manner as the *kin-term product* of that pair of kin terms.[12] We may formally define (compare with the quote above from Good 1981) the kin-term product as follows:

> **Definition**: Suppose K and L are kin terms, then the *kin term product* of the kin terms K and L, is a kin term M that speaker would (properly) use (if any) for alter 2 when alter1 (properly) refers to alter 2 by the kin term K and speaker (properly) refers to alter 1 by the kin term L (Read 1984: 422).

I include, parenthetically, the expression 'properly' in the definition to indicate that the kin-term product refers to usage that most, if not all, culture bearers agree is correct, or view as being their way to use this kin term. I also include, parenthetically, the caveat 'if any' since even though the kin term product may be meaningful, it need not correspond to a kin term. For example, for English speakers, the product of the kin terms *father* and *father-in-law* does not correspond to an English kin term even though the kin-term product *father* of *father-in-law* is meaningful; that is, this corresponds, for English speakers, to a situation where speaker refers to a man [alter 1] as *father* and that man refers to another man [alter 2] as *father-in-law*, which is meaningful from a communication viewpoint, yet speaker does not have a kin term that refers to alter 2. Additionally, the definition states 'is *a* kin term' rather than 'is *the* kin term' since, in some situations (though not often) the kin-term product may correspond to more than one kin term. For example, for English speakers, the kin-term product *mother* of *1st-cousin-once removed* (where *mother* and *1st-cousin-once removed* are kin terms) may either be the kin term *1st-cousin* or the kin term *great-aunt* since *1st-cousin-once-removed* is a self-reciprocal kin term used either for speaker's first cousin's child or speaker's great-aunt's child.

---

12   Read (1984) introduced the expression *kin-term product* to designate computations with kin terms in place of the expression *relative product* since the latter does not specifically refer to kin-term computations and is generally used to refer to the concatenation of genealogical relations.

We will formally denote that the kin-term product of the kin terms K and L leads to the kin term M by the equation, K o L = M (read: 'the product of the kin term K with the kin term L, denoted by K o L, is the kin term M' or in simple word form, 'K of L is M.' Here 'of' is formally denoted by the symbol 'o', 'is' by the symbol '=', and K, L and M are kin terms, not persons or genealogical relations. Thus (for English speakers), if alter 1 refers to alter 2 by the kin term *daughter* (= K) and speaker refers to alter 1 by the kin term *aunt* (= L), then speaker, drawing upon her or his cultural knowledge, knows that she or he may properly refer to alter 2 by the kin term *cousin* (= M) and so the kin-term product of *daughter* and *aunt* is *cousin* (see Figure 1); more formally, *daughter* o *aunt* = *cousin*. What we derive or express through the kin-term product is, or can be, expressed in a culturally salient manner.[13] This does not mean that results obtained through the equivalence rules lack cultural saliency, only that the latter must be demonstrated and not assumed.

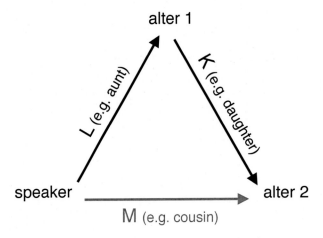

Figure 1. Kin-term product of L (aunt) and K (daughter) is M (cousin)
Labelled (black) arrows show the reference kin term (properly) used by speaker and alter 1 and by alter 1 for alter 2. The grey arrow shows the term known from cultural knowledge to be (properly) used by speaker for alter 2.
Source: Constructed by © Dwight Read.

---

[13] Kin-term product equations can be elicited systematically from informants as Leaf (2006) discusses in detail and illustrates with the Punjabi terminology (see also Leaf and Read 2012).

Assumed genealogical basis for kin terms contradicted by ethnographic evidence

The fact that culturally meaningful computations are made consistently by culture bearers through the kin-term product strongly suggests that a kinship terminology is not simply a list of terms corresponding to already determined categories of genealogical relations, as has generally been assumed, but has an underlying computational logic that enables culture bearers to make kin-term computations in a consistent and noncontradictory manner without reference to genealogical definitions of kin terms. From this perspective, a kinship terminology would be structured through kin-term products made with primary kin terms, where the primary terms are terms for the family relations, rather than through an ontological sequence beginning with genealogical relations. For English speakers, the primary terms include the kin terms *father*, *mother* (or *parent*), *brother*, *sister* (or *sibling*), *son*, *daughter* (or *child*), *husband* and *wife* (or *spouse*).

Thus we need to reconsider the assumption that the ontological sequence for the kinship relations expressed through the terms making up a kinship terminology is: procreation → genealogical relations → categories of genealogical relations → kin terms. In this sequence, the genealogical relations are assumed to stem from procreatively determined parent/child connections, augmented by a marriage relation that links a putative father with a presumed mother. The first part of the sequence, procreation → genealogical relations, is not problematic so long as we include the caveat that it involves procreation as it is locally understood and culturally expressed (Scheffler and Lounsbury 1971: 37),[14] meaning

---

14   Going from procreation to genealogical relatedness is only problematic when one insists that the latter refers to a biological connection between speaker and referent; that is that a genealogy is the same as a pedigree. Numerous ethnographic accounts have established that biology is not a universal driver for genealogical relatedness, as it is locally recognised, if only because neither the statuses of motherhood nor of fatherhood from which genealogical connections are derived are constrained to biological mother and biological father. However, this does not imply the irrelevance of the biological facts underlying procreation, only that these biological facts do not universally determine cultural understanding of procreation; hence genealogical relatedness cannot be assumed universally to be constructed through biological parent and offspring. Local accounts of procreation are neither completely independent of, nor totally determined by, the biological facts. Instead, procreation is understood culturally and, while this understanding is not divorced from the biological facts, it may include aspects that are culturally recognised yet do not have a biological basis. This can be seen in the quite different accounts in various societies regarding who contributes what and under what conditions to the formation of an offspring recognised as a societal member and thereby understood to have genealogical connections to other societal members. For example, as Keen (1985) discusses,

that culturally understood procreative relations may be conceptually disconnected from biological procreation. What *is* problematic in this ontological sequence, though, is the assumption that genealogical relations are first categorised by generally unspecified criteria into a relatively limited number of categories, and these are then linguistically labelled and constitute the kinship terminology.

The fundamental assumption of this ontological sequence, namely that the meaning of a kin term is first and foremost genealogical, is contradicted by numerous ethnographic accounts regarding kinship systems in which genealogical relations are neither central nor even critical to how group members understand kinship relations. With regard to the !Kung San from Botswana, Africa, for example, Lorna Marshall comments:

> [They] were apparently not always assiduous in teaching their children the exact biological position of their kinsmen … and a person would not always know *why* he applied a certain term to someone, but he would know that the term he used was proper [emphasis in original] (1976: 204).

In other words, the underlying genealogical relations are not of primary concern to the !Kung San. Instead, what is of concern to them are aspects of their kinship system, such as the kin tie between two persons established through name giving, that do not have a direct counterpart in genealogical (let alone biological) relations. Similarly, Shapiro refers to the difficulty his informants had in making genealogical calculations, but not calculations based on kin-term products: Aboriginal Australians easily decode the messages '"aunt's children" and "X's children" but not the message "father's sister's children"' (1982: 274), and:

---

the Bahaya of Tanzania attribute fatherhood for a woman's first child to the man who first had intercourse with her even if that occurred more than nine months prior to her giving birth (Moller 1958), the Atta *negritos* in the Philippines allow for partible paternity in which more than one man can be considered to be the genitor of a child (Armando Marques-Guedes, personal communication to Ian Keen, n.d.), and the older Lusi people from Kaliai, West New Guinea assume that multiple copulatory acts are needed for foetal development, thus more than one man may contribute to this process (Counts and Counts 1983). Scheffler makes the distinction between genealogical relations and biological relations explicit when he says that for a critique made of his use of connotation and metaphor to be valid:

> [O]ne would have to accept the absurd assumption that kinship terms refer to biogenetic relationships of the sort known only to the sciences of biology and genetics. *The only tenable assumption is that they refer to relationships 'known' to or posited by the people who use the terms.* The components of their significata … are *cultural constructs* [emphasis added] (1972: 322; compare with Greaves and Kramer Chapter 4).

In dealing with such relatively remote kin-types and even with close collateral kin, informants were generally more comfortable operating through the relationship terminology: it made little or no personal or social difference to them whether (say) an alleged brother of the MM was in fact a MMB or a more remote 'brother' of the MM (ibid.: 275; see also Shapiro Chapter 1).

Scheffler and Lounsbury make much the same point with regard to formalisms such as componential analysis:

> [F]ew, if any informants ever offer statements about the meaning of their kin terms which correspond ... to the statements of these definitions as expressed in componential analyses ... If asked directly what the term 'cousin' means, a competent informant is likely to respond with 'my cousins are the children of my uncles and aunts', i.e. ... as a relative product [read: kin-term product] ... From our experience and that of other ethnographers (see Nayacakalou 1955), we know that in general that this is the way in which other peoples typically respond to direct questions about the 'meanings' of their kin terms (1971: 140).

They go on to discuss how children, when learning a kinship terminology, do not learn the meaning of kin terms and the relationships among terms by reference to genealogy, but directly through the kin-term product (relative product in their vocabulary):

> [For] a person from a society with an Iroquois-type terminology ... the son of any man he calls 'father' is to be called 'brother' ... He need not inquire into whether the [son] is his father's long-lost brother, or his father's FBS, or his father's FZS, etc., in order to know how to classify him (ibid.: 142).

In other words, the child only needs to know that the kin-term product equation, 'son' o 'father' = 'brother' (read: '"son" of "father" is "brother" for the kin terms translated as *son*, *father* and *brother*, respectively'), applies to any male he refers to as 'father'. He does not need to know the genealogical relation(s) involved, let alone the actual biological relations. Thus even Scheffler and Lounsbury, despite their emphasis on procreation as the basis for kinship relations, recognised that kin relations are not computed from genealogical relations simpliciter, let alone, as Jones (Chapter 11) points out, relations determined and structured by a biologically defined coefficient of relatedness. They did not explore the logic, though, of kin-term products and how this leads to a solution to the extension problem. It is this logic and its implications for solving the extension problem that I will now address in the remainder of this chapter.

The kin-term product logic of kinship terminology structures

I begin by graphically expressing the structure for the terms making up a kinship terminology by taking kin-term products with the primary kin terms for all of the kin terms in the terminology. Figure 2a shows the structure for the American/English kinship terminology formed in this manner using the primary terms *parent*, *child*, and *spouse*, along with *self*, where *self* provides the starting point for the structure.[15] The terminology has a ladder-like structure for both the lineal kin terms and the first line of collateral kin terms. Compare this with the very different, symmetric structure for the kinship terminology of the Shipibo (see Figure 2b). Yet other structural forms for kinship terminologies are presented in Read (2013). Note that the connector, 'of', in the kin-term product of a pair of kin terms, may be interpreted as a *binary operator* acting over each pair of kin terms making up a kinship terminology. With this interpretation, the kin-term product leads to expressing, in a natural way, a kinship terminology as having the structural form of an abstract algebra, where the latter consists of a set **S** of elements (here, **S** is the set of kin terms), at least one operator defined over that set of elements **S** (here, the kin-term product interpreted as a binary operator) and subject to a set of structural equations (here, the kin-term product equations giving the terminology its structural form, to be discussed below). Viewing a kinship terminology as having an algebraic structure (Read 1984) is culturally salient and leads to analysing a kinship terminology as a symbolic, computational system based on the kin-term product.

---

15   The American/English terminology has both sex-marked and neutral primary kin terms such as *mother*, *father* and *parent*. The generative logic of the American/English terminology shows that the terminology is based on the neutral primary kin terms, with sex marking introduced by bifurcating the lineal neutral kin terms such as *parent*, *grandparent* ... into sex-marked kin terms. In this way, *parent* becomes the 'covering' kin term for the kin terms *mother* and *father*, *grandparent* becomes the covering kin term for the kin terms *grandmother* and *grandfather*, and so on (see Read 2007; Read and Behrens 1990; and Leaf and Read 2012 for details). This, however, is not universally the means by which kin terms become sex marked.

2. EXTENSION PROBLEM

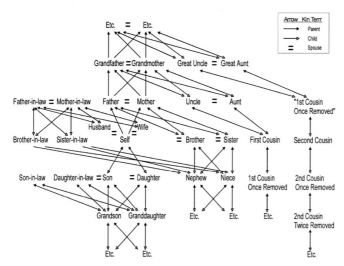

Figure 2a. Structure of the American/English kinship terminology
Source: Constructed by © Dwight Read.

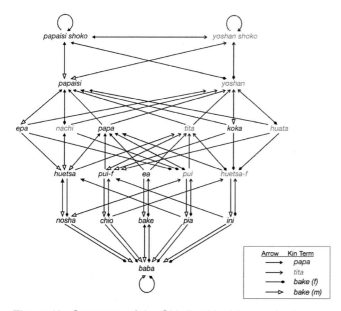

Figure 2b. Structure of the Shipibo kinship terminology

Both structures are based on kin-term products. Each arrow corresponds to a primary kin term, as shown in the key for each diagram, and shows the consequence of taking the kin-term product of a primary kin term with a kin term. Thus, the arrow with an open arrow head in Figure 2a going from the kin term *aunt* to the kin term *first cousin* shows that the kin-term product of the primary kin term *child* with the kin term *aunt* is the kin term *first cousin*: *child* o *aunt* = *first cousin*.

Source: Constructed by © Dwight Read.

Kinship terminologies viewed as symbolic, computational systems

Notably absent from the ontological sequence given above is the ontological basis for the various kinship terminology structures made evident through kin-term products of kin terms with primary kin terms. Morgan's attempt to account for the structural differences between the Roman terminology (used by him as a canonical example of a descriptive terminology) and the Seneca/Iroquois terminology led him to an unsuccessful excursion into hypothesised past marriage practices. Similarly, Scheffler and Lounsbury's subsequent attempt to resolve the extension problem through equivalence rules can justifiably be critiqued as insufficient for the reasons outlined above; nonetheless, their equivalence rules partially expose an underlying logic for the system of kin terms making up a kinship terminology. That there is an underlying logic is suggested by the fact that only a few rules are needed to describe the relationship between the secondary and the primary genealogical referents of the kin terms. Instead of referring to genealogical relations as a way to account for structural properties, though, the implied structural logic needs to be linked to fundamental kinship concepts, such as reciprocity of kinship relations; that is if speaker has a kinship relation to alter (expressed through the kin term K), then alter has a kinship relation to speaker (expressed through a kin term L), that may be expressed through kin-term products.[16] For example, for English speakers, if speaker refers to alter as *child*, then alter refers to speaker as *parent*, hence *parent* and *child* are reciprocal kin terms and *parent* o *child* = *self* (read '*parent* of *child* is *self*') since speaker refers to himself/herself as *self*. (Defining reciprocity of kin terms through the kin-term product in this manner will be discussed in more detail below.) A structure derived from kinship properties like reciprocity makes it possible, as we will see, to connect kin terms to genealogical relations rather than the reverse, as has generally been assumed, and from this the extension problem may be solved. Rather than staying with the assumption that kin terms are, first of all, genealogical relations, we need, as David Schneider phrased it (but without providing a means for implementation), a different way to consider kinship terminologies other than through genealogical relations:

---

16   The term L, in some cases, may be the same as K, as occurs with the kin term *sibling* (= K) for English speakers. When K and its reciprocal term L are the same term, then K is said to be self-reciprocal.

[T]he genealogically defined grid is the only analytic device that has been applied to most of the systems which anthropologists have studied. There has been almost no systematic attempt to study the question without employing this device. To put it simply, it is about time that we tested some other hypotheses (1972: 49).

The different way (contra the performatist view of kinship derived from Schneider and critiqued by Shapiro Chapter 1), which we will now discuss briefly (see Read and Behrens 1990; Read 2001, 2007; Leaf and Read 2012 for more complete discussions) to provide the background for resolving the extension problem, is to consider a kinship terminology as a (symbolic) computational system based on the logic of kin-term products and integrated with fundamental kinship concepts such as reciprocity of kin terms. The logic of this computational system underlies the computation of kinship relations through kin-term products in the manner well attested to in the ethnographic accounts mentioned above and leads us, as we will see, to resolution of the extension problem.

From procreation to the Family Space

As we have seen, the kin-term product enables determining kin-term relations among individuals even when relevant genealogical relations are unknown. We now turn computations like this around. Instead of kin-term products being computed using already known kin terms, we will use the kin-term product to *generate* new kin-term relations from the kin terms for primary relations. This enables us to use the kin-term product systematically as a way to generate the kinship relations corresponding to the terms of a kinship terminology from primary relations. In addition, the kin-term product enables prediction of the kin types (genealogical relations) subsumed under the kin terms for these generated kinship relations. The predictions are typically 100 per cent correct, thereby providing strong evidence for the validity of modelling a kinship terminology as a structure generated from primary relations. Once all of this is in place, we can then resolve the extension problem.

To carry out the argument, we first identify culturally salient, primary relations from which the kin-term relations making up a kinship terminology can be generated. These primary relations must be meaningful to culture bearers even absent the kinship terminology, just as we must have a beginning concept—the concept of singleness—for generating the counting numbers that is already understood prior to generating those numbers. The relations that will play an analogous role in the generation of kin-term relations will be the relations forming what we will refer to as a *Family Space* (Read, Fischer and Lehman 2014; see Figure 3). By a Family Space will be meant a mental construct, not the instantiation of a mental construct such as the nuclear family that is part of the phenomenal domain. As Shapiro has put it succinctly: '[the] Nuclear family is a proposition … it emphasizes Behaviour, not Mind' (1982: 260). The Family Space can be thought of as being composed of the relations expressed through a cultural representation of procreation, not as an encoding of, or elaboration on, the facts of biological procreation.

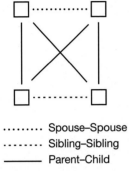

·········· Spouse–Spouse
········ Sibling–Sibling
———— Parent–Child

Figure 3. Minimal graph of the positions, indicated by boxes, making up a Family Space

Four positions are necessary as there is both a vertical (parent-child) division and a horizontal (husband–wife and sibling–sibling) division. A person(s) may be assigned to each position by cultural criteria.

Source: Constructed by © Dwight Read.

Just as 'singleness' is taken to be axiomatic for the purpose of formally generating the counting numbers, the relations making up the Family Space will be axiomatic for formally generating kin-term relations. By being axiomatic will be meant that these relations are self-evident to culture bearers without reference to a kinship terminology, in the same sense that 'singleness' is understood without reference to the counting numbers, as can be seen through the ways that 'singleness' is expressed linguistically for English speakers through phrases such as 'I have a book', 'the object over there', 'my dog is brown', and so on. Just as 'singleness' is understood without reference to the counting numbers generated from the concept of singleness, the relations of the Family Space are understood by culture bearers without reference to the kin-term relations generated from them and making up a kinship terminology. Instead, the

2. EXTENSION PROBLEM

family relations are understood through the way the biological facts of procreation are culturally understood and formulated. The relationship of mother to child (and reciprocally, of child to mother), for example, is initiated through (but need not be in complete accordance with) biological birth and mothering behaviours, hence does not require reference to kin-term relations to be understood. In all societies, culture bearers recognise a mother/child relation and its attendant behaviours however it may be culturally expressed and culturally instantiated (see Read 2002 for a discussion of cultural instantiation).

As shown in Figure 3, the Family Space has four positions: the mother, father, daughter and son positions, and three kinds of connections between the possible pairs of these positions.[17] The first kind of connection is shown by the four vertical connections (solid lines in Figure 3) determined through motherhood and fatherhood and their reciprocal concept of childhood. From a formal viewpoint, the logical possibility of a parenthood connection from a mother or father position back to itself is excluded by the fact that selfing does not occur under biological procreation. Further, and critically, motherhood involves not only the concept of giving birth to a child, but also the idea of engaging in mothering behaviour towards that child.[18] There are two child positions, indicating conceptually

---

17   Keen (1985) somewhat similarly builds a hierarchy of what he calls 'kin-relational expressions', starting with first-order expressions and their definitions (see his Table 1); for example, 'one's mother is the female person who gave birth to one' exemplifies what he considers to be a first-order kin-relational expression and its definition for English speakers. His goal, to establish a foundational basis upon which higher-order kin-relational expressions can be built, is similar to what is discussed here. However, Keen does not fully succeed in his endeavour since his first-order definitions are essentially biological definitions and thus take the endeavour outside of the cultural context that is germane to his task. As we know through reproductive technologies, adoption and the like, the English kin term *mother* does not simply refer to 'the female person who gave birth to one.' Indeed, any attempt to formally define a foundational concept such as *mother* runs into the problem of an infinite regress. For this reason, as has long been established in mathematics, an axiomatic system begins with terms undefined within the axiomatic system. Thus, for the Family Space we begin with, for example, *mother* as an undefined concept within the formalism, but a concept whose meaning is intuitively known to culture bearers. An enculturated individual 'knows' that someone is a mother, not because of a formal definition, but because of one's experience, and the experience of others, with regard to behaviours that are understood to be part of the essence of what it means to be a mother, hence mark the fact that one is dealing with an instance of the mother relation.

18   Surrogate mothers become biological mothers, but do not take on the status of motherhood by that fact alone. It is the female who has contracted for the offspring with a surrogate mother who takes on the status of motherhood, regardless of her biological connection to the offspring, by engaging in mothering behaviours legitimised through the contractual relationship with the surrogate mother. Who takes on the status of being mother, let alone motherhood, becomes uncertain, though, when the contractual relationship is violated or declared null and void. The latter has, in at least one case in Canada, led to a child not having a legally recognised mother (Baudouin and Blaikie 2014).

the procreative property of being able to have more than one child. Second, there is a horizontal connection between the two child positions (see dashed line in Figure 3) that we can refer to as a sibling connection. From a formal viewpoint, the logical possibility of the sibling connection coinciding with the parent/child connection is excluded by the facts of biological procreation. However, the sibling connection would, according to procreation alone, still allow for three possible modalities: (1) a shared mother but not a shared father, (2) a shared father but not a shared mother, and (3) a shared mother and a shared father. Third, the first two modalities are culturally erased by marriage establishing a spouse connection between the mother and father positions and the cultural assignment of birth legitimacy through the presumption of a parent/child connection from a child position to both a male marked position and a female marked position, themselves connected by a spouse relation (see dotted line in Figure 3).[19] Thus the act of marriage identifies a male as (putative) father for the future offspring-to-be of a female and her offspring are thereby culturally recognised as legitimate societal members for the social group in which the female is recognised as a proper societal member.[20] Fourth, from a formal viewpoint, marriage, in and of itself, does not exclude the possibility that the spouse connection coincides with either the parent/child connection or the sibling connection. These two possibilities are excluded by the universal incest taboos prohibiting marriage between parent and child and between siblings (see discussion in the chapter by Fadwa El Guindi), thus making the only structure consistent with the biological constraints on procreation and the cultural constraint on marriage between parent and child or between siblings expressed through the universal incest taboos be the one shown in Figure 3. This suggests that the incest taboo prohibitions on marriages between parent and child and between siblings may be universal for the reason discussed by Mary

---

19 In the United States, most states legally make the husband of a woman the presumed (legal) father of her child unless the presumed father has challenged that status on the grounds that the child was not the consequence of sexual intercourse between him and his wife.

20 With the exception of commoners among the Mosuo of China for whom marriage is not required for the child of a woman to be recognised as legitimate (Shih 2010), the common (though not exclusive) means across societies for a community to legitimate a female as bearer of children (that is for her children to be considered legitimate from the viewpoint of the community) is through marriage, however it may be locally construed (Malinowski 1927b, 1929, 1930; Gough 1959; Lehman 2011).

Douglas (1966) regarding the food taboos of the Old Testament, namely that which would violate the understood order is made taboo in order to prevent it from being perceived as a possibility.[21]

The words naming the relations making up the Family Space, whether or not, in any particular instance, all of the positions defining the relations are instantiated and given content, are (in English) father, mother (or parent), son, daughter (or child), brother, sister (or sibling, a recent addition to the English vocabulary), and husband, wife (or spouse) (see Figure 4). These English words are also polysemic in the manner discussed by Scheffler since they refer to both genealogical and kin-term relations. For example, consider English 'mother'. Alone, the word 'mother' does not distinguish whether a pedigree relation, a genealogical relation or a kin-term relation is involved. Thus when an English speaker says: 'Mary is my mother', we do not know from that statement alone and without further elaboration, whether the speaker is saying that Mary begat speaker, or if speaker is saying that the kinship relation between Mary and speaker is that of mother, and reciprocally, child, even though Mary is not the begetter of speaker. It may be that Mary is being recognised as mother of speaker in the genealogical sense of a presumed begetter (even if she is not, factually, the biological mother), or it may be that she is being recognised as mother of speaker in a kin-term sense, in which case procreation need not be involved; for example, speaker was adopted by Mary. For clarity, as discussed in footnote 3, I will italicise the word denoting a relation when it is being used in a kin-term sense; for example, *mother*, when the word 'mother' is being used in a kin-term sense.

---

21 The claim that the parent-child and sibling incest taboos are the consequence of the presumed Westermarck Effect (see, e.g. Wolf and Durham 2004; and Turner and Maryanski 2005) can be discounted on the grounds that there is (1) no unequivocal evidence supporting the assertion that persons raised together will have abhorrence (not just indifference) at the idea of having sex together (Leavitt 2005; Shor and Simchai 2009, 2012; Rantala and Marcinkowska 2011; El Guindi and Read 2012; Read 2014) and (2) under genetic equilibrium conditions, the frequency of phenotypes expressing deleterious effects due to the formation of homozygous genotypes for recessive, deleterious alleles is independent of the mating system (Read 2014), hence over evolutionary time scales sufficient to reach genetic equilibrium, inbreeding alone does not select for a particular mating type. The upsurge in deleterious effects that occurs with a shift to inbreeding from outbreeding is due to the *change* in mating type, not to inbred matings, per se. Under genetic equilibrium conditions, the rate of occurrence of homozygous genotypes for deleterious alleles tracks the mutation rate for the appearance of deleterious alleles, not the mating type.

From the Family Space to genealogical tracing

Consider first the recursive process of genealogical tracing. Genealogical tracing, which we will only consider briefly, begins by cultural instantiation of the positions making up the Family Space. Under the presumption that procreation takes place in the context of marriage, there will be assigned both a female, call her B, recognised as the mother and a male (call him C) recognised as the father of the individual A instantiated as self (see Figure 4). Let us refer to the former two individuals as the genealogical mother and the genealogical father, respectively, of person A instantiated as self. Genealogical tracing now proceeds recursively. We apply the same argument to each of B and C; e.g. for societal member B, there is understood to be person D who is the genealogical mother of B and person E who is understood to be the genealogical father of B. We may now apply recursively the same argument to each person that has just been identified, and so on.

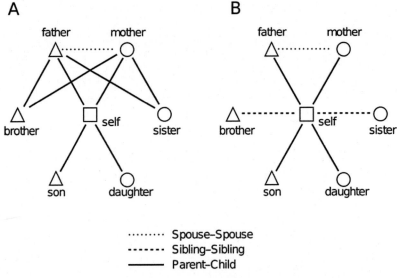

Figure 4. Graph of the Family Space with a self position for reference

There are two ways the sibling positions may be represented: (A) The sibling positions are related to the parent positions via the parent/child relation. (B) The sibling positions are related to the self position directly and to the parent position indirectly. In both (A) and (B), the spouse relation identifies the person instantiated as spouse to be the 'other (legitimate) parent'.

Source: Constructed by © Dwight Read.

Similar arguments apply to the son and daughter reciprocal positions for the parental positions in the Family Space, except that there need not be a person culturally instantiated as son or daughter in an instance of a family, and similarly for the affinal positions of wife and husband. Note that while many authors have assumed, as discussed by Schneider (1984), that genealogical relations are biological, there is nothing in the recursive procedure for genealogical tracing that requires genealogical mother or genealogical father to be instantiated by biological mother or biological father, respectively, of the person instantiated as self. Thus, contrary to Schneider's assumption, kinship may involve genealogical relations without, at the same time, presuming that these are necessarily biological relations. To put it simply, a genealogy based on genealogical parent and genealogical child need not be a pedigree. Nonetheless, there is still a biological substrate due to the fact that the status of, for example, motherhood in the Family Space is modelled on biological mother and the behaviours presumed to be associated with being a biological mother.

From the Family Space to a kinship terminology

Now consider how kin-term relations can be generated from the relations in the Family Space through the kin-term product. I will not provide a full account here (for a more detailed account see, e.g. Read 2000, 2007; Leaf and Read 2012; Read, Fischer and Lehman 2014). Instead, I shall limit myself to deriving only what is needed to resolve the extension problem through showing how the extension from close to more distant genealogical relations follows directly from the way kin-term relations are generated from the relations in the Family Space. The latter will also provide the basis for making predictions of the genealogical relations corresponding to a kin-term relation. Though I will illustrate the argument using the American/English terminology, it applies equally to other terminologies (Read 2007; Leaf and Read 2012).

Generation of an ascending kin-term structure; predicted categories of genealogical relations

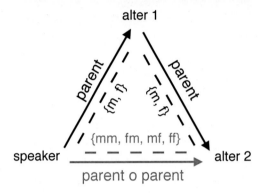

Figure 5. Kin-term product of *parent* with itself generates a new kin-term relation, *parent* o *parent*, given the name *grandparent*

The kin types subsumed under the kin terms corresponding to the black arrows are marked with a black dashed line. The predicted kin types (in grey) associated with the generated kin term *grandparent* = *parent* o *parent* are determined by taking the product of the sets of kin types subsumed by the kin terms in the kin-term product *parent* o *parent*: {m, f} × {m, f} = {mm, fm, mf, ff}.

Source: Constructed by © Dwight Read.

Let us begin with *self* and the kin terms corresponding to the non sex-marked, primary kinship relations of the American/English terminology, namely the primary kin terms *parent, child,* and *spouse*.[22] Start with the ascending primary term, *parent*, and form the kin-term product *parent* o *parent* determined by alter 1 referring to alter 2 by *parent* and speaker referring to alter 1 by *parent* (see Figure 5). Then *parent* o *parent* will be the generated kinship relation between speaker and alter 2. This generated relation has the name *grandparent*, which indicates that the kin-term

---

22   The choice of non sex-marked primary relations stems from the fact that all of the sex-marked terms in the American/English terminology come in pairs for which a kin-term product that terminates at, or begins with, one term of the pair is matched precisely by a kin-term product that terminates at, or begins with, the other term of that pair. For example, for the pair *grandmother, grandfather*, each kin-term product with one term of the pair, such as *son* o *grandmother* = *uncle,* is matched by a corresponding kin-term product, in this case *son* o *grandfather* = *uncle,* with the other term of the pair. For products in the other direction, *father* o *mother* = *grandfather* = *father* o *father* is matched by *mother* o *mother* = *grandmother* = *mother* o *father*. Thus the sex-marked primary terms can be considered to be the bifurcation of neutral terms into male and female marked terms. Were we to use the sex-marked (rather than the neutral) primary terms as generators, we would end up with a generative account that requires introducing numerous ad hoc equations solely to 'force' the generated structure to match the observed structure, whereas with the neutral primary terms, no ad hoc equations are needed.

product, *parent* o *parent*, determines a kinship relation recognised as such by culture bearers. This also establishes the meaning of the kin term *grandparent* to be the name for the generated kinship relation, *parent* o *parent*. Note that constructing new kinship relations from primary kin terms through the kin-term product parallels the process of generating new symbolic numbers from the symbolic primary counting number 1 through the binary operation '+'; that is, from the primary symbolic number 1, construct the new symbolic number 1 + 1 and give it the name *two* and symbolise it by '2'. From the symbolic number 2, construct the new symbolic number 1 + 2 and give it the name *three* and symbolise it by '3', and so on.

The kin-term product also predicts a category of genealogical relations corresponding to a kin term such as *grandfather* generated as the kin-term product of primary kin terms, or more generally, a category of genealogical relations corresponding to a kin term that is the kin-term product of a primary kin term with an already generated kin term. (In the following discussion, for succinctness in referring to the members of a genealogical category, I will use kin-type notation, using lower case letters, for the genealogical relations: for example, f, m, s, and d will be the kin types corresponding to genealogical father, mother, son and daughter, respectively.) The predicted category is determined by computing, in the order corresponding to that of the kin terms in the product of the kin terms generating the kin term in question, all possible products of kin types, one from each category of genealogical relations corresponding to each primary kin term in the kin-term product generating the kin-term relation, with each product formed in the order of the kin terms in the kin-term product. Thus for *grandparent* = *parent* o *parent*, we form the category of predicted genealogical relations for *grandparent* by computing {m, f} × {m, f} = {mm, fm, mf, ff}, using the formal brace notation for sets, since the category of kin types corresponding to the primary kin term, *parent*, is, from the Family Space, the category consisting of the kin types m and f and can be denoted by the set {m, f} (see Figure 5, dashed lines).[23] The predicted set of genealogical referents, {mm, fm, mf, ff}, is precisely the actual set of genealogical referents for the kin term *grandparent*.

---

23 I use the convention that kin-term products are written from right to left so that a kin-term product may be read directly as an English phrase by substituting 'of' for the kin-term product symbol 'o'. Thus *daughter* o *aunt* may be read '*daughter* of *aunt*', and this corresponds to alter 1 referring to alter 2 by the kin term *daughter* and speaker referring to alter 1 by the kin term *aunt*. In contrast, products of

We continue the construction process for kin terms by forming, recursively, all possible products of the primary kin term *parent* with each term that is generated, and giving each new product a name when it generates a kin-term relation recognised as such by culture bearers. Thus, following this procedure, we next introduce *great-grandparent* as the name for the kin term corresponding to the kin-term product *parent* o *grandparent* since the kin-term relation corresponding to this kin-term product is recognised as such by culture bearers; that is *great-grandparent* is the kin term that speaker properly uses to refer to alter 2 when alter 1 refers to alter 2 as *parent* and speaker refers to alter 1 as *grandparent*. To form the predicted set of genealogical referents corresponding to the kin term *great-grandparent* = *parent* o *grandparent*, we compute the product of the categories of kin types corresponding to *parent* and *grandparent*, respectively, and obtain {m, f} × {mm, fm, mf, ff} = {mmm, fmm, mfm, ffm, mmf, fmf, mff, fff} as the set of genealogical referents for the kin term *great-grandparent*. Next, we introduce *great-great-grandparent* as the name for the kin-term relation given by the kin-term product *parent* o *great-grandparent* (since this kin-term product is recognised as a kin-term relation by culture bearers) and determine the set of genealogical referents for the kin term *great-great-grandparent* by computing {m, f} × {mmm, fmm, mfm, ffm, mmf, fmf, mff, fff} = {mmmm, fmmm, ..., mfff, ffff}, which is precisely the category of genealogical referents for the kin term *great-great-grandparent*, and so on. For the American/English terminology, this process continues indefinitely, hence a new kin term is included for each additional product with the primary kin term *parent*.

In other terminologies, the sequence of new kin terms does not continue indefinitely and the kin-term products eventually become reflexive, or are not considered to determine a kinship relation, or make a closed

---

kin types are written from left to right so that a kin-type product string can be read using the possessive form for each kin type in the product except the last one; thus 'fm' is read as the genealogical relation f's m, or 'father's mother', With this convention, the product of the categories of kin types formed by taking the product of the category of kin types corresponding to each term in the kin-term product becomes reversed from that of the kin-term products. For example, the kin-term product *father* o *mother* (read *father* of *mother*) corresponds to the kin-type category product {f} × {m} = {mf} (read 'the category of kin types whose only member is m's f, or mf, for short'). That is, the category in question is formed by first taking a kin type from the first category in the product of categories and then taking the kin-type product of it with a kin type from the second category, with the order of the kin-type products reversed from that of the kin-term products. Hence the predicted genealogical relations for the kin term *grandfather* = *parent* o *parent* (read, using sex-marked kin terms in place of *parent*, '*mother* or *father* of *mother* or *father*') is the category of kin types given by {mm, fm, mf, ff}, where the kin-type products are read in the indicated order: 'm's m, f's m, m's f, or f's f'.

loop as occurs when the kin-term product of a primary ascendant kin term with the most ascendant kin term in the terminology is equated with the most descendant kin term, as happens in the terminology for the Kariera, a hunter-gatherer group in Western Australia (Radcliffe-Brown 1913; see discussion in Leaf and Read 2012). Reflexivity can be represented structurally by an equation that defines the next product in the sequence of products to be equal to the current product. Thus, in the Tongan terminology with primary ascending male-marked kin term *tamai* ('father'), we generate the sequence of ascending kin terms given by: *tamai*, *tamai* o *tamai* = *kui* ('grandparent'), and *tamai* o *kui* = *kui* (see Bennardo and Read 2007). The last equation indicates that *kui* is used in all ascending generations from the second generation upwards.

Here, corresponding to *tamai* o *tamai* = *kui*, we have the predicted category of genealogical relations given by $\{f\} \times \{f\} = \{ff\}$, which obviously is not the full set of genealogical relations for the kin term *kui*. We also need to consider other products of primary ascending terms equal to *kui*. For the Tongan terminology, this includes kin-term products using the primary female-marked kin term *fa'e* ('mother') as well. We find that *kui* is also generated by *fa'e* o *fa'e* = *kui*, *fa'e* o *tamai* = *kui*, and *tamai* o *fa'e* = *kui*, which implies that the kin-type products $\{m\} \times \{m\} = \{mm\}$, $\{m\} \times \{f\} = \{fm\}$ and $\{f\} \times \{m\} = \{mf\}$ are also referents of the kin term *kui*, hence ff, mm, fm, and mf are included in the predicted category of kin types corresponding to *kui*. In other words, included as genealogical referents of a kin term are the kin-type products corresponding to *any* kin-term product that equals (that is, is reducible to, using the structural equations) the kin term in question. We will use this property below to show how the extension problem is resolved through the generative logic for classificatory terminologies. Before doing so, we need to continue further with this overview of the process by which a kinship terminology is generated from primary kin terms.

Structural equations are crucial to this generative process as they can be used to express cultural concepts regarding kinship relations embedded within the kinship terminology. Whereas English speakers consider kinship relations to extend indefinitely in an ascending direction and are labelled with a new kin term in each generation, Tongans consider, as noted above, each of these kinship relations to be marked with a new kin term only up to the +2 generation, with the kin term in the +2 generation repeated in subsequent generations. This reflexive property may be denoted, as indicated above, by introducing the structural equations *tamai* o *kui* = *kui* and *fa'e* o *kui* = *kui* into the generative process for the Tongan terminology. Note that structural equations like this that express differences between English and Tongan speakers in their respective ideas about kinship relations are taken as axiomatic in the formal representation. The reason for differences like this among kinship terminologies is an interesting question in its own right whose (as yet uncertain) answer lies outside the immediate purview of the generative logic for a kinship terminology or that of any account of kinship terminologies for that matter.

Generation of a descending kin-term structure; predicted categories of genealogical relations

Typically (see discussions in Read 2007; Leaf and Read 2012), the generation of a kinship terminology continues by next generating a descending structure isomorphic to the ascending structure that has just been generated. The isomorphic descending structure is formed by introducing a (generally distinct) primary descending term for each primary ascending term used to generate the ascending structure.[24] The primary descending term corresponding to a primary ascending term will be said to be *structurally isomorphic* to that ascending term, and vice-versa. For the American/English terminology, the structurally isomorphic primary descending term corresponding to the (single) primary ascending term *parent* will be the primary term *child*. For the American/English terminology, the descending structure isomorphic to the ascending structure with terms *parent, grandparent* (= *parent* o *parent*), *great-grandparent* (= *parent* o *grandparent*) ... will be the isomorphic structure with terms *child, grandchild* (= *child* o *child*), *great-grandchild* (= *child* o *grandchild*) ... In addition, the isomorphic version of any structural equation that is part of the ascending structure will be included in the descending structure. For the Tongan terminology, an isomorphic copy of the ascending structural equation *tamai* o *kui* = *kui*, (read: 'father' of 'grandfather' is 'grandfather'), namely (for a male speaker) *foha* o *mokopuna* = *mokopuna*, where *foha* ('son') is structurally isomorphic to *tamai* ('father') and *mokopuna* ('grandson') = *foha* o *foha*, is included in the descending structure. The predicted categories of kin types corresponding to the descending kin terms are then generated in a manner analogous to the way the predicted categories of kin types are generated for the ascending kin terms.

---

24   For the English terminology, there is but one primary ascending term, namely *parent*, but in other terminologies such as the Tongan terminology, more than a single ascending primary term is used to generate the ascending structure (see Bennardo and Read 2007 for details).

Reciprocal kin terms

Not yet included in the construction is a structural criterion that defines the structurally isomorphic English kin terms, *parent* and *child,* introduced, respectively, in the generation of the ascending and the descending structures, to be reciprocal terms and not just isomorphic corresponding kin terms. With regard to usage, if speaker refers to alter by the kin term L (e.g. *child*), then the reciprocal term for L is the term K (i.e. *parent*) that alter properly uses for speaker. In addition, when considering reciprocal kin terms, the sex of speaker may need to be taken into account, as well as whether the reciprocal is determined within just the domain of consanguineal relations, or in the domain of both consanguineal and affinal relations, which depends on whether affinal relations have yet been introduced in the construction process.

The definition of reciprocal terms determined through usage can be transformed into a structural equation. To do this, note that when generating a kinship terminology by first generating a structure of ascending terms and next an isomorphic structure of descending terms, the genealogical references for the kin terms constructed so far will just be consanguineal genealogical relations since affinal kin terms have not yet been introduced, hence we will identify the structural equation that defines kin terms K and L to be reciprocal terms in the domain of consanguineal relations.

The usage definition for K and L to be reciprocal kin terms can be restated using the kin-term product. For example, if L = *child* and K = *parent*, suppose alter 1 refers to alter 2 as *parent* and speaker refers to alter 1 as *child*. Then since *child* and *parent* are reciprocal terms and we are only considering (so far) consanguineal genealogical relations for speaker, alter 2 must be speaker. We now ask: What expression does speaker use for alter 2 = speaker? and the answer, obviously, is *myself* (or *self*, for short). Thus, *parent* o *child* = *self* is the kin-term equation corresponding to the fact that *parent* and *child* are reciprocal kin terms. Note that if we reverse *child* and *parent* in this equation and alter 1 refers to alter 2 as *child* and speaker refers to alter 1 as *parent*, then alter 2 need not be speaker and if alter 2 is not speaker, then speaker refers to alter 2 as *sibling*. Thus, *child* o *parent* = *sibling* for English speakers. Observe that the predicted kin-type referents for *sibling* derived from the kin-term equation *child* o *parent* = *sibling* are given by {s, d} × {f, m} = {fs, ms, fd, md} = {b, z}, where b (z) is the genealogical relation standing for fs or ms (fd or md). Thus, the kin-term product *parent* o *child* = *self* defines *parent* and *child* to be reciprocal kin terms, whereas the kin-term product *child* o *parent* defines a new kin-term relation, *sibling*, with predicted genealogical referents {b, z}. In algebraic terms, we have also established that the kin-term product is not commutative for the American/English kinship terminology since *parent* o *child* ≠ *child* o *parent*.

The *form* of the structural equation, *parent* o *child* = *self*, that defines *parent* and *child* to be reciprocal kin terms is not specific to the American/English terminology or to these primary kin terms, but is a general property of kinship terminologies and primary kin terms. The structural form of the equation, *parent* o *child* = *self*, defining *child* to be the reciprocal of *parent* is (in words): *ascending primary term* of *descending primary term* is *self*, where the descending primary term is structurally isomorphic to the ascending primary term. In general, if K and L are structurally isomorphic primary ascending and descending kin terms, respectively, and if alter 1 refers to alter 2 by K and speaker refers to alter 1 by L, then the structural equation K o L = *self* defines K and L to be reciprocal kin terms. In some cases, such as with the primary kin term *spouse* that expresses the affinal relation for English speakers, the kin term is self-reciprocal, meaning that we have, for the kin term *spouse*, the structural equation *spouse* o *spouse* = *self*. A self-reciprocal primary kin term is neither an ascending nor a descending kin term, just as 0 is neither a positive nor a negative number.

We may structurally define the reciprocal kin term for a nonprimary kin term K as follows. Since K is not a primary kin term, it is generated from primary kin terms, so we may write K as a product of primary kin terms, say $K = P_1$ o P_2 o ... o P_n, where each P_i is a primary kin term and the same primary kin term may appear more than once in a sequence of kin-term products of primary terms. The reciprocal kin term for K, which we will denote by K^r, is given by the kin-term product of the reciprocal terms for the primary kin terms but in reverse order: $K^r = P_n^r$ o P_{n-1}^r o ... o P_1^r, where P_i^r denotes the reciprocal kin term for the primary kin term P_i. For example, from *sibling* = *child* o *parent*, we determine that the reciprocal of *sibling* is given by $sibling^r$ = $parent^r$ o $child^r$; that is by the kin-term product of the reciprocal of *parent* (= *child*) and the reciprocal of *child* (= *parent*), in that order, so the reciprocal of *sibling* is given by *child* o *parent* = *sibling*, hence *sibling* must be a self-reciprocal kin term and so is neither an ascending nor a descending kin term.

2. EXTENSION PROBLEM

American/English Kinship Terminology

Primary Kin Terms
  Self, Parent, Child, Spouse
Structural Equations
  Reciprocal Definition Equation for Child and Parent
    Child o Parent = Self
  Spouse Definition Equation
    Spouse o Spouse = Self
  Affinal Equations
    Spouse o Parent = Parent
    Spouse o Child o Parent = Child o Parent o Spouse
  Affinal Restriction Equations
    Parent o Spouse o Child = 0
    Parent o Parent o Spouse = 0
Structural Rules
  Sex Marking of Kin Terms
    Kin term K is sex marked if Spouse o K is a kin term or Spouse o K^r is a kin term, where K^r is the reciprocal term for K

Generated Kinship Terminology Structure

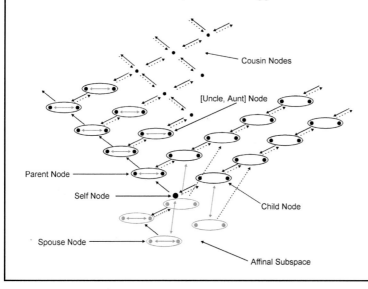

Figure 6. Primary kin terms and structural equations for generating the American/English terminology

Bottom graph: Generated structure isomorphic to the kin-term map for the American/English terminology (see Figure 2a).

Source: Constructed by © Dwight Read.

Though *sibling* and *spouse* are both self-reciprocal, *sibling* differs structurally from *spouse* due to the (axiomatic) kin-term product equation *spouse* o *parent* = *parent* (see Read 2007; Leaf and Read 2012) corresponding to the cultural knowledge of culture bearers that '*spouse* of *parent* is *parent*', whereas *sibling* o *parent* defines a new kin term for English speakers. For this latter kin-term product, we have for its name and using sex-marked kin terms, either *sibling* o *parent* = *aunt* or *sibling* o *parent* = *uncle*. These examples show how, through the generative logic for the kinship terminology, we can account for properties of the kin terms making up a kinship terminology and the way kin terms in this terminology are structurally linked to one another.

Generation of the complete American/English kinship terminology

We will not go through the entire process of generating the American/English terminology through kin-term products, a process that uses, as shown above, the set G of generating terms given by G = {*self, parent, child, spouse*}. Interested readers can consult Read (1984, 2000, 2007); Read and Behrens (1990); Bennardo and Read (2007) or Leaf and Read (2012) for details. We only present here the final set of structural equations used to generate the American/English kinship terminology and the structure generated from these structural equations (see Figure 6). As can be seen from Figure 6, the structural equations for the American/English terminology are culturally salient and express properties of the terminology familiar to the users of the terminology. This is no coincidence, but stems from the kinship terminology being generated through structural properties (primary terms and structural equations) that are culturally salient.

The generated structure can be shown to be isomorphic to the empirically derived structure for the American/English kinship terminology shown in Figure 2a, hence we now have an explanation for the structural form of the American/English kinship terminology by reference to the cultural knowledge shown in Figure 6. Other terminologies will differ from the American/English kinship terminology by different choices of primary terms used to generate the terminology and/or in the equations that express structural properties embedded in the kinship terminology.

Two culturally salient definitions for sibling in the Family Space

One additional property of the Family Space is needed before we can account for the extension of the referents of kin terms from closer to more distant genealogical relations. Structurally, there are two ways that a sibling may be defined: (A) speaker's sibling is the child of speaker's parent other than speaker and (B) individuals A and B are siblings when the parents of A are also the parents of B (see Figure 4). Empirical justification for these two ways to conceptualise sibling comes from ethnographic observations regarding the importance of the sibling relation when sibling is conceptualised through shared parents, as occurs, for example, with the Kaluli and the Tangu groups of New Guinea (see also Knight 2011). According to Edward Schieffelin, when the Kaluli work out kin relations:

> [They] frequently invoke a sibling relationship as the link that explains the application of a term – 'I call him brother because my father calls his father brother' ... *[T]he sibling relationship takes precedence over descent [parent-child links] whenever the principles are in conflict* [emphasis in original] (1976: 54–55).

Likewise, Kenelm Burridge notes the Tangu consider that:

> [S]iblingship is the determinant that descent [parent-child links] might have been expected to be ... descent was probably always calculated from siblingship ... and siblingship rather than descent always provided the definitive norms of social behavior (1959–1960: 128, 130).

R.R. Nayacakalou, an indigenous Fijian ethnographer, makes a similar comment for the Fijian classificatory terminology: '[I]f A is a classificatory father to B, and C is also a classificatory father to B, then A and C are classificatory brothers, even if no genealogical tie can be traced between them' (1955: 48).

He also identifies conceptualising siblings in Fiji through what he calls the 'principle ... of common parentage, which binds together the members of a sibling group' (ibid.: 46) (see Figure 4(B)). German Dziebel finds that both definitions (A) and (B) of sibling are needed to accommodate differences among terminologies regarding sibling kin-term relations. He then links siblings defined through common parents with classificatory terminologies: '[I]f alternatively Ego prefers to think that he shares ... common ascent with his siblings, 0 generation terminology will be Bifurcate Merging [i.e. classificatory]' (2007: 233).

These two ways of conceptualising sibling shown in Figure 4 correspond to a compound kin term (Figure 4(A)) versus a primary generating kin term (Figure 4(B)). Definition (A) implies that the kin term translated as 'sibling' is a compound kin term: 'sibling' = 'child' o 'parent'. Definition (B) implies that 'sibling' is a primary generating kin term.[25]

Generating a classificatory terminology

We next consider the structural properties introduced logically when 'sibling' is one of the primary generating terms. As we will see, the addition of 'sibling' as a generating term leads to classificatory terminologies. For simplicity of notation in the following, we will use capital letters F, M, S, D, B, B+, B-, Z, Z+, Z- to denote the kin terms for the father, mother, son, daughter, brother, older brother, younger brother, and sister, older sister, and younger sister relations, respectively, in the Family Space. We begin by generating male marked kin terms (or equivalently, we begin by generating female marked kin terms).[26] Let **A** = {*male self*, F, B+} be the

---

25   Keen (1985) incorrectly assumes *sibling* must be a second-order kin relationship; that is, sibling, as a kin-term concept, must be conceptualised through the kin-term product, 'child' of 'parent.' This ignores the ethnographic evidence, a small part of which has been presented here, showing that, for many groups, sibling is conceptualised as a first-order kin relationship (to use Keen's vocabulary), and hence is a primary generating term. Wierzbicka (2016) makes a related error by assuming that the prerequisite for having a 'sibling' kin term is having a linguistic term for a sibling concept in which sibling is 'undifferentiated in gender and relative age' (ibid.: 412). Since such a sibling concept is not universally given linguistic recognition, she argues that sibling is not a universal concept. Her assertion, however, confounds *sibling* as a structural relation in the Family Space that may, on the one hand, be incorporated into a system of kin-term relations expressed through the kin terms making up a kinship terminology in different ways (see Read 2011, 2014 for examples), with, on the other hand, *sibling* as a genealogical relation undifferentiated in gender or by relative age. 'Sibling' from the perspective of the conceptual system of kin-term relations making up a KTS expressed through a kinship terminology, and 'sibling', from the perspective of the conceptual system of genealogical relations making up what Lehman and Witz (1974) referred to as a PGS, are not one and the same thing. In her example of Kyardild kin terms, Wierzbicka provides definitions for their 'sibling' terms that do not require the use of the technical construct, ego, or the kin-type, sibling; that is, her definitions reinforce the incorrectness of the ontology going necessarily from procreation to genealogy to kinship terms. For the Kyardild sibling kin term *wakatha*, she gives the definition (contra Keen's assumption): 'a man can say about a woman "this is my *wakatha*" if he can think about her like this: "her mother is my mother, her father is my father"'—but this just defines one of two structural ways the sibling relation can be part of the Family Space (see Figure 4), each of which can be defined (as must be the case) without using concepts that depend upon already having the KTS or the PGS in place. In other words, her argument validates taking the Family Space to be axiomatic. Further, since she has provided a definition of their kin term, *wakatha*, that does not require reference to a KTS or to the PGS, *wakatha* is a linguistically recognised primary kin-term concept, hence a generating term for their kinship terminology.

26   The rationale for first generating structures of male marked, or female marked, terms has been discussed extensively, and illustrated with the Tongan, the Kariera, the Trobriand and the Dravidian terminologies in: Read and Behrens 1990; Bennardo and Read 2007; Read 2010a; Leaf and Read 2012.

2. EXTENSION PROBLEM

generating set for the ascending, male-marked kinship terms and include both the structural equation F o B+ = F ('father' of 'older brother' is 'father'), in agreement with the second definition for *sibling* given above, and the structural equation B+ o B+ = B+ ('older brother' of 'older brother' is 'older brother') that structurally identifies B+ as a sibling kin term in the ascending structure.

Typically, classificatory terminologies become reflexive beyond the +2 generation, so we also include the equation F o (F o F) = F o F, or more succinctly, $F^3 = F^2$. The distinct kin terms we generate from A and the structural equations F o B+ = F, B+ o B+ = B+ and $F^3 = F^2$ are:

F, F^2, B+, B+ o F, and B+ o F^2 ('father', 'grandfather', 'older brother', 'older brother' of 'father', and 'older brother' of 'grandfather', respectively).

Note that at this stage in the construction, B+ o F ('older brother' of 'father') and B+ o F^2 ('older brother' of 'grandfather') are each distinct kin-term relations since no structural equations that would reduce these kin-term products to a simpler form have yet been introduced.

Next, we generate an isomorphic structure of descending terms using the generating set D = {*male self*, S, B-}. Then we introduce the structural equations F o S = *male self* and B+ o B- = *male self* = B- o B+ to define F and S as a pair of reciprocal kin terms and B+ and B- as a second pair of reciprocal kin terms. Since the descending structure will be isomorphic to the ascending structure, we also include the structural equations $S^3 = S^2$ and S o B- = S that are isomorphic to $F^3 = F^2$ and F o B+ = F, respectively. Note that the equations isomorphic to the two equations B+ o B- = *male self* = B- o B+ are just these two equations again, so no new equations would be introduced through including the isomorphic forms of these two equations.

One other general property of kinship terminologies needs to be introduced, namely that the reciprocal version of a structural equation is also a structural equation for the terminology (see Scheffler 1986), which follows from the isomorphism between the ascending and the descending structures. Thus, from the equation S o B- = S, we include the reciprocal structural equation $B{-}^r$ o $S^r = S^r$, which corresponds to B+ o F = F. This last equation introduces the structural equation, 'older brother' of 'father' = 'father'. Further, from B+ o F = F, it follows that B- o B+ o F = B- o F, and since B- o B+ = *male self*, we have:

B- o F = B- o B+ o F
= *male self* o F.

Since *male self* o F = F,[27] it follows that B- o F = F, and so B o F = F, where B is either B+ or B-; that is 'brother' of 'father' is 'father'. From the equation B o F = F, it follows that the reciprocal of this equation, namely F^r o B^r = F^r; i.e. S o B = S, is also a structural equation for the terminology. Thus, the structural equations, B o F = F ('brother' of 'father' is 'father') and S o B = S ('son' of 'brother' is 'son'), fundamental to distinguishing classificatory terminologies as a distinct class of terminologies, *are the logical consequence of generating a kinship terminology when a sibling term is also a generating term*. Hence Morgan's distinction between descriptive and classificatory terminologies can now be expressed structurally through whether the terminology has 'sibling' as a primary, generating term (classificatory terminologies) or whether 'sibling' is a compound kin term of the form 'child' of 'parent' is 'sibling' (descriptive terminologies).

For our purposes here, I need not carry out the generation of a classificatory terminology any further. Interested readers can consult Bennardo and Read (2007) for the generation of the Tongan classificatory kinship terminology, Read (2010b) for the generation of a Dravidian terminology, and Leaf and Read (2012) for the generation of the Kariera kinship terminology for examples of generating a classificatory terminology. I now assume that we have done the rest of the construction and turn to resolving the extension problem, using the classificatory kin term 'father'. The means for so doing with the kin term 'father' will also serve as a canonical procedure for showing how the extension problem is resolved, in general, through the logical consequences of having a sibling term as one of the generating terms. I carry out this demonstration in three parts.

---

27 The kin-term product *male self* o F means alter 1 refers to alter 2 as F and male speaker refers to alter 1 as *male self*. The kin-term product, *male self* o F, will be equal to the kin term M that speaker (properly) uses for alter 2. Since speaker refers to alter 1 as *male self*, then alter 1 is speaker, hence the fact that alter 1 refers to alter 2 as F means that speaker refers to alter 2 as F, thus *male self* o F = F. The equation, F o *male self*, may be shown in a similar manner. In general, the term, *self* will be an identity element for the kin-term product; that is, for any kin term K, *self* o K = K = K o *self*. The sex-marked terms *male self* and *female self* will be identity elements for kin-term products of kin terms with the same-sex marking, as shown above for *male self* and F.

2. EXTENSION PROBLEM

Resolution of the extension problem

Part 1: Primary kin types for the lineal kin terms

I begin by noting that the generating term, F, generates the lineal sequence of ascending kin terms given by F, F^2, $F^3 = F^2$, with predicted, corresponding categories of kin types {f} and {ff, fff, …} for F and F^2, respectively. Let S be the descending generating term isomorphic to F. The term S generates the lineal sequence of descending kin terms, S, S^2, and $S^3 = S^2$, with {s} and {ss, sss, …} as the predicted genealogical categories of kin types corresponding to S and S^2, respectively. This part of the construction structurally subsumes the reduction made by Scheffler and Lounsbury of the genealogical categories corresponding to lineal terms to their primary (lineal) kin types, except whereas they needed to rationalise the reason for so doing, the generation of a classificatory terminology already provides the underlying structural basis for distinguishing the primary kin types for the lineal kin terms (see also the discussion of this topic by Shapiro Chapter 1).

Part 2: Extension of 'father' to father's brother

The structural equations B+ o F = F = B- o F, with corresponding kin-type products:

$$\{b+\} \times \{f\} = \{b-\} \times \{f\}$$
$$= \{fb-, fb+\}$$
$$= \{fb\},$$

extend the category of genealogical kin types corresponding to 'father' to include fb, where b refers either to genealogical older brother, b+, or genealogical younger brother, b-. Similar arguments may be made for other kin terms expressed as products of primary terms.

Part 3: Extension of 'father' to same generation, male collateral relations

We still need to establish the structural basis for F including the male collateral genealogical relations fffss (= ffbs), ffffsss (= fffbss) … within the domain of referents for F. We do this as follows. We map any genealogical string expressed as a product of kin types to a corresponding kin-term product formed by mapping each kin type in the product of kin types to the kin term that subsumes that kin type, then we compute the reduction of the resulting kin-term product to an irreducible kin term using the structural equations for the terminology, and lastly we assign the genealogical string in question to this kin term. Thus, from the kin type product, fffss (father's father's father's son's son), for example, we form the corresponding kin-term product S o S o F o F o F ('son' of 'son' of 'father' of 'father' of 'father').[28] Observe that:

S o S o F o F o F = S o (S o F) o F o F
= S o B o F o F
= S o (B o F) o F
= S o F o F
= B o F
= F (since S o F = B and B o F = F),

hence the genealogical relation given by the kin-type product fffss corresponds to the kin-term product S o S o F o F o F = F, and so the genealogical relation fffss is included under the kin term F. By a similar argument, any genealogical string of the form, f(n times)s(n - 1 times), corresponds to a kin-term product that reduces to F, hence in addition to the genealogical relations f and ffs = fb, the sequence of male collateral genealogical relations fffss (= ffbs), ffffsss (= fffbss), ... are also genealogical relations included under the kin term F. In a similar manner, we may determine the predicted assignment of *any* genealogical string to a kin term by reducing the corresponding kin-term product with the structural equations for generating the kinship terminology to a kin term K that is irreducible, then assigning the genealogical string to K. We find that the predicted assignments matches the observed assignments for all kin terms, consequently we have an explanatory argument (see Read 2008) for the categories of genealogical relations associated with the kin terms in a classificatory kinship terminology.

It follows, then, that terms such as *no-yeh'* ('mother') and *hä-nih'* ('father') in the Iroquois terminology do not refer, as discussed by Shapiro (Chapter 1), to a unitary class of undifferentiated, co-equal members, but to a class with a natural differentiation, starting with a class member who is in a lineal relation to speaker that is then extended to include other members who have a genealogical relationship to speaker in accordance with the

---

28 As discussed in footnote 23, I use the convention that the order for the product of the kin terms is reversed from that of kin-type products when going from kin-type products to kin-term products.

computational logic of the kinship terminology for that kin term. Whether we think of the former as the focal member of the class or in some other manner is not critical. What the generative logic makes clear is that the members of the class instantiated through procreation (as it is culturally understood) are necessarily differentiated according to genealogical criteria.[29] Further, cultural recognition of this differentiation may be made to varying degrees, as exemplified by the Siriono who linguistically mark the differentiation through modifiers meaning 'real' (Scheffler and Lounsbury 1971; see discussion by Shapiro Chapter 1) and by the Tiwi for whom marking, or even acting on, the differentiation, appears to be unimportant (Goodale 1971). In both of these cases, the differentiation derives from the generative logic of a classificatory terminology.

The use of modifiers seems to be a way to resolve the difference between the generative logic that categorises individuals (some with lineal and others with collateral relations to speaker) in the same manner and the genealogical framework that distinguishes between lineal and collateral relations. It is the generative logic that requires the assignment of individuals, some with lineal, or others with collateral, relationship to the same kin-term category. From the perspective of class logic, being assigned to the same class makes them coequal as class members, but the genealogical logic still requires that they be differentiated. Resolution of this disjunction, when it is culturally salient, is achieved by using modifiers that differentiate the primary class members as focal or 'real' kin, thereby distinct from the secondary class members.

Yet why should there be terms requiring this differentiation in the first place? If it is necessary to use a modifier to distinguish genealogical father (mother) from other genealogical relations also referred to by the same kin term, why not simply have a kin term that refers just to the genealogical father (mother) in the first place? Or, if what a kin term designates could change, essentially independent of the other terms, then why have not the kin terms in question each bifurcated into one term that refers only to genealogical father (mother) and a second term that refers to the other genealogical referents? The extensive evidence regarding what seems to be a common practice of using modifiers to make a distinction not otherwise made within the kin terms (see Shapiro Chapter 1) strongly

---

29 Of course, additional individuals may also be recognised as members of a class through nongenealogical cultural instantiation of kin terms, as discussed by Andrew Strathern (1973) for the Melpa of the New Guinea Highlands.

suggest that modifiers come into play because making such a change is not possible without violating the logic of the terminology. As shown here, making a distinction between genealogical father (mother) and other genealogical referents through different kin terms would violate the internal consistency of the terminology in question due to the logical connection between conceptualising sibling as a primary relation and having a classificatory terminology. Thus, the frequent use of modifiers may be less a confirmation of a procreative basis for kinship relations and more a way to maintain the logical consistency of a kinship terminology, yet recognising the primacy of the father (mother) relation as it is expressed in the Family Space.

Conclusion

The explanatory argument presented here resolves the extension problem through appeal to the generative logic of a terminology and whether or not the sibling relation is conceptualised as a primary kinship relation. The generative logic is expressed using culturally salient kin-term products and structural equations. These equations suffice to account for the regularities expressed through the equivalence rules for classificatory terminologies in the following manner. When there is a sibling generating term, the lineal terms are generated not only by an ascending generator, and reciprocally by a descending generator, but also by products with the sibling generator. These products reduce to lineal kin terms, thereby bringing collateral relations into the scope of the genealogical relations subsumed under lineal kin terms, thus accounting for the equivalence rules that extend lineal to collateral genealogical relations, or vice-versa. Consequently, the extension of the genealogical referents of kin terms from lineal to collateral genealogical relations is not mysterious. It follows from the sibling relation being conceptualised (through procreation) by shared parentage. What has, heretofore, hindered recognition of this underlying logic has been the invalid presumption that genealogical kinship relations are first established through procreation and then categorised in some manner, usually by a means assumed to be external to the terminology, with kin terms playing a secondary role as a linguistic labelling system for those categories.

Rather than being based on external factors, the underlying generative logic is based on culturally salient ideas about kinship relations applied to the primary relations making up the Family Space. This leads to clarification of the relationship that kinship terminologies have to local ideas about procreation and kinship. The kinship ideas do not simply give biological procreation a cultural overlay. Instead, they lay the foundation for a generative logic that incorporates nonbiological properties such as isomorphism between ascending and descending kin-term structures, reciprocity among kin terms, structural criteria for distinguishing between male-marked and female-marked kin terms, introduction of affinal kin terms either through structural criteria (see, for example, the analysis of the Kariera terminology in Leaf and Read 2012) or through expansion of the core kinship terminology by including an affinal kin term as a generating term (see Read 2007; Leaf and Read 2012 for details), and the culturally different ways that siblings are conceptualised. The last property leads to the disjunction between genealogical structure and the structure of the classificatory kinship terminologies that concerned Morgan, and was addressed formally, though incompletely, through the equivalence rules introduced by Lounsbury and elaborated upon by the work of Scheffler. While the concept of a sibling relation may ultimately have developed from the facts of biological reproduction, viewing kinship terminologies as symbolic (in a mathematical/linguistic sense) computational systems makes evident the way kinship terminology structures can deviate from their biological underpinnings. This allows us to bypass Schneider's antigenealogical position and does not require appeal to other formalisms such as the natural semantic metalanguage formalism developed by Wierzbicka (1992) and co-workers. It permits us to recognise what derives from our biological heritage directly and, at the same time, to appreciate what is new by virtue of our cognitive ability to construct symbolic systems, from whence derives the inherent mathematical character of kinship terminologies.

Acknowledgements

I would like to thank one of the reviewers of the book manuscript for suggesting that a post-Lounsbury context for the extension problem would be useful, including reference to the writings of Kris Lehman, Ian Keen, the mathematical formalism of Sydney Gould, and further elaboration on the relationship of the work of David Kronenfeld to the ideas of Floyd Lounsbury. This led me to expand the sections titled 'Previous attempts to solve the extension problem' and 'A formal attempt to resolve the extension problem'.

References

Allen, Nicholas J., Hilary Callan, Robin Dunbar and Wendy James (eds). 2011. *Early Human Kinship: From Sex to Social Reproduction*. London, Wiley-Blackwell.

Ballonoff, Paul A. (ed.). 1974. *Genealogical Mathematics*. The Hague: Mouton.

Barnard, Alan. 2010. 'When individuals do not stop at the skin'. In *Social Brain, Distributed Mind*, edited by Robin Dunbar, Clive Gamble and John Gowlett, 249–67. London: Oxford University Press. doi.org/10.5871/bacad/9780197264522.003.0012

Baudouin, C. and H. Blaikie. 2014. 'Surrogacy in Quebec: First legal case'. *Canadian Fertility and Andrology Society*. Online: www.cfas.ca/index.php?option=com_content&view=article&id=772&Itemid=523.k (accessed 23 September 2014).

Behrens, Clifford Allen. 1984. 'Shipibo ecology and economy: A mathematical approach to understanding human adaption'. PhD dissertation. Department of Anthropology, University of California, Los Angeles.

Behrens, Clifford and Dwight Read. 1993. 'Anthropology: Moving from task-driven to science-driven computing'. *Social Science Computer Review* 11(4): 429–51.

Bennardo, Giovanni and Dwight Read. 2005. 'The Tongan kinship terminology: Insights from an algebraic analysis'. *Mathematical Anthropology and Culture Theory* 2(1). Online: www.mathematicalanthropology.org/Pdf/Bennardo&Read1205.pdf (accessed 22 September 2010).

———. 2007. 'Cognition, algebra, and culture in the Tongan kinship terminology'. *Journal of Cognition and Culture* 7(1–2): 49–88. doi.org/10.1163/156853707X171810

Biersack, Aletta. 1982. 'Tongan exchange structures: Beyond descent and alliance'. *The Journal of the Polynesian Society* 91(2): 181–212.

Buchler, Ira R. and Henry A. Selby. 1968. *Kinship and Social Organization: An Introduction to Theory and Method*. New York: The Macmillan Company.

Burridge, Kenelm O.L. 1959–1960. 'Siblings in Tangu'. *Oceania* 30: 127–54. doi.org/10.1002/j.1834-4461.1959.tb00215.x

Chomsky, Noam. 1963. 'Formal properties of grammars'. In *Handbook of Mathematical Psychology*, edited by Robert Duncan Luce, Robert R. Bush and Eugene Galanter, vol. 2, 323–41. New York: Addison Wesley.

Counts, Dorothy Ayres and David R. Counts. 1983. 'Father's water equals mother's milk: The conception of parentage in Kaliai, West New Guinea'. *Mankind* 14(1): 46–56. doi.org/10.1111/j.1835-9310.1983.tb01250.x

D'Andrade, Roy G. 1970. 'Structure and syntax in the semantic analysis of kinship terminologies'. In *Cognition: A Multiple View*, edited by Paul L. Garvin, 87–143. New York: Spartan Books.

Douglas, Mary. 1966. *Purity and Danger: An Analysis of the Concepts of Pollution and Taboo*. London: Routledge & Kegan Paul. doi.org/10.4324/9780203361832

Dousset, Laurent. 2005. 'Structure and substance: combining "classic" and "modern" kinship studies in the Australian Western Desert'. *The Australian Journal of Anthropology* 16(1): 18–30. doi.org/10.1111/j.1835-9310.2005.tb00107.x

Dunbar, Robin, Clive Gamble, John Gowlett (eds). 2010. *Social Brain, Distributed Mind*. London: Oxford University Press.

Dziebel, German Valentinovich. 2007. *The Genius of Kinship: The Phenomenon of Human Kinship and the Global Diversity of Kinship Terminologies*. Youngstown: Cambria Press.

El Guindi, Fadwa and Dwight Read. 2012. 'Westermarck hypothesis reconsidered: A comment on Kushnick and Fessler'. *Current Anthropology* 53(1): 134–35. doi.org/10.1086/663576

Evans-Pritchard, E.E. 1929. 'The study of kinship in primitive societies'. *Man* 29: 190–94. doi.org/10.2307/2789028

———. 1932. 'The nature of kinship extensions'. *Man* 32: 12–15. doi.org/10.2307/2789766

Feinberg, Richard and Martin Ottenheimer (eds). 2001. *The Cultural Analysis of Kinship: The Legacy of David M. Schneider*. Urbana, IL: University of Illinois Press.

Freire-Marreco, B.W., Sir J.L. Myres and the British Association for the Advancement of Science (eds). 1912. *Notes and Queries on Anthropology*. London: Royal Anthropological Institute.

Garvin, Paul L. (ed.). 1970. *Cognition: A Multiple View*. New York: Spartan Books.

Good, Anthony. 1981. 'Prescription, preference and practice: Marriage patterns among the Kondaiyankottai Maravar of South India'. *Man* (N. S.) 16(1): 108–29. doi.org/10.2307/2801978

Goodale, Jane C. 1971. *Tiwi Wives: Study of the Women of Melville Island, North Australia*. Seattle: University of Washington Press.

Goodenough, Ward Hunt (ed.). 1964. *Explorations in Cultural Anthropology: Essays in Honor of George Peter Murdock*. New York: McGraw Hill.

Goody, Jack (ed.). 1973. *The Character of Kinship*. Cambridge: Cambridge University Press.

Gough, E. Kathleen. 1959. 'The Nayars and the definition of marriage'. *Journal of the Royal Anthropological Institute of Great Britain and Ireland* 89(1): 23–34. doi.org/10.2307/2844434

Gould, Sydney Henry. 2000. *A New System for the Formal Analysis of Kinship*. Edited, annotated and with an introduction by David B. Kronenfeld. Lanham: University Press of America.

Gow, Peter. 1991. *An Amazonian Myth and its History*. Oxford: Oxford University Press.

Hocart, A.M. 1937. 'Kinship systems'. *Anthropos* 32: 545–51.

Jones, Doug and Bojka Milicic (eds). 2010. *Kinship, Language, and Prehistory: Per Hage and the Renaissance in Kinship Studies*. Salt Lake City: University of Utah Press.

Kaplan, Joanna O. 1975. *The Piaroa: A People of the Orinoco Basin—A Study of Kinship and Marriage*. Oxford: Clarendon Press.

Keen, I. 1985. 'Definitions of kin'. *Journal of Anthropological Research* 41(1): 62–90. doi.org/10.1086/jar.41.1.3630271

Kelly, Raymond C. 1977. *Etoro Social Structure: A Study in Structural Contradiction*. Ann Arbor, MI: University of Michigan Press.

Knight, Chris. 2011. 'Early human kinship was matrilineal'. In *Early Human Kinship: From Sex to Social Reproduction*, edited by Nicholas J. Allen, Hillary Callan, Robin Dunbar and Wendy James, 61–82. London: Wiley-Blackwell.

Kroeber, A.L. 1909. 'Classificatory system of relationship'. *Journal of the Royal Anthropological Institute* 39: 77–84. doi.org/10.2307/2843284

Kronenfeld, David B. 1980. 'Particularistic or universalistic analyses of Fanti kin-terminology: The alternative goals of terminological analysis'. *Man* (n.s.) 15(1) (1980): 151–69. doi.org/10.2307/2802007; republished in *Fanti Kinship and the Analysis of Kinship Terminologies*, edited by Kronenfeld, 53–70. Urbana: University of Illinois Press, 2009 (page references to 2009 edition).

Kronenfeld, David B. (ed.). 2009. *Fanti Kinship and the Analysis of Kinship Terminologies*. Urbana: University of Illinois Press.

Kronenfeld, David B., Giovanni Bennardo, Victor C. de Munck and Michael D. Fischer (eds). 2011. *A Companion to Cognitive Anthropology*. London: Blackwell Publishing Ltd.

Leach, Edmund R. 1958. 'Concerning Trobriand clans and the kinship category tabu'. *The Developmental Cycle Domestic Groups*, edited by Jack Goody, 120–45. Cambridge: Cambridge University Press.

Leaf, Murray J. 2006. 'Experimental-formal analysis of kinship'. *Ethnology* 45(4): 305–30. doi.org/10.2307/20456604

Leaf, Murray J. and Dwight Read. 2012. *The Conceptual Foundation of Human Society and Thought: Anthropology on a New Plane*. Lanham, MD: Lexington Books.

Leavitt, Gregory C. 2005. *Incest and Inbreeding Avoidance: A Critique of Darwinian Social Science*. Lewiston: Edwin Mellen Press.

Lehman, Frederick K. 2011. 'Kinship theory and cognitive theory in anthropology'. *A Companion to Cognitive Anthropology*, edited by David B. Kronenfeld, Giovanni Bennardo, Victor C. de Munck and Michael D. Fischer, 254–69. London: Blackwell.

Lehman, F.K. and K.G. Witz. 1974. 'Prolegomena to a formal theory of kinship'. In *Genealogical Mathematics*, edited by Paul A. Ballonoff, 11–134. The Hague: Mouton.

Levinson, Stephen C. 2006. 'Matrilineal clans and kin terms on Rossel Island'. *Anthropological Linguistics* 48(1): 1–43.

Liu, Pin-Hsiung. 1986. *Foundations of Kinship Mathematics*. Taipei: Academia Sinica Press.

Lounsbury, Floyd G. 1964. 'A formal account of Crow- and Omaha-type kinship terminologies'. In *Explorations in Cultural Anthropology: Essays in Honor of George Peter Murdock*, edited by Ward Hunt Goodenough, 351–93. New York: McGraw Hill.

———. 1965. 'Another view of the Trobriand kinship categories'. In *American Anthropologist* 67(5):142–85. doi.org/10.1525/aa.1965.67.5.02a00770

Luce, Robert Duncan, Robert R. Bush and Eugene Galanter (eds). 1963. *Handbook of Mathematical Psychology*. New York: Addison Wesley.

Malinowski, Bronisław. 1927a. *Sex and Repression in Savage Society*. London: Routledge.

———. 1927b. *The Father in Primitive Psychology*. New York: W.W. Norton and Company.

———. 1929. 'Marriage'. *Encyclopedia Britannica* 14: 940–50.

———. 1930. 'Kinship'. *Man* (n.s.) 30: 19–29. doi.org/10.2307/2789869

———. 1962. *Sex, Culture and Myth*. New York: Harcourt, Brace & World, Inc.

Marshall, Lorna. 1976. *The !Kung of Nyae Nyae*. Cambridge: Harvard University Press. doi.org/10.4159/harvard.9780674180574

Moller, M.S.G. 1958. 'Bahaya customs and beliefs in connection with pregnancy and childbirth'. *Tanganiyka Notes and Records* 50: 112–17.

Morgan, Lewis H. 1871. *Systems of Consanguinity and Affinity in the Human Family*. Washington, DC: The Smithsonian Institute.

Murdock, George Peter. 1949. *Social Structure*. New York, Macmillan.

Nayacakalou, R.R. 1955. 'The Fijian system of kinship and marriage (Part I)'. *Journal of the Polynesian Society* 64(1): 44–55.

Newton, Sir Isaac. 1782 [1672]. *Isaaci Newtoni Opera Quae Exstant Omnia. Commentariis illustrabat Samuel Horsley*, Tomas 4. London: Excudebat Joannes Nichols.

Radcliffe-Brown, A.R. 1913. 'Three tribes of Western Australia'. *Journal of the Royal Anthropological Institute* 43: 143–94. doi.org/10.2307/2843166

——. 1950. 'Introduction'. In *African Systems of Kinship and Marriage*, edited by A.R. Radcliffe-Brown and Daryll Forde, 1–85. Oxford: Oxford University Press.

Radcliffe-Brown A.R. and Daryll Forde (eds). 1950. *African Systems of Kinship and Marriage*. Oxford: Oxford University Press.

Rantala, Markus J. and Ursula M. Marcinkowska. 2011. 'The role of sexual imprinting and the Westermarck effect in mate choice in humans'. *Behavioral Ecology and Sociobiology* 65: 859–73. doi.org/10.1007/s00265-011-1145-y

Read, Dwight W. 1984. 'An algebraic account of the American kinship terminology [and comments and reply]'. *Current Anthropology* 25(4): 417–49. doi.org/10.1086/203160

——. 2000. 'Formal analysis of kinship terminologies and its relationship to what constitutes kinship (complete text)'. *Mathematical Anthropology and Cultural Theory* 1(1): 1–46.

——. 2001. 'What is kinship?' In *The Cultural Analysis of Kinship: The Legacy of David M. Schneider*, edited by Richard Feinberg and Martin Ottenheimer, 78–117. Urbana, IL: University of Illinois Press.

——. 2002. 'Cultural construct + instantiation = constructed reality'. *Human Complex Systems*. Paper DWR2002. Online: repositories.cdlib.org/hcs/DWR2002 (accessed 31 May 2017).

——. 2007. 'Kinship theory: A paradigm shift'. *Ethnology* 46(4): 329–64.

———. 2008. 'A formal explanation of formal explanation'. *Structure and Dynamics* 3(2): 1–16. Online: escholarship.org/uc/item/91z973j6 (accessed 14 July 2017).

———. 2010a. 'The generative logic of Dravidian language terminologies'. *Mathematical Anthropology and Cultural Theory* 3(7). Online: www.mathematicalanthropology.org/pdf/Read.0810.pdf (accessed 24 September 2010).

———. 2010b. 'The logic and structure of kinship terminologies: Implications for theory and historical reconstruction'. In *Kinship, Language, and Prehistory: Per Hage and the Renaissance in Kinship Studies*, edited by Doug Jones and Bojka Milicic, 152–72. Salt Lake City: University of Utah Press.

———. 2011. 'Mathematical representation of cultural constructs'. In *A Companion to Cognitive Anthropology*, edited by David Kronenfeld, Giovanni Bennardo, Victor C. de Munck and Michael D. Fischer, 229–53. London: Blackwell Publishing Ltd. doi.org/10.1002/9781444394931.ch13

———. 2013. 'A new approach to forming a typology of kinship terminology systems: From Morgan and Murdock to the present'. *Structure and Dynamics* 6(1). Online: escholarship.org/uc/item/0ss6j8sh (accessed 9 August 2017).

———. 2014. 'Incest taboos and kinship: A biological or a cultural story?' *Reviews in Anthropology* 43(2): 150–75. doi.org/10.1080/00938157.2014.903151

Read, Dwight W. and Clifford A. Behrens. 1990. 'KAES: An expert system for the algebraic analysis of kinship terminologies'. *Journal of Quantitative Anthropology* 2(4): 353–93.

Read, Dwight W., Michael D. Fischer and Kris Lehman (Chit Hlaing). 2014. 'The cultural grounding of kinship: A paradigm shift'. *L'Homme* 210(2): 63–89. doi.org/10.4000/lhomme.23550

Reining, Priscilla (ed.). 1972. *Kinship Studies in the Morgan Centennial Year*. Washington: The Anthropological Society of Washington.

Rivers, William H.R. 1910. 'The genealogical method of anthropological enquiry'. *Sociological Review* 3(1): 1–12. doi.org/10.1111/j.1467-954X.1910.tb02078.x

———. 1912. 'A general account of method'. In *Notes and Queries on Anthropology*, edited by B.W. Freire-Marreco, Sir J.L. Myres and the British Association for the Advancement of Science, 108–27. London: Royal Anthropological Institute.

———. 1914. *The History of Melanesian Society*, vol. 1. Cambridge: Cambridge University Press.

Sahlins, Marshall. 1962. *Culture and Nature on a Fijian Island*. Ann Arbor, University of Michigan Press. doi.org/10.3998/mpub.9690566

Scheffler, Harold W. 1972. 'Kinship semantics'. *Annual Reviews in Anthropology* 1: 309–28.

———. 1978. *Australian Kin Classification*. Cambridge: Cambridge University Press. doi.org/10.1017/CBO9780511557590

———. 1986. 'Extension rules and "generative models"'. *American Ethnologist* 13(2): 369–70. doi.org/10.1525/ae.1986.13.2.02a00130

———. 2002. Review of *A New System for the Formal Analysis of Kinship* by Sydney H. Gould. *Journal of Anthropological Research* 58: 295–96. doi.org/10.1086/jar.58.2.3631055

Scheffler, Harold W. and Floyd G. Lounsbury. 1971. *A Study in Structural Semantics: The Siriono Kinship System*. Englewood Cliffs, NJ: Prentice Hall.

Schieffelin, Edward L. 1976. *The Sorrow of the Lonely and the Burning of the Dancers*. New York: Palgrave Macmillan. doi.org/10.1057/9781403981790

Schneider, David M. 1972. 'What is kinship all about?' In *Kinship Studies in the Morgan Centennial Year*, edited by Priscilla Reining, 32–63. Washington: The Anthropological Society of Washington.

———. 1984. *A Critique of the Study of Kinship*. Ann Arbor: University of Michigan Press. doi.org/10.3998/mpub.7203

Seligman, Brenda Z. 1929. 'Incest and descent: Their influence on social organization'. *Journal of the Royal Anthropological Institute of Great Britain and Ireland* 59: 231–72. doi.org/10.2307/2843567

Shapiro, Warren. 1982. 'Review: The place of cognitive extensionism in the history of anthropological thought'. *The Journal of the Polynesian Society* 91(2): 257–97. www.jstor.org/stable/20705647

Shih, Chuan-kang. 2010. *Quest for Harmony: The Moso Traditions of Sexual Union and Family Life*. Stanford: Stanford University Press.

Shor, Eran and Dalit Simchai. 2009. 'Incest avoidance, the incest taboo, and social cohesion: Revisiting Westermarck and the case of the Israeli *kibbutzim*'. *American Journal of Sociology* 114(6): 1803–842. doi.org/10.1086/597178

———. 2012. 'Exposing the myth of sexual aversion in the Israeli *kibbutzim*: A challenge to the Westermarck hypothesis'. *American Journal of Sociology* 117(5): 1509–513. doi.org/10.1086/665522

Sigarimbun, Masri. 1975. *Kinship, Descent and Alliance among the Karo Batak*. Berkeley, CA: University of California Press.

Strathern, Andrew. 1973. 'Kinship, descent and locality: Some New Guinea examples'. In *The Character of Kinship*, edited by Jack Goody, 21–34. Cambridge: Cambridge University Press.

Turner, Jonathan H. and Alexandra Maryanski. 2005. *Incest: Origins of the Taboo*. Boulder: Paradigm.

Unwin, J.D. 1929. 'The classificatory system of relationship'. *Man* 29: 164.

Vilaca, Aparecida. 2002. 'Making kin out of others in Amazonia'. *Journal of the Royal Anthropological Institute* 8(2): 347–65.

Wierzbicka, Anna. 1992. *Semantics, Culture, and Cognition: Universal Human Concepts in Culture-Specific Configurations*. New York: Oxford University Press.

———. 2016. 'Back to "mother" and "father": Overcoming the Eurocentrism of kinship studies through eight lexical universals'. *Current Anthropology* 57(4): 408–29. doi.org/10.1086/687360

Wolf, Arthur P. and Willian H. Durham (eds). 2004. *Inbreeding, Incest, and the Incest Taboo: The State of Knowledge at the Turn of the Century*. Stanford: Stanford University Press.

Part III. Ethnographic Explorations of Extensionist Theory

3

Action, Metaphor and Extensions in Kinship

Andrew Strathern and Pamela J. Stewart

In this chapter we honour the fundamental and enduring contributions of Harold Scheffler to the study of kinship in human societies. Scheffler has vigorously pursued the topic of the primary reference of kin terms, and it is on this topic that the most controversy has tended to emerge. We recognise the force of Scheffler's arguments, and we seek to mediate between the different viewpoints on the fundamental issues at stake by considering the evidence further from contexts of action and from some aspects of linguistic theory. Scheffler also made important contributions to the study of descent and the question of cognatic descent as a category of analysis (e.g. Scheffler 1965, 2001), changing his mind about this arena of discussion in his 2001 book. We do not engage with this issue here, but it remains important, especially in the analysis of Pacific Island societies and their flexible systems of affiliation (see e.g. Strathern and Stewart 2004a on the Duna case from Papua New Guinea).

In our book *Kinship in Action* (Strathern and Stewart 2011) we argued that an important focus in kinship studies is found in the context of action as well as in linguistic classifications of kin types, foundational as these are for general frameworks of action. An action-based approach enables us to understand the pragmatic issues behind ways in which kin classifications are applied in practice. This argument is relevant for the long-standing debates in kinship studies regarding the 'meaning' of kinship terms;

do they refer to primary kin types of a genealogical kind or do they refer to broad classifications? Clearly, in practice they can do both, depending on contexts of action. However, there is another way to enter the discussion. Language is intrinsically influenced by metaphorical applications of meanings, seen as 'extensions' from elementary structures that are tied to embodied experience. The 'extended mind' that evolutionary thinkers have identified as crucial for the development of human culture and language lends itself well to a context of sociality in which kin terms are applied both to close bodily relations and to wider sets of persons with whom cooperation is advantageous. 'Extensions', added to primary points of reference, are intrinsic to the whole process of human development. This viewpoint mediates between the opposing ideas of primary kin types versus kin classifications.

Kinship studies in anthropology, seen as being at the heart of the discipline in its early phases, have gone through a number of changes. Kinship terminologies were at first taken as proxy evidence for states of evolution of society. Theories of 'group marriage', for example, were broached as a means of apparently explaining classificatory terminologies. In these and other approaches one viewpoint tended to prevail: that a distinction between genealogical usages deriving from immediate links of reproduction (and marriage) and extended classificatory usages is to be found universally. In this viewpoint, the genealogical ties are implicitly taken as basic and self-explanatory and it is the classificatory usages that require further explanation. This explanation can then be found in terms of local logics of the equivalence of persons within genealogical grids or in terms of group or category membership and potentiality for marriage affiliations. While the concern for using kin-term structures as evidence for social evolution fell away, basic assumptions about the subject matter of kinship continued, and fed into a further phase of in-depth modelling of the putative logics of extension and equations between kin types. In the United States (US), this analytical method reached its climax in the work of the ethnoscientists who tended to equate 'culture' with linguistic classifications and developed extensionist kin-term analysis as a master art for revealing kinship structures. Among the many prominent exponents of this approach, the work of Floyd Lounsbury (e.g. Lounsbury 1964) clearly stood out, enabling a method of positing extension rules that could order the distribution of kin-term assignments over a set of genealogical positions, starting from basic genealogical foci. ('Genealogy', however, can itself also be an ambiguous term, referring either to ideas of biological procreation or to legal principles, or to both of these semantic domains.) Harold Scheffler and Floyd Lounsbury collaborated on a sophisticated analysis of the Siriono kinship system, exploring the strengths of this mode of analysis (Scheffler and Lounsbury 1971; see also Scheffler 1978 on *Australian Kin Classification*).

A strongly negative reaction against this method, and all other approaches that assumed a genealogical grid, came also from within the US with the work of David M. Schneider. Schneider's deconstructive strategy was to question the whole category of 'kinship' as a universal, genealogy-based grid of relations (Schneider 1984). In Schneider's view, the category was to be seen as ethnocentric, tied to English-language usages, and inapplicable as a general model. Schneider used the example of his work on Yap in Micronesia to question the genealogical basis of paternal filiation there, because the spirits of children were thought to come as a gift or form of bestowal from the ancestors (*thagith*), not from sexual procreation. A new child's name was accordingly given to it by male elders of the *tabinau* (local group) to which it was affiliated, acting in the place of the ancestors in this regard. Dogmas of this kind are common enough in societies with matrilineal descent (e.g. the famous but often misconstrued case of the Trobrianders of Papua New Guinea). The important thing is that they are dogmas, and that in practice and informally there is ample evidence of knowledge among the Trobrianders that sex and procreation are linked (see a discussion in Strathern and Stewart 2011: 36–38 and also 39–41 on the Yapese case with critiques of Schneider's argument). Schneider's stance, however, and his influence over others, gave rise to a school of cultural relativistic work on kinship that dissolved it as a category under sociality in general. Kinship studies as a separate domain of enquiry appeared to have suffered a serious blow.

More nuanced and thoughtful reconstructive approaches have since emerged. What we call kinship, in its social sense, can be composed of several elements, from basic significata, however these are formulated, to extended considerations of practice, embodiment, emplacement, consumption of food, political solidarity and the like. Especially food giving, care and identifications with locality have long been recognised as important for many New Guinea societies (see e.g. Strathern 1973; also Meigs 1984; Kahn 1986). What we call 'adoption' is another complicating factor in analysis, which can be resolved in various ways by stressing that kin terms refer to roles and statuses and in adoption the assumption of a parental role gives access to parental status. None of these complications necessarily validates or invalidates the general arguments about whether kinship is to be seen as based on genealogy or not. Rather, they obviate this argument by concentrating on practice as a domain in its own right. Among Melpa speakers of Mount Hagen in the Papua New Guinea Highlands, people will privilege either genealogical classifications or local solidarity, depending on circumstances. People also supplement kinship with friendship ties based on food sharing and the adoption of food names to make a more personal and special relationship of solidarity than a kin term alone can convey (see Strathern 1977). For the most part, then, a contemporary approach is to situate kinship relations within broader fields of sociality without, however, dissolving them entirely. The phenomenon of kin terms is culturally widespread, if not universal. It must obviously be rooted in embodied ('biological') facts that cannot be ignored. Kinship therefore survives as a living category of cross-cultural human behaviour and practice in spite of Schneider's deconstruction.

Warren Shapiro, editor of this volume, (pers. comm., n.d.) has pointed out to us, referring to one of his own writings (Shapiro 2009) that 'adoptive kinship is usually (always?) lexically marked, i.e. nonfocal'. The observation is true for the Melpa speakers of Papua New Guinea. A child taken over by someone else after the demise of its original parental figures is described as *mbo nunggökli*, 'nurtured'. Adoption was considered in some nuanced detail in various places in Strathern (1972), and also more recently in Strathern and Stewart (2011). Our point here is not to contest this issue, but to extend the argument into considerations of practice, while not denying the focal character of primary kin terms as Scheffler, and Shapiro following in the same vein, have done. We acknowledge here the arguments put forward by Shapiro in the present volume. Our own observations here about the importance of practice are also in effect fundamental to the topic of kinship at large.

The overall theoretical question nevertheless remains. Is there an essence of kinship that is culturally universal, and does it reside in the recognition of sexual and procreative relationships and the ties that derive from these as they are culturally defined? Our approach to this general issue is to deflect it further again, not just into the character of social practice but into the domain of linguistic practice. This can easily be justified by pointing out that the classic arguments have revolved around the interpretation of linguistic usages, specifically in relation to kin. The arguments have been all about semantics or meanings, and since the question of meaning is complex and disputed, it is little wonder that disagreements remain. Two further linguistic approaches are available. One is linguistic pragmatics. How do people use terms in practice? Clearly, they extend them in ways that suit their own pursuits of interests. Clearly, also, this cannot be done with total fluidity. Pragmatics require plausibility, and this means that some semantic principle has to be invoked to justify the usage. Gender, age, locality, marriage, or religion may all be called into play, leading to or resulting from ties of exchange. Indeed, for Papua New Guinea, exchange is certainly as fundamental a principle as any other, so it must be reckoned with in any consideration of the bases for sociality as well as the manipulation of these bases by aspiring leaders. Generally, then, contemporary ethnographic analyses of kinship as a topic have been guided by an exposition of cultural pragmatics.

Another resource from linguistic theory can be brought to bear on the problem in hand. This has to do with the meaning of the term meaning itself. There are endless arguments about this, implicating both philosophers and linguists. In general, these debates mirror the fundamental matters at stake in kinship theory. Do words have a core referential meaning which then can be extended by means of transfers or extensions, including to the realm that we call metaphor? This, again perhaps with an English language bias, might appear to be a common-sense statement. In fact, the whole idea of a metaphor, something carried over from one domain into another, tends to suggest this stance although the technical sense of the term 'extension' in kinship analysis is not identical with the term 'metaphor'. The one-to-one correspondence between words and things they ostensibly name in the world of observation and experience fails to take into account the much greater human capacity to build complex meanings through imagination and association. As one theorist, Robert Logan, put it, words can be 'strange attractors' of meanings (2007: 45–50). Also, as they are tools to explore human experience, words and the larger utterances in which they appear, as in poetry and song, acquire a power that goes far beyond their ability to name things. These observations suggest, in turn, that a tendency to accrete rich and complex meanings around at least certain terms in a given language is fundamental to the development of language itself as a consistent part of experience. This observation, then, can be applied to kinship terms. Such an observation in no way invalidates the notion of elementary meanings of kin terms, but it does suggest that *because* of their fundamental primary significance they lend themselves to productive extensions, and that their full range of meanings resides in such extensions as well as in an elementary referential or naming grid of references. Again, this does not amount to a denial of the theory of focal meanings for kin terms as classificatory devices. It does indicate that the extensions beyond such a focality are also socially important. This is *not* a trivial point, because it enables us to place debates about meaning in a broader context of action.

This chapter is not intended as a detailed exposition of the kin terms in a given societal area, such as among the Melpa speakers of Mount Hagen in Papua New Guinea. This kind of exposition was made in an earlier publication (Strathern 1980a). Nevertheless, we give here a few examples of how the analytical scheme we have outlined can be applied. We take the Melpa terms that are glossed under the rubric of 'father' (summarised in Strathern and Stewart 2011: 185). The basic reference term involved is *tepam*, while the address form is *ta*. In order to distinguish an 'immediate' sense of the term from other usages, the qualifier *ingk*, glossed as 'genuine', 'true', can be added, in a general contrast with *tepam mburlukna*, 'backside father', referring to same-generation collateral male kin on the father's side. *Mburlukna* thus operates as a modifier in conjunction with *ingk*. These two terms form an implicit semantic pair, mutually defined. So far, this clearly corresponds to the 'focal-meaning' theory of kin terms, as well as the theory of extensions. The extensions depend on the wider social structure of subclans and clans within which social relations modelled on the focal usages are extended. It is perhaps unnecessary to add that the extension of the term to lineal male collaterals in no way implies that the relationship of the propositus or hypothetical ego is the same with all of those classified in this way. Equally, however, the sheer fact of such a classification implies some basis of solidarity that is marked out, or made available, through the terminology itself. The classification lays out a determinate area of potentiality, demarcated from other arenas of the kin universe. From a sociocentric standpoint what is significant is that all those included in the class are *tepamal*, 'fathers' (in the plural form), and can be invoked or referred to as such, without any necessity for cited genealogical reckoning (although this may be known, if not to ego, then to others, and may be detailed in accordance with the situation). From an egocentric viewpoint, this class of *tepamal* also refers to a field of objective potentiality within which subjective affiliations can be sought or may be brought into play by the fathers/*tepamal* themselves. Obligations to help, support, or protect in warfare, disputes, or exchanges go with the classification. The extensions are cognitively 'real', and from this perspective they are important in the sociocentric context of clan relationships. The *ingk* classification, equally, is fundamental from the egocentric viewpoint. The overall logic has to be found in the combination of the egocentric and sociocentric domains, and it is this logic that provides the grounding for 'kinship in action' (the title of our book, Strathern and Stewart 2011).

Our observations here are founded on a detailed knowledge of social life and the place of kinship in it in the Melpa (Hagen) area, dating from 1964 to very recent times. They are not impressionistic or fleeting suggestions. When we write that kinship includes both egocentric and sociocentric aspects, we are also following in a tradition of writing that recognises these two domains of usage. However, we note that sociocentric usages among the Melpa are also founded on putative procreative relationships centring on ancestral figures.

Further classifications present other dimensions of complexity. *Tepam* as a reference term can also be applied to MZH, normatively outside of the lineal clan relationship. How is this to be explained? The first example we gave depends on an equation in egocentric terms of F with FB; this further example rests on an equation between female siblings, such that M = MZ, and also F = MH, so we arrive at the proposition MZH = F. This is pure classification. In action terms MZH does not carry the same weight as F or FB; but again it marks out a field of potentiality, based as much on the presumed solidarity of sisters as on anything else. In essence, when we assess the social significance of these kinship classifications we have to go to the sphere of action in order to find the answers. This may be an obvious point, but it has to be borne in mind as a counter to analyses based purely on linguistic classifications.

Address terms present another level of cultural complexity. The term *ta* is used reciprocally between father and son and between father and daughter. The address usages, signalling immediacy and intimacy of relationship, express the sameness of the relationship with the father among brothers and sisters, while the reference term is geared to differences in inheritance and succession associated with gender. In addition, however, the fact that the address terms are reciprocal points up another cultural value: the tendency to pair units. *Ta* indicates the shared relationship between father and child. As an extra marker the father may say *kang ta* or *ambokla ta* (boy-*ta*, girl-*ta*), and the child may say *wuö ta* (man-*ta*). What, then, is the focal meaning of *ta*? It seems to be the relationship F-Child rather than an elementary kin-type (such as F or S). The reciprocal address term for M-Child is *ma* (again, specifiable as *ambokla ma* or *kang ma*). Taking this into account reveals something important about the way the Melpa think of kin terms, which can be recognised only if we free ourselves from the assumption that the elementary units must always be markers belonging to a universal analytic language. Over and above this point there is the fact of divergence between address and reference contexts. The reference contexts do lend themselves to being parsed via single kin-type categories. Two separate modes of classification thus operate within what we delimit as the kinship system. Moreover, as we have noted, the equations between kin types must not be taken as expressing complete identifications. Finally, here, 'father' terms are inflected also in terms of sibling order. *Tepam komone* is 'elder father', that is FeB, and *tepam akele* is 'junior father', that is FyB. The overall outcome of these explorations into what we have deliberately picked out as very obvious aspects of the wider kin term system is that by this means it is evident *both* that focal meanings are present and important *and* that extensions are readily made and follow a grid that is stamped with wider structural relations. As well, there is the somewhat more radical point that Melpa address terms signalling shared intimacy or closures of relationship must be understood as elementary reciprocal pairs.

There is another way we can put all this, also derived from linguistic theory and its application to discussions of ritual action. Recent theories of ritual have concentrated on performativity and efficacy. Ritual actions that have performative effects have to be seen as comparable to what the philosopher J.L. Austin called 'illocutionary statements' (Austin 1962). Austin classified linguistic statements—and note here that we are discussing statements, not isolated lexemes or 'words'—as constative, illocutionary and perlocutionary. Constative statements were, for him, simple statements about the world, like referential namings. Illocutionary statements, by contrast, created situations in the world by their social performativity. It turns out that these kinds of statements tend to be important because of being constitutive of ritual actions. Statements in rituals, as well as nonverbal actions, create or affirm social realities and changes in these realities. Initiation rituals that confer a new status on people are iconic examples of this process. Perlocutionary statements are ones that have further consequences beyond, or separately from, illocutionary effects. They relate to possibly unintended but implicated results of statements.

Perlocutionary effects are examples of the complex consequences of actions. In Austin's terms, the phrase 'You're fired' is an illocutionary statement, but the perlocutionary effects of such a statement may include a protest strike by a workers' union or the suicide of the person who is fired. Similarly a statement such as 'The argument of your paper is wrong' may result unintentionally in provoking enduring enmity or retaliation.

We can now apply a version of this tripartite classification of statements to the question of kinship terms. Some usages of terms may be simply constative, statements of a perceived or asserted naming of self-evident realities. These usages would correspond to what have been called 'focal' meanings. Other contexts of usage may have an illocutionary dimension. In other words, by naming someone as a kinsperson, they creatively make them so in the local context. As with all ritualised usages, this will work only if an authorisation of it is present in the overall context; but the statement itself is constitutive. For example, in certain field contexts, fieldworkers are defined as kin once they are taken in by a family. (This does not, of course, mean that they are confused with procreative kin.) An illocutionary moment occurs when a kin term is used and establishes this relationship. Kin terms in practice then operate across a constative-illocutionary continuum. Perlocutionary effects follow, because exchange relationships flow from such illocutionary moments. Interestingly, such moments are ritually displayed in the Mount Hagen society among local people themselves most strongly when two people decide to adopt food names, because a special ritual must be performed in order to make this relationship come into being, perhaps in addition to an existing kinship tie (see again Strathern 1977 for details of these remarkable practices of ritualised identity creation).

By bringing to bear these concepts from linguistic theory, then—pragmatics, theories of meaning, and the theory of illocutionary statements—we can situate arguments about kin terms in a way that is helpful and reformulates or adds to arguments about primary versus extended meanings. A virtue of this deployment of linguistic theory is that it resonates with a theory of kinship in action, the viewpoint we advocated in our book on kinship (Strathern and Stewart 2011). Kinship in action is not simply about meanings of terms, but about how people use these terms for vital purposes in practical lives. This approach both decentres kinship studies away from an exclusive concern with kin terms and recentres kinship as social action at the heart of ethnographic work, so that kinship is as kinship does, to adapt an expression ('handsome is as handsome does'). (For further instances of our examinations of issues in kinship analysis see Strathern 1972, 1973, 1980a, 1980b; Strathern and Stewart 2000a, 2000b, 2004b, 2006, 2010a, 2010b.)

Maurice Godelier's book on *The Metamorphoses of Kinship* is another sign of renewed interest in the topic of kinship studies (Godelier 2011). Godelier seeks to revisit all the classic sites of debate and to add some reflections on the state of kinship relations in developed, urbanised social contexts in the contemporary world. His work takes us away from the negative and deconstructive concerns of David Schneider's writings and back into discussion of major issues around the world, including the relationship between terminologies of kinship and social action. In a work of this scope, both the overall approach and the analysis of detailed cases are bound to be contested. Our own viewpoint enters into this domain from the side, as it were. We argue that to understand how kin terminologies work in practice, we must understand them in terms of general linguistic theories of meaning and also in terms of theories of social action. A combination of these viewpoints leads us to infer that kinship implies both a set of focal meanings and an important plasticity of usages in practice, modelled on the flexibility of social practice. Flexibility of the applications of meanings, in other words, goes hand in hand with the flexibility of practice, while such flexibility has to be modelled on a certain semantic grid that governs the extension of meanings. The argument between extensionism versus categories can therefore be reformulated so as to illuminate how social life operates. Instead of pitting these viewpoints against each other, we need to combine them into a single empirical and explanatory model of what kinship is all about, that is, linguistic and social practice.

Kinship studies, as we have noted at the outset, also began as a kind of handmaiden to discussions about social evolution. The approach we have advocated here resituates kinship in a kind of evolutionary context based on language. Evolutionary theorists such as Logan (2007: 241–51) have suggested the idea of the 'extended mind' as the means whereby shared language usages could have contributed to the emergence of human communities. Since this extension is an extension beyond each individual mind, to which each such mind contributes and from which it draws, it is clear that extension as such is an important cognitive basis for social life. (Our usage here is of course not the same as Scheffler's technically impeccable use of this term, but it does help to draw out the broad significance of such an idea.) It would seem highly appropriate, then, that one of the dimensions in which such an important extension could take place would be in the realm of kinship. In other words, the extensions of kinship terms were probably crucially instrumental in the evolution of the cognitive basis of solidarity in human communities—which is why the idiom of kinship continues to carry symbolic power in social rhetorics of unity and shared identity.

References

Austin, J.L. 1962. *How to Do Things with Words*. Oxford: Oxford University Press.

Babidge, Sally (ed.). 2010. *Aboriginal Family and the State*. London: Ashgate.

Comaroff, John L. (ed.). 1980. *The Meaning of Marriage Payments*. London: Academic Press.

Cook, Edwin A. and Denise O'Brien (eds). 1980. *Blood and Semen: Kinship System of Highlands New Guinea*. Ann Arbor: The University of Michigan Press.

Godelier, Maurice 2011. *The Metamorphoses of Kinship*, translated from the French original by Norah Scott. London: Verso.

Goodenough, Ward Hunt (ed.). 1964. *Explorations in Cultural Anthropology: Essays in Honor of George Peter Murdock*. New York: McGraw Hill.

Goody, Jack (ed.). 1973. *The Character of Kinship*. Cambridge: Cambridge University Press.

Kahn, Miriam 1986. *Always Hungry, Never Greedy*. Cambridge: Cambridge University Press.

Logan, Robert K. 2007. *The Extended Mind: The Emergence of Language, the Human Mind, and Culture*. Toronto: University of Toronto Press.

Lounsbury, Floyd G. 1964. 'A formal account of Crow- and Omaha-type kinship terminologies'. In *Explorations in Cultural Anthropology: Essays in Honor of George Peter Murdock*, edited by Ward Hunt Goodenough, 351–93. New York: McGraw Hill.

McKnight, David. 2004. *Going the Whiteman's Way. Kinship and Marriage among Australian Aborigines*. London: Ashgate.

Meigs, Anna. 1984. *Food, Sex, and Pollution: A New Guinea Religion*. New Brunswick, NJ: Rutgers University Press.

Scheffler, Harold W. 1965. *Choiseul Island Social Structure*. Berkeley: University of California Press.

———. 1978. *Australian Kin Classification*. Cambridge Studies in Social Anthropology No. 23. Cambridge: Cambridge University Press. doi.org/10.1017/CBO9780511557590

———. 2001. *Filiation and Affiliation*. Boulder, CO: Westview Press.

Scheffler, Harold W. and Floyd G. Lounsbury. 1971. *A Study in Structured Semantics: The Siriono Kinship System*. Englewood Cliffs, NJ: Prentice Hall.

Schneider, David M. 1984. *A Critique of the Study of Kinship*. Ann Arbor: University of Michigan Press. doi.org/10.3998/mpub.7203

Shapiro, Warren 2009. 'A.L. Kroeber and the new kinship studies'. *Anthropological Forum* 19(1):1–20. doi.org/10.1080/00664670802695418

Strathern, Andrew. 1972. *One Father, One Blood: Descent and Group Structure among the Melpa People*. Canberra: The Australian National University Press.

———. 1973. 'Kinship, descent, and locality: Some New Guinea examples'. In *The Character of Kinship*, edited by Jack Goody, 21–34. Cambridge: Cambridge University Press.

———. 1977. 'Melpa food-names as an expression of ideas on identity and substance'. *Journal of the Polynesian Society* 86(4):503–11.

———. 1980a. 'Melpa kinship terms'. In *Blood and Semen: Kinship System of Highlands New Guinea*, edited by Edwin A. Cook and Denise O'Brien, 329–70. Ann Arbor: The University of Michigan Press.

———. 1980b. 'The central and the contingent: Brideweath among the Melpa and the Wiru.' In *The Meaning of Marriage Payments*, edited by John L. Comaroff, 49–66. London: Academic Press.

Strathern, Andrew and Pamela J. Stewart. 2000a. 'Kinship and commoditization: Historical transformations. *Question de parenté*. Special issue of *L'Homme* 154–55, 373–90.

——. 2000b. 'Creating difference: A contemporary affiliation drama in the highlands of New Guinea'. *The Journal of the Royal Anthropological Institute* 6(1):1–15. doi.org/10.1111/1467-9655.t01-2-00001

——. 2004a. *Empowering the Past, Confronting the Future: The Duna of Papua New Guinea*. New York: Palgrave-Macmillan. doi.org/10.1057/9781403982421

——. 2004b. 'Preface: Anthropology and cultural history in Asia and the Indo-Pacific'. In *Going the Whiteman's Way. Kinship and Marriage among Australian Aborigines*, David McKnight, xv–xviii. London: Ashgate.

——. 2006. 'Preface: Anthropology and cultural history in Asia and the Indo-Pacific.' In *Family, Gender and Kinship in Australia*, Allon J. Uhlmann, vii–ix. London: Ashgate.

——. 2010a. 'Kinship, ritual, cosmos'. *Journal de la Societe des Oceanistes* 130–131: 79–90. doi.org/10.4000/jso.6011

——. 2010b. 'Anthropology and cultural history in Asia and the Indo-Pacific, series editors' preface: Kinship, process and history'. In *Aboriginal Family and the State*, edited by Sally Babidge, xi–xvi. London: Ashgate.

——. 2011. *Kinship in Action: Self and Group*. Upper Saddle River, NJ: Prentice Hall.

Uhlmann, Allon J. 2006. *Family, Gender and Kinship in Australia*. London: Ashgate.

4

Should I Stay or Should I Go? Hunter-Gatherer Networking Through Bilateral Kin

Russell D. Greaves and Karen L. Kramer

Introduction

Mobility and shifting kin associations structure a range of subsistence, sharing, and cooperative support networks in traditional human societies. Both traditional ethnographic interests in familial alliance and behavioural ecology's comparative focus view postmarital residence as fundamental in determining kin associations and group composition. Despite the long history of interest in environmental and behavioural factors that influence postmarital residence, results from cross-cultural research differ in their characterisation of predominant patterns and causal relationships between environment, social organisation, coalitionary activities, and residence (Ember 1978; Ember and Ember 1971, 1972; Marlowe 2004; Otterbein and Marlowe 2005; Quinlan and Quinlan 2007; Rodseth et al. 1991).

In the spirit of Harold Scheffler's perspective that kinship stems from biological relatedness (Scheffler 2001), we see the interactions between individuals in Pumé forager communities to be constructed primarily according to genetic distance and secondarily through self-interested participation in cooperative subsistence efforts. We support the view that facultative adaptations of kinship systems are always based in recognition that they primarily derive from and describe genealogical kinship. Kinship classifications are not cultural constructs unrelated to descent and genetic kinship as has been suggested by Schneider (1972, 1984). The extension of these biological terms as facultative kin (that fictively assign individuals' relationships beyond their actual genetic relationship to others) creates relationships that are then subject to behavioural and social expectations determined by the roles of biological kin. Far from denying the importance of descent, such facultative links use biology to structure the many uniquely human cooperative behaviours in relation to the kinds of self-interested interactions of both close and distant kin. Living with an array of recognised close and more distant kin is one way that humans structure the cooperative behaviours that are central to our species' unique adaptations. Our perspective in this chapter looks at the advantages that bilateral kinship systems have in providing maximally extensive familial support networks for hunter-gatherer adaptations. This longitudinal study of camp associations among mobile, foraging Pumé of Venezuela permits investigation of how long-term residential patterns compare with other hunter-gatherer groups living in contrasting environments.

Hunter-gatherer residence

Distinguishing how humans use kin associations may also help understand how human life history and complex cooperative behaviours evolved as distinct and highly successful strategies. One important source of these cooperative activities is through elective membership in a community that provides alliances and fall-back options based on kinship. In many group-living animals, including primates, individuals emigrate at sexual maturity and join new communities. Dispersal patterns lay much of the foundation for sociality and are important in the formation of both kin and nonkin associations. In humans much debate has surrounded postmarital residence and identifying whether a single pattern typifies hunter-gatherers. While human dispersal was traditionally portrayed as being male-biased, the model of the patrilocal band (Radcliffe-Brown 1930; Service 1962; Steward 1955) has long been questioned (Ember 1975; Helm 1965; Hiatt 1962; Lee 1972, 1979; Lee and DeVore 1968; Meggitt 1965; Murdock 1949; Shapiro 1973; Turnbull 1965). Matrilocality generally has been considered less prevalent among hunter-gatherers (Walker et al. 2013) and is associated with particular activities resulting in male absenteeism, such as external warfare (Divale 1974;

Ember and Ember 1971), long distance hunting (Perry 1989) and reliance on female subsistence (Scelza and Bliege Bird 2008). A number of recent case studies have pointed out that residence patterns among foragers are flexible, facultative and may vary across the life course (Blurton Jones et al. 2005; Marlowe 2010). Several recent cross-cultural studies that synthesise much of the comparative data on hunter-gatherers have highlighted the importance of bilocal and multilocal residence (Alvarez 2004; Costopoulos 2005; Gray and Costopoulos 2006; Kelly 1995; Marlowe 2004, 2005). The results from these general analyses dispute many earlier expectations that most hunter-gatherers can be characterised by sex-biased postmarital residence (Cavalli-Sforza 1997; Ember 1978; Ember and Ember 1971; Rodseth et al. 1991) and are a provocative contrast to traditional perceptions of hunter-gatherer social organisation.

Cross-cultural studies

While cross-cultural studies are critical to uncovering large-scale patterning, they also have limitations. The cross-cultural databases are derived from ethnographies in which postmarital residence classifications are taken primarily from interviews and culturally stated marriage rules rather than from observation. These norms often do not account for intragroup variation in postmarital residence that arises to cope with diverse environmental and demographic conditions in traditional societies. Informants often describe current conditions that may not include temporal histories or account for lifetime changes in residence. Because cross-cultural comparisons depend on aggregate data, they necessarily overemphasise cultural norms and underrepresent both individual and group variation. The coding of ethnographic case studies for use in standard comparative samples (Binford 2001; Murdock 1949; Murdock and White 1980) involves further abstraction from sources that contain inherent differences in data collection methods, thoroughness of ethnographic observation and other sampling idiosyncrasies.

To balance the challenges posed by cross-cultural comparisons, longitudinal and individual-level data provide an important temporal view on marriage dynamics at a time depth unavailable in aggregate comparisons. They also are able to capture variability in postmarital residence arrangements both within groups and across the life course.

The combination of large-scale comparisons across multiple societies with focused individual-level longitudinal data is crucial in reexamining hunter-gatherer social organisation.

In this chapter we compare postmarital residence patterns among mobile Pumé foragers of Venezuela in order to investigate the prevalence of sex-biased and nonsex-biased residence using detailed data spanning 25 years. We first situate the problem of postmarital residence and discuss why we expect bilateral kin networks to be key for mobile hunter-gatherers. Analyses using the longitudinal Pumé data demonstrate a strong residence pattern of natolocality. The discussion turns to environmental influences on residence patterns and how different hunter-gatherer mobility can accomplish similar ends in maximising bilateral kin affiliations compared to sex-biased residence. The Pumé example emphasises ways that men and women may strategise opportunities to retain extended kin access in the face of stochastic demographic variation in a small-scale foraging society.

Human dispersal and postmarital residence

Historical background

Humans exhibit a broad range of dispersal and postmarital residence patterns. This is reflected in the rich anthropological terminology describing residential affiliations, social assortment options and the obligations and opportunities they provide. While many aspects of reproductive behaviour have become important areas of human behavioural ecology research (Rodseth et al. 1991), kinship and residence studies have languished with less attention. Although a range of hunter-gatherer behaviours formerly characterised as determined by static cultural norms (i.e. sharing, marriage, cooperation) have been reevaluated using behaviour observation methods, perspectives on residence patterns have remained within the grip of assumed conformity with normative practice.

Early hunter-gatherer studies (Radcliffe-Brown 1930; Service 1962, 1966) and some kinship studies appealed to by researchers seeking broad cross-cultural regularities among all hunter-gatherer populations (i.e. Lévi-Strauss 1949) emphasised patrilocal organisation as the dominant form of social organisation that structured territoriality and exogamous marriage. Interest in modern hunter-gatherers during the 1960s challenged this assumption and recognised that many groups maintain very flexible social organisation that emphasises association with bilateral kin (Helm 1965; Hiatt 1962; Lee and Devore 1968; Turnbull 1965). More recent cross-cultural surveys emphasise the importance of multilocality rather than sex-biased dispersal among hunter-gatherers. Unfortunately the exchanges (Costopoulos 2005; Gray and Costopoulos 2006; Marlowe 2005; Otterbein and Marlowe 2005) following Frank Marlowe's (2004) cross-cultural study of postmarital residence focused on sampling and the use of the Standard Cross-Cultural Sample, rather than on his demonstration of the predominance of multilocality among foragers. Marlowe's approach is a valuable way to try and extract the dynamics of residential variation from data collected under assumptions of strict and static cultural norms of residential behaviour.

Despite these reanalyses, patrilocality remains a common characterisation of foragers (Cant and Johnstone 2008; Cavalli-Sforza 1997; Di Fiore and Rendall 1994; Ember 1975, 1978; Otterbein and Marlowe 2005; Rodseth et al. 1991). For example, a number of recent genetic studies that address residence patterns assume that patrilocality is common among hunter-gatherers. Patterns of sex-biased dispersal appear evident based on greater diversity in mtDNA compared with low variance in Y-chromosome expression (Destro-Bisol et al. 2004a; Oota et al. 2001; Seielstad et al. 1998). Some results are ambiguous (Langergraber et al. 2007; Kumar et al. 2006; Wilder et al. 2004) and interpretations of patrilocality may not consider whether potentially highly differential male reproductive success compared to lower female variance could produce similar patterns (however, see Destro-Bisol et al. 2004a).

While kin often are implicated in these interactions (food sharing, cooperation, allocare, resource and labour transfers), few quantitative data are available for postmarital residence patterns that form the basis of these kin associations. Among any foraging population, longitudinal observational data are necessary to capture both the variation in camp memberships and long-term kin associations that can be evaluated as potential strategies of cooperation with relatives. Although interview questioning can elicit stated preferences for matrilocal or patrilocal residence, it is unclear whether this supports the concept of cultural norms or describes situational and variable kin associations. We feel that greater time investment is needed to collect empirical data on residential patterns.

Bilateral kin networks

Comparative data suggest that many foraging societies practise situational flexibility in the kin with whom an individual or family lives (Alvarez 2004; Marlowe 2004). Viewed from both male and female perspectives, a residence pattern that maintains access to bilateral kin is advantageous in many ways. In the absence of compelling reasons to associate more closely with virilocal or uxorilocal kin, or for one sex to preferentially disperse from their natal communities, bilocal residence creates the broadest base of potential kin interaction for mobile foragers. In addition to providing opportunities for interactions with parents of both husband and wife, bilaterality broadens access to collateral kin—siblings, in-laws, cousins, nieces, nephews, and other more distant kin referent to both members of the couple (Silberbauer 1972). While in some societies close association with certain kin may augment potential conflicts (between brothers, or sisters, or in reference to downwardly directed resources from wives' or husbands' parents), there is no a priori reason to expect that conflict is a more important determinant of residence than opportunities for cooperation.

In some societies, preferred lineality is an important means of recruiting or obliging particular kin to cooperate (Alvard 2003; Alvard and Nolin 2002). Because lineality incorporates individuals beyond closely related kin (Dunbar 2008), it can bring large numbers of individuals together where certain tasks require articulation of larger work groups or material capital than a nuclear or extended family can muster (Donald 1997; Kan 1989; Mauss 1967; Oberg 1973). This is pertinent in large village communities, with greater resident populations than are represented by most mobile foragers' camps. In small-scale populations with smaller or changing resident membership, preferred lineality would limit the number of potential collaborators whereas bilaterality is maximally inclusive of kin (Alvard 2002; Ember 1975). This is one reason why the characterisation of hunter-gatherers as predominantly patrilineal or matrilineal has been challenged (Blurton Jones et al. 2005; Hiatt 1962; Lee 1972, 1979; Marlowe 2004, 2010; Scelza and Bliege Bird 2008; Turnbull 1965; Woodburn 1972).

The flexibility of bilateral residential organisation may be especially important in small-scale societies where stochastic variation in birth and survivorship can result in skewed age and sex distributions (Ember 1975). For example, between 1990 and 1993, in one Savanna Pumé community short-term asymmetries in birth and survival rates resulted in four boys between the ages of zero and seven, in contrast to 17 girls between these same ages (Greaves 1997a). Bilateral residence options permit a facultative means to adjust uneven age and sex ratios, either to balance production and consumption ratios or to facilitate mating opportunities. Maximising rather than biasing potential kin association may be especially relevant for foraging economies where subsistence often changes throughout the year, and oscillations in residential organisation can respond to changes in labour organisation and sharing patterns.

Bilateral kin affiliation also can permit greater potential flexibility in residence. In many groups of hunter-gatherers, parents and other relatives help support young couples, who may not yet be mature food producers (Bogin 1999; Hrdy 2005; Kaplan 1996; Kramer 2008; Kramer and Greaves 2010; Kramer, Greaves and Ellison 2009). Rather than restricting access to kin, bilateral association can make it possible for couples to situationally locate with the kin of either spouse in response to demographic changes in family composition. Parents also are expected to be self-interested in maintaining potential relationships with both their sons and daughters. Parents may manipulate the potential mate pools for their children by choosing residences with the highest number (or value) of potential mates. These examples are far from exhaustive, but they illustrate the benefits of bilateral kin associations. It is not clear whether multilocal residential organisation causes such flexibility or reflects extant practices. However, situationally responsive kinship options in relation to subsistence, marriage, or labour can provide hunter-gatherers with more diverse means of confronting environmental variability. In the Lamalera example (sedentary Indonesian fisher-traders) a large population is required to maintain diverse roles within a unilineal system that structures food access through stringently fixed rules of participation and rewards (Alvard 2003; Alvard and Nolin 2002). Such conditions are rarely encountered in small populations of hunter-gatherers (Alvard 2002).

Given the potential benefits of residential flexibility in small-scale foraging populations, we test the prediction that Pumé postmarital residence will be minimally sex-biased. Although early ethnographic descriptions identified the Pumé as generally matrilocal (Leeds 1964; Mitrani 1975, 1988; Orobitg Canal 1998; Petrullo 1939), we anticipate that sex-biased residence will be less common than bilateral association. The Pumé are mobile foragers. In contrast to known associations with sex-biased residence, the Pumé have a general equality of male and female dietary contributions, food excesses are uncommon, long-distance hunting is rare, opportunities for heritable property or status are minimal; there is no evidence of coercion or violence toward women and no institutional aggressive conflicts with other Pumé or non-Pumé. Additionally, the Pumé live in small groups of four to 13 extended families and are subject to stochastic variation in age and sex distribution. Given these conditions, we expect that bilateral affiliations will be maintained either through multilocal or natolocal postmarital residence.

Methods

Study population

The Pumé are indigenous to the low plains, or *llanos*, in the western portion of the Orinoco basin of west central Venezuela. Recent indigenous census figures from Venezuela (INE 2001, 2011) significantly over count many native groups because of changing recognition of indigenous rights following constitutional changes under the Chavez regime. We focus on the Savanna Pumé, who are mobile foragers with an estimated population of 800 individuals (Gragson 1989; Greaves 1997a, 1997b, 2006). The Savanna Pumé are a subset of the much larger Pumé ethnic and language group (OCEI 1985: 38, 1995: 32), which also includes sedentary horticultural villages and more acculturated towns. The Pumé linguistically recognise these three subsistence distinctions in their population.

The llanos are an extensive hyper-seasonal savanna, with approximately 85 per cent of the annual precipitation falling in the wet season from June to November. These grasslands are associated with very low diversity and densities of terrestrial fauna. Extreme rainfall variation dramatically alters the flora and fauna during each season. The wet season is associated with low protein returns (mean = 2 kg/hunter/trip), substantial reliance on wild tubers (mean = 12 kg/woman/trip) and small inputs of cultivated manioc. Food availability increases during the dry season when men focus on aquatic resources. Although the mean fishing returns per trip are similar to hunting, more men fish each day, some men fish every day, multiple fishing trips by individuals are common on some days, and most boys contribute equivalent returns to adult efforts from this low-skill foraging activity. Tubers also are an important dry season food. Women, and a few men, collect large amounts of feral mangos (mean = 27 kg/woman/trip). Both male and female-contributed foods are critical to the diet and widely shared.

The Savanna Pumé move residential camps throughout the year in response to seasonal subsistence and variation in water availability. For example, Russell Greaves followed 11 main camp moves over 24 months between 1990 and 1993 (Greaves 1997a) and we identified six main residential moves for the same community over the 12-month period of the dry season of 2004 through the dry season of 2005. Camp moves are associated with changes in the spatial configuration of houses and members within the community. Despite these frequent changes in family and individual distributions across different camps, the overall camp population remains quite stable. Small groups of individuals may leave these residential camps and establish temporary camps for a few days to a couple of weeks for focused subsistence activities or raw material exploitation. Small, short-term fishing camps are particularly common during the dry season. Temporary camps can include both spouses' kin, less closely related individuals with close subsistence or labour relationships, or other opportunistic arrangements. Membership in these temporary camps had few regular associations, except that husbands and wives always accompany each other. While we refer to these small, short-term camps in the discussion, we use the residence patterns of the main camps from each of the two seasons for the purpose of the analyses.

Pumé kinship

The Pumé language (*Pumé mai*) is usually considered to be a language isolate (Mosonyi 1975; Obregón Muñoz 1981; Perez de Vega 1960). It may have been related to the now extinct Esmeralda or Otomaco languages (Hervás y Panduro 1979; Leeds 1964; Loukotka and Wilbert 1968), but it is completely unrelated to the Guahiboan (Arawak) languages of the dominant ethnic groups of the Venezuelan and Colombian llanos. Some linguists have suggested that Pumé may be classified as macro-Chibchan (Key 1979; Loukotka and Wilbert 1968; Tovar and Tovar 1961), Jivaroan (Key 1979), or might be similar to some Andean languages (Key 1979). Most discussions of the language affiliation of Pumé are simply repeating earlier classifications (de Carrocera 1980; Rey Fajardo 1979; Perez de Vega 1960). Vincenzo Petrullo (1939) erroneously reported the existence of moieties, a point refuted by Anthony Leeds

(1964). Philippe Mitrani (1988: 188–95, tabla 2, figuras 1–3) presents the clearest outlines of Pumé kinship as reported by horticultural River Pumé. These terms are not very different from those employed by the hunting-and-gathering Savanna Pumé. Most researchers (excepting Gragson and Greaves) have only reported kinship terminology as a static descriptive system, but have not had opportunities to study nuances of its use. This is because investigators did not conduct their research using the Pumé language and spent little time in the field. All information about Pumé kinship terminology presented in this paper is based on research performed solely in the Pumé language over the 30 months of cumulative fieldwork.

Pumé kinship has been identified as bifurcate merging (Mitrani 1988), a Dravidian form of Dakota-Iroquois classification with some additional generational distinctions of ego's grandparents referent to parental sex. Dravidian systems are associated with kinship that is not matrilineal or patrilineal among indigenous Venezuelan populations including the Pumé, although this is not universal in other parts of South America (J. Shapiro 1984). The Pumé also distinguish birth-order age differences among siblings and parallel cousins that permit checking of relative ages within our samples. They do not recognise lineages, clans, or moieties (Leeds 1964).

The extension of Pumé kinship terms to parents' same-sex siblings does not indicate unilineal descent, as Warren Shapiro (1995) has demonstrated. As has been noted for many traditional societies (Scheffler 1970, 1972, 1973; Shapiro 2008 Chapter 1), the Pumé apply the term 'true' or 'real' (*tamó*) to distinguish biological mothers and fathers from parallel uncles and aunts, to name full and half siblings as distinct from parallel cousins, and to discriminate parents' biological children from parallel nieces and nephews. The qualifier is rarely applied to distinguish close biological kin such as aunts and uncles (or other ascendant or descendant relatives) who are siblings of parents from those of more distantly related individuals who share merged kinship-term designations.

Kinship is the crucial description of social relationships among the Pumé. The Pumé only use kin terms to address each other. No indigenous names or nicknames were encountered in our work with the Savanna Pumé. Names of adults are used only for interactions with outsiders. They are derived from Pumé adaptations of Spanish names, but the Pumé do not use Spanish or indigenous surnames. Among the Savanna Pumé, only kin terms are employed both within the community and in reference to the normal spheres of interactions with individuals in other communities. Only men and women who are rarely encountered (less than once every few years) are occasionally referred to by both their kin term and Spanish names for clarification. Pumé use names only in reference to children under the ages of approximately 11 years. We believe this is because the kin terms for nephews, nieces and grandchildren contain minimal distinctions of these young people.

The Pumé daily discuss individuals they identify only by kin terms, each of which could equally apply to dozens of individuals resident within a camp and hundreds of people in other communities. Geographic residence of the person being described helps clarify whom the kin term refers to. Another way that these references may be distinctive is that speakers use terms appropriate to the ego-centric kin network of the listeners. The convergence of terms in a discussion helps to identify one particular person within the web of networks represented by a particular audience.

Also common in many other kinship systems (Scheffler 1965, 1972), Pumé occasionally use a diminutive form of 'mother' (literally 'little mother') to reference ego's biological mother's sisters (MZ). This is not necessarily an age distinction among women. The 'little mother' term is occasionally extended to co-wives of ego's father, even when they are not ego's MZ. However, the meaning of the term is clearly anchored in its use as a linguistic alternative to identifying all of mother's sisters as 'mother'. No comparable term distinguishes male kin. Although older and younger siblings are used to identify ego's brothers, sisters and parallel cousins, there is no birth-order terminology.

As in many other cultures (Lowie 1920; Marshall 1976; Needham 1954), Pumé women often are referred to within camp using a teknonym, although the term does not literally translate as 'mother of x (child)'. These teknonyms incorporate the name of a mother's most recent child's Spanish-based name. As with the 'little mother' term applied to MZ, no such teknonymic identification of 'father of x' is employed for men. These kin conventions make greater distinctions between women than men. This was initially thought to reflect a matrilocal residential focus where potentially larger female family units result in more diverse referent terms.

This diversity in reference to women is an interesting contrast to the lack of such terms for men. In addition to their potential use in matrilocal residence, such markers used only to distinguish women might be expected in societies with high levels of recognised infidelity and paternal uncertainty. However, among the Savanna Pumé we have not identified any instances of acknowledged or suspected adultery. This is not due to prudery by the Pumé. Topics of social, sexual, or bodily functions are readily discussed by the Pumé and no apparent secret knowledge is held outside of the public sphere. Such linguistic conventions may be a remnant of past social organisation, with comparable levels of infidelity to those found among many tropical South American groups (Gregor 1977; Hill and Hurtado 1996). There are some suggestions that the Pumé are a population that moved into their current territory in the llanos of Venezuela from another region, possibly as refugee former agriculturalists (Leeds 1961; Greaves and Kramer 2014). However, aside from genetic differences (blood group, Layrisse et al. 1961, 1964) and the significant linguistic distinctions from the adjacent Guahiboan populations in the llanos, no secure data can be brought to address this question of past Pumé economics. As noted, we felt that this term diversity might reflect matrilocality. Our observational data and additional census data prior to Greaves's initiation of research in 1990 provide a longitudinal view to address the question of Pumé postmarital residential associations.

Marriage and postmarital residence

Our goal in this chapter is to address how kinship is used in relationship to cooperation and subsistence in a challenging environment. To understand how the Pumé live in relation to kin networks, we use census data collected over a 25-year period to look at postmarital residence and long-term data on camp membership. This allows us to document whether community associations represent shifting or consistent access to bilateral kin, or are biased towards living with particular kin. We explore how mobility, camp membership and relatedness among Savanna Pumé foragers demonstrate ways that hunter-gatherer populations maximise obligations across broad kinship networks. We contrast the Pumé with other well-known hunter-gatherer groups to show that there is no single pattern in how foragers associate with and interact with kin. As with many aspects of modern human behaviour and culture, it is the flexibility in recognising the genetic relatedness of other individuals that structures cooperative interactions and makes human sociality a highly successful means of surviving in diverse environments.

Among the Pumé, marriage is not formalised through ceremony, but is socially recognised when a man or woman move in together. Divorce likewise is informal and may be instigated by either spouse. Parents and other adult kin have major influences on determining initial marriage partnerships for young people. However, couples autonomously decide whether they remain with their first partners. Subsequent marriages, and first marriages of younger men to older women, are initiated by the couple. Pumé girls marry and initiate reproduction on average at age 15.5 (Kramer 2008). Although many girls are betrothed or cohabit before menarche, coital relations are not initiated before sexual maturity. We have witnessed no examples of coercive sex within the Savanna Pumé, nor heard of any such events from informants. Many young men are married either before sexual maturity or just after puberty. Young couples often initially live in the houses of their parents or other close kin, or in close proximity to them. Postmarital residence with a relative does not have a fixed duration. Following this period, couples may establish their own houses or live in flexible association with younger and older generations. Coresidence of opposite-sex siblings and their spouses within a single household also has been observed. Household kin associations are commonly re-sorted during seasonal camp moves when new structures or house arrangements are made that realign former camp arrangements.

Data collection

Detailed census and genealogical data collected between 1982 and 2007 are used to examine residential patterns among Pumé foragers. Residence data are extracted from two primary sources: our own census data and Venezuelan indigenous censuses. Greaves conducted censuses and genealogical interviews in 1990, 1992–93 and 2005–07. These interviews were conducted in the Pumé language. The Pumé do not reckon ages but identify life stages associated with specific behaviours (i.e. walking or talking for infants, menarche, marriage, or having had a child), height, or very broad relative age classes (childhood, maturity, and old age). Genealogical data are freely and enthusiastically discussed about both living and dead individuals. Interview methods to determine ages and kin relations are detailed in previous studies (Kramer 2008; Kramer and

Greaves 2007, 2010; Kramer, Greaves and Ellison 2009). Indigenous censuses of the Pumé were carried out in 1982, 1986, 1988, 1989 and 1992 (Lizarralde and Gragson n.d.). These censuses were collected primarily in Spanish with the assistance of bilingual River Pumé. We use these censuses to extend our residential data and as anchoring events that help determine ages for younger individuals. Both sources of census data are comparable in including names, ages, genealogical data, identification of co-residential units, and past marriage and camp residential histories. The time depth of this detailed sample allows us to examine postmarital residence, shifts in kin associations and stability in residence throughout individual marriages.

Residential data are analysed for two Savanna Pumé villages (Doro Aná and Yagurí) that are part of our current demographic and economic research and for which we have the highest quality data regarding parentage, lateral kinship, and longitudinal data on marriage, reproductive histories, ages, subsistence activities and residence. These two communities are of equivalent size and have a total population of 164 individuals. The sample includes all married adults (105) and all marriages (78) that have occurred or were established since censuses were first collected in 1982. Both villages interact frequently, have close kin ties, and some migration occurs between them as part of postmarital residence. Greaves has worked with both communities since 1990. Both villages were established as part of a migration to this area approximately 45 years ago from the southern portion of Pumé territory near the Cinaruco River.

It is also important to emphasise what we mean by community, village and camps in the context of mobile foragers. The terms community and village refer interchangeably to an association of people that are relatively constant at the scale of the seasonal round. They do not refer to geographic or physical locations. Community or village is the group of people that moves as a population unit during camp residential moves (*sensu* Binford 1980). Within this broad temporal association, there may be seasonal household reshuffling within a community and the formation of small temporary logistic task groups. Camps identify short-term clusters that may contain various members from the larger community. We return to the issue of hunter-gatherer mobility in the discussion and interpretation of Pumé postmarital residence patterns.

Data analysis

Postmarital residence is coded in two ways. First, we identify whether an *individual* dispersed from his or her natal village at marriage. Individual-focused observation is consistent with how ethologists and primatologists think about dispersal at sexual maturity. Each adult is coded as dispersing or not dispersing from their natal village for their first and all subsequent marriages. Because traditional ethnographic classifications are based on *marriage* as the unit of analysis, the second way we record postmarital residence is with respect to where a couple resides relative to their kin. Marriages are coded as virilocal, uxorilocal, neolocal or natolocal. We use the term virilocal to identify postmarital residence referent to the husband's kin. Uxorilocal refers to postmarital residence in relation to the wife's kin. A marriage is coded as neolocal if the couple moved to a community separate from close kin of either husband or wife. In a small-scale society this does not mean that they would necessarily move to a community where they have no kin ties. Neolocality identifies couples who disperse away from their natal or closest kin. We use these terms both because they are consistent with how Frank Marlowe (2004) and others (Ember and Ember 1972) coded their cross-cultural samples and because they are a simplification of the complex anthropological vocabulary of postmarital residence in being more inclusive of male and female kin associations. A fourth category, natolocal, is added to refer to endogamous marriages, where both partners remain within their natal community (camp or village) after marriage. Marlowe (2004) notes that natolocality is much more difficult to identify from the Standard Cross-Cultural Sample for foragers than it is for more sedentary societies. This is partly because the Standard Cross-Cultural Sample presents a static characterisation of societies that cannot systematically address temporal changes in residence and because of the more shifting membership among many foragers. As noted in Figures 7 and 9, we distinguish natolocality referent to foragers' birth village, not just the household in which that individual was born. This modification is necessary among mobile foragers as neither houses, locations, nor intrahousehold membership remains stable across the changes in camp moves. As an example of how to interpret these two coding schemes, if a young woman marries a man from another community and he moves to her community, she is coded as not dispersing, and the marriage is coded as uxorilocal. However, if she married someone within her village, she would be coded as not dispersing and the marriage as natolocal.

Because the Pumé sample has precise information on where couples live at different points in their adult lives, we track residential stability at two levels. An individual's residential stability is coded both for changes in community affiliation at marriage and for residential moves during a marriage union. The latter records multilocality directly from longitudinal observation. (The terms multilocality and bilocality are used here interchangeably.) Movement within a marriage is recorded for a subset of the population (community of Doro Aná) for whom we have the most continuous observational data.

We clarify that dispersal and postmarital residence are referent to the community in which an individual resided as a juvenile. We refer to this as the natal village because in most cases this is the birth village. To reduce overcategorisation, natolocality includes individuals who have lived in one of the two communities since childhood, but were born elsewhere. In the sample, 18 adults (17 per cent) moved into their 'natal community' as young children. Some of these (33 per cent) moved with their parents during the large migration from the south 45 years ago. Most children, however, joined the study communities because they were orphaned (67 per cent). All computations, descriptive and statistical analyses were preformed in SAS version 9.1.3.

Results

Postmarital residence was coded for 105 individuals (55 women and 50 men) and 78 marriages (Table 1). This included all marriages from two Savanna Pumé villages with a total population of 164 individuals. For all individuals, 32 per cent of men and 22 per cent of women have been married more than once. A nonparametric one-sided Wilcoxon-Mann-Whitney test shows that while males tend to remarry more often, this difference is not significant ($z = 1.2006$, $p = .1149$, $n = 105$). Although many young adults have been married more than once, age is obviously a significant determinant of times married (model $f = 5.58$, $df = 3$, $p = .0007$, $n = 105$ for a multivariate general linear model [GLM] including age [$p = .0002$] and a quadratic term for age [$p = .0002$]). Older individuals are more likely to experience multiple marriages, but sex is not significant when added to the model ($p = .2741$). Men (15.5 per cent) more commonly than women (6.5 per cent) have been polygynously married at some point in their adult lives. Of the 78 marriages, 62 are first marriages, 14 are second marriages and two are third or more marriages.

Table 1. Pumé sample description

Married individuals (n=105)	Males	Females
	50	55
Times married 1 2 3+	34 14 2	43 11 1
Polygynously married	15.5%	6.5%
Marriages (n=78)		
1st marriage	62 (79.5%)	
2nd marriage	14 (17.9%)	
3rd+ marriage	2 (2.6 %)	

Source: Constructed by © Russell D. Greaves and Karen L. Kramer from their fieldwork data and the Lizarralde and Gragson n.d. census data-RG.

Figure 7 shows individual dispersal patterns for Pumé males (n = 49) and females (n = 54). The precise dispersal history of two older adults was unclear despite multiple interviews. The majority of men (86 per cent) and women (76 per cent) marry endogamously and remain in their natal village, at least for the entire duration of their first marriage. While more females disperse than males, this difference is not significant (Chi-sq = 1.5730, df = 1, p = .2098).

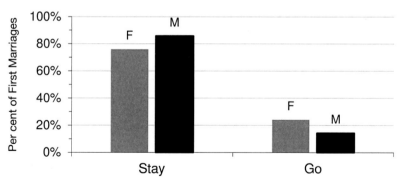

Figure 7. Pumé postmarital dispersal patterns from natal village for first marriage

(n = 49 males, black bars; n = 54 females, grey bars)

Source: Constructed by © Russell D. Greaves and Karen L. Kramer from their fieldwork data and the Lizarralde and Gragson n.d. census data-RG.

To situate postmarital residence patterns as they are commonly coded in ethnographic studies, marriage as the unit of analysis is stratified by postmarital residence. Of first marriages ($n = 62$), 66 per cent are natolocal (Figure 8). Virilocality, where wives emigrate to their husbands' community, occurs in 19 per cent of marriages. Uxorilocality, where husbands move to their wives' communities, occurs in 15 per cent of marriages.

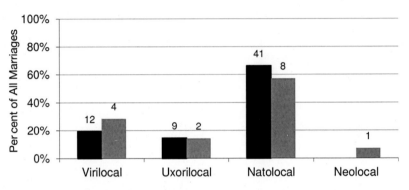

Figure 8. Pumé postmarital residence patterns

Marriages stratified by whether the couple resides with the husband's relatives (virilocal), the wife's relatives (uxorilocal), in their natal village (natolocal), or in a village where neither has close relatives (neolocal). Shown for first marriages (black bars; $n = 62$), and second marriages (grey bars; $n = 15$).

Source: Constructed by © Russell D. Greaves and Karen L. Kramer from their fieldwork data and the Lizarralde and Gragson n.d. census data-RG.

Residence decisions during second marriages are examined separately for several reasons. To maximise sample size, individuals of different ages and couples at different stages in their reproductive careers are included. First marriages are overrepresented since all couples have at least one marriage to be included in the sample, but not all couples have completed their marital history. First and second marriages may show different residential choices, with distinctions between younger and older individuals based on number of children, extent of within-community alliances, or mate availability. Despite these potential differences of residence selection following divorce or at initiation of a subsequent union, the pattern for second marriages is remarkably similar to that of first marriages (Figure 9). Although a slightly higher proportion of individuals emigrate following a second marriage, this difference is not significant (Chi-sq = .6043, $df = 2$, $p = .7392$). The majority of second marriages are natolocal, with both partners continuing to remain associated with their natal community and that of their first marriages. Only one case of neolocality was identified in our sample.

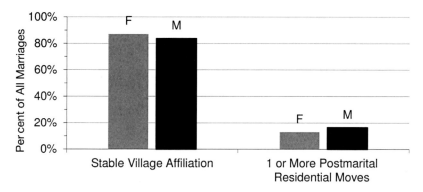

Figure 9. Postmarital residential stability for Pumé residents
(n = 49 males, black bars; n = 54 females, grey bars)
Source: Constructed by © Russell D. Greaves and Karen L. Kramer from their fieldwork data and the Lizarralde and Gragson n.d. census data-RG.

Postmarital residential stability evaluates the extent to which Pumé men and women shift their kin associations with subsequent marriages. Figure 7 shows the frequency distribution for males and females who remain in the community where they first reside after marriage (whether it is natolocal, virilocal, or uxorilocal) compared to those who make one or more additional residential moves during subsequent marriages. All first marriages within both communities are shown in Figure 9. Most Pumé women (87 per cent; n = 54) and men (84 per cent; n = 49) remain affiliated with the same community where they lived at the time of their first marriage. Postmarital residential stability is independent of sex (Chi-sq = .2336, df = 1, p = .6289). When the probability that someone who dispersed at first marriage will continue to move during subsequent marriages is modelled, results are insignificant (Wald chi-sq = .9781, p = .3227, n = 103). While exogamous dispersal at first marriage is not a significant predictor of subsequent community shifts for later marriages, it is notable that the several individuals who have been married three or more times have made multiple residential moves during their adult lives.

Residential changes within a marriage also are rare. Ninety-one per cent (n = 42 marriages) of couples remain associated with the same community throughout their marriage. Couples that do move tend to be young and the wife and husband each have at least one living parent (so that such a move is not neolocal). These couples move infrequently between their parents' communities. While the Pumé have a strong bilateral residence pattern, there is a low incidence of multilocality.

In sum, although the Pumé have been culturally characterised as a matrilocal foraging society, longitudinal census data and residential analyses provide a different and more nuanced view of postmarital decisions. There is no evidence of predominantly sex-biased dispersal. Neither men nor women preferentially relocate from their village residence following marriage. Most marriages in our sample are natolocal, both spouses remaining in the community where they grew up throughout their adult lives. Individuals that do move after their first marriage exhibit minimal subsequent residential reshuffling. Although the incidence of bilocality at the scale of community relocation is low, we emphasise in the discussion that natolocality is functionally a similar strategy that maintains bilateral kin affiliations.

Discussion

The perception that hunter-gatherers are patrilocal persists in many formulations about human social organisation despite numerous ethnographic examples to the contrary. Recent cross-cultural comparisons demonstrate that the predominant residential pattern among modern foragers is neither male- nor female-focused, but bilateral, in which ties to both male and female kin are maintained (Figure 10). Foragers also trace descent bilaterally more frequently than do nonforagers (Marlowe 2004). Together these patterns strongly suggest that an important general characteristic of hunter-gatherer social organisation is access to a broad pool of kin through flexible residential association and recognition of more kinds of kin than seen among nonforaging groups. Even in societies that may be characterised as patrilocal or matrilocal, the recognition that they still calculate bilateral kin has become a mundane anthropological assumption. However, recognition of bilateral kin is a unique behaviour even among the most social of other animals (Alexander 1979; Alexander and Noonan 1979; Rodseth et al. 1991). The Pumé results complement cross-cultural studies in using individual-level, longitudinal behavioural data to show that postmarital residence is organised to maintain strong bilateral kin ties.

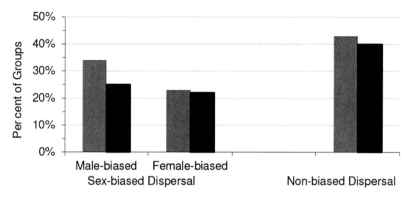

Figure 10. Reassessment of hunter-gatherer postmarital patterns from Marlowe (2004: 280)

Source: Constructed by © Russell D. Greaves and Karen L. Kramer from Marlowe (2004: 280), n = 36 groups from the Standard Cross-Cultural Sample, grey bars (Alvarez 2004); n = 48 groups from Murdock's 1967 Ethnographic Atlas, black bars.

Results show a clear pattern of natolocality among the Savanna Pumé that keeps both spouses across most marriages in close association with their immediate and extended families. Although cross-cultural analyses show that the proportions of male contributions to the overall forager diet do not result in higher levels of virilocality (Marlowe 2004), there are suggestions that uxorilocality may be associated with higher amounts of women's contributions (Korotayev 2001; Marlowe 2004; Scelza and Bliege Bird 2008). Given the characterisation of the Pumé as matrilocal and the relative equality in importance of male and female foods to their diet, we expected that there might be some biases in the variation toward that pattern. Although there is much reliance on female food contributions, residence favouring association with more female kin is not apparent.

We expected that there might be differences in postmarital residence between first and subsequent marriages. Residential decisions may be made for various reasons, and second marriages may be made for different reasons than initial unions. Younger individuals may be less tethered to one community because they have fewer child-support demands and less-developed adult relationships. Older individuals may be more interested in remaining in the village they first marry into because of children, offspring support from former spouses or other kin, extant friendships, labour or sharing alliances that are costly to abandon. Divorce could engender potential conflicts resulting in more exogamous second marriages compared with first unions. However, these life-history changes appear to have little effect on residence location following remarriage. For all marriages, natolocal and exogamous, lifetime association most commonly remains with the community of initial postmarital residence. This suggests that established adult relationships, which involve frequent labour and sharing interactions, are important considerations in decisions about where to live following divorce. Although there is lability in group composition during temporary camps, visits or seasonal household reorganisation, primary village associations are remarkably stable.

While natolocality and postmarital residential stability are strong patterns, some Pumé do separate from their kin and emigrate to households within their husbands' or wives' communities (20 individuals' first marriage, 19.4 per cent of males and females in the sample). Three of these are older individuals who emigrated from the parent population that formed the communities of Doro Aná and Yagurí 45 years ago. Two individuals represent the one neolocal marriage in our sample. One woman and her younger brother moved in as young orphans and both married within this adoptive group. While multivariate analyses might bring greater insight into the conditions under which individuals deviate from the natolocal pattern, the sample of exceptions is too small. However, in examining these exogamous marriages, we found a suggestive patterned difference between men and women that provides a direction for future research.

Of the remaining 13 men and women whose first marriages were non-natolocal (four men and nine women), the majority of the exceptions fall into two general categories. Most males who relocate into uxorilocal postmarital residence are part of large families. They appear to emigrate because their available mating options are already coopted by older siblings and male parallel cousins. All four men who married exogamously had at least three living siblings in their natal communities. In contrast, women who emigrate into the communities of their husbands tend to have few close kin of their own, and gain larger kin networks through alliances with their husbands' families. Two of the women had no living siblings and small families. Another young woman married exogamously when she had only one full sibling in her natal group, her mother had recently remarried and the family's status was relatively low. Three women who initially resided virilocally during their first marriages have subsequently divorced and returned to their natal communities. One woman had been raised for most of her life in the non-natal community where she married, her father still lives there and her mother lived there for approximately 13 years. One woman followed her husband's relocation to a village where his brother lived, although they both initially resided in her birth community. The remaining woman's situation does not appear to fit our generalisation about exogamous marriage. There is no indication that sororal polygyny is associated with exogamous female marriage among the Savanna Pumé, as found among other foragers (Scelza and Bliege Bird 2008). Additional support of these patterns is apparent in exogamous third and fourth marriages.[1] In mobile hunter-gatherers the complexities of residential shifts across the life span reinforce the importance of bilateral kin association. For example, the three women who returned to their natal communities subsequent to dissolution of an exogamous postmarital residence and the one woman who had lived as a child in the nonnatal community where she married (also see two similar exceptions in footnote 1) demonstrate a preponderance of bilateral kin proximity.

In small populations, low levels of exogamous marriage persisting over a long period raise obvious concerns about incest avoidance (Bittles 2004; Durham 2004). One observation from our fieldwork may address this concern and provide insight into a less appreciated form of mobility in small-scale societies. Although Pumé community associations are relatively stable both at marriage and throughout the duration of a marriage, major reshuffling of kin affiliations does occur at a deeper temporal scale.

Both study communities moved to their current territory approximately 45 years ago from further south near the Cinaruco River. The adults in the generation who moved state that they represent more distantly related individuals from less intermarried lineage segments who fissioned from their parent community. Additionally, following this fission, some individuals from nearby villages joined these new communities. This move occurred before the data collection used in these analyses, and

---

1   The importance we infer for bilateral kin access is also supported by the 12 examples of non-natolocal second–fourth marriages in our sample. Four (three men, one woman) of the eight individuals with two non-natolocal marriages initiated their first union natolocally, and subsequently sought mates in other communities. Two of those same men, and another woman with exogamous second marriages had lived in the community they married into as pre-adolescent children for at least 10 years before moving away with their parents. One other man's second marriage took place uxorilocally within the same community that he had married into 13 years previously. One woman's second and third marriages were both exogamous (as was her first), although she had lived extensively in the two communities where her second–third marriages occurred. She also had a small number of relatives in both groups. Only one woman exhibited both marriages that were virilocal without having local kin. The other non-natolocal third ($n = 2$) and fourth ($n = 1$) unions (representing two men) were by individuals whose first marriages were natolocal. Both of these men with the highest number of exogamous marriages come from a family with a large number of surviving full and half-brothers (and natolocally resident sisters).

confirmation of the relatedness of individuals in this founder group compared to their original community membership is beyond the reach of the current genealogical data. Following the consequences of the *Darkness in El Dorado* scandal (Borofsky 2005; Gregor and Gross 2004; Tierney 2000), genetic testing is unlikely to be permitted by government ministries in Venezuela to resolve this issue. Informants, however, are clear in their statements that they moved to their current location as less-related families from their source residence. This recent migration offers new marriage options through a temporal and geographic reassortment of the population. These two communities retain ties with each other and with other families who also dispersed into other Pumé villages. These provide an additional destination and source for low-frequency exogamous marriages. For example, as noted above in the discussion of exogamous marriages, some camp moves do bring in new members whose children marry natolocally (by our coding criteria) but represent individuals from outside family groups. While it is unknown whether such reshuffling is a consistent feature of Pumé demography or explains natolocality in other contexts, such large-scale population shifts are known for other foragers (Blackburn 1996; Denbow 1984; Wilmsen 1989).

Another question raised by these analyses, is the role of affinal kin in comparison to the apparent importance of bilateral kin access. Both male and female resources are widely shared within Savanna Pumé communities (Gragson 1989; Greaves and Kramer 2014; Kramer and Greaves 2010; Mitrani 1988), and there is no evidence of strict in-law avoidance or preferential association in relation to subsistence work or food sharing (Mitrani 1988). Quantitative time allocation data would further clarify whether the strength of interactions varies between affines and consangual kin. Time allocation data on sharing and other interactions, the spatial proximity of wives' and husbands' parents or other in-laws (data available from one Pumé community), and longitudinal persistence (potentially available for some of the 25-year genealogical sample) could contribute to an improved understanding of affinal roles and variation by sex and generation (Coall and Hertwig 2010; Euler and Weitzel 1996; Euler and Michalski 2007).

Environmental influences on bilateral kinship organisation

The observation that hunter-gatherers exhibit greater bilateral kin identification and more bilaterally referenced residence than nonforaging societies (Marlowe 2004) suggests that reliance on wild foods is related to broad kinship networks (Ember 1975; Lee 1972, 1979; Silberbauer 1972). Many foragers exploit a wide diversity of food resources with distinct and variable distributions, return payoffs, access and processing requirements. Resource variation must be mediated through an array of mobility, labour and group size changes (Binford 2001; Kelly 1995; Panter-Brick, Layton and Rowley-Conwy 2001; Quinlan and Quinlan 2007; Scelza and Bliege Bird 2008; Smith 1991; Winterhalder and Smith 1981). Seasonality influences all of these changing needs, including the sex of primary producers and their labour (i.e. multiple female or male membership groups) and support (i.e. childcare, food processing, mobility, auxiliary help roles) demands. Kinship association is an important means to assemble and alter social memberships, at potentially different geographical and temporal scales, in response to these changes. Foragers living in small communities necessarily cope with variation in sex ratios, age profiles, productivity and generosity of kin, as well as both anticipated and unforeseen changes in environmental conditions affecting subsistence, stress, and future options. In addition, hunter-gatherers may use mobility or kinship to change relationships between producers and consumers, to recruit labour groups appropriate for particular tasks or to adjust for food availability during certain times of the year.

If foragers tend to be more inclusive of bilateral kin relationships than nonforagers, is this evident in the different kinds of camps they make? We use the Savanna Pumé results to address how bilateral kin affiliation can be broadly similar across hunter-gatherers despite differences in mobility, camp size and residence patterns. We contrast pumé natolocality with the multilocal residence and uxorilocal bias of the Hadza of Tanzania to demonstrate how both of these apparently distinct and different living arrangements each accomplish similar maximisation of lifetime association with a broad set of bilateral kin.

Membership at Pumé main residence camps is stable across all seasonal moves. Except for short-term camps, almost identical groups are present in each co-resident association across our 25-year sample. The predominant pattern of Pumé natolocality appears to be a response, in part, to their marginal environment. Six months of each year are associated with seasonal shortfalls in food availability, nutritional stress and increased epidemiological challenges. During this season, few men hunt on any particular day and returns are normally much smaller than among many foragers (Greaves 1997b). Low wet-season inputs of protein and fat are offset by highly predictable and larger returns by women collecting tubers (Greaves and Kramer 2014; Kramer and Greaves 2017). Unlike many other foragers, female foods are extensively shared. These factors may condition living with as broadly inclusive a male and female kin base as possible. Smaller camps might have fewer consumers, but they also would have fewer hunters, smaller areas searched by hunters and lower male food returns. In a relatively depauperate terrestrial environment, wet-season camps may not atomise because a certain threshold number of men are necessary to realise any hunting success. Because husbands and wives are always co-resident, this results in a matched labour force. The stability of natolocality appears to be an outcome of living in aggregate groups of bilateral kin, which may be favoured to minimise resource shortfalls. It is notable that smaller temporary camps are common only during the dry season, when food is more widely available and parts of the community move to productive fishing locations for one to three weeks.

Comparisons to other hunter-gatherers

In contrast, the Hadza rotate membership across a range of smaller short-term camps (Marlowe 2006, 2010; Woodburn 1968, 1972). Unlike the Venezuelan savanna, the Hadza environment has a greater availability of large game, tubers of larger package size and reliable sources of densely caloric honey. Individual camps are generally smaller (~20–60 individuals) than most Savanna Pumé residential camps, and potential kin associations at any particular camp are less diverse. Hadza men and women move between several small camps on average 6.5 times a year ranging between 4–20 camp moves per year (Marlowe 2010). The Hadza calculate bilateral kinship and have generally uxorilocally referenced camp residence (Woodburn 1972). The differences between Hadza and Pumé camps on the ground reflect distinct ways of employing bilateral kin (Figure 11), which are linked to differences in camp size, aggregation and the higher productivity of the Hadza environment. Only a minority of Hadza camp moves appear to be related to food shortages, partly because small numbers of producers can have an assurance of returns and smaller camp size reduces the numbers of consumers (Woodburn 1972).

Although each individual Hadza camp may be composed of a narrower range of kin, individuals or couples, they associate with a broad range of bilateral kin throughout their lives. At a deeper temporal scale, each of these temporary camps combines into a larger bilateral kin network (Wood and Marlowe 2011).

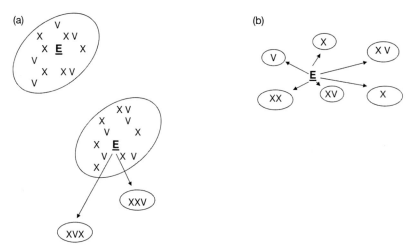

Figure 11. Schematic model of a married hunter-gatherer's relationship to bilateral kin under two common residential patterns

(a) natolocal residence and stable camp composition, showing occasional temporary camps (Pumé-type pattern); (b) multilocal residence and a shifting camp composition (Hadza-type pattern). Each model represents ego's (E) residential mobility and the hypothetical assortment of kin (X=uxorilocal, V=virilocal) within individual camps across an unspecified time period.

Source: Drawn by © Russell D. Greaves and Karen L. Kramer.

The schematic differences between two residential systems such as those practised by the Pumé or the Hadza are shown in Figure 11. The figure outlines kin associations in a natolocal and a multilocal residential system as they might appear across time. The view shows ego's (E) relationships to uxorilocal (X) and virilocal (V) kin who are resident in each camp. Because a hunter-gatherer's individual residential events are subsumed within a larger pattern of lifetime interactions, this is a useful scale to examine the cumulative system effects of forager residential organisation. Figure 11 illustrates how both natolocal and multilocal residence affect a similarly broad set of bilateral kin associations.

The residential variation seen among Ju/'hoansi foragers, who live in comparable savanna settings, also emphasises the importance of maintaining access to bilateral kin. Researchers working with Ju/'hoansi recognise the importance of variable residence associations across a broad suite of potential bilateral kin that are responsive to environmental, social, and life history changes in foraging opportunities. Richard B. Lee (1976, 1979) contradicts Lorna Marshall's (1960) position on patrilineal control over waterholes and associated resource areas. Lee explicitly underlines the flexible associations among kin across !Kung camp moves (1979: 61–67, tables 3.13–3.14, figures 3.4–3.6). Marshall (1976) describes highly variable potential kin associations, even with an expected period of residence with uxorilocal kin for bride service. Lee (1979) agrees with this point and indicates that even bride service may include the relocation of a husband's kin to create a bilateral kin-based residential camp rather than a strictly uxorilocal-referenced postmarital residence. Looking at women's residence choices among the !Kung, Howell (2001) states that post-divorce residence may be determined by the amount of time in a particular community before divorce, whether the woman has kin in that group, if her parents are still living, whether her children were married or the possibility of remarriage to a brother of her ex-husband. Polly Wiessner (2002) also emphasises the egalitarian options of men and women in choosing associations with particular kin. She identifies group membership as facultative and at least partially related to hunting ability of central males. Wiessner (ibid.: 422–27, tables 2–4) calculates that productive males also have significantly more sharing partners among distant kin than poorer hunters, indicating opportunities to extend their networks well beyond those of less-skilled hunters who primarily have support relationships only with more closely related individuals.

Like the Hadza example outlined above, temporal changes in camp membership result in multiple patterns of residential association with bilateral kin, not an adherence to any strict and biased norm of preferential residence with a more limited set of relatives. For Ju'/hoansi, food shortages are not uncommon and a similar shifting residential pattern to that employed by the Hadza in a more resource-rich environment is used as a social means of accessing variable returns from men and women who are both close and more distant kin. The variability in Ju'/hoansi seasonal subsistence activities, fluctuating annual and interannual rainfall, and occasionally extreme differences in resource availability, appears to result in a flexible residential system that maximises potential access to diverse locations through fluid tactical associations with a range of kin.

Conclusions

Our goal in this chapter is to further investigate the challenge from recent cross-cultural comparisons that bilateral rather than sex-biased kin affiliations are an important pattern in human postmarital residence using longitudinal and individual observations for a group of mobile foragers. The Savanna Pumé combine close and more distant biological kin, along with affines, into networks that generally persist for life. Long-term shifts in population reorganise mobile Pumé communities so that natolocality is a stable strategy maintaining broad bilateral kin associations. Cross-cultural studies have shown that bilateral kin associations are more common in forager than food-producing populations. Additionally, such broad access to kin is associated with a range of environments, resource productivity, and hunter-gatherer subsistence practices. We emphasise that natolocality, bilocality and multilocality accomplish similar ends in maximising bilateral kin affiliations compared to sex-biased kin affiliations. Distinctions between hunter-gatherer residential organisations appear to be responses to environmental differences that adjust labour groups and camp size through manipulation of kin associations. Such flexible changes in forager group composition are possible because humans recognise a broad range of relatives.

Descent and genetic relatedness are the bases for these kinship systems that secondarily link affines into an extensive network. The additional layering of more facultative kinship extends the categories and obligations based on descent to individuals of economic value and interest (such as good producers or visiting anthropologists) to the cooperating community. Far from being a cultural construct of human ideation, human kinship is grounded in biology. Our unique human diversity employs myriad languages, forms of social organisation, knowledge systems, and subsistence adaptations across the world. However, a relatively limited number of ways to describe kin associations between individuals are flexibly used as critical components in those different behavioural strategies for social cooperation. In contrast, the more limited variety in kinship classification systems used globally reflects their biological basis in descent. However, how kinspeople distribute themselves in residential and subsistence groups is responsive to the broad range of environmental and social challenges that humans face.

References

Alexander, Richard D. 1979. *Darwinism and Human Affairs*. Seattle: University of Washington Press.

Alexander, Richard D. and Katherine M. Noonan. 1979. 'Concealment of ovulation, parental care, and human social evolution'. In *Evolutionary Biology and Human Social Behavior: An Anthropological Perspective*, edited by Napoleon A. Chagnon and William Irons, 402–35. North Scituate: Duxbury Press.

Allen, Nicholas J., Hilary Callan, Robin Dunbar and Wendy James (eds). 2008. *Early Human Kinship: From Sex to Social Reproduction*. Malden: Blackwell Publishing. doi.org/10.1002/9781444302714

Alvard, Michael S. 2002. 'Carcass ownership and meat distribution by big-game cooperative hunters'. *Research in Economic Anthropology* 21: 99–132. doi.org/10.1016/S0190-1281(02)21005-7

——. 2003. 'Kinship, lineage identity, and an evolutionary perspective on the structure of cooperative big game hunting groups in Indonesia'. *Human Nature* 14(2): 129–63. doi.org/10.1007/s12110-003-1001-5

Alvard, Michael S. and David A. Nolin. 2002. 'Rousseau's whale hunt? Coordination among big game hunters'. *Current Anthropology* 43(4): 533–59. doi.org/10.1086/341653

Alvarez, Helen Perich. 2004. 'Residence groups among hunter-gathers: A view of the claims and evidence for patrilocal bands'. In *Kinship and Behavior in Primates*, edited by Bernard Chapais and Carol M. Berman, 420–42. Oxford: Oxford University Press.

Barry, Herbert and Alice Schlegel (eds). 1980. *Cross-Cultural Sample and Codes*. Pittsburgh: University of Pittsburgh Press.

Berndt R.M. and C.H. Berndt (eds). 1965. *Aboriginal Man in Australia*. Sydney: Angus and Robertson.

Bicchieri, M.G. (ed.). 1972. *Hunters and Gatherers Today: A Socioeconomic Study of Eleven Such Cultures in the Twentieth Century*. New York: Holt, Rinehart and Winston.

Binford, Lewis R. 1980. 'Willow smoke and dogs' tails: Hunter-gatherer settlement systems and archaeological site formation'. *American Antiquity* 45(1): 4–20. doi.org/10.2307/279653

——. 2001. *Constructing Frames of Reference: An Analytical Method for Archaeological Theory Building Using Ethnographic and Environmental Data Sets*. Berkeley: University of California Press.

Bittles, Alan H. 2004. 'Genetic aspects of inbreeding and incest'. In *Inbreeding, Incest, and the Incest Taboo: The State of Knowledge at the Turn of the Century*, edited by Arthur P. Wolf and William H. Durham, 38–60. Stanford: Stanford University Press.

Blackburn, Roderic. 1996. 'Fission, fusion, and foragers in East Africa: Micro- and macroprocesses of diversity and integration among Okeik'. In *Cultural Diversity Among Twentieth Century Foragers: An African Perspective*, edited by Susan Kent, 188–212. Cambridge: Cambridge University Press.

Blurton Jones, Nick, Kristen Hawkes and James F. O'Connell. 2005. 'Older Hadza men and women as helpers'. In *Hunter-Gatherer Childhoods: Evolutionary, Developmental and Cultural Perspectives*, edited by Barry S. Hewlett and Michael E. Lamb, 214–36. New Brunswick: Aldine Transactions.

Bogin, Barry. 1999. *Patterns of Human Growth*. 2nd edition. Cambridge: Cambridge University Press.

Borofsky, Rob. 2005. *Yanomami: The Fierce Controversy and What We can Learn from It*. Berkeley: University of California Press.

Brown, Melissa J. (ed.). 2008. *Explaining Culture Scientifically*. Seattle: University of Washington Press.

Cant, Michael A. and Rufus A. Johnstone. 2008. 'Reproductive conflict and the separation of reproductive generations in humans'. *Proceedings of the National Academy of Sciences* 105(14): 5332–36. doi.org/10.1073/pnas.0711911105

Carroll, Vern (ed.). 1970. *Adoption in Eastern Oceania*. Honolulu: University of Hawaii Press.

Cavalli-Sforza, Luigi Luca. 1997. 'Genes, people, languages'. *Proceedings of the National Academy of Sciences* 94(15): 7719–24. doi.org/10.1073/pnas.94.15.7719

Chagnon, Napoleon A. and William Irons (eds). 1979. *Evolutionary Biology and Human Social Behavior: An Anthropological Perspective*. North Scituate: Duxbury Press.

Chapais, Bernard and Carol M. Berman (eds). 2004. *Kinship and Behavior in Primates*. Oxford: Oxford University Press.

Coall, David and Ralph Hertwig. 2010. 'Grandparental investment: Past, present and future'. *Behavioral and Brain Sciences* 33(1): 1–59. doi.org/10.1017/S0140525X09991105

Costopoulos, Andre. 2005. 'On comparative studies using Standard Cross-Cultural Sample data: Monte Carlo simulation of artificial trends'. *Current Anthropology* 46(3): 457–59. doi.org/10.1086/430014

de Carrocera, Buenaventura, O.F.M. (1980). 'Lingüística indígena venezolana y los misioneros Capuchinos'. *Montalban* 10: 203–530.

Denbow, J.R. 1984. 'Prehistoric herders and foragers of the Kalahari: The evidence for 1500 years of interaction'. In *Past and Present in Hunter-Gatherer Studies*, edited by Carmel Shrire, 175–93. New York: Academic Press.

Destro-Bisol, G., F. Donati, V. Coia, I. Boschi, F. Verginelli, A. Caglià, S. Tofanelli, G. Spedini and C. Capelli. 2004a. 'The analysis of variation of mtDNA hypervariable region I suggests that eastern and western Pygmies diverged before the Bantu expansion'. *American Naturalist* 163(2): 212–26. doi.org/10.1086/381405

———. 2004b. 'Variation in female and male lineages in Sub-Saharan populations: The importance of sociocultural factors'. *Molecular Biology and Evolution* 21(9): 1673–82. doi.org/10.1093/molbev/msh186

Di Fiore, Anthony and Drew Rendall. 1994. 'Evolution of social organization: A reappraisal for primates by using phylogenetic methods'. *Proceeding of the National Academy of Sciences* 91: 9941–45. doi.org/10.1073/pnas.91.21.9941

Divale, William Tulio. 1974. 'Migration, external warfare, and matrilocal residence'. *Behavior Science Research* 9(2): 75–133. doi.org/10.1177/106939717400900201

Donald, Leland. 1997. *Aboriginal Slavery on the Northwest Coast of North America*. Berkeley: University of California Press. doi.org/10.1525/california/9780520206168.001.0001

Dunbar, Robin. 2008. 'Kinship in biological perspective'. In *Early Human Kinship: From Sex to Social Reproduction*, edited by Nicholas J. Allen, Hilary Callan, Robin Dunbar and Wendy James, 131–50. Malden: Blackwell Publishing. doi.org/10.1002/9781444302714.ch7

Durham, William H. 2004. 'Assessing the gaps in Westermarck's theory'. In *Inbreeding, Incest, and the Incest Taboo: The State of Knowledge at the Turn of the Century*, edited by Arthur P. Wolf and William H. Durham, 121–38. Stanford: Stanford University Press.

Ember, Carol R. 1975. 'Residential variation in hunter-gatherers'. *Cross Cultural Research* 10(3): 199–227. doi.org/10.1177/106939717501000302

———. 1978. 'Myths about hunter-gatherers'. *Ethnology* 17(4): 439–48. doi.org/10.2307/3773193

Ember, Carol R. and Melvin Ember. 1972. 'The conditions favoring multilocal residence'. *Southwestern Journal of Anthropology* 28(4): 382–400. doi.org/10.1086/soutjanth.28.4.3629318

Ember, Melvin and Carol R. Ember. 1971. 'The conditions favoring matrilocal versus patrilocal residence'. *American Anthropologist* 73(3): 571–94. doi.org/10.1525/aa.1971.73.3.02a00040

Euler, Harald A. and Richard L. Michalski. 2007. 'Grandparental and extended kin relations'. In *Family Relationships: An Evolutionary Perspective*, edited by Catherine A. Salmon and Todd K. Shackelford, 230–55. New York: Oxford University Press. doi.org/10.1093/acprof:oso/9780195320510.003.0011

Euler, Harald A. and Barbara Weitzel. 1996. 'Discriminative grandparental solicitude as reproductive strategy'. *Human Nature* 7(1): 39–59. doi.org/10.1007/BF02733489

Gragson, Ted L. 1989. 'Allocation of time to subsistence and settlement in a ciri khonome Pumé village of the Llanos of Apure, Venezuela'. PhD thesis, Pennsylvania State University, Pittsburgh.

Gray, J. Patrick and Andre Costopoulos. 2006. 'On artificial trends in comparative studies using Standard Cross-Cultural Sample data'. *Current Anthropology* 47(1): 149–51. doi.org/10.1086/498954

Greaves, Russell D. 1997a. 'Ethnoarchaeological investigation of subsistence mobility, resource targeting, and technological organization among Pumé foragers of Venezuela'. PhD thesis, University of New Mexico, Albuquerque.

———. 1997b. 'Hunting and multifunctional use of bows and arrows: Ethnoarchaeology of technological organization among Pumé hunters of Venezuela'. In *Projectile Technology*, edited by Heidi Knecht, 287–320. Interdisciplinary Contributions to Archaeology Series. New York: Plenum Press. doi.org/10.1007/978-1-4899-1851-2_12

———. 2006. 'Forager landscape use and residential organization'. In *Archaeology and Ethnoarchaeology of Mobility*, edited by Frederic Sellet, Russell D. Greaves and Pei-Lin Yu, 127–52. Gainesville: University Press of Florida.

Greaves, Russell D. and Karen L. Kramer. 2014. 'Hunter-gatherer use of wild plants and domesticates: Archaeological implications for mixed economies before agricultural intensification'. *Journal of Archaeological Science* 41: 263–71. doi.org/10.1016/j.jas.2013.08.014

Gregor, Thomas. 1977. *Mehinaku: The Drama of Daily Life in a Brazilian Village*. Chicago: University of Chicago Press.

Gregor, Thomas A. and Daniel R. Gross. 2004. 'Guilt by association: The culture of accusation and the American Anthropological Association's investigation of *Darkness in El Dorado*'. *American Anthropologist* 106(4): 687–98. doi.org/10.1525/aa.2004.106.4.687

Helm, June. 1965. 'Bilaterality in socio-territorial organization of the Arctic Drainage Dene'. *Ethnology* 4(4): 361–85. doi.org/10.2307/3772786

Hervás y Panduro, Lorenzo. 1979. *Catálogo de las Lenguas de las Naciones Conocidas: y Numeración, División y Clases de Estas Según la Diversidad de sus Idiomas y Dialectos*, vol. 1. Madrid: Ediciones Atlas.

Hewlett, Barry S. and Michael E. Lamb (eds). 2005. *Hunter-Gatherer Childhoods: Evolutionary, Developmental and Cultural Perspectives*. New Brunswick: Transaction Publishers.

Hiatt, L.R. 1962. 'Local organization among the Australian Aborigines'. *Oceania* 32(4): 267–86. doi.org/10.1002/j.1834-4461.1962.tb01782.x

Hill, Kim and A. Magdalena Hurtado. 1996. *Ache Life History: The Ecology and Demography of a Foraging People*. New York: Aldine de Gruyter.

Hilton, Charles E. and Russell D. Greaves. 2004. 'Age, sex, and resource transport in Venezuelan foragers'. In *From Biped to Strider: The Emergence of Modern Human Walking, Running, and Resource Transport*, edited by D. Jeffrey Meldrum and Charles E. Hilton, 163–81. New York: Kluwer. doi.org/10.1007/978-1-4419-8965-9_10

———. 2008. 'Seasonality and sex differences in travel distance and resource transport in Venezuelan foragers'. *Current Anthropology* 49(1): 144–53. doi.org/10.1086/524760

Hohmann, Gottfried, Martha Robbins and Christophe Boesch (eds). 2006. *Feeding Ecology in Apes and Other Primates*. Cambridge: Cambridge University Press.

Honigmann, John J. (ed.). 1973. *Handbook of Social and Cultural Anthropology*. Chicago: Rand McNally.

Howell, Nancy. 2001. *Demography of the Dobe !Kung*. 2nd edition. New York: Aldine de Gruyter.

Hrdy, Sarah Blaffer. 2005. 'Comes the child before the man: How cooperative breeding and prolonged postweaning dependence shaped human potential'. In *Hunter Gatherer Childhoods: Evolutionary Developments and Cultural Perspectives*, edited by Barry S. Hewlett and Michael E. Lamb, 65–91. New Brunswick: Transaction Publishers.

INE (Instituto Nacional de Estadística-Apure). 2001. *Censo comunidades indígenas, pobalción indígena empadronada por grupo segun sexo y pueblo indígena de pertenencia el el esatdo Apure*. Online: www.portalapure.com/INDIGENAS.html (accessed 16 January 2005, no longer available).

———. 2011. *Censo nacional de pobalción y vivienda. Empadronamiento de la pobalción indígena.* República Bolivariana de Venezuela, Ministerio del Poder Popular de Planificación, Instituto Nacional de Estadística (INE), Gerencia General de Estadísticas Demográficas, Gerencia de Censo de Pobalción y Vivienda. Online: www.ine.gov.ve/index.php?option=com_content&view=category&id=95&Itemid (accessed 14 July 2017).

Kan, Sergei. 1989. *Symbolic Immortality: The Tlingit Potlatch of the Nineteenth Century.* Washington, DC: Smithsonian Institution Press.

Kaplan, Hillard. 1996. 'A theory of fertility and parental investment in traditional and modern human societies'. *Yearbook of Physical Anthropology* 39: 91–135. doi.org/10.1002/(SICI)1096-8644(1996)23+<91::AID-AJPA4>3.0.CO;2-C

Kelly, Robert L. 1995. *The Foraging Spectrum: Diversity in Hunter-Gatherer Lifeways.* Washington, DC: Smithsonian Institution Press.

Kensinger, Kenneth M. (ed.). 1984. *Marriage Practices in Lowland South America.* Urbana: University of Illinois Press.

Kent, Susan (ed.). 1996. *Cultural Diversity among Twentieth-Century Foragers: An African Perspective.* Cambridge: Cambridge University Press.

Key, Marie Ritchie. 1979. *The Grouping of South American Indian Languages.* Tübingen: Ars Linguistica 2. Gunter Narr Verlag.

Knecht, Heidi (ed.). 1997. *Projectile Technology.* Interdisciplinary Contributions to Archaeology Series. New York: Plenum Press.

Korotayev, Andrey. 2001. 'An apologia of George Peter Murdock. Discussion of labor by gender and postmatital residence in cross-cultural perspective: a reconsideration'. *World Cultures* 12(2): 179–203.

Kramer, Karen L. 2008. 'Early sexual maturity among Pumé foragers of Venezuela: Fitness implications of teen motherhood'. *American Journal of Physical Anthropology* 136(3): 338–50. doi.org/10.1002/ajpa.20817

Kramer, Karen L. and Russell D. Greaves. 2007. 'Changing patterns of infant mortality and fertility among Pumé foragers and horticulturalists'. *American Anthropologist* 109(4): 713–26. doi.org/10.1525/aa.2007.109.4.713

———. 2010. 'Synchrony between growth and reproductive patterns in human females: Early investment in growth among Pumé foragers'. *American Journal of Physical Anthropology*. 141(2): 235–44. doi.org/10.1002/ajpa.21139

———. 2017. 'Why Pumé foragers retain a hunting and gathering way of life'. In *Hunter-Gatherers in a Changing World*, edited by Victoria Reyes-García and Aili Pyhälä, 109–26. Cham: Springer. doi.org/10.1007/978-3-319-422-71-8_7

Kramer, Karen L., Russell D. Greaves and Peter D. Ellison. 2009. 'Early reproductive maturity among Pumé foragers: Implications of a pooled energy model to fast life histories'. *American Journal of Human Biology* 21(4): 430–37. doi.org/10.1002/ajhb.20930

Kumar, Vikrant, Banrida T. Langstieh, Komal V. Madhavi, Vega M. Naidu, Hardeep Pal Singh, Silpak Biswas, Kumarasamy Thangaraj, Lalji Singh, and B. Mohan Reddy. 2006. 'Global patterns in human mitochondrial DNA and Y-chromosome variation caused by spatial instability of the local cultural processes'. *PLoS One* 2(4): e53. doi.org/10.1371/journal.pgen.0020053

Langergraber, Kevin E., Heike Siedel, John C. Mitani, Richard W. Wrangham, Vernon Reynolds, Kevin Hunt and Linda Vigilant 2007. 'The genetic signatures of sex-biased migration in patrilocal chimpanzees and humans'. *PLoS One* 2(10):e973. doi.org/10.1371/journal.pone.0000973

Layrisse, Miguel, Zulay Layrisse, E. Garcia and Johannes Wilbert. 1961. 'Blood group antigen tests groups of the Yaruro Indians'. *Southwestern Journal of Anthropology* 17(2):198–204. doi.org/10.1086/soutjanth.17.2.3629143

Layrisse, Miguel, Zulay Layrisse and Johannes Wilbert. 1964. 'Variaciones genéticas de grupos sanguíneos en 12 tribus de Caribes en Venezuela y Guayana Británica'. *Actas y Memorias del 25 Congeso Internacional de Americanistas* 3: 49–55.

Lee, Richard B. 1972. 'Work effort, group structure, and land-use in contemporary hunter-gatherers'. In *Man, Settlement, and Urbanism*, edited by Peter J. Ucko, Ruth Tringham and G.W. Dimbelby, 177–85. London: Gerald Duckworth.

———. 1976. '!Kung spatial organization: An ecological and historical model'. In *Kalahari Hunter-Gatherers: Studies of the !Kung San and Their Neighbors*, edited by Richard B. Lee and Irven DeVore, 73–97. Cambridge: Harvard University Press. doi.org/10.4159/harvard.9780674430600.c6

———. 1979. *The !Kung San: Men, Women, and Work in a Foraging Society*. Cambridge: Cambridge University Press.

Lee, Richard B. and Irven DeVore. 1968. 'Problems in the study of hunter-gatherers'. In *Man The Hunter: The First Intensive Survey of a Single, Crucial Stage of Human Development—Man's Once Universal Hunting Way of Life*, edited by Richard B. Lee and Irven DeVore, 3–12. Chicago: Aldine.

Lee, Richard B. and Irven DeVore (eds). 1976. *Kalahari Hunter-Gatherers: Studies of the !Kung San and Their Neighbors*. Cambridge: Harvard University Press. doi.org/10.4159/harvard.9780674430600

Leeds, Anthony. 1961. 'The Yaruro incipient tropical forest horticulture: Possibilities and limits'. In *The Evolution of Horticultural Systems in Native South America: Causes and Consequences*, edited by Johannes Wilbert, 13–46. Antropológica Supplement no. 2. Caracas: Editorial Sucre.

———. 1964. 'Some problems of Yaruro ethnohistory'. *Actas y Memorias del 25 Congreso International de Americanistas* 2: 157–75.

Lévi-Strauss, Claude. 1949. *Les Structures élémentaires de la parenté*. Paris: Presses Universitaire de France.

Lizarralde, Roberto and Ted Gragson, unpublished data; portions published in OCEI 1985 and 1995.

Lizot, Jacques (ed.). 1988. *Los Aborígenes de Venezuela*, Vol. III, *Etnología Contemporánea II*. Caracas: Fundación La Salle de Ciencias Naturales.

Loukotka, Čestmír and Johannes Wilbert. 1968. *Classification of South American Indian Languages*. Reference Series vol. 7. Los Angeles: Latin American Center, University of California.

Lowie, Robert H. 1920. *Primitive Society*. New York: Boni and Liveright.

Marlowe, Frank W. 2004. 'Marital residence among foragers'. *Current Anthropology* 45(2): 277–84. doi.org/10.1086/382256

———. 2005. 'Hunter-gatherers and human evolution'. *Evolutionary Anthropology* 14(2): 54–67. doi.org/10.1002/evan.20046

———. 2006. 'Central place provisioning: The Hadza as an example'. In *Feeding Ecology in Apes and Other Primates*, edited by Gottfried Hohmann, Martha Robbins and Christophe Boesch, 359–77. Cambridge: Cambridge University Press.

———. 2010. *The Hadza: Hunter-Gatherers of Tanzania*. Berkeley: University of California Press.

Marshall, Lorna. 1960. '!Kung Bushman bands'. *Africa* 30(4): 325–55. doi.org/10.2307/1157596

———. 1976. *The !Kung of Nyae Nyae*. Cambridge: Harvard University Press. doi.org/10.4159/harvard.9780674180574

Mauss, Marcel. 1967. *The Gift: The Form and Reason for Exchange in Archaic Societies*, translated by I. Cunnison. New York: Norton.

Meggitt, M.J. 1965. 'Marriage among the Walbiri of Central Australia: A statistical examination'. In *Aboriginal Man in Australia*, edited by R.M. Berndt and C.H. Berndt, 146–66. Sydney: Angus and Robertson.

Meldrum, D. Jeffrey and Charles E. Hilton (eds). 2004. *From Biped to Strider: The Emergence of Modern Human Walking, Running, and Resource Transport*. New York: Kluwer. doi.org/10.1007/978-1-4419-8965-9

Mitrani, Philippe. 1975. Remarques sur l'organisation sociale, la parenté et l'alliance des Yaruro de l'Apure. *Antropológica* 40: 3–23.

———. 1988. 'Los Pumé (Yaruro)'. In *Los Aborígenes de Venezuela*, Vol. III, *Etnología Contemporánea II*, edited by Jacques Lizot, 147–213. Caracas: Fundación La Salle de Ciencias Naturales.

Mosonyi, Esteban Emelio. 1975. *El Indígena Venezolano en Pos de su Liberación Definitiva*. Cracas: Universidad Central de Venezuela, Facultad de Ciencias Económicas y Sociales, División de Publicaciónes.

Murdock, George Peter. 1949. *Social Structure*. New York: Macmillan.

Murdock, George Peter and Douglas R. White. 1980. 'Standard cross-cultural sample'. In *Cross-Cultural Sample and Codes*, edited by Herbert Barry and Alice Schlegel, 3–43. Pittsburgh: University of Pittsburgh Press.

Needham, Roger. 1954. 'The system of teknonyms and death names of the Penan'. *Southwestern Journal of Anthropology* 10(4): 416–31. doi.org/10.1086/soutjanth.10.4.3628836

Oberg, Kalvero. 1973. *The Social Economy of the Tlingit Indians*. American Ethnological Society Monograph 55. Seattle: University of Washington Press.

Obregón Muñoz, Hugo. 1981. 'En torno al alfabeto de las lenguas indígenas de Venezuela a propósito de la reducción del Pumé a la escritura'. *Revista Latinoamericana de Estudios Etnolingüísticos* 1: 25–46.

OCEI (Oficina Central de Estadística e Informática). 1985. *Censo Indígena de Venezuela*. Caracas: Taller Gráfico de la Oficina Central de Estadística e Informática.

——. 1995. *Censo Indígena de Venezuela 1992*. Tomo I. Caracas: Taller Gráfico de la Oficina Central de Estadística e Informática.

Oota, H., W. Settheetham-Ishida, D. Tiwawech, I. Takfumi and M. Stoneking. 2001. 'Human mtDNA and Y-chromosome variation is correlated with matrilocal versus patrilocal residence'. *Nature Genetics* 29(1): 20–21. doi.org/10.1038/ng711

Orobitg Canal, Gemma. 1998. *Les Pumé et Leurs Rêves: Étude d'un Groupe Indien des Plaines du Venezuela*. Amsterdam: Éditions des Archies Contemporaines.

Otterbein, Keith F. and Frank W. Marlowe. 2005. 'On hunting and virilocality'. *Current Anthropology* 46(1): 124–27. doi.org/10.1086/427097

Panter-Brick, Catherine, Robert Layton and Peter Rowley-Conwy (eds). 2001. *Hunter-Gatherers: An Interdisciplinary Approach*. Cambridge: Cambridge University Press.

Perez de Vega, F. 1960. *Las lenguas aborigenes*. Caracas: Editorial Ciencia.

Perry, Richard J. 1989. 'Matrilineal descent in a hunting context: The Athapaskan case'. *Ethnology* 28(1): 33–51. doi.org/10.2307/3773641

Petrullo, Vincenzo. 1939. *The Yaruros of the Capanaparo River, Venezuela. Anthropological Papers 11, Bureau of American Ethnology Bulletin* 123: 161–290. Washington, DC: Smithsonian Institution.

Quinlan, Robert J. and Marsha B. Quinlan. 2007. 'Evolutionary ecology of human pair bonds: cross-cultural tests of alternative hypotheses'. *Cross-Cultural Research* 41(2): 149–69. doi.org/10.1177/1069397106298893

Radcliffe-Brown, A.R. 1930. 'The social organization of Australian tribes'. *Oceania* 1(2): 206–46. doi.org/10.1002/j.1834-4461.1930.tb01645.x

Reining, Priscilla (ed.). 1972. *Kinship Studies in the Morgan Centennial Year*. Washington: Anthropological Society of Washington.

Rey Fajardo, José del. 1979. 'Los Jesuitas y las lenguas Indígenas Venezolanas'. *Montalban* 9: 357–478.

Reyes-García, Victoria and Aili Pyhälä (eds). 2017. *Hunter-Gatherers in a Changing World*. Cham: Springer. doi.org/10.1007/978-3-319-42271-8

Richerson, Peter J. and Robert Boyd. 2008. 'Cultural evolution: Accomplishments and future prospects'. In *Explaining Culture Scientifically*, edited by Melissa J. Brown, 75–99. Seattle: University of Washington Press.

Rodseth, Lars, Richard W. Wrangham, Alisa M. Harrigan, Barbara B. Smuts, Ron Dare, Robin Fox, Barbara J. King, P. C. Lee, R. A. Foley, J. C. Muller, Keith F. Otterbein, Karen B. Strier, Paul W. Turke and Milford H. Wolpoff. 1991. 'The human community as a primate society'. *Current Anthropology* 32(3): 221–54. doi.org/10.1086/203952

Ruvolo, M. 1997. 'Genetic diversity in hominoid primates'. *Annual Review of Anthropology* 26: 515–40. doi.org/10.1146/annurev.anthro.26.1.515

Salmon, Catherine A. and Todd K. Shackelford (eds). 2007. *Family Relationships: An Evolutionary Perspective*. New York: Oxford University Press. doi.org/10.1093/acprof:oso/9780195320510.001.0001

SAS. 2002–2003. Cary, NC: SAS Institute, Inc.

Scelza, Brook and Rebecca Bliege Bird. 2008. 'Group structure and female cooperative networks in Australia's Western Desert'. *Human Nature* 19: 231–48. doi.org/10.1007/s12110-008-9041-5

Scheffler, Harold W. 1965. *Choiseul Island Social Structure*. Berkeley: University of California Press.

———. 1970. 'Kinship and adoption in the northern New Hebrides'. In *Adoption in Eastern Oceania*, edited by Vern Carroll, 369–89. Honolulu: University of Hawaii Press.

———. 1972. 'Baniata kin classification: The case for extensions'. *Southwestern Journal of Anthropology* 28(4): 350–81. doi.org/10.1086/soutjanth.28.4.3629317

———. 1973. 'Kinship, descent, and alliance'. In *Handbook of Social and Cultural Anthropology*, edited by John J. Honigmann, 747–93. Chicago: Rand McNally.

———. 2001. *Filiation and Affiliation*. Boulder, CO: Westview Press.

Schneider, David M. 1972. 'What is kinship all about?' In *Kinship Studies in the Morgan Centennial Year*, edited by Priscilla Reining, 32–63. Washington: Anthropological Society of Washington.

———. 1984. *A Critique of the Study of Kinship*. Ann Arbor: University of Michigan Press. doi.org/10.3998/mpub.7203

Seielstad, Mark, Eric Minch and L. Luca Cavalli-Sforza. 1998. 'Genetic evidence for a higher female migration rate in humans'. *Nature Genetics* 20(3): 278–80. doi.org/10.1038/3088

Sellet, Frederic, Russell D. Greaves and Pei-Lin Yu (eds). 2006. *Archaeology and Ethnoarchaeology of Mobility*. Gainesville: University Press of Florida.

Service, Elman R. 1962. *Primitive Social Organization: An Evolutionary Perspective*. New York: Random House.

———. 1966. *The Hunters*. Engelwood Cliffs: Prentice Hall.

Shapiro, Judith R. 1984. 'Marriage rules, marriage exchange, and the definition of marriage in lowland South American socieites'. In *Marriage Practices in Lowland South America*, edited by Kenneth M. Kensinger, 1–30. Urbana: University of Illinois Press.

Shapiro, Warren. 1973. 'Residential grouping in northeast Arnhem Land'. *Man* (n.s.) 8(3): 365–83. doi.org/10.2307/2800315

——. 1995. 'Fuzziness, structure-dependency, and "structural anthropology": An extended reply to Parkin'. *Journal of the Anthropological Society of Oxford* 26(2): 197–214.

——. 2008. 'What human kinship is primarily about: Toward a critique of the new kinship studies'. *Social Anthropology* 16(2): 137–53. doi.org/10.1111/j.1469-8676.2008.00038.x

Shrire, Carmel (ed.). 1984. *Past and Present in Hunter-Gatherer Studies*. New York: Academic Press.

Silberbauer, George B. 1972. 'The G/wi bushmen'. In *Hunters and Gatherers Today: A Socioeconomic Study of Eleven Such Cultures in the Twentieth Century*, edited by M.G. Bicchieri, 271–326. New York: Holt, Rinehart and Winston.

Smith, Eric Alden. (1991). *Inujjuamiut Foraging Strategies: Evolutionary Ecology of an Arctic Hunting Economy*. New York: Aldine de Gruyter.

Steward, Julian Haynes. 1955. *Theory of Culture Change: The Methodology of Multilinear Evolution*. Urbana: University of Illinois Press.

Tierney, Patrick. 2000. *Darkness in El Dorado: How Scientists and Journalists Devastated the Amazon*. New York: Norton.

Tovar, Antonio and Consuelo Larrucea de Tovar. 1961. *Catálogo de las Lenguas de América del Sur*. Buenos Aires: Editorial Sudamericana.

Turnbull, Colin M. 1965. *Wayward Servants: The Two Worlds of African Pygmies*. Westport: Greenwood Press.

Ucko, Peter J., Ruth Tringham and G.W. Dimbelby (eds). 1972. *Man, Settlement, and Urbanism*. London: Gerald Duckworth.

Walker, Robert S., Stephen Beckerman, Mark V. Flinn, Michael Gurven, Chris R. von Rueden, Karen L. Kramer, Russell D. Greaves, Lorena Córdoba, Diego Villar, Edward H. Hagen, Jeremy M. Koster, Lawrence Sugiyama, Tiffany E. Hunter and Kim R. Hill. 2013. 'Living with kin in lowland horticultural societies'. *Current Anthropology* 54(1): 96–103. doi.org/10.1086/668867

Wiessner, Polly. 2002. 'Hunting, healing, and *hxaro* exchange: A long-term perspective on !Kung (Ju/'hoansi) large game hunting'. *Evolution and Human Behavior* 23(6): 407–36. doi.org/10.1016/S1090-5138(02)00096-X

Wilbert, Johannes (ed.). 1961. *The Evolution of Horticultural Systems in Native South America: Causes and Consequences*. Antropológica Supplement no. 2. Caracas: Editorial Sucre.

Wilder, Jason A., Sarah B. Kingan, Zahra Mobasher, Maya Metni Pilkington and Michael F. Hamme. 2004. 'Global patterns of human mitochondrial DNA and Y-chromosome structure are not influenced by higher migration rates of females versus males'. *Nature Genetics* 36: 1122–25. doi.org/10.1038/ng1428

Wilmsen, Edwin N. 1989. *Land Filled with Flies: A Political Economy of the Kalahari*. Chicago: University of Chicago Press.

Winterhalder, Bruce and Eric A. Smith (eds). 1981. *Hunter-Gatherer Foraging Strategies*. Chicago: University of Chicago Press.

Wolf, Arthur P. and William H. Durham (eds). 2004. *Inbreeding, Incest, and the Incest Taboo: The State of Knowledge at the Turn of the Century*. Stanford: Stanford University Press.

Wood, Brian M. and Frank W. Marlowe. 2011. 'Dynamics of postmarital residence among the Hadza: A kin investment model'. *Human Nature* 22(1–2): 128–38. doi.org/10.1007/s12110-011-9109-5

Woodburn, James. 1968. 'Stability and flexibility in Hadza residential groupings'. In *Man The Hunter: The First Intensive Survey of a Single, Crucial Stage of Human Development—Man's Once Universal Hunting Way of Life*, edited by Richard B. Lee and Irven DeVore, 103–17. Chicago: Aldine.

——. 1972. 'Ecology, nomadic movement and the composition of the local group among hunters and gatherers: An East African example and its implications'. In *Man, Settlement and Urbanism*, edited by Peter J. Ucko, Ruth Tringham and G.W. Dimbelby, 193–206. London: Gerald Duckworth.

5

Properties of Kinship Structure: Transformational Dynamics of Suckling, Adoption and Incest

Fadwa El Guindi

Introduction

It is fitting in a volume edited by Warren Shapiro honouring the groundbreaking contribution by Harold Scheffler to the study of kinship semantics (Scheffler 1972; Scheffler and Lounsbury 1971 among other works) to present an analysis[1] that integrates meaning and semantics of kinship terms, concepts and practices, in ways that reveal the logical properties of kinship structure, which is my primary concern.

---

1   This grew out of a systematic empirical study of kinship practices in Qatar carried out over a period of seven years (between 2006 and 2013). The primary data derive from systematic ethnographic observations made by the author on Qatari kinship practices and in-depth data obtained by a research team headed by the author on the subject of suckling kinship, including elicitation of Qatari kinship terms, over a period of three years. The research team consisted of colleague Wesam al-Othman (former Associate Professor of Anthropology, Qatar University), and undergraduate students from the Department of Social Sciences majoring in Sociology and Anthropology, namely Sara al-Mahmoud, Alanoud al-Marri, Raneen Najjar, Dana al-Dossary and Fatima Abed Bahumaid. The field project was funded by two grants from the Qatar National Research Fund under its Undergraduate Research Experience Program: (a) UREP 06-012-5-003 (Milk Kinship: The Khalij Case) and (b) UREP 09-051-5-013 (Blood, Milk and Marriage: Kinship Behavior and Kinship Terminology in Qatar). The grant contents are solely the responsibility of the lead principal investigator and do not necessarily represent the official views of the Qatar National Research Fund. I especially thank colleague Wesam al-Othman for being a willing mentored and mentoring partner on the research project. Ego's case was elicited in parallel with the research team project.

The ethnographic focus of this analysis is a phenomenon I call suckling, which relates to, but is separable from, the complex of practices commonly labelled 'milk kinship' (Altorki 1980; Conte 1987; Giladi 1998, 1999; Héritier-Augé and Copet-Rougier 1995; Héritier 1994; Khatib-Chahidi 1992; Lacoste-Dujardin 2000; Long 1996; Parkes 2004a, 2005). The latter is reported as historically common in the wider region covering the Balkans, the Mediterranean, and the Arab and the Islamic East (Parkes 2001, 2003, 2004b).

Suckling refers to a practice by which lactating women breastfeed babies who are not their own by birth, engendering new kin relations and networks, and generating new transformations that shift kin status among birth and marital kin (El Guindi 2011, 2012a, 2012b, 2013; El Guindi and al-Othman 2013). Studying suckling, a practice that is quite prevalent in contemporary Arab society, particularly among kinship-intensive Arabian Arabs living in the regions of Arabia and the Arabian Gulf, led to new insights and perspectives on old issues, some of which are shared in this work. The thrust of analytic conceptualisation derives from primary data, but additional data were located in secondary sources such as existing studies and literature, religious documents, poetry and prose, as well as various visual sources.

I propose to establish two points: (1) that suckling, unlike other practices of breastfeeding, is kinship, thus belonging in kinship study not social relations; and (2) how integrating insights from the analysis of primary data about practices of suckling, adoption and incest in Qatar reveals general properties of kinship structure. The structure is described in this paper.

What is suckling?

It is interesting that the data collected show how suckling kin terms and categories are lexically marked relative to procreative kin terms and categories. Relatives among themselves and their familiars introduce relatives by suckling saying 'this is my mother, this is my sister', etc. Noticeably, the marker 'by suckling' is used in the presence of strangers to convey the exact nature of the relationship, but is dropped in ordinary, daily interactions among familiars. More can be said but this has to await analysis of the body of kin terminology data I gathered as part of the kinship project on Qatar,[2] which cover Qatari Arabic kin terms of reference and address for kin by birth, marriage and suckling. I contend, however, from preliminary analysis that there is sufficient support for the modelling notion held by Scheffler, which considers nonprocreative kin to be 'as though' or 'modeled after' kin by birth (Scheffler 1970: 370). In this case, the reference is about suckling kin terms.[3] Support for modelling is also found in Islamic Hadith (Prophetic Narratives, considered sacred but not divine) which quotes Muhammad (Islam's Prophet) as having stated that 'suckling prohibits what birth prohibits' (al-Tarmathi n.d.: 129–35; Sallama 2006). In the course of my fieldwork people often brought up this Hadith passage to emphasise suckling kinship's similarity in kinship character to birth kinship.

Equally compelling is the observation that the incest taboo applies equally to birth and suckling according to the Qur'an, the Hadith, and the ethnography. But, unlike the Qur'an, the Hadith, like the ethnography, recognises the attribute of lineal and lateral extensions beyond the suckling dyad. The notion of modelling in this case conveys analytic significance to the interrelationship among the three kinship practices recognised among the population of Qatar, and elsewhere as indicated. The analysis goes further by contending how aspects of the practice of women's suckling of nonbirth infants reveal a transformational character of kinship. This chapter builds on, but goes further than, descriptive and analytic accounts which I have recently published, based on primary field data and conclusions from various sources on local knowledge and cultural tradition, including original Islamic sources (El Guindi 2011, 2012a, 2012b, 2013, 2016; El Guindi and al-Othman 2013).

I have argued in earlier publications that sufficient analytic evidence supports the cultural view that the kind of suckling (Ar. *rida'a*) explored in the research project is considered kinship, alongside procreative (Ar. *nasab*[4]) and marital kinship (Ar. *musahara*). This claim of kinship status is not only culture-derived, but is also based on analytic criteria shared by kinship specialists. These criteria include classification in terminology (from

---

2 Most of it sits in a trunk shipped recently to my home in Los Angeles.
3 Arabic terms for marital kin are distinct from birth kin, and do not carry a marker such as 'in-law' as used in other terminological systems. The significance of the difference between the two kin-term sets, that of suckling and that of marriage, will be the subject for another work.
4 The Arabic term *nasab* is multivocal, sometimes used to refer to genealogical affiliation, other times to kin by marriage versus kin by birth. Formally, and as used in this account, it refers to procreative kin versus marital or suckling kin.

preliminary analysis), observations of behavioural reciprocity, and the feature of lineality and laterality of recursions in marital prohibitions. It is observed that suckling extends links and prohibitions lineally and laterally beyond the original suckling dyad, and lifts avoidance and constructs new taboos that enable and disable marriage possibilities.

Here I seek to show that the structural property of transformationality is key to revealing a kinship structure integrating procreative, marital and suckling elements. The analysis draws upon field-derived ethnographic cases, which includes adoptive practices, an element in the process which made manifest the way prohibitions and avoidances are created and lifted. Adoption processes affirm suckling to be not only as an additional way whereby persons are incorporated as kin members, itself considered important, but also, if not more importantly, it becomes itself a process by which a transformational property of kinship structure is revealed. This leads to fresh insights into the construct of the incest taboo, and perhaps also into adoption.

Three decades before my field study on suckling in Qatar, Soraya Altorki published an article in 1980 entitled 'Milk-Kinship in Arab society: An Unexplored Problem in the Ethnography of Marriage', based on her field study of the practice of suckling in Saudi Arabia. This practice is also quite pervasive in other parts of the contemporary Arab world. But my decision to study suckling kinship independently grew out of an anthropological curiosity from directly observing and experiencing the intensity of such kinship activity in Qatari life. The constant encounter with lived kinship and especially the linguistic, ritual and interactional manifestations of suckling kinship (whether in classrooms or weddings) aroused my research interest and inspired my seeking two consecutive grants from the Qatar National Research Fund to systematically study suckling as it relates to kinship in general.

To capture the feel for the kinship-intensive environment among Arabs, I venture out of ethnography and into the memoir by Anthony Shadid, the late *New York Times* reporter who died covering the battlefield in Syria, in which he vividly describes, in what was to be his last book, his days in the hometown of his ancestors in Lebanon uncovering his roots as he participates in the project of remodelling his grandfather's house of stone. He covers ordinary daily life, familiar in any Arab society:

5. PROPERTIES OF KINSHIP STRUCTURE

> As we sat there [the author writes], he kept introducing people to me, usually with a reference to their root in our family ... 'This man's grandmother is a Shadid' ... 'This man's mother is a Shadid' ... No conversations ... more common, more authoritatively deliberated ... more steeped in encyclopedic knowledge than those about genealogy... intermarriages ... that connected everyone to everyone else ... Tracking one's surname was a constant activity: Hikmat belonged to Bayt Farha, Isber to Bayt Samara ... names themselves were clues to the stories of origins' (Shadid 2012: 74).

As if in response to the view from afar, as it were, about kinship as mutuality of being (Sahlins 2013), Shadid goes on: 'Families always have conflict, he told me ... from the outside it looks okay' (2012: 109). It is not that the romanticised view of kinship, that 'people ... live each other's lives and die each other's deaths' (Sahlins 2013: 28), is wrong. It is incomplete. Some relatives behave kindly to each other, others do not. Perhaps this is what Marilyn Strathern means when she writes, 'Mutuality's largely benign connotations lead to some special pleading when it comes to malevolent or negative consequences' (1988: 392).

This analytical approach situates suckling in kinship as conventionally construed. It is thus indebted to Harold Scheffler's critique of kinship 'dismantlers' as he called them (Scheffler 2004: 294), and to Warren Shapiro, who has argued convincingly, using ethnographic evidence, against Janet Carsten's analysis of Malaysian ethnography (Shapiro 2011), an example of the so-called 'new kinship studies'. I shall show that radical claims of the new kinship studies do not adequately address the complexity of the phenomenon of kinship among Qataris.

To return to Altorki. She recognised suckling as a kinship practice, referring to it by the local Arabic term *rida'a* ('suckling'). Her article drew scholarly attention to the practice, otherwise neglected in anthropology, leading to further explorations. A century earlier than Altorki's study, William Robertson Smith briefly wrote on suckling in his classic publication on kinship and marriage in early Arabia (1885). Presumably he used information from the Qur'an, which is considered by Muslims to be the most sacred and divinely revealed source. There is significance to the fact that Qur'anic passages explicitly define kinship and recognise three forms: procreative, marital and suckling. This inclusive quality is further supported by other sources, including primary field-derived ethnography by Altorki on Saudi Arabia among others, and, independently, in my field-derived ethnography on Qatar.

Peter Parkes (referenced earlier) was moved by Altorki's article to explore the phenomenon further.[5] He conducted a search of the literature and contributed a synthesis of historical materials describing the distribution of apparently similar practices, such as fosterage and wet-nursing, extending beyond Arab and Islamic regions, to include Christian groups in the Balkans. Some practices, he found, existed prior to Islam. Ethnographic accounts of social life in Hijaz during the first two centuries after Hijra (roughly the seventh and eighth centuries CE) suggest a pervasiveness of the practice of wet-nursing. The record, Parkes further found, points to a much earlier presence, as for example, in the Babylonian code of Hammurabi—the oldest comprehensive set of written laws, which gives a prominent position to 'Adoption and Wet-nursing' (Driver and Miles 1952: 383–406; Goody 1969).

Drawing on ethnographic insights, I contend that not differentiating among forms such as 'adoption', 'wet nursing', 'fosterage,' etc. results in confusion and ambiguity. Instead, I propose here that the 'milk phenomenon' subsumes a variety of traditions by which women breastfed infants who are not their own. The anthropological literature often refers to wet-nursing and suckling interchangeably. I maintain that such grouping may be a result of focusing on the substance of milk rather than on the properties of the kinship structure.

In his brief discussion on suckling kinship Smith brought out the link between the taboo against marriage and the practice of suckling. It could simply be a labelling problem when he chose to use the terms 'foster-mother', 'foster-child', 'foster-brothers' but these are terminologically and semantically imprecise, since the Arabic original *ridā'a* stands for nursing or suckling, not fostering. My preference is for the term *suckling*, to distinguish the phenomenon of my research focus from nursing one's own babies. It seems too that Smith's categorisation is ambiguous, particularly when he fluctuates among 'milk kinship', 'foster parenthood' and a combined 'milk-fosterage'. In Arabic there are two derivatives from the same linguistic root for nursing *r-d-'*: *istirdā'* and *ridā'a*, which refer to two identifiably different practices, wet-nursing and suckling.

---

5   At a reception at Kent University and before my own interest in the subject, Peter Parkes (see references) mentioned his interest in milk kinship, which a few years later turned into several publications.

5. PROPERTIES OF KINSHIP STRUCTURE

By converting the three kin positions specified by Smith into two dyadic relationships of mother–child and sibling–sibling, we can draw a parallel with the relations in the Qur'anic text as illustrated in Figure 16. The Qur'an expresses suckling relations in terms of dyads: 'suckling mothers', that is mother–child and 'sisters-in-suckling', that is sibling dyads. Smith wrote of 'foster-brothers' as well, but this is inaccurate: in the *sura* 4:23, sexually prohibited kin are positioned from a male reference point that, accordingly, refers to sisters and not brothers—that is, it assumes heterosexuality. Smith makes no reference to other sources like Shari'a, Jurisprudence, or extant ethnographic records.

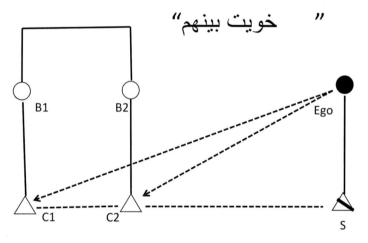

Figure 12. Brothering matrilateral parallel cousins
Source: © Fadwa El Guindi, 2014.

Arabs put much stress on mother's milk. When possible, nursing one's own infants is both desirable and preferred. However, since before Islam, women from wealthy families (as is the case with families of wealth elsewhere, including Europe) were not expected or obligated to nurse their own babies. Whether due to a mother's death, ill health, or wealth, urban Arabs frequently resorted to Badawi (Bedouin) women for nursing and early nurturing services, and this led to the development of an institution of wet-nursing or *istirda'* in the Arabian region. It was common and preferred at that time for families in urban centres such as Makka to utilise the service of Badawi women. Newborns were delivered to nonresident wet-nurses, to nurse for two years and be nurtured for several years beyond that. Wet-nursing was also carried out by resident slave women and household help, the latter continuing to this day in different parts of Arabia and the Gulf. Although, as already noted, this custom was practised prior to the advent of Islam, the Qur'an validated it as shown earlier by sacred text.

I distinguish wet-nursing as a paid service, whether in cash or kind, from the kind of suckling practices among women in the Arabian area and elsewhere in the larger Arabic-speaking region. Until empirical studies prove otherwise, I shall contend that most of these forms subsumed within the 'milk phenomenon' do not adequately qualify to be considered kinship.

Scholarly Arabic works suggest that suckling practices similar to those studied in my research project on Qatar existed in urban centres such as Makka[6] at the beginning of Islam (for some references on these observations see al-Samhoudi 1505; Ibn Manthur 1311; Ibn Sa'd 844). It is also reported that suckling kinship varies in ethnographic details within the same region in Saudi Arabia as well as between the larger regions of Najd and Hijaz (Altorki 1980: 238).

Groin, womb and nerve

To convey the similarity of suckling to kin by birth, Smith wrote:

> There is a real unity of flesh and blood between foster-mother and foster-child, or between foster-brothers; and so we find among the Arabs a feeling about milk-kinship so well established that Mohammed's law of forbidden degrees gives it all the effects of blood-relationship as a bar to marriage (1885: 176).

---

6   Reports of life in Yathrib, or Madina, to which Muslims immigrated escaping from Makka mention Jewish wet-nurses among the women suckling Arab infants during early Islam. See al-'Ayashi, Abdullah, bin Muhammad (1679); and Ibn Manthur, Mohammad bin Makram (1311). Lisan al-Arab is a comprehensive classical Arabic dictionary completed in 1290 CE, by the Arabic lexicographer Ibn Manthur (1233–1312 CE), al-Maṭba'a al-Kubra al-Amirīya, Bulaq 1883–1890 (20 volumes).

His phrase 'Mohammed's law' indicates that he was referencing the Qur'an, probably through secondary information. His Biblical imagery—'real unity of flesh and blood'—to describe suckling kinship relations is inaccurate, because it suggests identity with those of procreative kinship. The imagery of flesh and blood is used in very specific and limited circumstances among Arabs. Moreover, ethnography-based conceptualisations of Arabian kinship convey an alternative set of concepts: groin-womb-nerve.

Parentation is construed as both paternity in terms of 'groin' (*solb*) and maternity in terms of 'womb' (*rahm*). Thus among prohibited kin to a male are the wives of his 'sons by groin'. This phrase is employed in the text. 'Womb' is mentioned in the ethnographic interview in Figure 14 describing a relation forged by suckling as analogous to that by birth. More extended genealogical bonds are construed in terms of 'nerve' (*'asab*)—an observation widely supported by ethnography.

In an earlier publication I describe how the complementary duality of groin-womb represents how Arabs construe procreation (El Guindi 2012a), an idiom expressing the process of becoming 'birth kin'. By contrast, in the context of descent groups, genealogical relations are construed as generative with ascendants (see El Guindi 2012a for argument for ascent over descent) connected by *'asab* (S1, 'nerve').[7] This is a point confirmed in numerous studies describing Badawi (or Bedouin) groups, notably in the ethnography by Ahmad Abu-Zeid (1991a: 213) on the Egyptian Sinai, where the local terms *'asib* (S1, meaning 'nerve bound') and *'asiba* (S1, 'nerve binding') are used to describe agnatic relations. He aptly describes (1991a, 1991b) *'Asab* (S1, 'nerve') as the principle agnatically bonding Bedouin groups. Here, genealogy becomes the framework for corporateness and unity and the idiom by which relations are expressed, while, in reality, practices would be generatively fluid. Significantly, reputation and honour constitute the core elements for corporateness, which incorporated outsiders do not and cannot share or transmit (on this, see Lancaster 1997).

---

7   Syllable stress in the Arabic language is relevant to the meaning of the term. Henceforth stress will be marked in parentheses following the term by S for stress and a number designating the syllable (1, 2, 3) to which the stress applies.

Crisscrossing paths of milk

I was struck during fieldwork on suckling by a comment made by a Qatari woman, henceforth Ego, during an interview about her own suckling practices.[8] Casually, Ego recounted: 'By suckling them, I brothered them.' She used the term *khawithom*, a gender-neutral Arabic verb form, meaning 'turned them into siblings'. After giving birth to a son of her own, Ego herself suckled two other male infants unrelated to her by birth or marriage, but related to each other as matrilateral parallel cousins. She went on to say: 'this way I also *siblinged* my son', meaning she gave brothers to her son by birth. These became her sons. This relationship is diagrammed in Figure 12.

One primary data-gathering technique I devised during the UREP kinship project was aimed at eliciting data on suckling. The research team was also seeking local knowledge among women who are the memory bearers of the paths of suckling, and who thus hold the key to decisions on permitted or prohibited spouses. The technique consists of templates designed on the basis of needed data about all possible suckling kin positions. Student researchers went to the field with these templates as a guide to elicit data on specific suckling kin positions, using unstructured open-ended interviews. In the case where the interviewee is not a participant or directly familiar with the kind of suckling represented in the template, the student interviewer was trained to construct a hypothetical case matching that of the template.

Both formulated techniques—the template and the hypothetical case—constitute a methodological innovation meant to fulfil the need of eliciting particular kinship data. The specific template in Figure 13 was designed to elicit data by interviewing women (and occasionally men) about situations in which a male ego has a brother-in-suckling and a brother's son-in-suckling. This is demonstrated in Figure 13.

---

8   The extended interview was carried out over several months by myself and my colleague, Dr Wesam al-Othman, sometimes together and sometimes separately. This observation was made to me directly.

5. PROPERTIES OF KINSHIP STRUCTURE

Field Kinship Elicitation

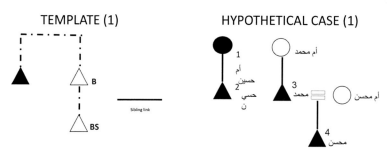

Figure 13. Template 1 and Hypothetical Case 1, employed in UREP project as a kinship elicitation method
Source: Designed by © Fadwa El Guindi, 2014.

The interview itself, translated from Arabic by author, went as follows, with Raneen being the student interviewer and Ne'ma, a Palestinian-Jordanian living in Qatar, the interviewee. The interview is presented in Figure 14. To clarify, numbers next to names correspond to numbers in the diagram in Figure 13 assigned to kin positions:

> **Raneen:** Um Husein (mother of Husein) (1) suckled at the same time as her own (2) another infant called Muhammad (3). What would be the relation between the two boys?
> **Ne'ma:** Brothers-in-suckling.
> **Raneen:** What do you mean by brothers-in-suckling?
> **Ne'ma:** It means that had they been cross-sex they would not be able to marry each other, like **real** brothers.
> **Raneen:** What do you mean by real brothers?
> **Ne'ma:** Procreative brothers from same mother and father, or from mother, or from father.
> **Raneen:** Why would they not be able to marry, had they been cross-sex?
> **Ne'ma:** Because in the Islamic religion siblings-in-suckling are tabooed to each other.
> **Raneen:** Do you know why Islam prohibits such marriage?
> **Ne'ma:** Yes, because they become womb.
> [skip].
> **Raneen:** Had Muhammad had a son called Mohsen (4), what would be the relation between Mohsen (4) and Husein (2)?
> **Ne'ma:** Husein is Mohsen's paternal uncle-in-suckling.
> **Raneen:** So, how is Mohsen (4) referred to?
> **Ne'ma:** Brother's son.
> **Raneen:** Do they behave as paternal uncle and brother's son to each other?
> **Ne'ma:** They should.
> **Raneen:** In what way?
> **Ne'ma:** They visit each other.

Figure 14. Ethnographic interview conducted by Raneen, student researcher on the project
Source: Translation and presentation by author. © Fadwa El Guindi, 2014.

A number of observations can be made from this interview:

a. Suckling is culturally considered kinship.

b. Kinship is defined by the incest taboo.
c. Suckling terms are derivative from procreative terms and expected conduct is that expected between procreative kin.
d. Procreative siblings share mother and father, mother only, or father only.
e. Suckling relations go beyond the giving–receiving dyad, extending prohibitions horizontally and vertically.

Tahrim: Prohibition and avoidance

The Arabic word *tahrim*, with stress on the last syllable, signifies prohibition. I identify syllable stress for semantic reasons. In a kinship context *tahrim* means prohibition from marriage and derives from the root *h-r-m* which 'is among the most important Arabic roots in the vocabulary of Islamic practice', according to some scholars (Reinhart 1995). Kevin Reinhart uses the terms 'forbidden' or 'taboo', evoking constraint and heightened sanctity (ibid.: 101). I have previously discussed the multivocal, interrelated derivatives of this root and their significance in Arab cultural conceptualisation (El Guindi 2003: 82–96). '*Haram* means forbidden, prohibited, unlawful, taboo, sacred,' I wrote. 'It is a word widely used in the Arabic vocabulary ... [It] refers to all that is prohibited by divine authority' (ibid.: 84).

My monograph on privacy, first published in 1999, included analysis of Arabic-term concepts that are derivatives from the root *h-r-m*. Among these are: *hurma* (S1), *harim* (S2), *ihram* (S1), *haram* (S1), *haram* (S2), *maharim* (S2), *mahram* (S1), *muharram* (S2). There is also *tahrim*, the subject of this section. The key meaning, shared by these derivatives, is embedded in the notion of sacred sanctity, implying respect.

Tahrim denotes the quality of sacred sanctity, of forbidding or prohibiting. This denotation is confirmed by ethnographic data and ethnographic analysis of other records. The suckling field project shows that analysis of suckling must include *tahrim* as an interrelated process. As Figure 15 illustrates in graphics and text, two kin whose relationship is culturally established as characterised by the incest taboo would not be in an avoidance relationship.

5. PROPERTIES OF KINSHIP STRUCTURE

How Incest Taboo & Avoidance Work

- Incest taboo prevents mother–son marriage (*maharim*)
  - Incest taboo lifts mother–son avoidance

➤ Space Can Be Shared
➤ Behavioral & Sartorial Avoidance Lifted

Incest Taboo = Lifting Avoidance
Avoidance = Absence of Incest Prohibition

Figure 15. Depiction of mother–son and text illustrating incest and avoidance
Source: © Fadwa El Guindi, 2014.

Two Qur'anic verses (*suras*) deal with *tahrim*: *sura* 4:23 (al-Nisa') and *sura* 24:3 (al-Nur). The point of reference in the former is male, the latter female. Both are about kin prohibitions, but only *sura* al-Nisa' (4:23) includes references to suckling. The other *sura* (24:3, al-Nur) uses a female reference point that does not include suckling relations and is charted in an earlier publication (El Guindi 1999: 86). In Figure 16, I present an original graph of *sura* 4:23 (al-Nisa'), using standard notational symbols based on the text and maintaining the male reference point, in order to illustrate prohibited kin in relations of *tahrim*.[9] Also included in Figure 16, at the top, is my original passage, which I have translated into English.

All prohibitions specified in *sura* 4:23 and illustrated in Figure 16 are reported to have been in effect in Arabia prior to Islam, except two: marrying two sisters (diagrammed in Figure 16) and a son's claim to his deceased father's wife. Sources indicate that both practices existed legitimately and pervasively in Arabia before new prohibitions became imposed in accordance with the relevant Qur'anic passages (Al-Magdoub 2003: 32).

---

[9] I had employed conventional charting kin relations from Qur'anic texts previously, for the first time in 1999, primarily to clarify relations specified in Qur'anic passages in order to enhance analysis. It probably had the consequence of breaking any implicit taboo against such nonreligious use of the sacred text.

Qur'anic *sura* 4:23, al-Nisa'
Prohibitions

Prohibited to you are your mothers, daughters, sisters; father's sisters, mother's sisters; brother's daughters, sister's daughters; **suckling mothers, sisters-in-suckling**; *your wives' mothers; wives' daughters in your care, wives of your sons by groin, and combining two sisters in marriage [translation by author from the original Arabic; emphasis added].*

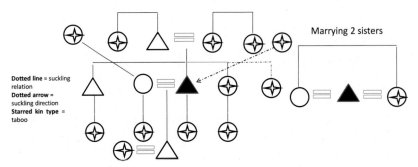

Figure 16. Depiction by author representing kin positions in the *sura* to demonstrate prohibitions
Source: © Fadwa El Guindi, 2014.

The incest taboo and adoption revisited

I find it remarkable that despite the universality of the incest taboo in human kinship, a significant anthropological discovery, two widely read volumes on kinship—the early compendium by Paul Bohannon and John Middleton (1968) and the more recent one by David Parkin and Linda Stone (2004)—do not include any chapters on incest. Perhaps this relates to the path taken in theorising the incest taboo, namely with focus on the hypotheses about its origin as contrasted with its occurrence in ongoing social life. Both have received attention in the history of our discipline (Cooper 1932; El Guindi and Read 2012; Fortune 1932; Freud 1831; Kuper 2002; Lévi-Strauss 1949; McCabe 1983; Turner and Maryanski 2005; Van Gelder 2013; Wilgaux 2000; Wolf 2014). Noticeably, discussion often blurs incest occurrence and incest taboo. The rule of prohibition is of great importance for understanding social organisational forms in anthropology.

5. PROPERTIES OF KINSHIP STRUCTURE

Dictionary and encyclopaedia definitions present incest as sexual intercourse between individuals related in certain prohibited degrees of kinship, and they note that every society has rules prohibiting incestuous unions. My concern here is with socially or legally recognised unions rather than statistical occurrences of sex among prohibited relatives. While sexual avoidance between primary kin is a near-universal in human society, cross-cultural studies show diversity in the content of the prohibited pool beyond parents and siblings.

In Islamic law *maharim* refers to a sexually prohibited pool. Muslims are minimally bound by the pool specified in the Qur'an. In a book dedicated to the topic of incest (Al-Magdoub 2003), referring to it as *zina*[10] *al-maharim* (adultery among prohibited kin), the term *maharim* is defined as 'females prohibited to males, by legislation, laws and customs, from having sexual relations whether in marriage or outside it' (ibid.: 87, my translation from Arabic).[11] *Al-maharim* constitutes a set of kin (birth, marital and suckling) subject to marital prohibitions. By contrast, marriage between patrilateral parallel cousins, prohibited in some societies, is considered a desirable and preferred union and thus not subject to taboo.

Avoidances are manifested as formal behaviours, separation of spaces, and appearances in clothing and gestures that communicate distancing, such as the widely discussed practice of veiling by women. The Arabic for this kind of ritual avoidance is *ihtijab*, sharing the same root *h-j-b* from which *hijab* ('Muslim woman's head-cover') derives (for a full discussion, see El Guindi 2003: 77–115).

Both revealing and puzzling in this connection is an incident reported in Hadith as having occurred in seventh-century Makka. I translate its recorded description this way: a Makkan woman called Zainab al-Usdiyya came to the Prophet seeking guidance regarding the fact that her father died, leaving behind an owned slave who bore his son. He requested to see the son. Upon looking at him he declared him heir to the deceased, then asked Zainab to 'avoid' him (Ibn 'Abdul Birr 1070 (463 A.H.): 321–323/4). By declaring him heir the boy was acknowledged as 'son of groin' of the deceased, but imposing avoidance by Zainab toward him means that he was not 'admitted' as her brother. Hence Zainab was

---

10   *Zina* is usually used to mean adultery, in this case adultery with prohibited women, while the term *sifah* is more appropriate for reference to incest.
11   For an extended analysis of the derivatives of *h-r-m* see El Guindi (2003).

instructed to ritualise space and appearance and to maintain distancing behaviours toward him. In other words, they were not recognised as siblings, and thus were not in a relationship of *maharim* to each other, in which case the incest taboo cannot apply and hence avoidance (*ihtijab*) is prescribed. Without access to independent additional details about this case, I would guess that the absence of marriage between genitor and slave, and the genetrix's status as slave, are the reasons behind the puzzling anomaly of being declared son with full inheritance rights but not brother to a 'daughter of groin'.

Why adoption?

The ethnography of Oceania has contributed in many ways to kinship debates (Berman 2014; Brady ed. 1976; Carroll 1970; Goodenough 1956; Malinowski 2001; Rivers 1914; Scheffler 1970; Schneider 1984; Silk 1980; Strathern 1988). Much of it centred on the pervasive phenomenon of the circulation of children in Oceania, referred to in scholarly works as 'adoption'. That most circulation was among procreative relatives generated much dispute on the relative importance of biology and culture. Other explanations have been social organisational (affiliation, succession, inheritance), transactional (as exchange), psychological (belonging and tension between givers and receivers), and sociobiological (predictability on sociobiological grounds of adoptive decisions). Jack Goody (1969) contributed a cross-cultural synthesis of the legal aspects of adoption and Vern Carroll edited a volume pulling together many ethnographic studies on this phenomenon (Carroll 1970).

In his introduction to that volume Carroll defined adoption as 'any customary and optional procedure for taking as one's own a child of other parents' (Carroll 1970: 3). In the United States, 'adoption' involves securing a child of unknown parentage from an 'adoption agency', and resorting to complicated legal proceedings (Carroll 1970: 4). Carroll goes on to write that American adoption is often a transaction involving total strangers, whereas adoption in Oceania is generally a transaction between close relatives (Carroll 1970: 7).

But data systematically gathered in the field, as well as secondary data from Arab ethnography, can shed a different light on the notion of adoption. Adoption occurs among Arabs, but it is not recognised as kinship. It is not socially admissible as a means to incorporate nonkin into an existing

5. PROPERTIES OF KINSHIP STRUCTURE

kinship network. Nonetheless, the sociological question emerging from my data is: Can adoption somehow bring about a transformation from stranger to kin?

Let me return to Ego, the woman who 'brothered' two infants. Her son by birth had died shortly after birth from some ailment and, after deliberation with her husband, she began the process of adoption, since her advanced age would prevent another pregnancy. Adoption is problematic—Islam does not legalise it and, as noted, society does not recognise it as a means to incorporate new kin. Relating how adoption in Ego's case was calculated conveys processes central to the analysis of kinship structure.

After a long delay Ego succeeded in, officially but not legally, adopting a male baby. By then her lactation had stopped. Why is lactation important in this case? Ego and her husband are not genetrix and genitor (procreative mother and father) to the baby, and since adoption is not recognised as creating kinship, the boy remains a 'stranger' even after he is adopted. Hence the incest taboo cannot apply, and since he is male, avoidance is required from resident females. The incest taboo would then be the only means for the adoptee to become a kinsman. The activation of the incest taboo lifts prescribed, ritualised avoidance among strangers. The other means to lift avoidance is marriage, irrelevant to this case. In order to become mother to her adopted son a woman has to nurse him, which was no longer a possibility for Ego since her lactation phase had ended.

Since suckling is not confined to procreative mothers and since any lactating woman qualifies to suckle within accepted social and cultural norms, Ego's calculation involved locating an appropriate lactating woman at the time the baby boy was adopted. What she did was to time adoption with the expected birth by her brother's wife. So once adoption actually took place the brother's wife was lactating, and was asked to nurse the adoptee along with her own child. Given the cultural rule discussed earlier, adoptee and birth son who cosuckle become siblings. This way the suckling brother's wife became the adoptee's mother, and by extension Ego's brother became father, and by further extension, Ego became paternal aunt to the adopted boy. And the cosuckled infants became siblings.

Given the cultural importance of enforcing cross-sex avoidance in cases of nonincestuous relations, Ego continued to have doubts about the sufficiency of suckling by her brother's wife for lifting the otherwise prescribed avoidance. Becoming paternal aunt might be adequate, but

193

there was uncertainty as to its sufficiency. Ego wanted to 'mother' the adoptee, as if she were his birth mother; that is, to nurture him without the constrictions of avoidance. The solution was to resort to a means which would 'double lock' incest, as it were.

The granddaughter of Ego's husband from a previous marriage (who lived in another country) was lactating and she was asked to nurse the adoptee. By doing so, Ego's husband (grandfather of the suckling woman) became grandfather to the adoptee (who is now sibling to his birth great-grandson) and, by extension, Ego became the adoptee's grandmother. Ego is now both paternal aunt via suckling through the procreative chain of kin, and grandmother through the affinal chain of kin. This doubly-secured lifting of avoidance enabled Ego to proceed with 'mothering' the adoptee.

However, even though Ego was able to become the adoptee's procreative kin through both birth and marital channels, the ethnographic case shows that without direct suckling of the adoptee she could never become his mother. The only means for transforming stranger to kin are marriage, where applicable, or suckling, when possible. Suckling, carefully calculated, re-categorises procreative kin and lifts avoidance when it activates the incest taboo. It can construct and reconstruct kin by birth or kin by marriage. It can convert maternal kin into paternal kin and vice versa. The details of the ethnographic case presented here reveal structures and transformations with implications for kinship by birth, by marriage and by suckling. Finally, it invites reconsiderations of both anthropological notions of adoption and the incest taboo.

General conclusions

In conclusion, I restate what my analysis in this chapter sought to convey. First, I distinguished suckling as studied in Qatar and practices in contiguous areas from other practices of the 'milk phenomenon' in the region and those reported as having existed historically. Analysis of the practice reveals properties necessary as criteria of kinship among Qataris.

Second, analysis of ethnographic data on suckling showed interrelatedness among procreative, marital, and suckling kinship practices, which therefore constitute an integrated structure of kinship for Qataris. Third, and finally, I conclude that studying kinship and the process of 'kinshipping', as it were, using in-depth primary data, can tell us something about what kinship 'is all about': namely a dynamic system of relations and transformations, a structure and a social reality in human life considerably more complex than reductionist claims can reveal. Suckling has a transformative function in kinship relations, constructs new links, creates new relations, transforms existing ones, intensifies and interlocks kin relations, prohibits some relations and creates others. It categorises and re-categorises kinship by birth and kinship by marriage. Adoption in Qatar poses a challenge to the cultural system, which legally disqualifies it but allows it to occur.

References

Abu-Zeid, Ahmad. 1991a. *al-Mujtama'at al-sahrawiyya fi-Misr: shamal sina', dirasa etnographiyya lil-nuthum wal-ansaq al-ijtima'iyy*a (Desert Communities in Egypt, North Sinai – Ethnographic Study of Social Structure and Organization). Cairo: al-Markaz al-Qawmi lil-Buhuth al-Ijtima'iyya wal-Jina'iyya, Qism Buhuth al-Mujtama'at al-Rifiyya wal Sahrawiya (National Centre for Social and Criminological Research – Research on Rural and Desert Communities Section).

——. 1991b. *al-Mujtamaat al-sahrawiyya i Misr. shamal sina, dirasa etnographiyya lil-nuthum wal-ansaq al-ijtimaiyya* (Desert Communities in Egypt, North Sinai – Ethnographic Study of Social Structure and Organization). Cairo: al-Markaz al-Qawmi lil-Buhuth al-Ijtimaiyya wal-Jinaiyya, Qism Buhuth al-Mujtamaat al- al-Rifiyya wal Sahrawiya (National Centre for Social and Criminological Research – Research on Rural and Desert Communities Section).

al-'Ayashi, Abdullah, bin Muhammad. 1679. *al-Madina al-munawwara fi rihlat al-'ayashi*; reprint 1988, edited by Muhammad Amahzun. Kuwait: Dar al-Arqam (page references are to the reprint edition).

Al-Magdoub, Ahmad. 2003. *Zina al-maharim: al-shaytan fi buyutna* (Incest: The Devil in our Households) (Arabic). Cairo: Maktabat Madbouli.

al-Samhoudi, Ali Bin Abdullah. 1972 [1505]. *Khulasat al-wafa' bi-akhbar dar al-mustafa. al-Madina al-Munawwara.* Saudi Arabia: al-Maktaba al-'Ilmiyya.

al-Tarmathi. n.d. *Sunan al-tarmathii: The Book on Suckling* (Arabic), Book 12. Dar Al-Gam'a al-Gadida.

Altorki, Soraya. 1980. 'Milk-kinship in Arab society: An unexplored problem in the ethnography of marriage'. *Ethnology* 19(2): 233–44. doi.org/10.2307/3773273

Berman, Elise. 2014. 'Holding on: Adoption, kinship tensions, and pregnancy in the Marshall Islands'. *American Anthropologist* 116(3): 578–90. doi.org/10.1111/aman.12116

Bohannon, Paul and John Middleton (eds). 1968. *Kinship and Social Organization*. Garden City, NY: American Museum Sourcebooks in Anthropology, the Natural History Press.

Bonte, Pierre (ed.). 1994. *Epouser au plus proche: Inceste, prohibitions et strategies matrimoniales autour de la Méditerranée*. Paris: Editions de l'Ecole des Hautes Etudes en Science Sociales.

Brady, Ivan (ed.). 1976. *Transactions in Kinship: Adoption and Fosterage in Oceania*. Association for Social Anthropology in Oceania Monograph 4. Honolulu: University of Hawaii Press.

Carroll, Vern. 1970. 'Introduction: What does "adoption" mean?' In *Adoption in Eastern Oceania*, edited by Carroll, 3–17. Honolulu: University of Hawaii Press.

Carroll, Vern (ed.). 1970. *Adoption in Eastern Oceania*. Association for Social Anthropology in Oceania Monograph 1. Honolulu: University of Hawaii Press.

Carsten, Janet. 1997. *The Heat of the Hearth: The Process of Kinship in a Malay Fishing Community*. Oxford: Clarendon Press.

———. 2000. *Cultures of Relatedness: New Approaches to the Study of Kinship*. Cambridge: Cambridge University Press.

Code of Hammurabi of Babylon. ca. 2250 B.C.; reprint 1952, as *The Babylonian La*ws, Oxford: Clarendon Press, 1952, edited by G.R. Driver and John C. Miles (page references are to the reprint edition).

Conte, Eduoard. 1987. 'Alliance et parenté élective en Arabie ancienne. Éléments d'une problématique'. *L'Homme* 27(102): 119–38. doi.org/10.3406/hom.1987.368814

Cooper, John M. 1932. 'Incest prohibitions in primitive culture'. *Primitive Man* 5(1): 1–20. doi.org/10.2307/3316422

Driver, G.R., and J.C. Miles. 1952. *The Babylonian Laws*, vol. 1. Oxford: Clarendon Press.

El Guindi, Fadwa. 1999. *Veil: Modesty, Privacy and Resistance*. Oxford and New York: Berg.

———. 2011. 'Kinship by suckling: Extending limits on alliance in endogymous systems'. In *Anthropologicheskii Forum* (Forum for Anthropology and Culture), *Peter the Great Museum of Anthropology and Ethnography ((Kunstkamera), Russian Academy of Sciences, Special Forum on Kinship* 15(7): 381–84.

———. 2012a. 'Milk and blood: Kinship among Muslim Arabs in Qatar'. *Anthropos* 107(2): 545–55.

———. 2012b. 'Suckling as kinship'. *Anthropology Newsletter* 53(1): n.p.

———. 2013. 'Inceste, adoption et allaitement: logiques et dynamiques de l'évitement'. *Incidence Revue* 19: 121–37.

———. 2016. 'Beyond fitness and nurture: The kinship paradox'. *Structure and Dynamics: eJournal of Anthropological and Related Sciences* 9(2): 66–78.

El Guindi, Fadwa and Wesam al-Othman. 2013. 'Transformationality and dynamicality of kinship structure'. *Structure and Dynamics: eJournal of Anthropological and Related Sciences* 6(1). Online: escholarship.org/uc/item/98z0r296 (accessed 6 June 2017).

El Guindi, Fadwa and Dwight Read. 2012. 'Westermarck hypothesis reconsidered: A comment on Kushnick and Fessler'. *Current Anthropology* 53(1): 134–35. doi.org/10.1086/663576

Fortune, R. 1932. *Encyclopedia of the Social Sciences*, vol. VII, s.v. Incest. New York: Macmillan.

Freud, Sigmund. 1831. *Totem and Taboo*. New York: The New Republic Edition.

Giladi, Avner. 1998. 'Breast-feeding in medieval Islamic thought: A preliminary study of legal and medical writings'. *Journal of Family History* 23(2): 107–23. doi.org/10.1177/036319909802300201

———. 1999. *Infants, Parents and Wet Nurses: Medieval Islamic Views on Breastfeeding and their Social Implications*. Leiden: Brill.

Goodenough, Ward H. 1956. 'Componential analysis and the study or meaning'. *Language* 32(1): 195–216. doi.org/10.2307/410665

Goody, Jack R. 1969. 'Adoption in cross-cultural perspective.' *Comparative Studies in Society and History* 11(1): 55–78. doi.org/10.1017/S0010417500005156

Héritier, Françoise. 1994. 'Identité de substance et parenté de lait dans le monde arabe'. In *Epouser au plus proche: Inceste, prohibitions et strategies matrimoniales autour de la Méditerranée*, edited by Pierre Bonte, 149–64. Paris: Editions de l'Ecole des Hautes Etudes en Science Sociales.

Héritier-Augé, Françoise and Elizabeth Copet-Rougier. 1995. *La Parenté Spirituelle*. Paris: Éditions des archives contemporaines.

Ibn 'Abdul Birr, Yusuf bin Abdullah. 1070. *al-Isti'ab fi asma' al-ashab, bi-hamish kitab al-isaba libn hagar*. Dar el-Fikr.

Ibn Manthur, Mohammad bin Makram. 1311. *Lisan al-Arab al-muhit*. Beirut, Lebanon: Dar Lisan al-Arab.

Ibn Sa'd, Muhammad. 844. *al-Tabaqat al-kubra*; reprint 1985, Beirut: Dar Sadir (page references are to the reprint edition).

Jones, Doug and Bojka Milicic (eds). 2011. *Kinship, Language, and Prehistory: Per Hage and the Renaissance in Kinship Studies*. Salt Lake City: University of Utah Press.

Khatib-Chahidi, Jane. 1992. 'Milk-kinship in Shi'ite Islamic Iran'. In *The Anthropology of Breast-feeding: Natural Law or Social Construct*, edited by Vanessa Maher, 109–32. Oxford: Berg.

Kuper, Adam. 2002. 'Incest, cousin marriage and the origin of human sciences in nineteenth century England'. *Past and Present* 174(1): 158–83. doi.org/10.1093/past/174.1.158

Lacoste-Dujardin, Camille. 2000. 'La filiation par le lait au Maghreb'. *L'Autre. Cliniques, Cultures et Societe* 1: 69–76. doi.org/10.3917/lautr. 001.0069

Lancaster, William. 1997. *The Rwala Bedouin Today*. 2nd edition. Prospect Heights, Illinois: Waveland Press.

Lévi-Strauss, Claude. 1949. *Les structures élémentaires de la parenté*. Paris: Presses Universitaires Françaises; rev. and trans. James Harle Bell and John Richard von Sturmer, edited by Rodney Needham as *The Elementary Structures of Kinship*. Boston: Beacon Press, 1969 (page citations are to the translated edition).

Long, Debbi. 1996. 'Milky ways. Milk kinship in anthropological literature and in a Turkish village community'. MA thesis, University of Nijmegen.

Malinowski, Bronisław. 1927. *Sex and Repression in Savage Society*. Kegan Paul, Trench, Trubner and Co. Ltd; reprint 2001, Chicago: University of Chicago Press (page references are to the reprint edition).

McCabe, Justine. 1983. 'FBD marriage: Further support for the Westermarck hypothesis of the incest taboo?' *American Anthopologist* 85(1): 50–69. doi.org/10.1525/aa.1983.85.1.02a00030

Parkes, Peter. 2001. 'Alternative social structures and foster relations in the Hindu Kush: Milk kinship allegiance in former mountain kingdoms of northern Pakistan'. *Comparative Studies in Society and History* 43(1): 4–36. doi.org/10.1017/S0010417501003565

——. 2003. 'Fostering fealty: A comparative analysis of tributary allegiances of adoptive kinship'. *Comparative Studies in Society and History* 45(4): 741–82. doi.org/10.1017/S0010417503000343

——. 2004a. 'Fosterage, kinship, and legend: When milk was thicker than blood?' *Comparative Studies in Society and History* 46(3): 587–615. doi.org/10.1017/S0010417504000271

——. 2004b. 'Milk kinship in Southeast Europe: Alternative social structures and foster relations in the Caucasus and the Balkans'. *Social Anthropology* 12(3): 341–58. doi.org/10.1111/j.1469-8676. 2004.tb00112.x

———. 2005. 'Milk kinship in Islam: Substance, structure, history'. *Social Anthropology* 13(3): 307–29. doi.org/10.1111/j.1469-8676.2005.tb00015.x

Parkin, David and Linda Stone. 2004. *Kinship and Family: An Anthropological Reader*. Oxford: Blackwell Publishers.

Reinhart, A. Kevin. 1995. 'Ḥarām'. In *The Oxford Encyclopedia of the Modern Islamic World*, 4 vols, edited by John L. Esposito, vol. 2, 101. New York: Oxford University Press.

Rivers, William H.R. 1914. *The History of Melanesian Society*, 2 vols. Cambridge: Cambridge University Press.

Sahlins, Marshall. 2013. *What Kinship Is – And Is Not*. Chicago: University of Chicago Press. doi.org/10.7208/chicago/9780226925134.001.0001

Sallama, Amer Hussein. 2006. *al-Muharramat min-al-nisa' bi-sabab al-Musahara*. Alexandria: Dar al-Iman lil Tab' wal Nashr wal Tawzi'.

Scheffler, Harold W. 1970. 'Kinship and adoption in the northern New Hebrides'. In *Adoption in Eastern Oceania*, edited by Vern Carroll, 369–89. Association for Social Anthropologists in Oceania Monograph 1. Honolulu: University of Hawaii Press.

———. 1972. 'Kinship semantics'. *Annual Reviews in Anthropology* 1: 309–28. doi.org/10.1146/annurev.an.01.100172.005121

———. 2004. 'Sexism and naturalism in the study of kinship'. In *Kinship and Family: An Anthropological Reader*, edited by Robert Parkin and Linda Stone, 294–308. Malden, MA: Blackwell.

Scheffler, Harold W. and Floyd G. Lounsbury. 1971. *A Study in Structural Semantics: The Siriono Kinship System*. Englewood Cliffs, NJ: Prentice Hall.

Schneider, David M. 1984. *A Critique of the Study of Kinship*. Ann Arbor: University of Michigan Press. doi.org/10.3998/mpub.7203

Shadid, Anthony. 2012. *House of Stone: A Memoir of Home, Family, and a Lost Middle East*. Boston: Houghton Mifflin Harcourt.

Shapiro, Warren. 2011. 'What is Malay kinship primarily about? Or the new kinship studies and the fabrication of an ethnographic fantasy'. In *Kinship, Language, and Prehistory: Per Hage and the Renaissance in Kinship Studies*, edited by Doug Jones and Bojka Milicic, 141–51. Salt Lake City: University of Utah Press.

Silk, Joan B. 1980. 'Adoption and kinship in Oceania'. *American Anthropologist* 82(4): 799–820. doi.org/10.1525/aa.1980.82.4.02a 00050

Smith, William Robertson. 1885. *Kinship and Marriage in Early Arabia*. Cambridge: Cambridge University Press.

Strathern, Marilyn. 1988. *The Gender of the Gift: Problems with Women and Problems with Society in Melane*sia. Anthropology Series. Berkeley: University of California Press. doi.org/10.1525/california/9780520064232.001.0001

Turner, Jonathan and Alexandra Maryanski. 2005. *Incest: Origins of the Taboo*. Boulder, CO: Paradigm Publishers.

Van Gelder, Geert Jan. 2013. 'Incest and inbreeding'. In *Encyclopedia Iranica*, vol XIII, 5–6.

Wilgaux, Jérôme. 2000. 'Entre inceste et échange: Réflexions sur le modèle matrimonial athénien'. *L'Homme* 154–55: 659–76. doi.org/10.4000/lhomme.54

Wolf, Arthur P. 2014. *Incest Avoidance and the Incest Taboos: Two Aspects of Human Nature*. Stanford, CA: Stanford University Press.

6

Of Mothers, Adoption and Orphans: The Significance of Relatedness in a Remote Aboriginal Community

Victoria Katherine Burbank

Introduction: Mothers

One day, in 1978, I accompanied a woman I call Lily on a trip that took us from the remote Aboriginal community of Numbulwar up the coast to an outstation for a few days of respite from the demands and distractions of settlement life. We were accompanied by three of Lily's children and one of her sister's sons, all of whom were of primary-school age. I was driving, Lily sat beside me and the children were in the back of the Land Rover. Her sister's son was an active child and on the long and rough trip to the outstation appeared to annoy his 'brothers', one of whom may have smacked him. In any event, the sister's son began to cry and was rebuked, perhaps by his attacker, with, 'Stop crying, your mummy isn't here', clearly referring to the boy's biological mother who had remained in the township. Now according to the kinship nomenclature employed at Numbulwar, particularly that of the Indigenous language, his 'mother' was there, for as is the case with Aboriginal kin terminology more generally, there is an equation of same-sex siblings; hence all the children with us that day called both Lily and her sister, 'mother'. Still, this child's 'brothers' noted a distinction between their mother and his, and by extension, we may presume, between their cousin and themselves. Marshall Sahlins has decried the fact that 'kinship has too often been analysed from the way it is lived and learned by individuals' (2013: 66), but I do just that. Assuming that the locus of cultures is to be found in mind, rather than floating freely in a social ether (D'Andrade 1995; Shore 1996), the way something is 'lived and learned by individuals' is often just what anthropologists should be studying. Admittedly, as Melford Spiro pointed out with reference to a confusion between 'cultural conceptions of the person' and 'the actors' conceptions of the self' (1993: 117), we should not assume that an encoded system of kin terminology is isomorphic with the way that kinship is 'lived and learned' but this hardly means that the latter is not worthy of our attention. Lily's sons call her sister 'mother' and her son 'brother', but clearly they do not see Lily's sister in the same way they see their mother, or see her son as exactly like themselves. This, I argue, is a critical kind of observation for understanding sociality in this remote Australian community, and likely elsewhere.

The nature/nurture debate, while quiescent in some anthropological quarters, has been characteristic of what is referred to as the 'new kinship' in which writers, often inspired by David Schneider's (1968) discussion of American kinship, cast it as an entirely cultural construction (Sahlins 2013). Marshall Sahlins provides us with another classic example of this stance, notable both for its persistence and longevity. In a sociobiological treatment of 'Adoption in Oceania', Joan Silk (1980) may have been the first in these debates to challenge his claim, that 'kinship is a unique characteristic of human society, distinguished precisely by its freedom from natural relationships' (Sahlins 1976: 58; in Silk 1980: 800). Some 30 years later he continues to provide us with examples of the dichotomisations of a topic that, at least, some now think is better treated in an integrative manner. Although he pays attention to human psychology, he continues to sever 'meaningful social endowment' from 'mere physiological substance'; insisting that kinship is 'a thoroughly symbolic-cum-cultural phenomenon' (Sahlins 2013: 65–66). In so doing, Sahlins ignores what a number of anthropologists increasingly see as vital components of cultural experience, what some describe as our 'biogenetic heritage': the potentials and constraints of our bodies and brains arising from our evolutionary history (e.g. Downey and Lende 2012). In contrast to the 'new kinship', the 'extensionist' position in kinship studies calls for just such treatment. Warren Shapiro (e.g. 2005, 2009, 2012) has long and energetically defended extensionism, an approach which assumes that people in general are often, if not always, acute observers of human activity, including reproductive activity, and that a kinship term such as 'mother' derives its meaning from the observation that a specific woman gives birth to a specific child. While these terms may be applied to others, in the case of 'mother', say, to her sisters, in some cases, it is recognised that in its extended application the entirety of its original meaning no longer applies. In this paper, I join Shapiro's, and Silk's, efforts by drawing upon the thinking of several writers who have attempted to incorporate inclusive fitness theory into kinship exegesis, thus integrating the biogenetic with the social and cultural. It will soon become clear that when viewed from an evolutionary perspective, Harold Scheffler's defence of the 'kinship terms and extensions' (1978: 21) interpretation of Aboriginal kin classification, his ideas about polysemy, the focality of some kin, like fathers and mothers, and the extension of labels for them to less focal others makes perfect sense, at least in Aboriginal Australia. It also illuminates some of the behaviour associated with what I have labelled adoption/fosterage in the remote Aboriginal community of Numbulwar.

Inclusive fitness and cultural experience

William Hamilton's (1964a, 1964b) theory of inclusive fitness, or kin selection, as it is sometimes known, has found a place at the centre of contemporary evolutionary thinking. 'Fitness' is the number of copies of an individual's genes, relative to others of its kind that are passed on to the next generation. The idea that organisms increase their fitness insofar as they are able to increase that of their close kin, given a cost/benefit advantage to ego, helps us understand a great deal about human sociality. A brother, say, who instead of having children himself, provides the additional calories that his nieces and nephews need to survive, grow and reproduce, may well end up with greater fitness than he would were he to bring his own offspring into a world that could not support them, or if he were to contribute to the children of an unrelated individual. In discussions of inclusive fitness it is usually assumed that the probability of sharing alleles (a variant of a gene) with a parent or sibling is 0.5 or 50 per cent. The coefficient of relatedness between half siblings is 25 per cent, as is that of aunt/uncle and nephew/niece, grandparent/grandchild. That of first cousins is only 12.5 per cent (Buller 2005: 351–52; Daly and Wilson 1983: 28–31). When Lily's sister's son was crying, he may well have been appealing to her for help in a 'fraternal' rivalry, whatever that might have been. Crying can be a form of demanding, to which adults may choose to respond, or not. It seems a fair assumption that the sister's son's behaviour was seen by his 'brother' as an attempt to gain *his* mother's allegiance and hence an advantage over her own son. The rebuke, 'your mummy isn't here', can be read as a signal both to his rival and to his mother that her sister's child was, in relatedness terms, less worthy of her attention than his opponents, her own genetic offspring.

The idea of inclusiveness fitness, like much of evolutionary theory, does not require organisms to act consciously in terms of its principles, only that their behaviour contributes to their greater relative fitness. Just what mechanisms may be at play and just what their ontological status may be has been a focus of evolutionary psychology, and considerable debate, for several decades (e.g. Buller 2005; Pinker 2003). Ideas about evolved psychological potentials, however, do not exclude a role for culture. On the contrary, increasingly culture is understood to have been the critical component of the environment in which our bodies and brains originated and hence an intrinsic part of almost anything we are and do (e.g. Lende and Downey 2012; Richerson and Boyd 2005; Tomasello 1999). The tricky part is understanding how biology and culture work together in human experience.

Maurice Bloch and Dan Sperber (2002) posit a scenario in which species-specific, genetically inherited, and hence universal, 'dispositions' direct our interest and attention to the kind of information we once needed, and perhaps still need, in the evolutionary game of reproductive success. This may occur even where historical processes have created settings where such information is neither emphasised nor valued. These dispositions do not create cultural representations, though they may contribute to their creation, but rather bias the possibility that such representations may stabilise in a cultural community. For example, inclusive fitness theory predicts that, 'individuals would tend to show interest in evidence of relatedness, whether or not culturally codified' (Bloch and Sperber 2002: 732). Acting as attractors these dispositions create relative stability and limited variability in spite of processes—environmental and historical—that constantly introduce variation and change into any cultural system (ibid.: 727–28). We might then understand whatever neuropsychological mechanisms exist to implement kin selection strategies as the attractors of kin-based behaviour in the midst of stochastic variations introduced in historical and environmental processes.

6. OF MOTHERS, ADOPTION AND ORPHANS

The distinction between 'your mother' and the unspoken, though logically implied, 'my mother', suggests just such 'interest in evidence of relatedness' (Bloch and Sperber 2002: 732). Wubuy is the dominant Indigenous language of Numbulwar, though most people there today speak an English-based creole, called 'Kriol' by its speakers. In the Wubuy kinship terminology, same-sex siblings are equated linguistically as are their children. That is, the children of two sisters would call both of them, 'mother' and the children of both women, 'sibling'. However, while terms of address do not include words for distinguishing a biological mother from a classificatory one, the linguist Jeffrey Heath has made note of the word, *ardiya*. It is 'not morphologically a kin term', he says, but is used to designate an 'expecting mother' and distinguish a woman as the 'true (biological) mother (of a particular child)' (1982: 177).[1] Furthermore, 'expressions like mana-da:n-jinyung "of the guts"' (i.e. of the womb) can be used in conjunction with the word for "mother" or "MoBr" to specify "actual mother" or "full brother of actual mother"' (ibid.: 330). Shapiro has observed similar expressions in northeast Arnhem Land (1979: 8). In Wubuy only two terms, *rrigang* and *bibi*, are used for M, MZ, MB, MBD, MBS and MBSS in an Omaha-type skewing of the terminology. However, Kriol terms are used by many to distinguish M, MZ and MB from the remainder of these Wubuy categories. The former are designated as 'mummy' and 'uncle', the latter as the interchangeable terms 'barnga' or 'cuz'. While this may be an attempt to bring the local kin terminology more into accord with the English system—for Numbulwar is an intercultural environment and Aboriginal people often try to communicate in ways that English speaking outsiders will understand—we might note that the distinctions clearly reflect diminishing coefficients of relatedness: 50 per cent to 25 per cent for 'mummy' and 'uncle', but only 12.5 per cent to 3.13 per cent for 'barnga' and 'cuz' and that their use may well represent a welcome means of expressing an intuitive sense of these differences.

Given kin selection as a force in human history, it is not surprising that humans appear to have capacities for kin recognition (e.g. DeBruine et al. 2009; Lieberman, Tooby and Cosmides 2007a; Porter 1991), perhaps particularly those that enable phenotypic matching, the ability to

---

1   Heath also points out that Wubuy phrases that may be translated as 'to beget, sire, be the father of' or 'to give birth to, bear, be the mother of' 'are freely extendable to opposite-sex siblings of the designated parent; thus a woman can say … "I begat him" of her brother's child 'and a man can say … "I bore him" of his sister's child. The mother's clan or its territorial centre can also be said to have "borne" a given person' (1982: 330).

recognise kin on the basis of similarity, whether that of appearance, smell or sound. This is something that the people of Numbulwar believe they can do, on occasion with substantial consequences:

> Sometimes a family here don't like [an unmarried] girl in the first place. But when they get pregnant and they have that little baby and when they see that baby is true for their son, that baby has their son's face, they won't growl at that girl. They will feel ashamed [and let] them marry (Teenage girl, in Burbank 1988: 109).

Children, say women at Numbulwar, take their mothers' and fathers' bodies. When a child is a foetus both mother and father grow thin before they grow fat:

> The child takes mother and father's body and makes them weak. Like Margira and his wife. They are strong because they don't have any children.[2] They are a bit old but still strong, not like Margira's brother who has children. He is weak (Woman speaking, unpublished fieldnotes, 1978).

In particular, a man is said to give his children his face and his foot. Lest readers be confused by the word 'foot', let me explain that as far as the people of Numbulwar are concerned, feet mark the individuality of a person much as does a face. The footprints that each person leaves are regarded as distinctive and older people, at least, can identify the prints of close kin, if not of all familiar individuals. If a woman who is known to have a lover bears a child who does not look like her husband, its paternity may be suspect. Once, when I was accompanied in the field by my son and husband, a visiting neighbour emphatically declared that their feet were identical, a compliment, no doubt, on my marital fidelity (Daly and Wilson 1982). All of this is to reiterate that the people of Numbulwar appear to believe they have the means of distinguishing among actual and classificatory parents, children, siblings and other kin. They also, I argue, have the motivation to do so. The distinctions that people make between 'close family' and others are, not surprisingly, reflected in behaviour. For example, only 'close relations' would take part in each other's fights; should an outsider attempt to do so, he or she might well be attacked (Burbank 1994: 76). And as with linguistic distinctions, these are not a peculiarity of Numbulwar. A child socialisation practice at Yuendumu provides an example from another remote Aboriginal community. There, adults

---

2 The word 'strong' is more often used in the sense of selfish or unwilling, as in 'He is strong, he can't let them use that tractor' and is opposed to 'kind', giving or kind.

regularly engage in *lani-mani*, frightening toddlers with the explicit intent of warning them of dangers such as bullocks and snakes. According to the ethnographer, 'One only conducts *lani-mani* session with one's own children ... People say, "You gotta be close to that kid, it wouldn't be right to scare other people's children"' (Musharbash 2016: 175).

Adoption/fostering

The ways in which people at Numbulwar both embrace a greater circle of kin than is typical in the western world, yet distinguish among those kin, and the fact that both the embrace and discrimination can be linked to coefficients of relatedness, helps us understand some of the practices and ideas associated with adoption/fostering in such a community. As neither 'adoption' nor 'fosterage' provide an adequate translation of the kind of alloparental care I discuss (see Goody 1971), both terms are used interchangeably to indicate that I am talking about practices that resemble both western arrangements.

> If a woman has no babies and if another has plenty and if that woman with none likes one, she is going to ask, 'Could you give me one that I could look after?' The woman with plenty can't say no because she has too many [a lot]. That stepmother will keep that little girl for her own, and when she is big that woman will do all the talking for her marriage or if there is trouble ... If someone asks the mother [about the girl's marriage], she will say, 'Don't' ask me, ask her stepmother'. And if the girl makes trouble the stepmother will pay for it, like broken windows. If the mother goes [to] another place the stepmother will keep the girl with her. They give little boys too (Burbank 1980: 52).[3]

Alloparental care is a practice both of past and contemporary local scenes. A residence survey of the 800 or so people living at Numbulwar in 2003 indicates that there were at least 18 children under the age of 18 who were living apart from both of their biological parents, while life history accounts of adults sometime include mention that a child was raised by someone other than his or her mother and/or father. Children have been given to others when their mother dies or when a woman asks a kinswoman for one of hers, sometimes because she has none of her own. On more than one occasion, when a child was thought to be at risk due

---

3   I believe the word 'stepmother' used in this account was only for my benefit. It is not a word generally used to describe women looking after adopted/fostered children.

to neglect or abuse, a kinswoman has stepped in and taken the child to raise as her own, at least for as long as necessary. Often a close genetic relationship, a coefficient of at least 25 per cent, can be traced between the carer and the child. In all cases of which I am aware, fostered children continue to be regarded as the child of their biological parents; they call their foster parents by the kin terms they would have used should they have stayed with their birth mothers.

Along with the responsibilities of caring for a fostered child come some rewards; there are both observable and less tangible benefits to alloparenting. As the speaker above indicates, in the days when girls were bestowed in marriage, a foster mother would have the right to make the bestowal.[4] Today, women who foster infants and toddlers can anticipate 'respect' from them in future years. While 'respect' is a new word in the local idiom, people appear to use it to mean the help and support due to a person, especially a family member. Once, for example, a woman complained to me that a man she had once fostered as a child was not taking her side in an argument: 'They gave him to me' when he was little, after his mother died, 'I was looking after him, he should respect me' (2004).

Foster children can be of assistance to the fosterer, especially perhaps, if they are girls (see Hamilton 1981). A foster grandmother, for example, who had been looking after an adolescent girl until she moved on to live with other kin, told me how she had been talking to her other granddaughters: 'Because [my foster child is] gone now, you are going to help me, wash my clothes, cook' (2004). And foster parents may receive government 'child cheques', that is, Child Benefit money.

There are, of course, also costs to fostering children. Numbulwar, like other remote communities in Australia, is a poor community. There are few if any people living there who do not sometimes lack for money and the essentials it can buy. Perhaps even more critically, there is social want as well. David McKnight's (1986) 'relational density', a measure of the number of relationships characterised by kin-like rights and duties, is useful for visualising daily life at Numbulwar: so many relationships of material and emotional significance; so many people with so many needs. Looking at any kindred there, one can see, along with familial affection and

---

4 This is assuming that the child had not been assigned a husband via mother-in-law bestowal. On mother-in-law bestowal, see Shapiro (1970).

succour, myriad forms of trauma and disadvantage: premature mortality, mental and physical illness, disability, substance abuse, domestic violence, hunger, truancy, vandalism, unemployment, debt—the list could go on. As the speaker above indicates, along with other duties towards a child, fosterers may be held responsible for their misbehaviour, a responsibility that might, on occasion, even involve a caretaker in a physical fight (Burbank 1994). In such circumstances, the presence of a foster child might seem to be the straw that breaks the camel's back (see Silk 1990) and we could argue here that the hardship of fostering should disabuse us of the notion that inclusive fitness acts as an attractor in the development of human culture, that it is instead solely based on moral sentiments. Would not a carer be more likely to get more copies of her genes into the next generation if she directed resources exclusively to her own biological children? Why foster another, less related child? Inclusive fitness theory permits another view, however. A broad perspective on human affairs is one of its theoretical strengths (Burnstein, Crandall and Kitayama 1994). Winning the fitness game takes more than just winning a fitness round. And to understand winning even a single round requires knowledge of the context in which a contest takes place. In some circumstances, such as those found at Numbulwar, fostering has the potential to enhance a carer's fitness, and that of her close kin (see also Silk 1980).

There is considerable evidence that being seen as kin can be advantageous (e.g. Burnstein, Crandall and Kitayama 1994). Providing one's own children with additional 'siblings' may thus be a way of increasing one's own fitness and fostering may be a means of doing so (Silk 1980). Looking for 'kin detection mechanisms' among humans, Debra Lieberman, John Tooby and Leda Cosmides (2007a) provide empirical support for the possibility that 'mother/child perinatal association' and 'sibling coresidence' are two means by which humans are able to calculate relatedness. Some of their study subjects had step, adoptive or half siblings. Coresidence, in this case, better than belief in whether or not they were genetic kin, predicted altruism towards a step, half or adopted sibling (Lieberman, Tooby and Cosmides 2007b: 7) suggesting that early and sustained contact can lead both a woman's biological child and her foster child to see each other as 'close' kin, appropriate recipients of help and generosity. As in most of the cases I know, fostered children are already regarded as 'close family', and as such we can anticipate that reciprocal altruism would be reinforced, benefitting both the woman's biological child and the foster child throughout their lifetimes, increasing the reproductive success of each. Women then, we might also anticipate, should be motivated to treat foster children as their own, for this again would reinforce the lesson that all the children in her care are 'close family'. Children clearly can learn that unrelated individuals or lesser kin can be like siblings or 'close family'. But we need to ask why humans learn the kinds of things that they do (Bloch and Sperber 2003: 729). Were there not a disposition for kin discrimination, and associated neurobiological mechanisms for implementing it, could we learn to distinguish kin from nonkin, close kin from more distant kin, or care about doing so?

Orphans

In addition to children fostered as infants or toddlers, there are increasing numbers of older children at Numbulwar today who have lost one or both parents due to divorce, desertion or death. If they are left without adequate kin support, these children may become *wangulu*.

Wangulu is the word that Aboriginal people at Numbulwar use to translate the English word 'orphans'. But *wangulu* are not necessarily children without parents. They are people who have no one to look after them. Whether or not one is an orphan is determined by the presence or absence of 'support', a word I first noted hearing from an Aboriginal English speaker in 2005. Adolescents without mobile phones may be described as *wangulu*. Or, 'when you go anywhere and ask anyone for money and they can't give you, they say *wangulu*' (Burbank 2011: 151–52). Speaking of the Pintupi of Central Australia, Myers calls orphans *yapunta* and, much like the use of *wangulu*, says that *yapunta* may also signify that an object 'does not belong to anyone' or that 'it has no one holding or looking after it' (Myers 1988: 55). In the township of Borroloola, roughly 209 kilometres down the coast from Numbulwar, some adolescent suicide victims are described as 'poddy' girls or boys, that is, as young people who were neglected by their families, often because of parental substance abuse (McMullen 2014). Sue McMullen observes that the term 'poddy' appears to have been derived from '"poddy calf", a calf with no mother' (ibid.: 113). With long experience of the cattle stations in the surrounding countryside, Aboriginal people at Borroloola might well be familiar with this term. Of the Pintupi *yapunta*, Fred Myers has said that such individuals manifest 'an anger that is not appeased' and are more likely to become 'the most active petrol sniffing children' (1986: 178).

Maggie Brady (1992: 75) has observed something similar of adolescents in the Western Desert, though it is not clear if these are children without parents or children with parents who 'don't worry' about them (McMullen 2014: 113). I have found a somewhat more complicated picture of people who might be considered *wangulu* at Numbulwar: they may be petrol sniffers, but they may also be those who are relatively 'successful' according to western standards (Burbank 2006: 17, 11).

More than one observer of Aboriginal Australia has noted that the highly responsive and nurturing kind of infant care characteristic of their communities is followed by a period of lessened parental engagement expressed in an expectation that more mature children who are able to ask for something will do so. Subsequently, children are largely left to their own devices when it comes to satisfying their needs, including their need for food (see Brady 1992; Hamilton 1981; Myers 1986). Crying, as mentioned above, may be one means of asking for something, an action that enables an adult to decide whether or not to respond. Thus children who are fostered at a more advanced age may be less likely to receive the same degree of nurturing that a younger child receives. Between 2003 and 2005, I observed several children, both male and female, who appeared to be in just such a situation. For example, I repeatedly saw them wearing the same dirty clothing in contrast to the sometimes new and usually clean attire of their 'siblings'. This relative neglect may not simply be a function of an adult's awareness of a fostered child's more distant kin position, however. It may also be due to the behaviour of the children they now live amongst. Once, for example, I overheard two teenage 'sisters' reproaching a third, younger, cousin who was being looked after by their grandmother. All three wanted a 'cold drink' but the money they asked for was not forthcoming. The fostered child was then told by her cousins that she was 'a young girl' now, an adolescent, and should be doing work for her fosterer, not asking her for money (unpublished fieldnotes, 2003).

What may be of particular significance in this case is the fact that the fostered adolescent's father was from a distant community, and hence probably regarded, at best, as a distant sort of kin. As the theory of inclusive fitness goes, kin-based cooperation can be expected to reflect coefficients of relatedness. Like Eric Smith, those who work with evolutionary theory generally assume that 'kinship ... is a key organizing principle in all societies' but that 'coefficients of relatedness drop off rapidly outside a narrow orbit of close kin' (2003: 422). Stuart West, Claire El Mouden and Andy Gardner, however, have taken issue with the latter supposition, observing that we assume, sometimes mistakenly, that 'relatedness can only be high between close family relatives' (2011: 243). They point out that the 'well-known approximations of relatedness', such as I have used above, are based on an assumption that a population is large and genetically diverse. We need to ask if this is indeed the case for a community such as Numbulwar, or if it is better described as a 'viscous population', one which is relatively sedentary, with little in or out migration. If the latter is the case, then 'relatedness between group members can be relatively high because it will tend to increase the genetic similarity between interacting individuals' (ibid.: 243). Although genealogies show some community exogamy occurring over the last four generations, Numbulwar is a small and largely stable population, numbering between only about 400 and 800 people over the 30 years I have been working there. Given polygynous marriage, much of it sororal (Chisholm and Burbank 1991), and the leverate, practised until only a few generations ago, we might be right to assume a relatively high degree of relatedness as a characteristic of the community as a whole.[5] Thus the extension of focality to seemingly more distant genetic relatives may well make sense as much in fitness terms as in terms of social solidarity (Park, Schaller and Van Vugt 2008; Shapiro 2005). At the same time, someone like the adolescent cousin, with a parent from a distant population, may actually be less genetically related to her cousins at Numbulwar, and to her mother and grandmother, than she might have been had her father been a local man.

Close family

As should be apparent by now, people at Numbulwar take care to distinguish 'close family' from other kin and treat them differently, as a rule. A segment of people in every egocentric social environment at Numbulwar is described as 'close' or 'full relations'. The totality of these may be described as a personal kindred (Shapiro 1979: 57). One of the criteria for recognising someone as a 'full relation', or 'family' is the recognition of a genealogical link such as sharing a grandparent whether

---

5   I have undertaken fieldwork at Numbulwar on eight occasions between 1977 and 2007. The last series of trips took place between 2003 and 2007. White and Parsons' study of genetic differentiation in Arnhem Land 'confirmed the relative isolation of the extreme Arnhem Land tribes' (1973: 5). Although the Nunggubuyu were not included in this study, it is nevertheless suggestive in this context. A study in which the Nunggubuyu were included found notable genetic differentiation between groups in Arnhem Land and elsewhere in Australia (see Balakrishnan, Sanghvi and Kirk (1975).

MM, FM, FF or MF. All of the people in one's 'clan' are 'family' as are the people in one's mother's clan: 'My family is Nunggargalung [speaker's mother's "clan"], like mother and uncle, family. My [mother's mother] and [mother's father].[6] They feeling flesh. We say, "We all one race"' (1978). Someone may, however, be regarded as a 'full relation' because of a totemic connection: 'He is full relation to me because of that dreamtime story. Goanna comes from his country. I am goanna too, because goanna went from Wurindi to Hodgson Downs' (unpublished fieldnotes, 1978). The term 'close', however, may be reserved for people with a genealogical link; 'close' was explained to me with reference to a shared ancestor, as in, they are 'close family' because they are 'one granny'. And this in turn, as the spatial metaphor would suggest (Lakoff and Johnson 1999), is associated by some, at least, with greater cooperation and intimacy: 'We are same grandfather and grandmother, we like each other, we can share' (unpublished fieldnotes, 2005).

Sometimes, however, even 'close' family may not be close enough. The harsh language directed to the fostered adolescent from her older cousins, might be interpreted simply as older children directing a younger one to do the kinds of things expected of her (see Hamilton 1981). However, the teenagers' words did not strike me as this kind of instruction. They struck me as harassment, a mildly aggressive form of competition. I have seen too many contests between full siblings to say that competition is restricted to those who share smaller coefficients of relatedness. Nevertheless, it may be that children are the most active agents of kin differentiation when it comes to others who are not their parents' own. The fostered girl was the teenage sisters' 'close relation', but she may not, by virtue of her father's genetic contribution, have been as close to her cousins as they were to each other, and they, in turn, to her fosterer, for they were the children of two local brothers with spouses from 'clans' long associated with Numbulwar. The question, however, is how might this discrimination be made? Clearly the teens knew that the adolescent's father came from a distant community. But they also knew that the three of them shared grandparents. What form of information should take precedence? And how might this occur? Thinking again about mother/child perinatal association and sibling coresidence (Lieberman, Tooby and Cosmides 2007a), we might ask how much time the adolescent and her mother spent at Numbulwar during

---

6   'Clan' is what most people at Numbulwar call named groups associated with specific 'country' via patrifiliation, at least in conversation with whitefellas.

her early years. These authors have observed that 'when MPA [mother/child perinatal association] is absent and coresidence is used as a cue to relatedness' between '14–18 years of coresidence duration' is required to have the same effect on individuals who have not witnessed mother/child perinatal association (ibid.: 1). Coresidence, however, as mentioned above, can have powerful effects in creating a kin-like relationship between unrelated people (ibid.: 7). To judge by the frequency of the adolescent's visits to her father's community between 2003 and 2007, it is probable that the two teenage 'sisters' spent much more time together than they spent with their adolescent cousin. The children of siblings are often companions throughout their early years, as was the case with Lily's and her sister's sons, whereas the adolescent cousin was, most likely, only an occasional visitor. By the same token, observation of her perinatal association with her mother would have been less frequent as well, thus, perhaps, creating the overall impression of the adolescent cousin as less rather than more a family member.

Sibling rivalry is an old theme in the psychological literature on child development. Here in a community where kin terms clearly grounded in the reproductive unit are extended to a more extensive range of people, it should not be surprising to see that 'sibling rivalry' may take place between people who are not genetic siblings. What may be more interesting about this extended rivalry, however, is the way it enables a fosterer to advantage her closest kin, without obviously violating norms of 'caring and sharing' for members of the larger kindred. The teenagers' actions obscured the fosterer's reluctance to provide money for 'cold drinks', enabling her, perhaps, to put her limited resources to better purpose. Silk has observed that when children are unrelated to their adoptive parents 'the addition of a child is always costly for the existing children' (1980: 802). At least some children at Numbulwar seem able to recognise this as the case when children are less related to the carer, and to themselves, if not in the language of fitness, then in the economic language of scarce resources. When children who are more related to a carer compete with children who are less so, they may be acting not only in their own but also in the caregiver's reproductive interests.

Numbulwar is an environment in which even the unity of 'close family' might be disrupted for it is fairly described as an environment characterised by want. Yet its Indigenous inhabitants are surrounded by 'whitefella' wealth, much of which appears to be extremely attractive, whether this be a mobile phone or a 'cold drink' (Burbank 2011). For children especially, the inadequate incomes of their households and the dearth of adult carers, due to high rates of premature morbidity and mortality, create a scarcity of necessary and desired goods and adults they can turn to in times of need. In these circumstance it would not be surprising if the teenage 'sisters' saw themselves in competition with their adolescent cousin for essential resources. This observation and others like it suggests that it may be children rather than adults who are the primary agents of kin discrimination when a foster child is in the family.

Conclusion

In what may be a 'viscous population', the fact that kin terms for nuclear family members are often extended to others suggests an intuitive understanding that many if not most individuals in the community are relatively close, genetically speaking. Nevertheless, Aboriginal people, at least at Numbulwar, take pains to distinguish actual from classificatory kin, and 'close family', or just 'family', from others. These distinctions reflect both biological and sociocultural realities. In an environment of scarcity, competition is to be expected and, especially in cases where such competition may be critical not simply for quality of life, but for life itself, coefficients of relatedness are pertinent (see Burnstein, Crandall and Kitayama 1994). Just how relatedness is determined in this community can only be extrapolated from the experimental literature. Mother/child perinatal association and coresidence have a face validity for the situation at Numbulwar. However, the children there complicate a simple understanding of this process. They are not blank slates ready to receive information from something like coresidence without challenge. While addressing the topic of 'parent offspring conflict', several observers of infant behaviour have interpreted night waking as a means of delaying the arrival of the next child, an event which could compromise the health, or even life, of the existing one (Badcock 1990: 74–75). Here we might interpret night waking as an anticipatory form of sibling rivalry, suggesting a readiness to attend to information about threats of resource competition even from the closest of kin. Hence, other aspects of the environment, such as the abundance or lack of food and the presence or absence of nurturing adults may provide equally compelling information to which children are disposed to attend (see Burbank, Senior and McMullen 2015; Nettle, Coyne and Colléony 2013).

Some years ago, Daly, Wilson and Weghorst (1982) observed that male sexual jealousy was manifest in societies where its expression was contrary to social convention, suggesting that jealousy-like emotions were something more than cultural inventions. Similarly, Bloch and Sperber have postulated that dispositions exist apart from culture, and that when expressed they need not 'be reflected in a cultural norm' (2002: 731). We probably should not speak of a precultural human, however, for culture is so much a part of what we are; our species' heritage is inevitably assimilated into our cultural selves even before birth (Downey and Lende 2012; Richerson and Boyd 2005; Tomasello 1999). We are, however, also animals and hence our biogenetic heritage needs analytic space and attention as an agentic source of our behaviour. In pursuing this route, integrating what we know about biology and psychology into our ethnographic interpretations, I believe we gain a far more detailed understanding of what we currently regard as the cultural aspects of being human. Understanding that kin selection and kin recognition are a part of what we are and what we do enriches our understanding of our own and others' social arrangements just as Scheffler's support and elaboration of the extensionist position has alerted us to the potential significance of kin discrimination in Aboriginal Australian communities.

Acknowledgements

Fieldwork was supported by the then Australian Institute of Aboriginal Studies, now the Australian Institute of Aboriginal and Torres Strait Islander Studies, Canberra and by an Australian Research Council Discovery Project grant (DP0210203) received with Robert Tonkinson and Myrna Tonkinson in 2001.

References

Badcock, Christopher. 1990. *Oedipus in Evolution: A New Theory of Sex*. Oxford: Blackwell.

Balakrishnan, V., L. Sanghvi and R. Kirk. 1975. *Genetic Diversity among Australian Aborigines*. Canberra: Australian Institute of Aboriginal Studies.

Berndt, Ronald (ed.). 1970. *Australian Aboriginal Anthropology: Modern Studies in the Anthropology of the Australian Aborigines*. University of Western Australia, Perth: Australian Institute of Aboriginal Studies.

Bloch, Maurice and Dan Sperber. 2002. 'Kinship and evolved psychological dispositions: The mother's brother controversy reconsidered'. *Current Anthropology* 43(5): 723–48. doi.org/10.1086/341654

Brady, Maggie. 1992. *Heavy Metal: The Social Meaning of Petrol Sniffing in Australia*. Canberra: Aboriginal Studies Press.

Buller, David. 2005. *Adapting Minds: Evolutionary Psychology and the Persistent Quest for Human Nature*. Cambridge, MA: MIT Press.

Burbank, Victoria. 1980. 'Expressions of anger and aggression in an Australian Aboriginal community'. PhD thesis, Rutgers University, New Brunswick, NJ.

———. 1988. *Aboriginal Adolescence: Maidenhood in an Australian Community*. New Brunswick, NJ: Rutgers University Press.

———. 1994. *Fighting Women: Anger and Aggression in Aboriginal Australia*. Berkeley: University of California Press.

———. 2006. 'From bedtime to on time: why some Aboriginal people don't especially like participating in western institutions'. *Anthropological Forum* 16(1): 3–20. doi.org/10.1080/00664670600572330

———. 2011. *An Ethnography of Stress: The Social Determinants of Health in Aboriginal Australia*. New York: Palgrave Macmillan. doi.org/10.1057/9780230117228

Burbank, Victoria, Kate Senior and Sue McMullen. 2015. 'Precocious pregnancy: Sexual conflict and early childbearing in remote Aboriginal Australia'. *Anthropological Forum* 25(3): 243–61. doi.org/10.1080/00664677.2015.1027657

Burnstein, Eugene, Christian Crandall and Shinobu Kitayama. 1994. 'Some neo-Darwinian decision rules for altruism: Weighing cues for inclusive fitness as a function of the biological importance of the decision'. *Journal of Personality and Social Psychology* 67(5): 773–89. doi.org/10.1037/0022-3514.67.5.773

Chisholm, James and Victoria Burbank. 1991. 'Monogamy and polygyny in southeast Arnhem Land: Male coercion and female choice'. *Ethology and Sociobiology* 12(4): 291–313. doi.org/10.1016/0162-3095(91)90022-I

Daly, Martin and Margo Wilson. 1982. 'Whom are newborn babies said to resemble'. *Ethology and Sociobiology* 3: 69–78. doi.org/10.1016/0162-3095(82)90002-4

———. 1983. *Sex, Evolution and Behaviour*, 2nd edition. Boston: Willard Grant Press.

Daly, Martin, Margo Wilson and Suzanne Weghorst. 1982. 'Male sexual jealousy'. *Ethology and Sociobiology* 3(1): 11–27. doi.org/10.1016/0162-3095(82)90027-9

D'Andrade, Roy. 1995. *The Development of Cognitive Anthropology*. Cambridge: Cambridge University Press. doi.org/10.1017/CBO9781139166645

DeBruine, Lisa, Finlay Smith, Benedict Jones, S. Roberts, Marion Petrie and Tim Spector. 2009. 'Kin recognition signals in adult faces'. *Vision Research* 49(1): 38–43. doi.org/10.1016/j.visres.2008.09.025

Downey, Greg and Daniel Lende. 2012. 'Neuroanthropology and the encultured brain'. In *The Encultured Brain: An Introduction to Neuroanthropology*, edited by Daniel Lende and Greg Downey, 23–66. Cambridge, MA: MIT Press.

Goody, Esther. 1971. 'Forms of pro-parenthood: The sharing and substitution of parental roles'. In *Kinship* edited by Jack Goody, 331–62. Harmondsworth: Penguin.

Goody, Jack (ed.). 1971. *Kinship*. Harmondsworth: Penguin.

Hamilton, Annette. 1981. *Nature and Nurture: Aboriginal Child-Rearing in North-Central Arnhem Land*. Canberra: Australian Institute of Aboriginal Studies.

Hamilton, William. 1964a. 'Genetic evolution of social behaviour, I'. *Journal of Theoretical Biology* 7(1): 1–16. doi.org/10.1016/0022-5193(64)90038-4

———. 1964b. 'Genetic evolution of social behaviour, II'. *Journal of Theoretical Biology* 7(1): 17–52. doi.org/10.1016/0022-5193(64) 90039-6

Hammerstein, Peter (ed.). 2003. *Genetic and Cultural Evolution of Cooperation*. Cambridge, MA: MIT Press.

Heath, Jeffrey. 1982. *Nunggubuyu Dictionary*. Canberra: Australian Institute of Aboriginal Studies.

Ingold, Tim, David Riches and James Woodburn (eds). 1988. *Hunters and Gatherers: Property, Power and Ideology*, vol. 2. Oxford: Berg.

Lakoff, George and Mark Johnson. 1999. *Philosophy in the Flesh: The Embodied Mind and its Challenge to Western Thought*. New York: Basic Books.

Lende, Daniel and Greg Downey (eds). 2012. *The Encultured Brain: An Introduction to Neuroanthropology*. Cambridge, MA: MIT Press.

Lieberman, Debra, John Tooby and Leda Cosmides. 2007a. 'The architecture of human kin detection'. *Nature* 445 (February): 727–31. doi.org/10.1038/nature05510

———. 2007b. 'The architecture of human kin detection: Supplementary information'. *Nature* 445 (February): 1–10. doi.org/10.1038/nature 05510

McKnight, David. 1986. 'Fighting in an Australian Aboriginal supercamp'. In *The Anthropology of Violence*, edited by David Riches, 137–63. Oxford: Basil Blackwell.

McMullen, Sue. 2014. '"Growing up fast": The sexual and reproductive health of young women in a remote Aboriginal town'. PhD thesis. Charles Darwin University, Darwin.

Musharbash, Yasmine. 2016. 'Evening play: Acquainting toddlers with dangers and fear at Yuendumu'. In *Social Learning and Innovation in Contemporary Hunter-Gatherers*, edited by Hideaki Terashima and Barry Hewlett, 171–78. Tokyo: Springer. doi.org/10.1007/978-4-431-55997-9_14

Myers, Fred. 1986. *Pintupi Country, Pintupi Self: Sentiment, Place, and Politics Among Western Desert Aborigines*. Washington: Smithsonian Institution Press.

———. 1988. 'Burning the truck and holding the country: Property, time, and the negotiation of identity among Pintupi Aborigines'. In *Hunters and Gatherers: Property, Power and Ideology*, vol. 2, edited by Tim Ingold, David Riches and James Woodburn, 52–74. Oxford: Berg.

Nettle, Daniel, Rebecca Coyne and Agathe Colléony. 2012. 'No country for old men: Street use and social diet in urban Newcastle'. *Human Nature* 23(4): 375–85. doi.org/10.1007/s12110-012-9153-9

Park, Justin, Mark Schaller and Mark Van Vugt. 2008. 'Psychology of human kin recognition: Heuristic cues, erroneous inferences, and their implications'. *Review of General Psychology* 12(3): 215–35. doi.org/10.1037/1089-2680.12.3.215

Pinker, Steven. 2003. *The Blank Slate: The Modern Denial of Human Nature*. London: Penguin.

Porter, Richard. 1991. 'Mutual mother-infant recognition in humans'. In *Kin Recognition*, edited by Peter G. Hepper, 413–32. Cambridge: Cambridge University Press. doi.org/10.1017/CBO9780511525414.016

Richerson, Peter and Robert Boyd. 2005. *Not by Genes Alone: How Culture Transformed Human Evolution*. Chicago: University of Chicago Press.

Sahlins, Marshall D. 1976. *The Use and Abuse of Biology: An Anthropological Critique of Sociobiology*. Ann Arbor, MI: The University of Michigan Press.

———. 2013. *What Kinship Is – And Is Not*. Chicago: University of Chicago Press. doi.org/10.7208/chicago/9780226925134.001.0001

Scheffler, Harold W. 1978. *Australian Kin Classification*. Cambridge Studies in Social Anthropology No. 23. Cambridge: Cambridge University Press. doi.org/10.1017/CBO9780511557590

Schneider, David M. 1968. *American Kinship: A Cultural Account*. Englewood Cliffs, NJ: Prentice Hall.

Shapiro, Warren. 1970. 'Local exogamy and the wife's mother in Aboriginal Australia'. In *Australian Aboriginal Anthropology: Modern Studies in the Anthropology of the Australian Aborigines*, edited by Ronald Berndt, 51–69. University of Western Australia, Perth: Australian Institute of Aboriginal Studies.

——. 1979. *Social Organization in Aboriginal Australia*. New York: St. Martin's Press.

——. 2005. 'Universal systems of kin categorization as primitivist projects'. *Anthropological Forum* 15(1): 45–59. doi.org/10.1080/0066467042000336706

——. 2009. *Partible Paternity and Anthropological Theory: The Construction of an Ethnographic Fantasy*. New York: University Press of America.

——. 2012. 'Extensionism and the nature of kinship: Comment'. *Journal of the Royal Anthropological Institute* (n.s.) 18(1): 191–93. doi.org/10.2307/41350814

Shore, Bradd. 1996. *Culture in Mind: Cognition, Culture, and the Problem of Meaning*. Oxford: Oxford University Press.

Silk, Joan. 1980. 'Adoption and kinship in Oceania'. *American Anthropologist* 82(4): 799–820. doi.org/10.1525/aa.1980.82.4.02a00050

——. 1990. 'Human adoption in evolutionary perspective'. *Human Nature* 1(1): 25–52. doi.org/10.1007/BF02692145

Smith, Eric. 2003. 'Human cooperation: Perspectives from behavioral ecology'. In *Genetic and Cultural Evolution of Cooperation*, edited by Peter Hammerstein, 429–44. Cambridge, MA: MIT Press.

Spiro, Melford E. 1993. 'Is the western conception of the self "peculiar" within the context of the world cultures?' *Ethos* 21(2): 107–53. doi.org/10.1525/eth.1993.21.2.02a00010

Terashima, Hideaki and Barry Hewlett (eds). 2016. *Social Learning and Innovation in Contemporary Hunter-Gatherers*. Tokyo: Springer. doi.org/10.1007/978-4-431-55997-9

Tomasello, Michael. 1999. *The Cultural Origins of Human Cognition*. Cambridge, MA: Harvard University Press.

Tomasello, Michael, Malinda Carpenter, Joseph Call, Tanya Behne and Henrike Moll. 2005. 'Understanding and sharing intentions: The origins of cultural cognition'. *Behavioral and Brain Science* 28(5): 675–735. doi.org/10.1017/S0140525X05000129

West, Stuart, Claire El Mouden and Andy Gardner. 2011. 'Sixteen common misconceptions about the evolution of cooperation in humans'. *Evolution and Human Behaviour* 32(4): 231–62. doi.org/10.1016/j.evolhumbehav.2010.08.001

White, N. and P. Parsons. 1973. 'Genetic and socio-cultural differentiation in the Aborigines of Arnhem Land, Australia'. *American Journal of Physical Anthropology* 38(1): 5–14. doi.org/10.1002/ajpa.1330380106

Part IV. Extensionist Theory and Culture History

7

Enhancing the Kinship Anthropology of Scheffler with Diachronic Linguistics and Centricity

Patrick McConvell

Introduction

This chapter is an appreciation of a figure in the anthropology of kinship in general, and particularly of Aboriginal Australia: Hal Scheffler. Scheffler's brilliant work on the formalisation of types of kinship extension and his *Australian Kin Classification* (1978) have been less appreciated by some in the era of 'new kinship studies' but the 'renaissance of kinship' of recent years will certainly restore its currency. Two missing elements in Scheffler's work are the diachronic dimension, and the role of linguistic evidence in reconstructing paths of change: this chapter will show concretely how these elements add to a more complete kinship ethnology. Scheffler's concept of 'extension' and his application of it to Australian Aboriginal kinship remain the foundation for work in kinship change and reconstruction, and dovetail neatly with theories of semantic change via transitional polysemy applied in Australia. However, some types of semantic change in kinship terminology do not fit so easily within the framework. I argue here that these may be more tractable if we recognise variation in pragmatic usage of terms, caused by shifts in centricity (Garde 2013; Merlan 1982) as also leading to change in meaning of terms without such obvious evidence of transitional polysemy.

Extension

The Lounsbury/Scheffler approach

In the work of Scheffler, extension describes a purely synchronic relationship between a focal kin-term meaning and its other 'extended' meanings. In the formalism developed by Floyd Lounsbury and Scheffler, rules take kin-type strings as input and reduce them to the focal kin type. These are often referred to as 'equivalence rules' or 'reduction rules'. They are similar to rewrite rules in early generative phonology and syntax.[1]

Relationships between two or more meanings that are distinguished as different words in some languages, but merged as one in others, are described in various different ways also. The case where the two meanings are represented by one lexical item can be called a 'syncretism', or the word with two distinct senses can be termed 'polysemous'. The notion of 'extension' adds a further element to this by stating that one sense is 'focal' or 'core' and the others are extended from that. There is potential for confusion in that 'extension' can be interpreted as a diachronic process whereby at some point in time another meaning or other meanings are added; or as a notion defined without reference to change over time.[2] This chapter aims to distinguish and clarify this ambiguity for the realm of kinship terminology at least.

David Kronenfeld (1996) gives a summary of work in an extensionist framework and its advantages over a 'conjunctivist' approach such as componential semantics. He particularly focuses on kinship analysis including his own work on Fanti (2009), which uses a slight modification of the Lounsbury–Scheffler framework, enabling use of both reduction and expansion rules. He presents some examples of how the Lounsbury

---

1 Vladimir Pericliev (2013: 15–20) describes Lounsbury's extensionist approach and other theories that have built on componential semantics. He notes (2013: 16) that the extensionist approach to kinship in anthropology goes back to Bronisław Malinowski's (1929: 525–26) idea that children first acquire the terms for elementary relationships like 'mother', 'sister' then extend them to more distant relationships to form a classificatory system. It is incorrect that the extensionism of Lounsbury and Scheffler truly relies on componentialism in defining the basic elements of kinship strings: rather they arise from relative products of elements like 'mother', 'sister' etc. (see Kronenfeld 1996: 155).
2 'Extension' has a different meaning in the philosophy of language and often in linguistic semantics, where it is contrasted with 'intension' as two ways of defining the meaning of a word. In this sense 'extension' involves a listing of the referents of a word, while 'intension' defines the word in terms of some combination of concepts drawn from a semantic metalanguage. In this theoretical discourse, therefore, the 'extension' being discussed in this chapter is a variety of intensional definition. While this is confusing, it would be more confusing to change the theoretical terminology at this point.

approach handles Crow skewing (Figures 17–19; Lounsbury 1964).[3] Skewing is a form of extension in which members of adjacent generations are referred to by the same term. In order to describe skewing accurately, it is necessary to combine the actual skewing rule with other rules that are of more general applicability also in systems without skewing such as Merging (Figure 17), which is the rule that plays a part in defining, for instance, Bifurcate Merging systems.

Lounsbury's reduction rules for Crow-type kinship terminologies: Merging rule

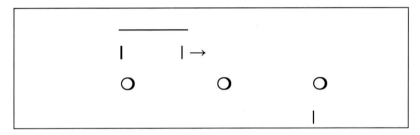

Figure 17. Somebody's mother's sister is equivalent to that somebody's mother, and reciprocally, some woman's sister's descendant is equivalent to that woman's own descendant
Source: Adapted from Kronenfeld (1996: 156, Figure 9.1) and used with permission.

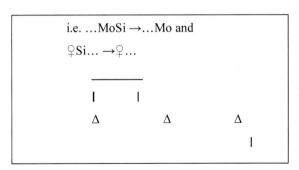

Figure 18. Somebody's father's brother is equivalent to that somebody's father, and reciprocally, some man's brother's descendant is equivalent to that man's own descendant
Source: Adapted from Kronenfeld (1996: 156, Figure 9.1) and used with permission.

---

3   The original notation of Lounsbury is used here. Elsewhere in this chapter, the kin abbreviations are changed from e.g. MoSi to MZ for 'mother's sister' etc. as used in the AustKin project.

FOCALITY AND EXTENSION IN KINSHIP

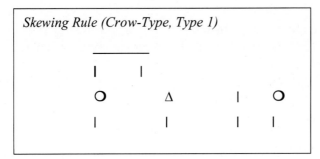

Figure 19. Somebody's mother's brother's child is equivalent to that somebody's own brother's child, and reciprocally, somebody's father's sister's child is equivalent to that somebody's father's sibling
Source: Adapted from Kronenfeld (1996: 156, Figure 9.1) and used with permission.

The extension rules can be classified into a small number of types. Such rules working together in constrained combinations can define the range of kinship systems that are known in world societies.

Extension rule types: Scheffler on Australia

Scheffler took on a major challenge in dealing with the range of Australian kinship systems in terms of the extensionist formalism in his *Australian Kinship Classification* (1978). The seeds of extensionism were present in A.R. Radcliffe-Brown but Scheffler went beyond the Radcliffe-Brown typology (1930–31), which had been dominant until that time.

Many found the prose of this book and the kinds of formal rules, as in the following example (Scheffler 1978: 145), dense and difficult.

Example of equivalence rules for a 'Kariera' system from Scheffler

Equivalence rules in Mari'ngar kin classification:

1. Half-sibling-merging rule
   (PC→Sb), self-reciprocal
2. Stepkin-merging rule
   (PSp→P) = (SpC →C)
3. Same-sex sibling-merging rule
   (...m/wSb // → m/w) = (m/wSb//... → m/w...)

4. Parallel-cross neutralisation rule
(FZ. → FB.) = (.wBC →.mBC)
(MB.→ MZ.) = (.mZC→.wZC)
5. Parallel-cross status extension rule
(FFSbxC→MSb) = (PSbxSC →ZC) (1978: 145, Table 4.4)

Nevertheless, the idea of extension and equivalence rules captured well the polysemies in these classificatory systems and the variations between the different systems in different groups. Others, including me, have tried to use the essential insights of these schemes to come up with more general and simplified schemes such as shown in Table 2.[4]

Table 2. Common equations and paths of semantic change in Australian kinship terms

Code	Name	Equation (example)	System type	Sheffler number: pp.	Scheffler name
A	Merger within parallel and within cross	FF = MMB ≠ MF = FMB	'Kariera'	5: 226	Parallel-cross status – extension
B	Merger of same gender	FF = MF ≠ MM = FM	'Aluridja'	4: 226	Parallel-cross neutralisation
C	Skewing (adjacent generation)	e.g. Omaha, mother = cross-cousin etc	'Ngarinyin'	5: 404	Omaha skewing
D	Alternate generation equivalence	sibling = parallel grandparent; cross-cousin = cross-grandparent		7: 226; 376	AGA
E	Consanguineal-affinal	FZ = WM		8: 226	Spouse-equation
F	Merger of opposite-sex siblings	MM = MMB			

Source: McConvell (2013c: 156).

---

4 The table has been slightly altered from the published version. AGA (Alternate Generation Agnatic) was included in the publication but not AGU (Alternate Generation Uterine).

Change in kinship

Extension in change

This 'extension' can, I propose, also be extended to describe diachronic change in kinship terms, which I shall call 'extension change'. The addition of the Omaha-skewing rule (Code C in Table 2) can, for instance, add the meaning MBS to a term meaning MB, and MBD to a term meaning M. Subsequently the original meaning may be lost in some languages. By hypothesis the change is unidirectional because the extension is from for instance MB to MBC, not the reverse. This is in fact what we find in all cases in Australia, based on linguistic evidence (McConvell and Alpher 2003; McConvell 2013b).

Similarly, other equivalences in Table 2 have their counterparts in diachronic change. For instance, D, Alternate Generation Equivalence, provides for the same term being used for grandparents and siblings or cousins, on a synchronic plane. There are also examples of words meaning parallel grandparent in some languages and siblings in others, for instance the widespread term *kaku* in Australia. By hypothesis this results from a transitional polysemy of this type in which only one meaning survives. This diachronic extension may or may not exhibit a fixed directionality of change: further research is needed to establish this empirically, for instance to determine which is the earlier meaning of *kaku* in Pama–Nyungan— elder sibling or father's father.[5]

'Transitional polysemy' mentioned above is therefore the stage in a change process in which two senses of a kinship term are found together in one language at one time. Figure 20 is the general form of the process, with stage 2 being the stage of transitional polysemy. An actual example is given of the change in *kaala due to Omaha skewing.

Stages:	1	2	3
Senses:	A	A + B	B
Example:	*kaala* 'MB'	*kaala* 'MB + MBC'	*kalay* MBC
	N. E. Qld.	N.W. Qld.	Yolngu

Figure 20. Transitional polysemy
Source: McConvell (2013b: 253–54).

---

5   *Kaku* for instance turns up as eB in Gumbaynggirr, on the north coast of New South Wales.

The following sections take a look at the relationship between extension and history in two North American language families, before discussing the relationship between extension as synchronic overlay and diachronic change in general, then returning to discussion of Australia.

Whistler on Wintun

1. Half-sibling merging rule		
(PC→ Sb) → Sb	self-reciprocal	
2. Parallel sibling merging rules		
(♂B. Pa♂...) ≈ (...♂B → ...♂)	all	
(♀Zll ...♀...) ≈ (...♀Z → ...♀)	WPR, WPH, WHHPas, WWMay2, WM	
(♂B+... → (♂...)+) ≈ (...♂B- → (...♂)-)	WWSac, WWMc	
(♀Z+... → (♀...)+) ≈ (...♀Z- → (...♀)-)		
3. Skewing rules affecting cross-collateral kin		
3A. Skewing rules affecting FZ etc.		
	• Type II Omaha Skewing rule	
3A.	(FZ. → Z+) ≈ (♀BC . ♀SB-)	WPR, WPH, WHHPas
	• Paternal cross-aunt merging rule	
3Ate	(FZ. → MBW.) ≈ (.♀BC → .HZC)	WWMay, WWMc (Gifford)
	(FZH. → MB.) ≈ (.♂WBC → .HZC)	
	• Cross-nuncle merging rule	
3Aoss	(PxSb → PP.) ≈ (.♂/♀xSbC) → PP♂/♀CC)	WWSac, WWMc (DuBois)
	(PxSbSp → PP.) ≈ (.♂/♀SpxSbC) → PP♂/♀CC)	
3B. Skewing rules affecting cross-cousins etc.		
	• Type III Omaha skewing rule	
3B.	(♂Z(.→(♂D...) ≈ (...♀B → ...♀F)	WPR, WPH,WHHPas, WWMay, WWMc (Gifford)

Figure 21. Extension in change: Whistler on Wintun
Source: Created by Patrick McConvell from information in Whistler (1980: 284).

The extensionist theory of Lounsbury and Scheffler has only rarely been applied to diachronic change. One example is the work of Ken Whistler in his PhD dissertation (1980) on Wintun kinship reconstruction (California). In Figure 21, the Lounsbury-style rules are listed on the left by name, then in the middle column the equivalence rules are stated formally. In the right-hand column are abbreviations for the languages or dialects in which each of the rule variants is found (Whistler 1980: 284).

The most important area of variation in equivalence relates to the skewing rules. These are all of 'Omaha' type but differ from the Omaha Type I found most generally in Australia (McConvell 2013b).

George Murdock (1949) proposed a prehistoric development of kinship systems in Wintu based on an evolution set out in Figure 22. This is what Whistler calls a 'non-lexical reconstruction'—it does not take account of the form of kinship terms. By contrast Whistler's (1980: 347) reconstruction in Figure 22 is based on lexical evidence, and on this basis Murdock's proposal can be shown to be false. Whistler's reconstruction (Figure 23) of the development of different types of Omaha skewing traces its stages through a phylogeny of Wintu languages.

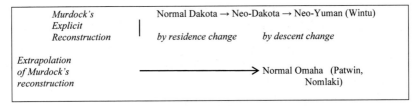

Figure 22. Murdock on Wintun kinship system reconstruction
Source: Created by Patrick McConvell from information in Whistler (1980: 345).

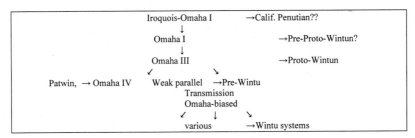

Figure 23. Whistler vs. Murdock on Wintun kinship system reconstruction
Source: Created by Patrick McConvell from information in Whistler (1980: 347).

Both Omaha and Crow skewing are found more widely in California, outside the Wintuan family. The combination of Omaha and Crow that Whistler calls 'parallel transmission' is found only in some of Northern Wintuan and is reconstructed back to pre-Wintuan by Whistler. With cautious queries Whistler roots the tree in a putative macrofamily of Californian Penutian.[6]

---

6   While evidence for Penutian seems to have grown since 1980, doubts linger over membership of Wintuan specifically, with suggestions that Wintuan is an independent intrusion from Oregon in the north.

This leaves intriguing questions about whether kinship system prehistory can be tied to proto-language stages or may involve areal groupings resulting from diffusion, or as I have proposed, from the type of migration involved (McConvell 2013b).

Change, variation and overlays

Kronenfeld: Stable core and unstable extensions

Kronenfeld (1996, cf. more general comments on change in Kronenfeld 2013) also touches on the themes of this chapter—diachrony and the contribution of historical linguistics—in a brief reference to Morgan's foundational comparative work in North America. He introduces an important hypothesis here, that 'core' meanings of terms are stable, but extensions are variable and unstable. As far as I know this has not been rigorously tested, but a number of the examples used in this chapter could be mustered to do this. His example is quite apposite for some of the material to be discussed, since it is about variation with a subgroup in North America that contains the Crow and Omaha people from whom the skewing patterns of the two types were named, as well as groups without skewing.

> When one examines data on kin terminologies for a large number of related languages and cultures—as is assembled, for example, in Morgan's data on the Dakota Indian groups (within his Ganowanian 'family' [1871: Table—Appendix to Part II, pp. 281–382])—the following facts emerge … if we use the full (that is, extended) range of referents (denotata) of these terms to infer their signifieds (related to their significata) we find a very bad match, since the languages show very different patterns of extension. Some of the languages have patrilineally skewed Omaha-type terminologies; some have matrilineally skewed Crow-type terminologies; and some have unskewed Iroquois-type terminologies. Indeed, the actual Omaha Indians and Crow Indians, for whom the two opposed types of skewing are named, are closely related members of a Dakota subgroup that also includes the Yankton and Oglalla Dakota (Sioux) Indians, who have unskewed terminologies. However, contrary to the picture we get for extended ranges, when we limit our comparison to kernel or focal kintype referents we find an extremely good match across the whole Dakota group …

Since the languages involved are fairly closely related, we know that they have each relatively recently developed out of a single, common ancestral language. The period of time involved has not been sufficient for the terminological labels (signifiers) or the focal referents (pointed to by the signifieds linked to each of these signifiers) to drift very far apart. But that same period of time has been quite adequate for great changes to occur in the extended ranges and thus in the extension operations (or rules) that produce these ranges (that is, extend them from the kernels). Thus we have diachronically based comparative data that supports the same contrast between relatively fixed, constant focal referents and more variable extended ranges that we found synchronically within the single Fanti system (Kronenfeld 1996: 164).

Kronenfeld on synchronic variability

This passage should be read in close association with Kronenfeld's other comments on synchronic variability. In Fanti, he identifies three types of patterning of kinship terminology in use in the community:

1. The 'courtesy' pattern: some terms are used to recognise relative age without genealogical specification.
2. The 'unskewed' pattern is restricted to actual kin, and includes more genealogical information on generation, relative age, gender and side of the family.
3. The 'skewed' pattern is most marked and is distinguished from 'unskewed' by the addition of a Crow-type skewing rule to the set of extension rules; Fanti say that the equation of 'mother's brother' and 'sister's son' exists because of inheritance by the latter from the former (1996: 161).

While there are factors which tend to induce one or other of these patterns to be used, he stresses that these are not unbreakable social rules but leave some role for individual choice and agency. He gives an enlightening example:

> In terms of usage and communication—Saussure's parole—we note that the use of particular patterns of extension is not limited to the social contexts that occasion them, but rather that every pattern is available at all times … Within a given conversation, different speakers may use terms from different extension patterns—that is, may use terms nonreciprocally—even if the one person's usage becomes part of the context for the other person's choice of term.

Thus the terminology with its variant forms as a part of *langue* provides sets of regularities, that is, patterns, which speakers are free to use as suits their purposes. This point was brought home to me when I observed a pair of Fanti cross-cousins nonreciprocally addressing each other—as 'father' in one direction, and as 'brother' in the other (see Kronenfeld 1970: 104–07). I knew from other interviews with them that both men knew (and stated) that the 'correct' reciprocal of 'father' was 'child' and of 'brother' was 'brother'; thus the usage I observed did not result from any lack of awareness of the pattern or from any resistance to it. Further investigation revealed that since they were close kin they felt they had to use kinterms in genealogically correct forms, instead of the nongenealogical mode of the courtesy pattern; such genealogically correct usage also emphasized the genealogical link, which, I gather, they wanted to do. At the same time, since they liked and respected each other, each man was anxious to show the other as much respect as he could—and so each man, in addressing the other, picked the highest status term out of the set available to him for that genealogical position. Thus, one man picked 'father' (from the skewed extension pattern) over 'brother' (from the unskewed pattern), while the other man picked 'brother' (from the unskewed pattern) over 'son' (from the skewed pattern). Their goal in this conversation was not to be correct, but to communicate their messages as effectively as possible with the resources that their language afforded them (Kronenfeld 1996: 162–63).

While this kind of flexibility is valuable in providing a means of sending subtle social messages to conversation participants and audiences, it may have a cost in the stability of the overall system (Kronenfeld 2013: 35). Children may reinterpret a system if its performance does not provide enough evidence for how it is operating to the children at the time when they are acquiring it.

It seems quite likely that such intergenerational mismatches lie behind the changes that I am discussing in this chapter. However, we do not in most cases have direct evidence of the social mechanisms of processes of change that may have occurred hundreds or thousands of years ago in such places as precolonial Australia or North America. We can know what happened, especially because of the evidence of historical linguistics, but finding out how it happened in social terms is more difficult.

Hypothesis that all changes are explained by extension

This chapter proposes a strong hypothesis that all diachronic changes in kin-term meanings in Australia can be explained as addition of, or loss of, reduction rules as formulated by Scheffler, or minor variations or sequential combinations of them. The ideas of Kronenfeld about contextual variation and overlays (section above) in extension patterns are also crucial in explaining transitions in kinship system change in Australia.

In the next section, examples of sequences of kinship system change that conform to this hypothesis in Australia are presented, introduced by an overview of the database tool we use to provide evidence, AustKin.

In the section following the next, examples are raised that do not conform to the hypothesis that all diachronic change in kin-term meanings results from extension. Possible reasons for such exceptions include altercentricity, such as filiocentricity.

Australian examples of semantic variation and change

The Austkin database

The kinship terminology data in this paper is obtained by standard linguistic comparison of forms of kinship terms across regions, and the whole of Australia, using the database AustKin (Dousset et al. 2010; McConvell and Dousset 2012). The searches used include equivalences (e.g. where does the word for MB also mean MBS?) and for forms of words (e.g. where is the form *kaala/kala+* found and what is its meaning?). These and other combinations and customised results can be matched and mapped using Google Earth, AustLang (ANU/AIATSIS) or other GIS programs.

Omaha skewing and asymmetry

Omaha skewing is a form of extension that has led to an extension change in Australia several times with different kinship-term forms. Figure 24 illustrates how the sequence plays out, beginning with 'overlay' skewing in which the skewed forms for MBS may only occur optionally or in particular context. In the next stage skewing may solidify so that the extension (MB to MBS, MBD in this example is always used) followed by loss of the form for the original meaning. We do not go into how this last stage happens in detail. In Yolngu Matha for instance, in most dialects a loanword has been brought in from a non-Pama–Nyungan neighbour, *ngapipi* for the meaning MB.

			→
MB	MB	MB	MB
MBS	MBS MBS	MBS	MBS
No skewing	Overlay skewing	Full skewing	Shift to skewed meaning
Two separate items	MB used for MBS under some conditions	MB used for MBS unconditionally	Original MB term replaced

Figure 24. A diachronic sequence of Omaha skewing in Australia
Source: McConvell (2013b: 253–54).

Figure 25 shows where reflexes of the term *kaala, originally MB in proto-Pama–Nyungan,[7] occur in Australia. The original meaning MB is found in northeast Queensland and there are some instances of skewing of this term to MBS or MBS in this area also. The unskewed meaning is also found in southeast Queensland, but other than that the meaning has changed; in the west (including Yolngu) and south, the skewed meaning (MBS, MBC) only is found.[8]

The diachronic interpretation is that skewing began in the northeast but as the term spread out to the west and south, with the expansion of Pama–Nyungan, the skewed meaning took over for the *kaala* reflexes and the MB meaning was lost (replaced by other forms).

In some cases the meanings of the skewed (cross-cousin) reflexes of the root have either the extension of spouse or some sibling-in-law or have changed completely to the affinal meaning. This type of extension is acknowledged by Scheffler as 'spouse-equation' and assigned Type E

---

7 Pama–Nyungan is by far the largest language family in Australia covering most of the continent except for the Central North. Yolngu Matha is an outlier of Pama–Nyungan surrounded by non-Pama–Nyungan languages in Northeast Arnhem Land.
8 In northern New South Wales between the areas of nonskewed meanings to the north and skewed meanings to the south, there is a case of active skewing in Gumbaynggirr (Morelli 2008). This involves the root *kawa* (probably cognate with *kaala (MB extended (as a contextual overlay) to MBC).

in Table 2. This provides an indication that either in the present or at some stage in history (some type of) cross-cousin was a marital partner, although marriage rules may have changed since that time.

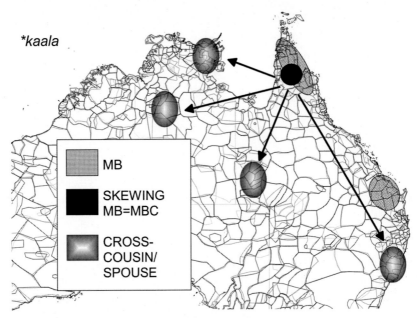

Figure 25. *Kaala* MB > Cross-cousin/spouse
Source: McConvell (2013b: 254). Mapping from AustKin © Patrick McConvell and William McConvell.

The Omaha extension has a corollary. Seen from the other end of the extension the female's child or sister's child extends up a generation, to mean father's sister's child (patrilateral cross-cousin). This too has a diachronic extension change. In the case of *kaala*, the corollary is found with *tyuwa+ proto-Pama–Nyungan for female's child. The pattern of spread and change in meaning of this root is quite similar to that of *kaala and is shown in Figure 26.

Again the original meaning (fC) is found in northeast Queensland, with skewing to FZC found in some languages, and to an extent south of there in Queensland. Other western attestations have changed to the skewed meaning FZC, as in Yolngu, which also has the meaning of husband (and his siblings) in the unilateral marriage system there. In the far west, cognate forms mean the affinal kin types HZ and BW, derived by the affinal extension change from the intermediate cross-cousin meaning.

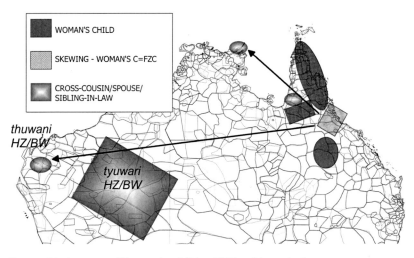

Figure 26. *tyuwa+: Woman's child > FZC > Sister-in-law
Source: McConvell (2013b: 255). Mapping from AustKin © Patrick McConvell and William McConvell.

Loss of cross-parallel distinctions

Another important type of extension change is the loss of cross-parallel distinctions, called 'parallel-cross neutralisation' by Scheffler, and listed as Type (Code) B in Table 2. This was a type of change which was proposed by the first scholars to work on Australian kinship, Fison and Howitt, in their book *Kamilaroi and Kurnai* (1880). The latter group, in Gippsland, Victoria, was notably different from the Kamilaroi and other groups known to them, because the Kurnai called their cross-cousins 'siblings', not some distinctive term. This is an example of cross-parallel neutralisation in the zero generation, but among the Kurnai this did not extend to other generations like the grandparents. This kind of restriction of cross-parallel neutralisation to the zero generation rather than the 'Hawaiian' system where there are no cross-parallel distinctions in any generation, is not uncommon world-wide: Gertrude Dole called it 'bifurcate generational' (1969: 118).[9]

---

9   Fison and Howitt did not have linguistic or convincing ethnological evidence of this direction of change in Gippsland but relied on assumptions that the Dravidianate systems elsewhere must have been primordial on the one hand, and a highly speculative story of how people arrived in Gippsland on the other (Fison and Howitt 1880; Gardner and McConvell 2015). Intriguingly, Lorimer Fison later rejected his own story about this, claiming that he had received 'new evidence'—but there is no account of this evidence (Fison 1892).

In the Western Desert, the so-called 'Aluridja' system also features cross-parallel neutralisation in the zero generation, but as Laurent Dousset (2003) has shown, it is actually a contextual overlay used to talk about people who are not marriageable, and this often depends on the state of relations between groups, not hard and fast rules. This kind of division of cross-cousins into the unmarriageable 'siblings' and the marriageable classificatory cross-cousins is found in other groups. Among the Kija the latter group are *thamany*- MF('s siblings). It may be though that for other groups like the Kurnai, this was once a transitional stage but then the naming of cross-cousin 'siblings' became categorical.[10]

The Western Desert (unusually for Australia) also has cross-parallel neutralisation in the +2 or grandparental generation, such that there is a term *tyamu*, which is like English 'grandfather' in referring to both maternal MF and paternal FF; and *kami* (and *kaparli* in different dialects) like English 'grandmother' referring to both maternal MM and paternal FM.

Omaha skewing, discussed earlier, seems to correlate with what I have called 'encroaching or downstream spread' and loss of cross-parallel distinctions with 'skirting or upstream spread'. Details of why these correlations are present still need to be worked out (McConvell 2013b).

Cross-parallel distinctions in grandparent terminology are also lost under apparently similar circumstances yielding grandfather/grandmother systems from systems which distinguished FF and MF and FM from MM, for example in the Chiracahua variety of Apachean (Dyen and Aberle 1974), and inland Northern Athapaskan (Ives 1998), as well as in the 'Aluridja' system of the Australian Western Desert. The restricted distribution of this kind of system in Australia can be seen in Figure 27.[11]

---

10   This kind of change does not seem to move on to a stage when the original meaning of the term is lost, as far as I know. That would mean that an original term meaning 'sibling' came to mean 'cross-cousin' only. Preliminary investigation does not reveal any such pathways.
11   It is also found to some extent in the Bandjalangic languages of the eastern Queensland–New South Wales border.

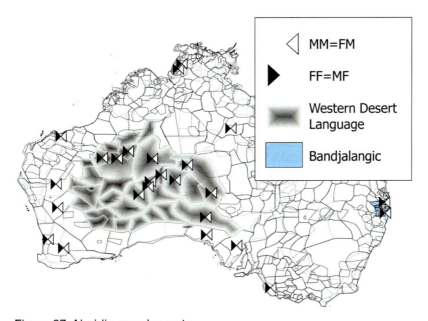

Figure 27. Aluridja grandparents
Source: Mapping from AustKin © Patrick McConvell and William McConvell.

Thanks to linguistic reconstruction we can be sure of the original sources in the proto-Pama–Nyungan or some high-level proto-language within Pama–Nyungan.

Tyamu clearly derived from an old Pama–Nyungan root meaning MF (McConvell 2013a) so was extended to FF in the Western Desert. In particular, *tyamu* or related forms are found in the Pilbara languages north of the Western Desert. The region where both icons are found for the same languages are where there is MF = FF, and MM = FM, which is roughly conterminous with the Western Desert (see Figure 28).

Kami is found in a wide area of Pama–Nyungan, including in the eastern states, in the meaning MM and can be reconstructed as MM, so must have been extended to FM in the Western Desert.[12] Similarly *kaparli* is found widespread as FM and must have been extended to MM (see Figure 29). The region where both icons are found for the same languages are where there is MM = FM, and is roughly conterminous with the Western Desert.

---

12 There is an area in Lake Eyre Basin where *kami* means FM, but this is clearly an innovation (McConvell 2013c) and is unrelated to the Western Desert change.

FOCALITY AND EXTENSION IN KINSHIP

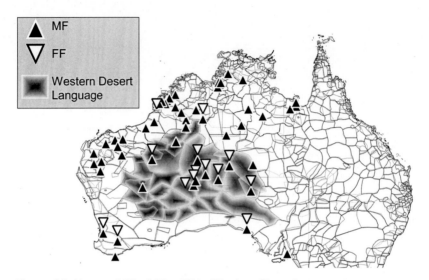

Figure 28. *tyamu MF > MF + FF in Western Desert
Source: Mapping from AustKin © Patrick McConvell and William McConvell.

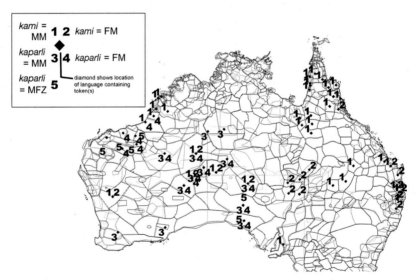

Figure 29. *Kami* and *Kaparli*
Source: Mapping from AustKin © Patrick McConvell and William McConvell.

Figure 30 shows how the extensions of grandparental terms occurred historically in the Western Desert. A hypothesis that the change went in the opposite direction would be completely implausible.

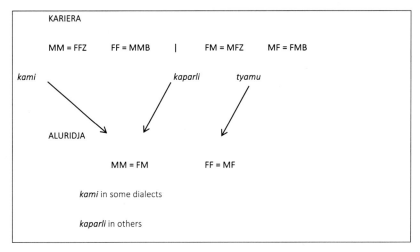

Figure 30. Kariera to Aluridja
Source: Drawn by © Patrick McConvell, 2017.

Cases not covered by the hypothesis

Introduction

This hypothesis, that changes in kinship meaning result from Schefflerian extensions that are found in transitional polysemies, stands up fairly well. But there are a number of cases where change of meaning of a term is evident but which cannot be explained in terms of Scheffler's proposed extension rules, and/or do not display evidence of the classic pattern of transitional polysemy.

Two types of change are noted here that do not display the classic pattern of transitional polysemy:

1. change of gender of +1 (parental) generation terms, affines or with affinal equivalences, and
2. change of one generation down, from sibling to child, unrelated to any known skewing pattern.

Change of gender of +1 (parental/affinal) generation terms

There is a term which began as *ramparr* in the North Kimberley region of Western Australia, diffused southwest, then, changing to *lamparr* due to a regular sound change, diffused west across the south Kimberley and a long distance into the Northern Territory (McConvell 2015).

The most problematic part of the history of *ramparr* is the change of the term from mother-in-law and her brother in west Worrorran and eastern Nyulnyulan to father-in-law in eastern Nyulnyulan. While these meanings both refer to parents-in-law, the change from WM(B) to WF is unexpected. Significantly, a change from mother-in-law to father-in-law apparently represents a contravention of a principle of transitional polysemy in semantic change set forth by Nicholas Evans and David Wilkins (2001) that I further developed in relation to kinship terms (McConvell 2013a). While many changes in kinship-term meanings do show these properties of transitional polysemy in Australia, there is doubt about whether mother-in-law and father-in-law share the same term anywhere, even in any of the Kimberley languages under discussion.

However, in this case, as we have noted, in its early history the term *ramparr* has a wider meaning of an avoidance relationship which encompassed several types of in-laws who may also be designated by more specific kinship terms, probably emerging from an original concrete meaning of 'barrier' extended metaphorically (McConvell 2015). This may be then a case of a term in which there is what we might call hypopolysemy. That is, one of two meanings involved is broader and includes the other narrower meaning. This is common as a synchronic pattern in fauna terms in Australia and also explains a semantic shift from the generic term for a life form to a species term or vice versa (McConvell 1997).

There is at least one more fairly clear case in Australian kinship where a similar change has happened. In Cape York Peninsula (Paman subgroup of Pama–Nyungan) the term *mukVr means 'mother's brother', but in the rest of the country where cognates of the term are found (mainly in Pama–Nyungan) it means 'father's sister and/or wife's mother' (McConvell and Keen 2011). Where the primary meanings of the terms seem to be consanguineal, they also both have affinal senses deriving from the rules of marriage: the equation FZ = WM is quite widely distributed in Australia especially where there is or was a Kariera system and cross-cousin marriage. The common ground between MB (WF) and FZ (WM) could be their key role as decision-makers about their daughter's marriage.[13]

Change of one generation down, from sibling to child

Another different kind of example that does not conform to what the hypothesis predicts is a change of the term *katya* from 'brother' quite generally, to 'son' in the Western Desert and neighbouring regions. Unlike the standard extension cases there appears to be nowhere where the term means both 'brother' and 'son'—but see the next section for a possible example of a parallel change in a root that gives insight into the process involved.

Figure 31 shows the distribution of forms cognate with *katya* in Australia. In Western Australia, the forms in the north in the Pilbara in the Ngayardic, Kanyara and Mantharda subgroups of Pama–Nyungan have the meaning 'elder brother'. Most of these have the form *katya* but some have *kaya* in languages in which there is a regular sound change of medial lenition *ty > y. South of there in the Wati (Western Desert) and Kartu subgroups, the form means 'son', with a couple of instances on the periphery where it is extended also to 'daughter'.[14]

There are a number of other instances of *katya* meaning 'elder brother' in eastern Pama–Nyungan subgroups which, taken together with the western distribution, open up the possibility that this is a proto-Pama–Nyungan form in this meaning. This reinforces the idea that 'elder brother' is the earlier meaning and the meaning 'son' or 'child' is the innovation in the Wati-Kartu subgroup.

---

13 However, unlike in the case of earlier broad meanings of *ramparr* that refer to a range of affines who have a hand in marriage decisions, there is no similar evidence to hand so far with regard to *mukr.
14 In a Nyungar dialect Minang, the form *kotya*, presumably cognate, means 'elder brother'. Unlike some other instances of *katya* in the Western Desert periphery, which are loans from Western Desert, this points to the 'elder brother' meaning being present in south-western as well as eastern Australia. Forms like *katyakatya* for 'child' are found areally around the southern Gulf of Carpentaria, but this may have a different etymology. Similarly, *kaathu* is 'man's child' in Yolngu Matha, but its cognacy with *katya elsewhere cannot be guaranteed.

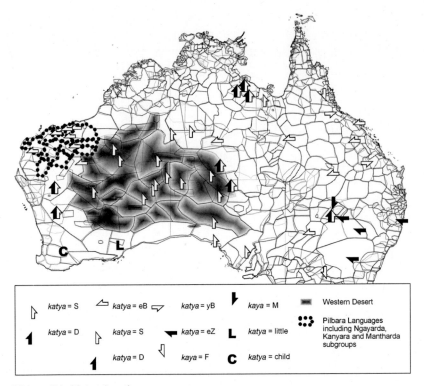

Figure 31. *Katya* brother > son
Source: Mapping from AustKin © Patrick McConvell and William McConvell.

In our extensive survey of kinship terms in AustKin, in no case does the reflex of *katya have both senses 'elder brother' and 'son/child' in the same language. This differs from the cases where there is such 'transitional polysemy' discussed above. Another difference is that while the earlier examples can be related to extensions proposed by Scheffler or similar, there is no known extension of 'elder brother' to 'son' discussed in the literature. This is a relationship between two adjacent generations but not any of the types of skewing have been analysed.

We now move on to examine what can be the cause of this meaning change if it is not related to standard types of extension. Other apparent examples of change from 'brother' to 'son/child' in Australia are then scrutinised for clues about the underpinnings of this process.

Altercentricity – filiocentricity

Altercentricity is a term usually used for where there is no propositus indicated (e.g. Where is Mum?) and where the propositus as pragmatically inferred is other than the speaker, for instance 'your' (e.g. Mum in the example is taken to be 'your mother').

Such pragmatic inference is commonly found in languages around the world. Francesca Merlan (1982, 1989), however, looked into whether there are general principles that predict whether such interpretation is egocentric or altercentric for the Australian Aboriginal language Mangarrayi. She proposes the Juniority–Seniority Principle:

> A senior speaker, in talking to a junior relative (especially a young child), tends to refer to third persons in terms of the junior's relationship to them.

> A junior person (again the norms are clearer where this is a young child) in speaking to a senior relative tends to refer to others in terms of his own relationship to them (Merlan 1982: 127–28)

Murray Garde confirms the general validity of this principle in Western Arnhem Land. In other words, children addressing senior relatives speak egocentrically in referencing others, and senior kin reply to them using altercentric terms, for example, (child to father) 'Where is Mum?' (father to child) 'Mum is in the garden' (Garde 2013: 119). This is not unfamiliar to speakers of English and many other languages around the world (see Agha 2007: 350, 63).

Filiocentricity is the resulting pattern where the term used converges on the form used to and by the child *in a parent-child dyad*. This is therefore a term used in a narrower sense than the term *teknocentricity*, which refers to a more general use of terms from the point of view of children in a wider grouping, say a whole family group. The particular type of historical shift between sibling and child meanings discussed here is related to the narrower type—filiocentricity. Whether there are other change phenomena related to the broader scope of teknocentricity is not investigated here.

In Garde's data from Bininy Gunwok (again not unfamiliar from many other languages), address (vocative) kin terms can be used as referential too (Garde 2013: 51, reporting a telephone conversation).

> Child: Ngudda ngabba?
> 2sg father VOC
> Is that you, Dad?

> DjNg: Yoh.
> Yes.

> Child: [to others] Ngabba … ngabba Manawukan
> F.VOC F.VOC [place]
> It's Dad, Dad in Maningrida

How does this relate to our problem of explaining the change of *katya* 'elder brother' to 'son' in the Western Desert? One possibility is that this change is mediated by a pragmatic context of 'filiocentricity', that is fathers, or more generally parents, were using the 'brother' term to their children to mean 'your brother/my son' and the main sense of the word became 'son'.

Robust reconstructions of the changes in meanings of kinship terms can be proposed based on linguistics. Most of these changes are diachronic versions of Schefflerian extensions. They involve transitional polysemies (equivalences).

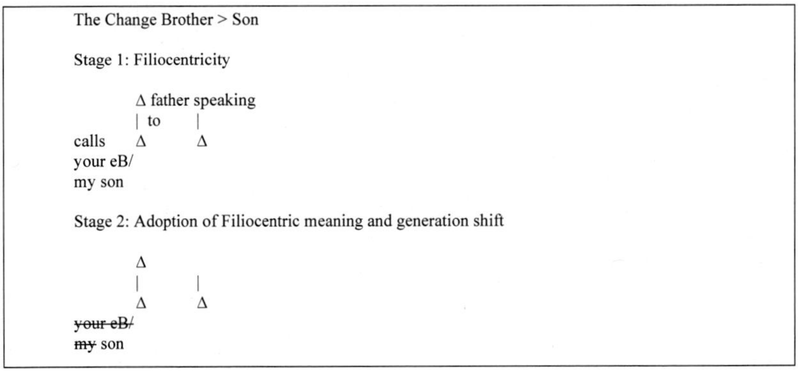

The Change Brother > Son

Stage 1: Filiocentricity

```
            Δ father speaking
            |  to   |
calls    Δ        Δ
your eB/
my son
```

Stage 2: Adoption of Filiocentric meaning and generation shift

```
            Δ
            |       |
            Δ       Δ
your eB/
my son
```
(with "your eB/" and "my" struck through)

Figure 32. The change brother > son
Source: Constructed by © Patrick McConvell, 2017.

However, filiocentric changes such as the one found in *katya* 'brother' > 'son' do not show the same kind of transitional equivalences. The two senses of the term that is changing are not found as alternatives in the same language in the intermediate stage in the same way. Rather, I propose that the source of the split is in the centricity of the term's use. This may be 'shifting' (Garde 2013) and the diachronic consequence of this may be a loss of the original meaning and replacement by a meaning associated with filiocentricity. The hypothesised process is shown in Figure 32.

The term for 'elder brother' in Western Desert was *kurta* subsequent to this change. This term is also found throughout the Pilbara mainly for 'elder brother' but occasionally for 'younger brother'. In those languages that have both *katya* and *kurta* in the meaning eB it would be useful to establish if there is or was a semantic difference or if there is a pragmatic difference of the two which contributed to the meaning change in *katya*.

There is one piece of evidence in a Western Desert language that may be relevant to this transition of *katya*, although it relates to *kurta*, the current word for eB. The Pintupi dictionary gives the phrase *kutyu kurta*, literally 'one elder-brother', as meaning 'oldest son' (Hansen and Hansen 1992: 43). This is taking a filiocentric view of relative age among brothers.

Brother > son elsewhere in Australia

There are a number of indicators that the kind of change from brother to son described in the last section for Western Desert is not alone of its kind in Australia. While the notes below on these other cases (drawn from the AustKin database) are of a preliminary nature, they do tend to support the idea that this is not an anomalous exception but part of a more general phenomenon.

In southeast Queensland the term *tyatya* is recorded as eB in a number of Waka-Kabi languages, with probable cognates elsewhere in southeast Australia. Nils Holmer (1983: 147–59) records the meaning 'son' in a Kabi language Gubbi-gubbi.

In Paman languages of northern Queensland, some (Kuku Ya'u, Umpila) have *yapu* in the meaning eB, while further south in the rainforest Wargamay has *yapu-tyu* as 'son' (*-tyu* being a common kinship suffix in Pama–Nyungan descending from an enclitic form of 'my' (McConvell 2008: 318–21). Another word for 'son' in neighbouring and related languages *yumurru*, has become a form for 'son' in Wargamay used by the referent's mother 'to avoid using his name' (Dixon 1981: 124).

In the Maric subgroup of languages, Warungu and Gugu-Badhun in northeast Queensland near to Townsville have *mukina* eB, and Gunya, a long distance away to the southwest has *mukana* 'son'. Between these, Wadjalang near Blackall has *mutyi(nu)* eB. This is a plausible cognate as k/ty correspondences are found in Maric and neighbouring languages. Further, there are possible cognates in Bandjalangic on the eastern Queensland–New South Wales border all in the meaning 'son', some *mutyum* with medial ty (Bundjalung, Waalubal, Yugambeh) and others *muyu(u)m* with medial y, due to regular lenition between the dialects.

In South Australia, in the Turra-Yurra subgroup, the form *yunga* (sometimes with a suffix) is the word for eB, but in one language at least, Turra, this means 'son'.

On the north coast of New South Wales, in Gumbaynggirr, there is an example which shows more variation in the forms used for kinship terminology, not only for elder brother and son, but other terms. This relates to the discussion earlier of 'overlays' in kinship, and may also illustrate at least a nascent form of a trirelational system. This has been discussed in some detail for some languages of northern Australia (e.g. Garde 2013 for a summary) but has not yet to my knowledge been positively identified for southern Australia. In a trirelational system the kinship terms vary not only according to the relation between the speaker and the referent, but additionally depending on the relation between the speaker and the propositus (or addressee).[15] So a term might be translated, for instance, 'my son, your brother' and a different term would be used for 'my son, your mother's brother'. This obviously adds a new dimension, and potentially many terms, to a kinship terminology.

This type of arrangement can be linked to the discussion of altercentricity. As Jeffrey Heath writes:

> Whenever speaker S and addressee A are both related to a referent R, there is a choice between egocentric ('my …') and altercentric ('your …') perspectives. Actual usage may be controlled by pragmatic principles, but these can be intricate (Merlan, 1982). The forced choice between the two perspectives is obviated in some Australian languages in which 'triangular' kin terms simultaneously specify S's and A's relationships to R (2006: 216; here 'triangular' is used instead of 'trirelational').

---

15 In some languages it seems the third factor is limited to the addressee but for others it includes third-person proposituses.

Some of the discussion of Gumbaynggirr suggests something akin to such a system, but calls the terms involved in the variation 'avoidance' (Williams, Walker and Morelli 2014).

Juulu is a word for 'brother' used by, or in the presence of, a person who is of the right section to marry the 'brother' (usually *gagu*). In the following a woman is introduced by the younger brother to his older brother (ordinarily called *gaguuga*) to her husband-to-be. It only occurs in Nymboidan.

Man to woman

(22) Yang   nganyu   juulu
      that   1SG.GEN   brother.AVOID

'That's my brother'

However, the avoidance term for 'brother' *juulu* is only used in the presence of the referent. Where a man talks about his **absent** brother to women marriageable to him he uses the nonavoidance term for 'brother', but with polite pluralising of the term for 'brother':

(23) Yarrang-anga   gagu-urra   ngayinggi-ng!
      that.there-PL.INDF   o.brother-PL.POL   sit-PST

'That's about where my brother lives.'

So, this is like a trirelational term which has a meaning 'my brother/your potential spouse' (with apparently additional conditions about presence/absence of the referent).

There are also other words apart from these two for 'elder brother' in Gumbaynggirr: *kuyu* 'brother' and *kuyumpan* 'elder brother' (Morelli 2008). Whether these are trirelational or under which conditions these are used is not clear.

There are other kinship terms in Gumbaynggirr that are more overtly recorded as having variants that are either vocative/addressee forms or depend on the addressee/propositus (i.e. quite likely trirelational), such as *kura* (Morelli 2008: *gura*, son, when parent talking to him). There is a possible cognate in Guwar of Moreton Island (which is connected to the languages further south) *kuran* meaning 'elder brother'. This could then be another example of a change from eB to S, and the reference to 'parent talking to him' would fit with the scenario proposed for the change.

Conclusions

This chapter began with acknowledging the ground-breaking contribution of Lounsbury and Scheffler in establishing the idea, and a formalism to express the idea, that extensions are a central part of kinship semantics. They are regular and logical and can be reduced to a small number of rules, which are in most cases found in many languages. Scheffler took this further and provided a thorough application of this idea and formalism to Australian Aboriginal kinship.

This chapter has referred to cases in which it has been shown, in the Australian context as well as elsewhere, that historical change in kinship-term meanings is also primarily based on the kind of extension Scheffler described. This is also allied to the notion that such changes pass through a stage of 'transitional polysemy' arising from kinship extension of a limited number of types.

Finally, cases were examined where these notions of extension and transitional polysemy are difficult to apply. Most emphasis was laid on the case of change from 'elder brother' to 'son' in the Western Desert (and quite probably in a number of other regions of Australia).[16] Here it is necessary to explore in more depth what the notion of synchronic variation between kinship terms and 'overlays' of different systems mean in terms of pragmatics and the social situation. In this case we need to broaden the idea of altercentricity and examine how filiocentricity (taking children as the pivot or propositus of the term chosen for use) may lead to such change. Another puzzle is why, unlike in the case of change following more standard extension paths, this kind of mechanism of change seems to leave no trace of transitional polysemy, at least as far as has been found so far.

References

Agha, Asif. 2007. *Language and Social Relations*. Cambridge: Cambridge University Press.

---

16   Harold Koch is currently engaged in researching instances of syncretism between adjacent generation kinship terms with a father–child relationship in south-eastern Australia, which are not examples of standard skewing systems but may be more closely related to filiocentricity as described here.

AustKin. *The Austkin Project: A Database of Australian Aboriginal Systems of Social Organization and Kinship*. Online: www.austkin.net (accessed 16 June 2017).

Bowern, Claire, Bethwyn Evans and Louisa Miceli (eds). 2008. *Morphology and Language History: In Honour of Harold Koch*. Amsterdam: Benjamins. doi.org/10.1075/cilt.298

Dixon, R.M.W. 1981. 'Wargamay'. In *Handbook of Australian Languages*, vol. 2, edited by R.M.W. Dixon and Barry J. Blake, 1–144. Canberra: ANU Press. doi.org/10.1075/z.hal2.06dix

Dixon, R.M.W. and Barry J. Blake (eds). 1981. *Handbook of Australian Languages*, vol. 2. Canberra: ANU Press. doi.org/10.1075/z.hal2

Dole, Gertrude. 1969. 'Generation kinship nomenclature as an adaptation to endogamy'. *Southwestern Journal of Anthropology*. 25(2): 105–23. doi.org/10.1086/soutjanth.25.2.3629197

Dousset, Laurent. 2003. 'On the misinterpretation of the Aluridja kinship system type (Australian Western Desert)'. *Social Anthropology* 11(1): 43–61. doi.org/10.1111/j.1469-8676.2003.tb00071.x

Dousset, Laurent, Rachel Hendery, Claire Bowern, Harold Koch, Patrick McConvell. 2010. 'Developing a database for Australian Indigenous kinship terminology: The AustKin project'. *Australian Aboriginal Studies* 1(1): 42–56.

Dyen, Isidore and David Aberle. 1974. *Lexical Reconstruction: The Case of the Proto-Athapaskan Kinship System*. London and New York: Cambridge University Press.

Evans, Nicholas and David Wilkins. 2001. 'The complete person: Networking the physical and the social'. In *Forty Years on: Ken Hale and Australian Languages*, edited by Jane Simpson, David G. Nash, Mary Laughren and Barry Alpher, 493–521. Canberra: Pacific Linguistics.

Fison, Lorimer. 1892. 'Address by the President to Section G Anthropology', *Report of the Australasian Association for the Advancement of Science*, 144–53. Hobart.

Fison, Lorimer and Alfred William Howitt. 1880. *Kamilaroi and Kurnai: Group Marriage and Relationship and Marriage by Elopement*. Melbourne: George Robertson.

Garde, Murray. 2013. *Culture, Interaction and Person Reference in an Australian Language.* Amsterdam: John Benjamins. doi.org/10.1075/clu.11

Gardner, Helen and Patrick McConvell. 2015. *Southern Anthropology: A History of Fison and Howitt's Kamilaroi and Kurnai.* London: Palgrave MacMillan. doi.org/10.1057/9781137463814

Godelier, Maurice, Thomas R. Trautmann and Franklin Edmund Tjon Sie Fat (eds). 1998. *Transformations of Kinship.* Washington: Smithsonian Institution Press.

Goodenough, Ward (ed.). 1964. *Explorations in Cultural Anthropology.* New York: McGraw-Hill.

Hansen K.C. and L.E. Hansen. 1992. *Pintupi/Luritja Dictionary.* Alice Springs: Institute for Aboriginal Development.

Heath, Jeffrey. 2006. 'Kinship expressions and terms'. In *Encyclopedia of Languages and Linguistics*, 214–16. Amsterdam: Elsevier. doi.org/10.1016/B0-08-044854-2/03026-1

Heath, Jeffrey, Francesca Merlan and Alan Rumsey (eds). 1982. *Languages of Kinship in Aboriginal Australia.* Oceania Monograph 24. Sydney: Oceania.

Holmer, Nils. 1983. *Linguistic Survey of South-East Queensland.* Canberra: Pacific Linguistics.

Ives, John. 1998. 'Developmental processes in the pre-contact history of Athapaskan, Algonquian and Numic Kin systems'. In *Transformations of Kinship*, edited by Maurice Godelier, Thomas R. Trautmann and Franklin Edmund Tjon Sie Fat, 94–139. Washington: Smithsonian Institution Press.

Jones, Doug and Bojka Milicic (eds). 2011. *Kinship, Language and Prehistory: Per Hage and the Renaissance in Kinship Studies.* Salt Lake City: University of Utah Press.

Kronenfeld, David B. 1970. 'The relationship between kinship categories and behavior among the Fanti', PhD dissertation, Stanford University, Ann Arbor: UMI.

———. 1996. *Plastic Glasses and Church Fathers : Semantic Extension From the Ethnoscience Tradition*. Oxford Studies in Anthropological Linguistics. New York: Oxford University Press.

———. 2009. *Fanti Kinship and the Analysis ff Kinship Terminologies*. Champaigne, IL: University of Illinois Press.

———. 2013. 'Kinship terms: typology and history'. In *Kinship Systems: Change and Reconstruction*, edited by Patrick McConvell, Ian Keen and Rachel Hendery, 19–42. Salt Lake City: University of Utah Press.

Laughren, Mary. 1982. 'Warlpiri kinship structure'. In *Languages of Kinship in Aboriginal Australia*, edited by Jeffrey Heath, Francesca Merlan and Alan Rumsey, 72–85. Oceania Monograph 24. Sydney: Oceania.

Lounsbury, Floyd. 1964. 'A formal account of the Crow- and Omaha-type kinship terminologies'. In *Explorations in Cultural Anthropology*, edited by Ward Goodenough, 351–93. New York: McGraw-Hill.

Mailhammer, Robert (ed.). 2013. *Beyond Word Histories: Lexical and Structural Etymology*. Berlin: De Gruyter. doi.org/10.1515/9781614510581

Malinowski, Bronisław. 1929. *The Sexual Life of Savages in North-Western Melanesia: An Ethnographic Account of Courtship, Marriage, and Family Life among the Natives of the Trobriand Islands, British New Guinea*. London: Routledge.

McConvell, Patrick. 1997. 'The semantic shift between "fish" and "meat" and the prehistory of Pama–Nyungan'. In *Boundary Rider: Essays in Honour of Geoffrey O'Grady*, edited by Darrell Tryon and Michael Walsh, 303–25. Canberra: Pacific Linguistics.

———. 2008. 'Grandaddy morphs: The importance of suffixes in reconstructing Pama–Nyungan kinship'. In *Morphology and Language History: In Honour of Harold Koch*, edited by Claire Bowern, Bethwyn Evans and Louisa Miceli, 313–28. Amsterdam: Benjamins. doi.org/10.1075/cilt.298.27mcc

———. 2013a. 'Proto-Pama–Nyungan kinship and the AustKin project: Reconstructing proto-terms for "mother's father" and their transformations'. In *Kinship Systems: Change and Reconstruction*, edited by Patrick McConvell, Ian Keen and Rachel Hendery, 192–216. Salt Lake City: University of Utah Press.

———. 2013b. 'Omaha skewing in Australia: Overlays, dynamism and change'. In *Crow-Omaha: New Light on a Classic Problem of Kinship Analysis*, edited by Thomas R. Trautmann and Peter M. Whiteley, 243–60. Tucson: University of Arizona Press.

———. 2013c. 'Granny got cross: Semantic change of *kami* in Pama–Nyungan from "mother's mother" to "father's mother"'. In *Beyond Word Histories: Lexical and Structural Etymology*, edited by Robert Mailhammer, 147–84. Berlin: De Gruyter. doi.org/10.1515/9781614510581.147

———. 2015. 'Long-distance diffusion of affinal kinship terms as evidence of late holocene change in marriage systems in Aboriginal Australia'. In *Strings of Connectedness: Essays in Honour of Ian Keen*, edited by Peter Toner, 287–316. Canberra: ANU Press. Online: press-files.anu.edu.au/downloads/press/p325141/pdf/ch131.pdf (accessed 14 July 2017).

McConvell, Patrick and Barry Alpher. 2003. 'The Omaha trail in Australia: Tracking skewing from east to west'. In *Kinship Change*, edited by Patrick McConvell, Laurent Dousset and Fiona Powell. Special issue of *Anthropological Forum* 12(2): 159–75. doi.org/10.1080/0066467023206227 89

McConvell, Patrick and Laurent Dousset. 2012. 'Tracking the dynamics of kinship and social category terms with AustKin II'. *Proceedings of the EACL 2012 Joint Workshop of LINGVIS and UNCLH*, 98–107. Avignon, France, 23–24 April.

McConvell, Patrick and Ian Keen. 2011. 'The transition from Kariera to an asymmetrical system: Cape York Peninsula to North-east Arnhem Land'. In *Kinship, Language and Prehistory: Per Hage and the Renaissance in Kinship Studies*, edited by Doug Jones and Bojka Milicic, 99–132. Salt Lake City: University of Utah Press.

McConvell, Patrick, Ian Keen and Rachel Hendery (eds). 2013. *Kinship Systems: Change and Reconstruction*. Salt Lake City: University of Utah Press.

Merlan, Francesca. 1982. '"Egocentric" and "altercentric" usage of kin terms in Mangarayi'. In *Languages of Kinship in Aboriginal Australia*, edited by Jeffrey Heath, Francesca Merlan and Alan Rumsey, 128–40 Oceania Monograph 24. Sydney: Oceania.

——. 1989. 'Jawoyn relationship terms: Interactional dimensions of Australian kin classification.' *Anthropological Linguistics* 31(3–4): 227–63.

Morelli, Steve. 2008. *A Gumbaynggir Language Dictionary*. 2nd edition. Nambucca Heads, NSW: Muurrbay Aboriginal Language and Culture Co-operative.

Morgan, Lewis Henry. 1871. *Systems of Consanguinity and Affinity in the Human Family*. Washington DC: Smithsonian Institute.

Murdock, George P. 1949. *Social Structure*. New York: Macmillan.

Pericliev, Vladimir. 2013. *Componential Analysis of Kinship Terminology: a Computational Approach*. Basingstoke: Palgrave MacMillan. doi.org/10.1057/9781137031181

Radcliffe-Brown, A.R. 1930. 'The social organization of Australian tribes'. *Oceania* 1(2): 206–46. doi.org/10.1002/j.1834-4461.1930.tb01645.x

Scheffler, Harold W. 1978. *Australian Kin Classification*. Cambridge Studies in Social Anthropology No. 23. Cambridge: Cambridge University Press. doi.org/10.1017/CBO9780511557590

Simpson, Jane, David G. Nash, Mary Laughren and Barry Alpher (eds). 2001. *Forty Years on: Ken Hale and Australian Languages*. Canberra: Pacific Linguistics.

Toner, Peter (ed.). 2015. *Strings of Connectedness: Essays in Honour of Ian Keen*. Canberra: ANU Press. doi.org/10.22459/SC.09.2015.

Trautmann, Thomas R. and Peter M. Whiteley (eds). 2013. *Crow-Omaha: New Light on a Classic Problem of Kinship Analysis*. Tucson: University of Arizona Press.

Tryon, Darrell and Michael Walsh (eds). 1997. *Boundary Rider: Essays in Honour of Geoffrey O'Grady*. Canberra: Pacific Linguistics.

Whistler, Kenneth. 1980. 'Proto-Wintun Kin Classification: A Case Study in Reconstruction of a Complex Semantic System'. PhD dissertation. University of California, Berkeley.

Williams, Gary, Dallas Walker and Steve Morelli. 2014. 'Different talk for different relatives: Relationships shown in restored stories from three Gumbaynggirr (N. Coast NSW) dialects.' Presentation at AIATSIS National Indigenous Studies Conference, Canberra. 28 March.

Part V. Questioning Extensionist Theory

8

Why Do Societies Abandon Cross-Cousin Marriage?

Robert Parkin

Professor Harold Scheffler's prominence in the anthropology of kinship is well established by virtue of his enormous corpus of written work on the subject, the logical rigour and scholarly care he evinced in his arguments and his influence over American anthropology in particular in promoting semantic analyses of kinship terms and terminologies. His studies of the latter were no doubt in part stimulated by his fruitful association with Floyd Lounsbury, but his independent work was nonetheless strikingly consistent in all these respects, and his other main claim to fame in kinship studies, his rethinking of the topic of descent, seems to have been entirely his own. There have, of course, been controversies and debates, some of them quite pointed, especially with various kinds of structuralists, who see things pretty much in a diametrically opposed fashion, though occasionally also with scholars who in general terms can be located within the Scheffler-Lounsbury 'camp' itself (see Scheffler and Lounsbury 1971: 73ff.).

At this point I should admit that for the most part my own training and longstanding views oppose me intellectually to that camp. I was trained at Oxford in the heyday of structuralism—with which Oxford anthropology at the time was widely associated elsewhere—and I was supervised for my doctorate on Austroasiatic kinship by N.J. (Nick) Allen, who once identified himself to me in conversation as an 'evolutionary structuralist'.

He had been a student of one of Scheffler's main adversaries, Rodney Needham, whom I knew personally and under whose influence I also fell, and who at the time counted as a leading British structuralist—less explicitly evolutionist than Allen, but still nonetheless interested in how both kinship terminologies and marriage practices change.[1] Given the structuralist aspect, there was also an explicit tendency to see kinship more as a matter of category words than of genealogy. Although genealogy was not dismissed entirely, it was not ordinarily seen as having much to do with how various indigenous peoples saw kinship; a position I adopted too at the time. More recently, however, I have moved away from this structuralist orthodoxy sufficiently to appreciate more how peoples the world over do think genealogically some of the time and that they are not as ignorant of the biological aspects of reproduction and parenthood as they are sometimes made out to be.[2] This has still not made me an extensionist, as I made clear in an article published in 1996 on the contextual uses of genealogy and category (Parkin 1996). Among other things, that article compared Scheffler's considerations of Tamil kinship with Louis Dumont's more ethnographically grounded studies, to the definite advantage of the latter. I suggested that genealogy and category are not mutually exclusive ways of interpreting kinship terminologies but rather two different forms of knowledge entirely, the latter being a form of classification, the former involving step-wise calculation to specify the details of a relationship more precisely; their difference is therefore ultimately a matter of the different contexts in which they are likely to be used.[3]

As I still adhere to this position, I do not want to return to this particular debate here, but instead will focus on the applicability of Scheffler's ideas to questions of change in kinship terminology and affinal alliance that have concerned Needham, Allen and myself for a number of years. That applicability is called into question, first by Scheffler's downplaying of the

---

1   I may therefore be said to represent the 'Needhamite' tendency in this volume; many of the other contributions are closer to the honourand's intellectual concerns. While I acknowledge Professor Scheffler's recent sad loss, in the remainder of this paper I will use the present tense to discuss his work and its impact.
2   For example, Parkin (2013a). I realise the importance of distinguishing between biology and genealogy in making this statement. The claim that genealogy does not matter to many peoples in the world and that it simply reflects western thinking is ironically the one major feature shared by both structuralist approaches to kinship and the Schneiderian cultural approaches that both rejected and replaced them.
3   For example, an English speaker may mention that someone is his cousin in ordinary conversation as a category, but resort to genealogy in order to spell out the exact route of the relationship for his interlocutor. I have briefly returned to these issues more recently (Parkin 2009).

importance of affinity in kinship terminologies associated with prescriptive alliance in favour of his focus on consanguinity; and second, by his scepticism, amounting in effect to a denial, that kinship terminologies reflect social morphology in any significant sense. These positions were largely established in Scheffler's debates with the structuralists, but among other things they minimise the potential significance of the most convincing starting point for theories of change, namely the existence of some form of cross-cousin marriage.[4] More generally, Scheffler's fundamentally synchronic approach cannot satisfactorily account for change almost by definition. I shall therefore return to essentially structuralist arguments in favour of both the existence of cross-cousin marriage (or 'prescriptive alliance' in Needham's early terminology) and systemic change by asking: first: Why do societies drift away from cross-cousin marriage?; and second, What changes when they do so—only 'the system' of cross-cousin marriage, or rather how key relatives are classified (especially, how they cease to be classified as cross-cousins)?

First, however, I will briefly review Scheffler's main arguments and targets, and also indicate my main sources, before setting out my own understandings of Scheffler's two positions just outlined above. Section II will discuss the central matter in this article, with examples, namely the circumstances in which a society may abandon cross-cousin marriage. Section III will examine the proposition that kinship terminologies also have a role to play here through the different ways in which they classify key relatives in systems of cross-cousin marriage and the practices that immediately evolve from them. Section IV provides a brief conclusion.

Section I

Throughout his career, Scheffler has rejected the structuralist position that kin terms should be seen as category words that do not primarily have genealogical referents. Instead he has consistently advocated the semantic theory of kin terms he worked out with the anthropological linguist, Floyd Lounsbury. For Scheffler, kin terms are precisely genealogical denotata

---

4   This has long been a controversial term for what is recognised to be a form of marriage into a category of kin with a wide range of possible genealogical referents, and not only first cross-cousin— assuming they can even be traced genealogically, or indeed will be, neither of which is necessarily the case. Nonetheless I choose it here for reasons of standardisation, and also because some of the data and arguments I am using assume a genealogically defined referent of this type. I will occasionally refer to alternatives (especially Needham's 'prescriptive alliance') where relevant.

focused on a single kin type of a sort found within the nuclear family. This focus on genealogy is tied to Scheffler's doctrine linking polysemy by sense generalisation to the extension of meaning of some terms outwards from such foci, as well as his rejection of structuralist and structural-functional assumptions that kinship terminologies reflect certain aspects of social morphology. For the Lévi-Straussian structuralist, the latter typically means cross-cousin marriage or prescriptive alliance in its various forms, which are seen precisely as a reflection of such category words and the systems they form. While Scheffler certainly recognises the facts of affinal alliance, his focus on genealogy also has the result that it renders affinity secondary to genealogy, whereas the structuralists do the reverse in making affinity primary in their models of prescriptive alliance. Thus, as I shall argue, the disjuncture that Scheffler tends to see between terminology and social morphology must be severely qualified in relation to prescriptive alliance, although it becomes more evident the more a society moves away from prescriptive alliance as the basis for its regulation of marriage.

Although Scheffler does deal with other structuralists such as Claude Lévi-Strauss and Edmund Leach on occasion, his key targets would seem to be Dumont and Needham.[5] His attack on Needham is particularly associated with a single book, *A Study in Structural Semantics: The Siriono Kinship System*, written with Floyd Lounsbury and published in 1971.[6] I have relied on it greatly here in setting out Scheffler's views as I see them, though I have also used other sources (Scheffler 1972, 1977, 1984) without (re-)reading the whole of Scheffler's vast corpus.

---

5   Needham mainly used other people's work, not his own, to provide the evidence for this view. However, Robert Barnes, one of his students, did provide an example from his own ethnography on the east Indonesian domain of Kédang (Barnes 1974), which is a structuralist ethnography in every way. He also contributed articles on prescriptive alliance based on his own ethnography (e.g. 1973, 1977), a path followed later by one of his own students, Penelope Graham (1987). Other students of Needham's included Peter Rivière (1969) on the Trio of Guyana, David Hicks, who wrote many works on Timor (see especially Hicks 1978, 1990), and Gregory Forth (e.g. 1985, 1988, 1990). Later Needham himself was to catch up with a book on the Sumban domain of Mamboru, based on fieldwork carried out some years before (1987).
6   The fact of coauthorship means we can never really know who wrote what in this book, but that still should not detract from its use here in a chapter dedicated to Scheffler specifically. The book appears under Scheffler's name as well as Lounsbury's, so one can assume that he agreed with its contents. Also, he and Lounsbury were obviously close intellectual allies in general, even though Scheffler (1971) did seek to reestablish the identity between Dravidian and Iroquois that Lounsbury (1964) had previously been at such pains to refute. See also Thomas Trautmann (1981: 85–88), who follows Lounsbury in respect of this disagreement; though otherwise he is critical of semantic analysis. Above all, the book on the Siriono handily brings together key Schefflerian perspectives on the categorical dimension of kinship.

8. WHY DO SOCIETIES ABANDON CROSS-COUSIN MARRIAGE?

I now return to the two main aspects of Scheffler's work, mentioned above, that I am dealing with in this chapter. I shall then address the key topic of this chapter, namely the circumstances in which a population may abandon cross-cousin marriage for a nonprescriptive form of affinal alliance that is no longer reflected in the kinship terminology and can therefore no longer be considered prescriptive. The overall arguments are first, that Scheffler's theories make more sense in respect of societies that do not pursue cross-cousin marriage than those that do; and second, that even so they cannot adequately account for systemic change between what are very definitely two different situations or stages.

Consanguinity and affinity

For Scheffler, kinship terms and terminologies are just that: they are predicated on local cultural views of procreation and its concomitant forms of consanguineal relatedness based on primary links of the sort one finds in the nuclear family (Scheffler and Lounsbury 1971: 63). These are generally considered 'focal' for Scheffler, and other consanguineal relationships and their denotata are treated as 'extensions' outwards from these foci. This is usually demonstrated in his analyses by a variety of 'extension' or 'equivalence' rules (they are apparently the same; see Scheffler and Lounsbury 1971: 51), expressed through a chain of genealogical symbols starting with a focal kin type (say, F) and leading to those kin types at a further genealogical distance from ego (e.g. FB, FFBS, etc.) with which the focal one is equated in the terminology. This is in effect the 'classificatory' idea, which, of course, has a long history of use in the anthropology of kinship. Scheffler also invokes the notion of polysemy a great deal; one of his criticisms of other schools of the anthropology of kinship being that they ignore it and assume that any kin term only has one intrinsic meaning; that is monosemic. For him this is connected, inter alia, with the structuralist doctrine that category is prior to genealogical position and that categories do not have a focal meaning (do not mean F, therefore, in our example), but an intrinsic, monosemic meaning along the lines of 'male patrikin of the previous generation' (i.e. F, FB, FFBS etc.). For Scheffler, when structuralists break down categories genealogically, they are relying on polysemy by sense specialisation, while at the same time denying the possibility of polysemy by sense generalisation, that is, the extensionism described above from F to FB, FFBS etc. Formally speaking both are possibilities, but it is clear that for Scheffler the latter is more important because he thinks that this is the way most kinship terminologies are structured, as well as accounting for—and making manageable, for both the anthropologist and the native informant[7]—all the denotata of an individual term. It is, in short, the way most people think most of the time: 'polysemy within the domain of kin classification is really what it is "all about"' (1972: 325).[8]

Three other points ought to be made here for purposes of clarification. First, while Scheffler certainly recognises change and history, he sees his analyses as basically synchronic in kind (1972: 313–14). This is another way in which he departs from the structuralists, especially perhaps Needham, who regularly invoked terminological change to explain internal inconsistencies in patterning between terminology and alliance (e.g. Needham 1966, 1967, 1974), without making that central to their work. Second, Scheffler is quite clear that his extensionism is not intended to explain how children learn kin-term use. However, they learn, they end up learning the adult classification, and that is what the analyst must focus on (Scheffler and Lounsbury 1971: 62). Third, Scheffler is clear that polysemy does not necessarily introduce metaphor (e.g. 1972: 318ff.). Kin terms certainly have metaphorical uses, but Scheffler conducts his semantic analyses on the basis that polysemy by sense generalisation is a matter of relating the genealogical denotata of kin terms to ordered sets of rules. The possible metaphorical aspects of kin-term use should, in his scheme, be subject to a separate study.

Since Scheffler sees kin terms as having primarily consanguineal significance, he is apt to view affinal denotata as secondary. It is not clear whether he thinks that affinal denotata can ever be focal denotata, though he appears to make an exception for H and W. However, extensions from H or W as focal kin types would not work in the same way as F > FB > FFBS links in the normal classificatory sense: one can get from H to HB, but then what? Logically, HBFBS etc., but these are not specifications the kinship analyst is ever likely to have to deal with. Thomas Trautmann was later to identify another problem in deciding, for example, the focal specification in equations like FZD = HZ, since neither is obviously prior, and positing such equations leads to a circularity in which each specification implies the other (1981: 59–60). In the case of prescriptive

---

7   Predictability is an aspect of this process that, by following the rules, both the anthropologist and the indigenous ego can predict what term will be used to or of a particular alter.
8   The words 'all about' were originally Needham's and are clearly being used ironically by Scheffler here. Unfortunately I have not been able to find the original reference in Needham's copious writings.

terminologies, which may well lack terms that are solely affinal, Scheffler chooses to view terms denoting affinal relatives as basically consanguineal. For a structuralist like Dumont, by contrast, they, like the terminology as a whole, may primarily express affinity, as he found was the case for ethnographically Dravidian terminologies like Tamil (Dumont 1953). For Scheffler, probably, the very invention of affinal specifications to attach to such terms is merely a function of the way the western analyst interprets and analyses nonwestern classifications; consanguinity and affinity are analytical concepts, but the former has more relevance than the latter because it is linked to genealogical ties connected with locally valid but still very general cultural ideas of conception and birth. While accepting the social uses of kinship terms and categories, Scheffler rejects the structuralist notion that kin terms must be considered primarily as 'social' categories both because of the potentially affinal denotations of some of them and because of their infinite extension from a specific genealogical base through the classificatory idea. That is, he disputes the idea that they are anything more than expressions purely of kinship in the narrow genealogical sense that he has always been keen to stress as primary. Thus, 'The spouse relationship is essential to any system of consanguinity *and affinity* … but not to systems of consanguinity, i.e. systems of *kin* classification *per se* [emphasis in original]' (Scheffler and Lounsbury 1971: 81 n11). And further, 'Relations of genealogical connection, or kinship proper, are fundamentally different from and are logically and temporally prior to any social relations of kinship' (Scheffler and Lounsbury 1971: 38)—of a jural kind, more especially (Scheffler and Lounsbury 1971: 39).

Do systems of prescriptive alliance exist?

While Scheffler does sometimes discuss the potential social morphology correlates of specific terminologies (see Scheffler and Lounsbury 1971: 151–228), his analyses of the latter do not require this and can be and normally are conducted in a sociological vacuum. In general, he is sceptical of views that particular types of terminology 'reflect' aspects of the social structure. One of his targets here is A.R. Radcliffe-Brown's suggestion (1952: 55–88) that Crow and Omaha terminologies reflect the principle of descent-group unity—matrilineal and patrilineal respectively—on the basis that some of their internal equations map this out to some extent (Scheffler and Lounsbury 1971: 15–18; also 63–64). Because they only do this 'to some extent', and because of the considerable variety of Omaha terminologies especially, Scheffler denies that this is a significant correlation; in addition, he has also deconstructed the idea of descent totally, clearly preferring the notion of filiation, that is, parent–child ties, as being more significant.[9] Another target of Scheffler's is the argument that cross-cousin marriage in Australia is invariably linked to section systems, which he dismisses because of the variation in both cross-cousin marriage and section systems that populations there exhibit (Scheffler 1977). One general principle invoked here (e.g. Scheffler and Lounsbury 1971: 152–53) is the well-known fact that similarly classified kin are not necessarily treated alike jurally; in particular, our obligations to a closely related individual in a particular kin class may be followed more diligently than in respect of someone in the same kin class who is more distantly related to us. To an extent, then, this is also a matter of behaviour as well as jural rights and obligations.

More important here, however, is Scheffler's dismissal of the notion of prescriptive alliance as a system reflected in particular forms of terminology. Scheffler does not deny that ego may have a claim in marriage on an alter who is usually going to be a cross-cousin of some description, but he also notes that such claims are rarely enforced across the whole society, that they may be evaded without detriment to the way the society defines itself, and that as a result the statistical count of such marriages may be very low indeed. In addition, societies united in their possession of a prescriptive terminology are scarcely similar in any other respect. For Scheffler, therefore, attempts by Needham and his followers to treat such societies as holistic in the Maussian sense, typically correlating prestations and dual symbolic classification to the principles of affinal alliance, are ultimately hollow.[10] While we may have a marriage rule predicated on cross-cousin marriage and the expected terminological equivalences, *systems* of asymmetric affinal alliance—or any other form of affinal alliance, for that matter—do not exist for Scheffler: 'the most distinctive feature of those [terminological] systems which do employ the MBD-FZS spouse

---

9   One might suggest that, as with extensionism related to the study of kinship terminologies, the focus on filiation reflects a preference for stepwise thinking, as well as, here, a recognition of the shallowness of genealogical memory that is frequently encountered and an appreciation that descent groups rarely act together, whence 'descent category' may be more useful. Scheffler's deconstructions of the notion of descent (e.g. 1966, 1985, 2001) are ultimately more cogent than, say, Adam Kuper's exaggerated dismissal (1982) of the whole idea of descent as an academic myth that has had to be deconstructed not just once but twice in anthropology's intellectual history.
10   Good examples are Needham's analyses of the Purum (Needham 1958) and Lamet (Needham 1960). Needham did in fact recognise that societies united by prescriptive alliance could vary in other ways. For him, principles of organisation—symmetry, asymmetry, transitivity—were more important than typologies of societies. See, for example, Needham (1971).

equation rule is that rule itself' (Scheffler and Lounsbury 1971: 220). Further, the reciprocal rights associated with affinal alliance exist between individuals, not social groups (ibid.: 223). In Scheffler's view it is therefore not correct of Needham to view prescriptive alliance as the cement of society, or as holistic in the sense that the whole of society is ordered by a simple relation of either symmetry or asymmetry between spouse-exchanging groups, expressed in symbolic values, as well as in actual exchanges of spouses and wedding prestations.[11] Also, for Scheffler the failure of all egos to marry, say, MBD/FZS, despite a rule enjoining them to do so, is to be seen as intrinsic to the way such rights and obligations are pursued, not interpreted as breaches of the rules requiring redefinitions of the relatives involved (ibid.: 223–24)—the latter being a key property of prescription for Needham (see further below).

Scheffler also evidently feels that Needham himself has caused confusion by first positing prescriptive alliance between groups (especially descent groups), then being forced to deny, in the face of contrary evidence, that groups of any sort were necessary for prescriptive alliance to be pursued. Scheffler and Lounsbury make much of this in relation to the Siriono of northeast Bolivia, where a rule of asymmetric cross-cousin marriage apparently occurs in the absence of any social groups like descent groups regularly exchanging alliance partners. As a result, 'it is not necessary to posit a system of affinal alliance between descent groups to give a reasonable and satisfactory account of the matrilateral cross-cousin marriage prescription of the Siriono' (Scheffler and Lounsbury 1971: 178). There is also a clear tendency in their discussions of some of the structuralist 'classics' for Scheffler and Lounsbury to stress the Crow–Omaha-type equations some of their terminologies make and to underplay the alliance aspects. Thus the Kachin are described as 'just an Omaha-type system with an overlaid MBD-FZS-spouse equation rule' (ibid.: 199), which itself merely 'has the status of a corollary of a more fundamental rule' (in this case an Omaha skewing rule; ibid.: 178).

Elsewhere (1971), Scheffler also denies that 'Dravidian' terminological patterns reflect the practice of bilateral cross-cousin marriage of which they are a logical expression. Indeed, he claims that there is no fundamental difference between Dravidian and Seneca–Iroquois terminologies,

---

11   Needham was following Lévi-Strauss here, but also seeking to go beyond him by listing key oppositions that expressed the structure (usually asymmetric). Examples of such 'total structural analysis' include Needham (1958) on the Purum and Needham (1960) on the Lamet.

despite his close collaborator Lounsbury (1964) already having shown that they were not identical. However, treating them as identical is precisely what Scheffler does on the basis of their focal kin specifications being identical, and despite Seneca–Iroquois terminologies not being considered prescriptive (unlike Dravidian terminologies), partly because Seneca–Iroquois terminologies typically have separate affinal terms, and partly because they are less consistent in how they treat the cross-parallel distinction; for Scheffler, these differences are secondary to what unites them, namely their focal kin types. As in the case of asymmetric alliance, Scheffler also pointed out that, even in the south Indian region that gave them their name, Dravidian terminologies can co-exist with a preference for marriage to MBD but not FZD, or vice versa, or no declared preference at all, as well as one for the bilateral cross-cousin that the terminology expresses (1971). His position here was rejected by Trautmann (1981: 60–62), after the latter had spent a dozen or so pages of his monumental study of Dravidian kinship submitting a logically consistent Dravidian-type terminology to semantic analysis in the manner of Scheffler and Lounsbury and then deciding that it was essentially a circular procedure: for instance (and as noted above), it could not handle consanguineal–affinal equations of the type FZD=HZ, as there was no way of deciding which of these kin types was the focal one (if any, as neither occurs within ego's nuclear family; see ibid.: 48–62).

As for the lack of fit between terminology and marriage patterns, Trautmann sought to deal with this by bringing in history and the probability that the situation has changed over time: 'I hypothesize that bilateral cross-cousin marriage is *ancestral* to all particular cognate Dravidian systems we find in the ethnographic present [emphasis in original]' (ibid.: 62), regardless of whether such systems have that form of marriage at the present day. This recalls a similar démarche made on a number of occasions by Needham in relation to asymmetric alliance. Thus in one double article (1966, 1967) Needham shows that MBD marriage can occur in three societies with a symmetric prescriptive, an asymmetric prescriptive and a nonprescriptive terminology respectively and postulates historical change to account for this. Another makes a similar historical argument in the case of the Warao of Venezuela (Needham 1974), who have moved away from bilateral cross-cousin marriage while retaining much of the terminology that hypothetically originally went with it. The same idea of change also underpins Allen's theory of the earliest human kinship system as tetradic, which he has put forward as a starting point for change of this type, involving a form of bilateral cross-cousin marriage closest to the Kariera system, though it is not attested ethnographically.[12]

Nonetheless, it is still possible to find societies with prescriptive terminologies where classificatory cross-cousin marriage clearly takes place on a regular basis, nullifying Scheffler's and others' objections to their existence on the basis of low rates of actual cross-cousin marriage and inconvenient unilateral preferences accompanying bilateral terminologies. Nevertheless, the argument that there is frequently a lack of fit between the patterns respectively of terminology and alliance has long been realised. Here Scheffler converges just slightly with his antagonists: the question is really what to do about it. Needham's answer (1973) was eventually to decide that, despite the word 'prescribe' logically being applied to the marriage rules, the notion of prescription was really to be located in the pattern of the terminology, not in that of alliances themselves. As a categorical system any kinship terminology defines how people, or rather the categories they belong to, are related, but a prescriptive terminology also *redefines* the kin involved in a marriage that breaks the rules; further, a terminology cannot be broken in the way that rules can. Moreover, one expects rules to be broken as a normal part of the operation of social life anywhere, therefore to expect anything approaching 100 per cent observance of them is simply unrealistic, just as it is equally naïve not to accept that, even while being observed, rules may well be manipulated to satisfy particular interests or simply to accommodate what is possible for particular egos.[13] As a result, one needs a third level of analysis, namely actual behaviour; that is, the extent to which people obey the rules.[14]

---

12   The original statement is Allen (1986, republished with revisions 2004). More recent versions include 1989 (written particularly with linguists in mind), 1998 and 2008. In the 2008 publication, Allen reviews and answers critiques of his theory (pp. 108–09). I return to his theory briefly below.
13   Prescriptive systems in particular, though not exclusively, often make it possible to trace ties with another relative down more than one pathway, for example, enabling one to find a reason for marrying alter, as well as for not doing so.
14   See Needham (1973). One example where this three-level analytical model is adopted in full for a particular ethnographic case is in Good's description (1981) of Tamilnad in south India, where there is a logically very consistent and 'pure' terminology of symmetric prescriptive type and where 95 per cent of the population marry someone in the prescribed category, though only 25 per cent of spouses are first cross-cousins, with a slight preference for FZDy/MBSe.

At this point, therefore, we can see that the positions Scheffler has adopted form a wide gulf from those of his structuralist opposite numbers, me included. In what follows, I will seek to take the matter forward both ethnographically and theoretically. Section II is more concerned with rules and behaviour, Section III with terminology or the level of classification. Section II is also much more rooted in ethnography, whereas the arguments in Section III are more general. This means that, apart from the occasional stray remark, I am not linking the data in Section II with an examination of any associated terminology. Rather, to repeat, my aim is to show that having cross-cousin marriage and not having it should be seen as two separate situations, possibly linked as stages; and that, despite Scheffler's argument to the contrary, they are not invariably to be interpreted simply in terms of a failure to observe marriage rules 100 per cent. If that were routinely the case, why have the rules and the associated terminology in the first place? Nonetheless, in Section III we return to the terminology as a possible explanation for, or at least associated feature of, such changes. Discussion here revolves around the insight—drawn partly from how prescriptive terminologies work in redefining kin who have married 'wrongly'—that classifications do not just reflect the world but determine in large measure how the world will be perceived. This insight can, in principle, be applied to kinship terminologies as much as anything else.

Section II

In pursuing such lines of enquiry myself, I have adopted structuralist paradigms in their essentials, as well as preferring to focus on cases where it is feasible, even necessary, to bring in a diachronic perspective to explain the synchronic analysis. Synchronic analysis itself often reveals inconsistencies in the logical patterning of the terminology,[15] which also involves relating actual kinship terminologies to a set of types against which ethnographic data can be measured. One can then test the basic hypothesis that change has taken place in order to account for the logical inconsistencies, possible redundancies, in the terminology, etc. There is sometimes resistance to such methods. For Ellen Basso (1970), in her debate with Gertrude Dole (1969), one needs to seek the reasons for a terminology having the pattern it does in present-day social practice,

---

15 North India has a number of examples, for example the Himalayan district of Kumaon (Krengel 1989) and the Malpahariya of Bihar (Parkin 1998).

not—as she alleged Dole was doing—rely on either theories of social change or alleged deviations from neat typologies to explain that pattern.[16] However, this does not always lead us very far, and when, for example, one finds evidence of prescription in the terminology but not the actual alliances or marriage rules that would logically correspond with it, then it is reasonable to posit that change has taken place in the latter but has not started or not been completed in the former.

One factor to be taken into account here is the persistence of theories that cross-cousin marriage, especially in its symmetric form, represents the original form of marriage in human history and that all other forms have derived historically from it. This was the underlying assumption of much of Needham's comparative work on kinship, but in the present day it is more usually associated with Allen's tetradic theory, already mentioned in passing in the previous section. This theory postulates a particular variant of bilateral cross-cousin marriage as the starting point for human kinship. It has become increasingly influential in recent years, though also controversial in the sense that its argument that it accounts for early human kinship has been questioned by others on ethnographic grounds (e.g. Barnard 2008; Layton 2008). Nonetheless, it forms a reasonable starting point for theories of the evolution of kinship systems.

Next, therefore, I consider what steps may lead from a system of cross-cousin marriage (Situation 1 below) to the 'open' arrangements of semi-complex and complex societies (Lévi-Strauss 1949), which lack them:

1. Cross-cousin marriage, with a sociocentric terminology to match, whether tetradic, that is with only four terms (Allen 1986) or not, and with everyone following the prescription generation after generation.
2. Possible evolution from symmetric to asymmetric prescriptive, or to an eight-section system assuming marriage consistently (and symmetrically) between genealogical second cross-cousins, or to some other system that can be described as prescriptive. These options may well be mutually exclusive.
3. Only one member of a group of siblings is required to follow the prescription; other siblings may or must marry into other families or kin groups (this is more often noted of asymmetric prescription

---

16 In the article Basso was criticising, Dole was suggesting yet another terminological 'type', namely bifurcate generational, that is Hawaiian in ego's level and bifurcate merging or bifurcate collateral in +1 and −1.

than symmetric) (see e.g. Hicks (1985: 77–78) on Mbae (Manggarai); and Lindell, Samuelsson and Tayanin (1979: 64, 66), on Kammu (Khmu)). Around this point, a class of nonrelatives might emerge that is not covered by the terminology. I am treating this as a separate stage from that in which everyone marries a classificatory cross-cousin.

4. Abandonment of cross-cousin marriage seen as a repeated practice of exchange between kin groups, but still a tendency, even a rule, for groups of siblings to marry exclusively and sometimes intensively with one another, for example through direct exchange within that generation. Such marriages may be expressed as taking place between siblings-in-law, and they are often associated with a ban on repeating alliances between any two groups in the immediately following generation(s). Some Munda peoples of central India provide examples (see Parkin 1992: 144–87). Terminological change of some sort (for example towards Iroquois or Hawaiian, or at least the emergence of specifically affinal terms) is likely as a result.

5. Though there are no longer any marriage prescriptions, marriage prohibitions continue to be framed in part by referring to kin categories and/or social groups, such as clans related in specific ways to ego. Often associated with Crow–Omaha terminologies (especially by Lévi-Strauss), but not only or necessarily.

6. Even social groups like clans cease to be relevant or even to exist and only certain categories named as unmarriageable are left of previous situations in which kin categories governed marriage options. Inter alia, the situation in most western societies, where for many people marriage partners are not supposed to be related prior to the marriage at all.

There is a certain tendency for later stages of this sequence to be associated with first, a greater dispersal of marriages between groups, and second, greater individual freedom of choice unrestricted by social obligations to marry in particular ways. Both assumptions have to be qualified. Cross-cousin marriage may appear excessively restrictive of choice to the western mind, but in fact first cross-cousin marriage could not work for simple demographic reasons, as not every ego will have a referent in that category. As a result, anthropologists soon realised that a wider range of equivalent kin is involved, such as second and remoter cross-cousins, or persons placed in the same categories but without traceable genealogical links to ego, and they developed the notion of the classificatory cross-cousin to cope with this. Later, especially after the structuralist revolution in kinship studies, it began to be recognised that suitable spouses need not be defined genealogically at all, but should rather be treated as members of a category that may be based, for example, on long-term inter-group relations: that is, ego seeks a spouse where other members of his or her group have done so already in the recent past, without needing to determine exact links genealogically with that spouse. In other words, choice is still possible with cross-cousin marriage, as 'cross-cousin' may actually be quite a large category in the indigenous view. Classificatory cross-cousin marriage also makes possible the dispersal of alliances between groups, though this may be ruled out or restricted where there is a set number of marriage classes (e.g. four or eight) or just two moieties. Situation 2 above involves such dispersal by definition, and within the same generation. Situation 3 enjoins dispersal in subsequent generations, by virtue of the ban on repeat alliances. Situation 4 ensures it by banning, for example, male ego from marrying into his mother's clan, which is where his father had sought a spouse, thus preventing the inter-generational repetition associated with cross-cousin marriage. With Situation 5 we arrive at the abandonment of any influence of category over marriage apart from the incest taboo. Even with cross-cousin marriage (Situation 1), but also more generally, the relevant categories may frequently be manipulated to justify technically 'wrong' marriages. Even if that is not the case, there may be more than one genealogical path linking ego to a desired spouse, which may provide a way of justifying an otherwise questionable match, or rejecting a perfectly sound one.

There is, nonetheless, the possibility that cross-cousin marriage still restricts alliances in ways that come to be seen as unacceptable and that this induces change. Why should this be? Despite Scheffler's scepticism, it has long been recognised that in most societies marriages are not just a matter of individual choice but are attached to social obligations between groups—indeed, individual choice may mean nothing, as in the very many societies where children are betrothed or bestowed on their spouses and the latter's social groups by their parents or other senior relatives (Needham 1986). These social obligations may be a matter of politics, especially as they may be manipulated to suit a particular political strategy—this is the concept of alliance, linked to marriage especially by French writers such as Lévi-Strauss (French *allié* = affine). To pursue political strategies effectively one needs flexibility, that is, the ability to choose from among several partners, whether the chosen partner is a spouse or a bestower of spouses. As already indicated, a system of strict cross-cousin marriage does not necessarily rule out choice, and the categories even of these systems are perfectly capable of manipulation in the interests of pursuing a political strategy; though the choice may not be ego's and alter's. However, as already noted too, choice may be limited if the number of social groups (classes or moieties) associated with cross-cousin marriage is also restricted. This may lead initially to such groups being abandoned but cross-cousin marriage continuing (also to the abandonment of tetradic society). However, even this situation will have restrictions that may eventually be seen as irksome, and the resulting tensions in the system may then set in train the sorts of changes listed above.

Political strategies will, of course, tend to be pursued by the leaders of society. However, ordinary members of society may also be led to pursue them in their own private interests or those of their immediate family. The interests involved may be relatable to notions of romantic love, as ideally in most western societies, but more usually they will be connected to considerations of one's future economic survival or appropriate social positioning—in some societies, ego may have closer relationships with siblings-in-law, who may also be cross-cousins, than with siblings (e.g. Sinhalese in Sri Lanka, Leach 1960). There is also a gender aspect here. Given that most societies have distinct regimes of male dominance, women are more likely overall to be the pawns in male games of marriage politics than vice versa. Age is yet another factor. Even males, as boys, may become pawns in the same game, while in societies where older men tend to monopolise marriages through polygyny, as among the Tiwi in Australia (Hart and Pilling 1979), younger men may be at the mercy of their elders' political arrangements well into middle life. The individual's desire for a perfect partner, often interpreted as a matter of romantic love, is certainly a factor demanding a degree of choice, but it is clearly more relevant in the west and societies that have been significantly influenced by it. Worldwide it is of less salience than the importance given to marriage, and to the use of women in marriage, as a mode of political alliance between social groups.[17]

---

[17] It is not that notions of romance are absent elsewhere, but they may well be placed in a different category than marriage, which is seen politically and socially as a more serious matter. The difference between the two domains may relate to stages in the life cycle, as with the Muria *ghotul* or youth dormitory in central India, where relationships between the genders formed in the youth dormitory are broken off when it comes to marriages, which should proceed in different directions (Elwin 1947). Other examples may relate rather to the different contexts of changing social events. For example, among the Miao of southwest China courting is placed in a different category than marriage, and even married men may take part in ritual events focused on courting (Chien Mei-ling 2013).

Missionary influence may also have an impact in drawing many societies away from cross-cousin marriage, as with at least some Lamaholot villages in eastern Indonesia (Barnes 1977: 137, after Raymond Kennedy's unpublished field notes). However, this is not always the case, despite the presence of missionaries (e.g. Désveaux and Selz (1998) deny this happened among the Cree and Ojibwa of Ontario and eastern Manitoba, Canada); similarly, cross-cousin marriage apparently survives among south Indian Christians, despite the Catholic Church not approving of it (Kapadia 1993: 46).

The Americas

Many sources on the Americas explain the retreat from cross-cousin marriage in terms of the physical expansion of hitherto small communities and/or their greater contact with neighbouring groups etc. One example is Paul Henley, in a brief but wide-ranging comparative study of Amerindian kinship in the Amazon (1996).[18] He points out that, where different populations are scattered along river systems, it tends to be those living up the headwaters that pursue cross-cousin marriage, while those downstream do not do so. The latter are more in contact with other groups, partly because of trade or political conflicts or alliances with such groups. However, Henley doubts that the usually suggested trajectory from cross-cousin marriage to its absence works in the Amazon, and indeed he seeks to reverse it, seeing his 'Amazonian type' as being more fundamental. This type:

> is similar to the canonical dravidianate insofar as the general distribution of terminological categories in the three medial generations is concerned, but it is very different in three other crucial and related respects: the absence of a positive rule of marriage, the absence of a category of cross-relative in Ego's own generation and the presence of a set of exclusively affinal terms (ibid.: 62).

It is also evident that both the intensification of sibling exchanges within a generation without cross-cousin marriage and the repetition of alliances after the elapse of a number of generations also occur in the Amazon, though Henley does not list these as features of his type (see Parkin 2013b). He does argue that the cross-cousin marriage of groups up the headwaters is an adaptation of his Amazonian type to cope with the consequences of

---

18   See also the excellent discussion of Henley's views in Harry Walker 2009: 65–66.

population decline and/or small populations, which have fewer options than those downstream. He also identifies groups on middle stretches of water that have Iroquois crossness, not Dravidian. The geographical transitions thus correlate with the typological ones. In particular, the upstream groups may be remoter, more peripheral, being those that went furthest into the interior, assuming, as is likely, that these river systems were the main means of access and movement to and in these areas.

More specific examples include the Urarina of lowland Peru (Walker 2009) and the various Jivaroan groups by Taylor (1998), also discussed in this context by Walker (2009: 65). Other anthropologists too have tried to connect geographical isolation of any sort with cross-cousin marriage. Needham noted that the Warao, who do not have or no longer have cross-cousin marriage, have been exposed to outside influences and contacts for centuries through their occupation of part of the Orinoco delta, whereas the Yanomamo, although perhaps closely connected with them in prehistory, have been much more isolated until recent times up the headwaters of the Orinoco and other rivers (1974: 27–29). Needham only notes that they also have a symmetric prescriptive terminology (ibid.: 28). His point would have been strengthened had he consulted their main ethnographer at the time, Napoleon Chagnon, who makes it clear that, unlike the Warao, they also have bilateral cross-cousin marriage (Chagnon 1968: 125ff.).

In the literature on North America, the explicit focus tends to be more on notions of endogamy and exogamy (e.g. Ives 1998; Smith 1974 on the Ojibwa), though arguments for their significance tend to resemble those made for the South American examples. While the type of group or unit to which the endogamy and exogamy apply is not always specified, a local residential community composed largely or entirely of recognised kin usually seems to be intended. The usual argument appears to be that cross-cousin marriage is pursued in such communities as a system of close-kin marriage. Conversely, in areas where both population and food resources are thinly distributed, cross-cousin marriage may be less viable as a basis for cooperation between widely dispersed groups. Also, the system becomes less and less attractive as individual communities expand demographically and/or geographically, for example, by moving into new hunting and foraging territories, whether in the plains or in forests, or by expanding trade relations. Under these circumstances a greater range of political and trading alliances with other groups becomes necessary, and as these are partly pursued through affinal alliance, close-kin marriage becomes a constraint, as cross-cousins tend not to be found in these other groups. Cross-cousin marriage is therefore progressively abandoned, although there may nonetheless be a tendency to marry known kin or affines from previous alliances in a more general sense. The terminologies are also modified, perhaps in only one or two levels to begin with, such as the Hawaiianisation of ego's level, but also a shift from Dravidian to Iroquois crossness, though this is difficult to document. For the Ojibwa (Smith 1974), one imperative historically may have been to use affinal alliance more widely than cross-cousin marriage to unite all Ojibwa groups in a single federation. However, contrary to Hickerson (1962), who saw cross-cousin marriage dying out among the Ojibwa in the late-seventeenth century for reasons that apparently had little to do with contact with Whites, Smith argues that the abandonment of this form of affinal alliance came much later, in the nineteenth century. It also had reasons very much associated with contact: a decline in hunting possibilities, itself a consequence of the excessive demands to supply the fur trade, which drove out food sources; the United States government's reservations policy and the consequent sedentarisation of Ojibwa and their dependence on government handouts; a population explosion; and the rise of individual trading and other forms of employment, with less sharing across kin groups and the dropping of traditional obligations to kin and affines. However, Smith is more inclined to accept the possibility that it was cross-cousin marriage itself that linked bands in the precontact period. He also argues that, in modern conditions, groups became more endogamous, as relations between groups became less important. However, he does not suggest that cross-cousin marriage was reverted to because of this.

Cross-cousin marriage may be linked to endogamy in this theory, but the indications are that, once this form of marriage has been abandoned there is no way back, whatever the circumstances. Similar models of small, isolated or dispersed populations practising cross-cousin marriage, larger, more consolidated ones abandoning it, can be found in John Ives's extensive comparative studies of Native American populations (e.g. 1998 on Athapaskan, Algonquian and Numan populations). Ives makes much of the modalities of what he calls 'sibling cores' and their residence patterns. In the case of bilateral cross-cousin marriage, where men exchange their sisters, it is claimed that they will live together and that their children may then marry in the same fashion. However, where the rule is that two brothers marry two sisters, it is linked in this theory with residential exogamy. And this seems to reflect deliberate decisions.[19] Writing of the Wrigley Slavey (after Asch 1998), Ives says that they:

> deliberately fashioned same-sex sibling cores that enforced local-group exogamy in the first descending generation. The entire logic of this framework is to keep potential affines outside the local group ... Asch found a distinct tendency to call even cross-cousins by sibling terms, widening the field for marriages (Ives 1998: 100).

Yet there is no intrinsic link between residence rules and marriage rules. Ives's theory may reflect local conditions (and his reconstructions are meticulous and detailed), but it cannot apply universally.[20]

The more general theory that cross-cousin marriage disappears with increases in group size and consolidation may have something to it, but it does rely on a notion of cross-cousin marriage as necessarily close-kin marriage, which, as argued above, it may not be. One countervailing theory, generally dismissed as unlikely by other anthropologists,[21] was put forward by Gertrude Dole (1969). She saw endogamy caused by population decline among the Kuikuru as forcing a change away from cross-cousin marriage, as cross-cousins would live in the same residential cluster and ultimately see each other as nonmarriageable kin. The terminology reflects this in its

---

19 This itself is not unusual, that is populations thinking about how they marry and asking themselves whether they could do it differently (see Layton 2008: 122). Theories of change in kinship sometimes forget this point and are often presented as if everything happens without those who are affected being aware of it.
20 Nonetheless, similar arguments are occasionally made in relation to other parts of the world. Thus R.H. Barnes doubts that change took place from symmetric to asymmetric prescription on Alor and Pantar in eastern Indonesia, where both forms occur:

> The symmetric systems of Alor and Pantar are found amongst trading populations situated along the coast and culturally distinct from the more anciently indigenous groups of the interior. They give the impression of being less permanently settled, and for a shorter time, than most Lamaholot communities. It would obviously demand a rather difficult historical argument to explain how they managed to retain the original form of social organisation, while the agricultural communities to the west of them shifted to asymmetric alliance (1977: 153).

The implication is that change, if change there was, proceeded in the opposite direction (this from a student of Needham's otherwise generally under the latter's influence at that time!). The theories of Ives, etc., for North America may also find resonance in the distinction in India between the Dravidian south, with bilateral cross-cousin marriage and village endogamy, and the Indo-European north, with no cousin marriage and village exogamy, the latter area also featuring dispersal of alliances and thus a greater distance between spouses, both genealogically and geographically.
21 One exception is Warren Shapiro, who uses Dole's theory to support an argument that the Siriono may have changed from a lineal (Lowie 1928: 266) or cognatic (Needham 1974: 18) terminology to a prescriptive one (Shapiro 1968: 52).

8. WHY DO SOCIETIES ABANDON CROSS-COUSIN MARRIAGE?

Hawaiianisation of ego's level, but not as yet the adjacent levels, a pattern Gertrude Dole called 'bifurcate generation'. This was immediately rejected by Basso (1970), from her work on the nearby Kalapalo, where she noted that, although here too cross-cousins could live in the same cluster, they still married one another. However, they also glossed over the fact so as not to draw attention to the reality of affinity (as elsewhere in this region, the Kalapalo seek to define affines as consanguines wherever possible).[22]

Another possible cause is hinted at very briefly by William Elmendorf (1961) in his comparison of interior and coastal Salish. While the former retains a bifurcate collateral terminology reminiscent of cross-cousin marriage, the coastal areas have a 'lineal' (or 'cognatic', to use Needham's more exact term) terminology and no cross-cousin marriage. The coastal areas also have more social and political stratification, with a stratum of chiefs. Elmendorf does not elaborate further on the implications of this, but he may well have in mind an idea that the constraints of cross-cousin marriage were found to restrict the sorts of political alliances in which the chiefs presumably indulged. However, South India is replete with stratified polities pursuing cross-cousin marriage; in any such society, people in lower social strata will refer to and address each other in kin-related ways, even if they do not do so when looking above them in the social scale.

South India

This has long been recognised as an area of extensive cross-cousin marriage, basically bilateral or symmetric prescriptive, but often with a preference for one or other cross-cousin without that upsetting the symmetric prescriptive terminology.[23] It has also given the name 'Dravidian' to this type of affinal alliance, as this is also an area of Dravidian speech communities, and there is indeed a high, though by no means invariable, association between language and type of affinal alliance here (see Trautmann 1981). However, some more recent ethnography (Fuller and Narasimhan 2008; Kapadia 1993) indicates clearly that cross-

---

22   Ellen Basso clearly prefers an explanation in terms of synchronic analysis and rejects the evolutionary implications of Dole's account. Both papers are summarised by Needham (1974: 32–35). See also Dole's (1984) reply to Basso.
23   To find asymmetric systems in South Asia, one has to look at the Himalayas, stretching from the Indo–Burmese borderlands, with groups such as the Purum and Garo (the latter a mixed system, however; see Needham 1958, 1966), to as far west as the Kham Magar in Nepal (Oppitz 1988).

cousin marriage is no longer being followed as consistently as in the past, for reasons ultimately connected to changes in attitudes to arranged marriages.

Before discussing these cases, we should turn briefly to the Nayar, historically a strongly matrilineal group of subcastes in Kerala with a very attenuated system of marriage not involving cross-cousins per se. In this system, Nayar women first attained marital status through a ritual involving a man from another lineage—a ritual marriage that is not necessarily consummated[24]—before being impregnated through sexual relations with a series of other, so-called *sambandham* partners in a relationship that is perhaps most suitably described as concubinage. The usual explanation for the emergence of this system is that while some Nayar were rulers others formed a military caste, and it was a way of protecting the *taravad* or matrilineal extended family from outside interference when Nayar men were absent on military service. Indeed, it had the effect of doing this more generally; being a matrilineal unit, the *taravad* was based on brother–sister ties, not husband–wife ties, the role of the *sambandham* partners merely being to impregnate Nayar women and nothing more.[25] Despite the peculiarities of this system, which has been treated as a test of the proposition that marriage is universal, both Dumont (1983) and Trautmann (1981: 208–14, 417–25) manage convincingly to show that it can be fitted into pan- or south-Indian norms respectively. Other reasons for thinking that it may represent a shift away from a more original system of bilateral cross-cousin marriage are its existence within an area that is strongly associated with the latter—the Nayar are also Dravidian speakers, after all—and the possibility that the Nayar only became matrilineal in historical times, perhaps in the tenth century AD (Moore 1985: 526).[26] Under legal changes introduced originally by the British, most *taravad*s have been dissolved, and kinship now basically consists of bilateral nuclear

---

24 At the heart of the ritual was the tying of a *tali* or silver or gold token around the neck of the bride by a man of a different lineage (or even caste in some cases, for example Nambudiri Brahmans), as is done in ordinary marriages across south India as well. These rituals linked so-called *enangar* relations between different matrilineages, likened by Dumont to the sort of inherited affinal relationships that one also finds with the regular relations of cross-cousin marriage, despite the latter's absence here (see Dumont 1983: 117ff.).
25 Often conjugal visits were very brief, not even sleepovers being necessary. At this extreme, matrilineal systems do seem to go along with a devaluation of marriage, let alone affinity; another example is the Mosuo of southwest China.
26 Moore prefers to see the *taravad* as a purely residential unit and downplays the matrilineal aspects accordingly, but she cannot deny them entirely. More conventional accounts of the Nayar system include Kathleen Gough (several works, but especially 1959) and Fuller (1976).

8. WHY DO SOCIETIES ABANDON CROSS-COUSIN MARRIAGE?

families. Chie Nakane, in a study carried out in the mid-1950s (1963: 24–25), indicated that some cross-cousin marriage was briefly being revived among the Nayar as the *taravad*s broke up, since it was a way of keeping property together that might otherwise have been dispersed between competing kin groups. However, she adds that 'the present younger generation strongly avoid cross-cousin marriage, as they think it is not good biologically' (ibid.: 25), perhaps a reference to folk theories of inbreeding emerging under western influence.

I turn at this point to more recent material on this region. C.J. Fuller and Haripriya Narasimhan (2008) discuss the case of another high-status Brahman subcaste, the Vattima of Tamilnadu, a state neighbouring Kerala. Here, the prevailing influences leading away from cross-cousin marriage appear to be exclusively modern, especially the intrusion of class values into caste practice. More specifically, these are middle-class values that are construed locally somewhat differently from their supposed Euro-American models, for example, in that they insist on withdrawing women from nondomestic labour.

The Vattima are influenced by north-Indian values—in their case by the *kanya dan* ideology of giving a virgin daughter to a family of higher status within the subcaste as a supreme gift to one's superiors—but they have traditionally pursued cross-cousin marriage as well.[27] However, there has recently been a shift in the ideal criteria adopted in seeking spouses, with traditional emphases on the importance of a suitable alliance, regardless of one's daughter's wishes, tending to be replaced by a greater stress on the personal characteristics and compatibility of prospective spouses. Added to this is a focus on education and employment prospects in India's modern economy, as well as the use of global networks, global forms of advertising, etc. to find the right match. Fuller and Narasimhan are careful to point out that these are not love marriages and that there is no conflict with the concept of arranged marriages; it is simply that those actually getting married are more likely to be involved in the arrangements themselves. The authors accordingly call these 'companionate marriages', to stress this new focus on the compatibility of spouses. There are now also more marriages to non-Vattima Brahmans, though much more rarely to non-Brahmans. There seems to have been a greater stress traditionally on patrilineal descent,

---

27 As Kapadia points out in an earlier article 'by consistently emphasising a "patrilateral" preference (with FZS as ideal spouse) [Tamilnad] Brahmins have made the cross-kin system hypergamous' (1993: 28).

as a bride would stay in her natal home until the birth of at least one child, though children were also fostered long-term to MB later. Now conjugal nuclear families are established immediately after marriage. The authors also state that there are now fewer close-kin marriages, only 10 per cent of their sample being with a cross-cousin or sister's daughter.[28] 'The last close-kin marriage in our genealogies occurred in 2002; we know of only two others since 1990' (Fuller and Narasimhan 1980: 742). This is said to reflect modern concerns about inbreeding and the greater concern for the compatibility of partners, but the imperative of keeping land together through cross-cousin marriage is no longer so strong now that so much land has been sold outside the community. Furthermore, it is said that a daughter-in-law now comes under less pressure from her natal family to knuckle under to her new affines if the two families are not already related through previous affinal ties. Conversely, north-Indian influence may be reflected in the circumstance that the groom's family is now expected to pay less of the wedding expenses. This entails a shift away from the rough balance of marriage prestations associated with cross-cousin marriage in the direction of an absolute imbalance between the bride's side giving everything as a dowry, while the groom's side gives nothing, as in classic north-Indian practice of *kanya dan* (lit. 'the gift of a virgin' in marriage).

An earlier article by Karen Kapadia (1993) on non-Brahman castes in Tamilnad also notes a decline in close-kin marriages, including between cross-cousins. As with the previous case, this is felt to reduce the influence of the bride's natal family over that of the groom, and it also means that women are left much more to their own devices in disputes with their husbands' families. Indeed, marriages not with close kin are advocated, even by women, as a way of reducing marital conflicts, as an aggrieved wife finds it less easy to get her natal family to support her if that family does not have an existing relationship with the husband's family. Again there is a shift away from a rough balance in marriage prestations to a north–India-style dowry, aggravated by the large-scale out-migration of men and concomitant shortage of husbands. Kapadia is much more concerned with the consequences of these changes for women, and she stresses in particular the greater seclusion of women, under the apparently mistaken

---

28   Sister's daughter's marriage is a widespread practice accompanying bilateral cross-cousin marriage in many communities in South India. It can be construed as male ego taking his sister's daughter as a wife for himself, not for his son, as with cross-cousin marriage. A useful account is Good (1980).

local assumption that withdrawing them from their traditional labour activities reflects western middle-class values—as if this were upper-class Victorian Britain rather than contemporary British society.

As with the previous case, Kapadia mentions education and employment prospects as more important considerations than the traditional emphasis on kin as marriage partners. The claims of such kin on one another are now being ignored in the pursuit of other, more modern, interests. One of these is certainly prospective husbands seeking the largest dowry, concomitant with their own rise of status in the labour market, as they abandon traditional agricultural labour for more comfortable jobs in the government service. However, Kapadia's statistics (1993: 44 ff.) indicate that it is the lower castes that are most likely to practice nonkin marriage, though still with considerable percentages marrying a close or classificatory cross-cousin or sister's daughter, and despite the latter being regarded as the ideal forms of marriage. However, this is not a new situation. As she explains, 'Right through the three generations considered … [i]t … is clear that there has been a striking discrepancy between marriage preference and marriage practice in the non-Brahman lower castes for at least five decades' (ibid.: 46). Only the wealthier Vellan Chettiar caste of landowners lived up to this preference, with over 97 per cent of marriages with cross kin. Despite the changes in lower-caste practices, however, there has been no change in the pattern of terminology (ibid.: 48–49), which is probably the case for the previous example also. This is hardly surprising in itself, given received wisdom that changes in terminology lag behind changes in alliance practice, though in Kapadia's case the changes in practice were evidently already in train around the time of World War II, 50 years before she wrote. In both these cases, modern changes are obviously having an impact. Among these are the development of the modern Indian economy; the sale of land; the out-migration of men especially; urbanisation and modern lifestyles generally; and the influence of ideas of class drawn ultimately, if in modified form, from the west. However, the spread of north-Indian values relating to kinship specifically, especially dowry marriage and marriage to cousins and other close kin, can also be detected.

A book by Isabelle Clark-Decès (2014) confirms the sudden and rapid move away from close-kin marriages currently among Tevar castes in Tamil Nadu. Like Anthony Good (1980), she sees elder sister's daughter marriage as traditionally more important than cross-cousin marriage generally in this area, but in respect of both forms she also rejects the alliance perspective deriving from Dumont (especially Dumont 1953), seeing Tamil attitudes to marriage much more as a matter of like marrying like, of marriage between status equals, not of structured oppositions between consanguines and affines who, potentially at least, are status unequals. This is especially true of elder sister's daughter marriage, which, she argues, represents a closed marriage within the kin group formed of opposite-sex siblings and their descendants, whereas cross-cousin marriage has at least the potential for extending links through marriage and negotiating status in the usual Indian fashion.

Clark-Decès also offers three explanations for the decline in all close-kin marriages in these castes (2014: 123–28). First, improved living conditions, public health campaigns and presumably (though not mentioned by Clark-Decès) 'modern'-style aspirations for education and steady employment have combined to lower family size and increase age differences between the generations, thus reducing the number of close kin one may marry, while at the same time making it less likely that a mother's brother and an elder sister's daughter will be of roughly the same age at marriage, despite the difference in genealogical level. Second, attitudes have been changed by the somewhat distorted ideas of the genetic damage caused by close-kin marriages that now circulate freely across India, whether in the media or through official public health campaigns. Third, considerations of the financial standing and educational levels of both bride and groom are replacing the generally very strong claims (Tamil *urimai*) that close kin formerly had on one another as spouses. Contra Kapadia (1995), however, Clark Decès does not attribute this change solely to the growing practice of dowry payments, which, unlike Kapadia, she does not see as a solely modern innovation, any more than are the negotiations over status with which the practice is intimately connected. Rather, it seems Clark-Decès is arguing that young women are catching up with young men in the educational stakes, making them a more valuable asset in the marriage market and thus contributing to changes in traditional marriage attitudes and practices generally.

I should mention one other case, or series of cases, here, namely the Munda speech communities further north in India, which were the subject of part of my doctoral thesis. I have discussed them on many occasions before in this context (see especially Parkin 1992: 144–87) and will only repeat here that, insofar as they have abandoned cross-cousin marriage, the impetus has almost certainly been the influence of the surrounding caste society, which typically marries in north-Indian fashion (that is no cousin marriage at all). It is, in short, an attempt to rise in the local hierarchy by imitating elite practice in what is a very status-conscious society, even in remote areas.[29]

Section III

In accounting for change in kinship systems, these examples indicate that we can only think in terms of local ethnographic reasons, not global or universal ones, for the abandonment of cross-cousin marriage. However, because many such changes are accompanied by changes in terminology, we may find that the more general explanations may lie in theories of classification, rather than of marriage per se. This conclusion is supported by the observation that categorical patterns are limited in number in a way that the details of actual marriage practices do not seem to be. To quote Needham, from his examination of the Warao case, 'very unlike social factors can produce like forms of classification' (Needham 1974: 40). In other words, while potential changes in social morphology and attitudes and the reasons for these changes are many, the logical possibilities in which a kinship terminology can be constructed are few,[30] meaning that exact correlations between these levels of analysis, though possible, are not inevitable (Good 1981). Needham continues, 'The decisive factors, I suggest, have been, not particular empirical circumstances or legislative motives, but general possibilities and constraints of a purely formal nature' (1974: 40).

Methodologically the restricted range of terminological possibilities makes it easier to control for variation, as well as to trace possible changes themselves, the future direction of which can, to some extent, be predicted. One possible approach is that of the lexical universalists, who might also be called lexical evolutionists. An early such work was Brent Berlin and Paul Kay's famous and influential study of colour terms (1969), which set out a predictive model of change in respect to the order in which some colour terms appear in evolutionary time. This methodology was followed in other work by, for example, Cecil Brown on life-form terms (1984) and Stanley Witowski on kin terms (1971, 1972). The latter

---

29 One should therefore add this to, for example, changing bride price for dowry, and burial for cremation, as well as giving up alcohol, youth dormitories and mixed-sex dancing, etc.
30 For example, for +1 male consanguines, only the following four patterns are attested: F = FB ≠ MB, F ≠ FB ≠ MB, F = FB = MB and F ≠ FB = MB. A fifth logical possibility, F = MB ≠ FB, is not.

in particular applied Berlin and Kay's insights to kinship terminologies regarding the predictability and order with which certain features disappear in circumstances of change. For example, prescriptive equations generally disappear before classificatory ones. Yet kinship terminologies are different from the sorts of classification studied by Berlin and Kay, and by Brown. The latter grow in number of categories over time, each category shrinking in its semantic range as other more specific categories emerge, as in the Linnaean classification of the natural world. This reflects the growth in knowledge about that world, or, for example, the range of colours recognised by a colour terminology.[31] Kinship, conversely, is not subject to such growth in knowledge—at a basic level, relationships and alters (relatives) have always been the same, though classified differently—so that change can only be effected in the form of how this finite knowledge is expressed by each emerging set of categories.[32]

Another possibly significant factor is the way in which categories and classifications can assume a very real concreteness in people's minds, despite their variations in form over both time and space. Edwin Ardener pointed out that 'worlds set up by categories bear all the signs of materiality to the untutored human being' (1982: 12).[33] Earlier in the same paper he suggests, 'Once the classification exists ... it is part of the total experience of unreflecting individuals' (ibid.: 6). Finally, as Needham remarks, 'In a prescriptive system especially there is an absolute categorical determination which is hard to evade or change [and] which tends towards conservatism' (1974: 41; also 1973). In other words, rules and behaviour are more labile than classifications: as already noted, rules can be broken, behaviour manipulated, but a classification is fixed, at least synchronically, and also diachronically within certain limits. When one adds to this the consideration, already noted, that because rules can be broken and behaviour manipulated complete uniformity between these

---

31 Sometimes traceable: for example, orange, lilac, and purple have known origins as loans into English.

32 One of the characteristics of prescriptive terminologies is that they are closed systems of classification, meaning that one can give any alter within them a term through a recursive process, however long the chain of genealogical symbols. With nonprescriptive systems this recursive process does not apply, but one can still locate any alter by using the chains of symbols themselves, however long. This has always conditioned knowledge of kin ties and it always will: it is not to be compared to the biologist continually finding new species in, say, the Amazon forests or the Mariana trench to add to Linnaeus's classification.

33 In Ardener's mind, this potentially objectionable word (untutored) probably meant little more than that in ordinary social practice ordinary human beings take their classifications for granted and are unaware both of this fact and of possible alternatives.

three levels is not to be expected and is rare in practice, then there is almost bound to be a time lag between changes in rules and practices and changes in terminology. But, as Needham also says:

> Yet prescriptive systems do change, and the problem is how precisely they do so. The crucial issue is the extent to which individuals make conscious alterations and adjustments; for the more deliberately they are supposed to act the more striking it is that their cumulative decisions should result in a common type of transformation (1974: 41).

This reference, to the possible impact of 'cumulative decisions', is itself striking in a paper by such a committed structuralist. However, it suggests that the cumulative impact of what are basically the same decisions being taken because individuals in a society are repeatedly faced with essentially the same circumstances may eventually make the lack of fit between terminology, on the one hand, and alliance rules and practice, on the other, intolerable. At this point the terminology may begin to change.

It is grasping these circumstances that is difficult. The necessary evidence for change is often circumstantial—the very fact of a mismatch between the respective patterns of terminology and alliance—while evidence for what may have caused it is even more often nonexistent or irrecoverable. However, there are exceptions, as in Europe and much of Asia, where there are written records. While there is no evidence that historical or prehistorical Indo–European speech communities had cross-cousin marriage,[34] it is a reasonable hypothesis, based on Han-yi Feng's careful study of kin terms (1937) that China had bilateral cross-cousin marriage into the early historical period. Historical records helped Trautmann immensely in fixing the limits of Dravidian kinship in South Asia (1981). In the Americas, finally, we do have some, often rather patchy written sources on Native American kinship patterns—dictionaries and word lists, travellers' and missionaries' accounts etc.—going back in some cases to the sixteenth century, of which anthropologists have made quite extensive use.[35]

---

34   There are exceptions in South Asia, most prominently Sinhalese (see Trautmann 1981: 153–55), but these are most probably due to a population retaining its kinship system on changing its language, with terms in the new language being invented or modified to suit. Indeed, this is strongly indicated in the Sinhalese by the circumstance that most of its kinship vocabulary is Dravidian, even though the Sinhalese language itself is Indo–European. See Edward Bruner (1955) on a lexically English but structurally Crow–Omaha terminology in North America.

35   This can be compared to Africa, Australia or Oceania, where contact has been much more recent on the whole and the time depth of such sources (if they exist at all) is far shallower. M.V. Kryukov (1998: 298–99) lists other techniques to which the analyst may have recourse in reconstructing the past.

However, the importance of classification ultimately lies in how kinship terminologies are articulated with marriage choices. While there has been a tendency since Morgan to see change in the former lagging behind change in the latter, we have also seen that, where they are congruent, the terminology will guide 'wrong marriages' (e.g. with a parallel cousin instead of a cross-cousin) into the right classificatory channels. Similarly, the terminology can be used to rule out all cousin marriage by the simple device of classifying cousins as siblings, as in north-Indian terminologies such as Hindi, Bengali or Gujarati. This can also have a knock-on effect on other parts of the terminology, in which the cross-parallel distinction may be modified or abandoned. Certainly the terminology may well be reacting to change elsewhere in the system, of the sort discussed in Section II. Nonetheless, we are justified in asking just what is meant by 'abandoning cross-cousin marriage' and whether it might not take the form of how genealogical cross-cousins are reclassified as kin prohibited in marriage, typically as siblings. Genealogically (i.e. analytically), therefore, cross-cousins do not disappear, but in the classificatory sense they are taken into other categories.

It is also in circumstances of flux and uncertainty that genealogy might become more important, since more exact calculations might have to be made regarding the suitability of potential spouses, for example, excluding genealogical cross-cousins but allowing classificatory ones. Both the terminology itself and genealogical reckoning by virtue of it have their own dynamics, not just the rules or practices of marriage; and this may even be reinforced by the limited number of patterns the terminology can assume, as well as by the propensity of any classification to appear concrete and 'natural', when in fact it is subject to cultural variation.

Section IV

To conclude, Scheffler's disinclination to see in cross-cousin marriage a 'system' is based on the inevitable failure of any society to reach a 100 per cent observance of the marriage rule and to that extent is understandable. However, although his approach is rooted in analysis of the terminology, it fails to recognise the extent to which classifications may be articulated in changes in how people marry, as well as in marriage practices at a particular point in time. In this respect his approach is quite different from the position that Needham eventually adopted (i.e. in Needham 1973), namely that the classification or terminology was where prescription should be identified, not the pattern or rule of marriages. Coupled with the synchronic bias in Scheffler's approach, which did not permit effective consideration of change, it can readily be seen how his debates with the structuralists could become largely a matter of the two sides talking past each other, with little hope of reconciliation.

References

Allen, Nicholas J. 1986. 'Tetradic theory: An approach to kinship'. *Journal of the Anthropological Society of Oxford* 13: 139–46.

——. 1989. 'The evolution of kinship terminologies'. *Lingua* 77(2): 173–85. doi.org/10.1016/0024-3841(89)90014-4

——. 1998. 'The pre-history of Dravidian-type terminologies'. In *Transformations of Kinship*, edited by Maurice Godelier, Thomas T. Trautmann and Franklin E. Tjon Sie Fat, 314–31. Washington: Smithsonian Institution Press.

——. 2004. 'Tetradic theory: An approach to kinship'. In *Kinship and Family: An Anthropological Reader*, edited by Robert Parkin and Linda Stone, 221–35. Oxford: Blackwell.

——. 2008. 'Tetradic theory and the origin of human kinship systems'. In *Early Human Kinship: From Sex to Social Reproduction*, edited by Nicholas J. Allen, Hilary Callan, Robin Dunbar and Wendy James, 96–112. Oxford: Blackwell. doi.org/10.1002/9781444302714.ch5

Allen, Nicholas J., Hilary Callan, Robin Dunbar and Wendy James (eds). 2008 *Early Human Kinship: From Sex to Social Reproduction*. Oxford: Blackwell. doi.org/10.1002/9781444302714

Ardener, Edwin. 1982. 'Social anthropology, language and reality'. In *Semantic Anthropology*, edited by David Parkin, 1–14. London: Academic Press.

Asch, Michael. 1998.' Kinship and Dravidianate logic: Some implications for understanding power, politics, and social life in a northern Dene community'. In *Transformations of Kinship*, edited by Maurice Godelier, Thomas T. Trautmann and Franklin E. Tjon Sie Fat, 140–49. Washington: Smithsonian Institution Press.

Barnard, Alan. 2008. 'The co-evolution of language and kinship'. In *Early Human Kinship: From Sex to Social Reproduction*, edited by Nicholas J. Allen, Hilary Callan, Robin Dunbar and Wendy James, 232–43. Oxford: Blackwell. doi.org/10.1002/9781444302714.ch13

Barnes, R.H. 1973. 'Two terminologies of symmetric prescriptive alliance from Pantar and Alor in eastern Indonesia'. *Sociologus* 23(1): 71–89.

———. 1974. *Kédang*. Oxford: Clarendon Press.

———. 1977. 'Alliance and categories in Wailolong, East Flores'. *Sociologus* 27(2): 133–57.

Basso, Ellen B. 1970. 'Xingu Carib kinship terminology and marriage: Another view'. *Southwestern Journal of Anthropology* 26(4): 402–16. doi.org/10.1086/soutjanth.26.4.3629368

Berlin, Brent and Paul Kay. 1969. *Basic Color Terms: Their Universality and Evolution*. Berkeley: University of California Press.

Brown, Cecil. 1984. *Language and Living Things: Uniformities in Folk Classification and Naming*. New Brunswick: Rutgers University Press.

Bruner, Edward M. 1955. 'Two processes of change in Mandan-Hidatsa kinship terminology'. *American Anthropologist* 57(4): 840–50. doi.org/10.1525/aa.1955.57.4.02a00080

Chagnon, Napoleon. 1968. *Yanomamo: The Fierce People*. New York: Holt, Rinehart and Winston.

Chien Mei-Ling. 2013. 'Tensions between romantic love and marriage: Performing "Miao cultural individuality" in an Upland Miao lovesong'. In *Modalities of Change: The Interface of Tradition and Modernity in East Asia*, edited by James Wilkerson and Robert Parkin, 93–116. New York and Oxford: Berghahn Books.

Clark-Decès, Isabelle. 2014. *The Right Spouse: Preferential Marriages in Tamil Nadu*. Stanford: Stanford University Press.

Cook, E.A. 1969. 'Marriage among the Manga'. In *Pigs, Pearlshells, and Women: Marriage in the New Guinea Highlands*, edited by Robert M. Glasse and Mervyn J. Meggitt, 96–116. Englewood Cliffs, NJ: Prentice Hall.

Désveaux, Emmanuel and Marion Selz. 1998. 'Dravidian nomenclature as an expression of ego-centered dualism'. In *Transformations of Kinship*, edited by Maurice Godelier, Thomas T. Trautmann and Franklin E. Tjon Sie Fat, 150–67. Washington: Smithsonian Institution Press.

Dole, Gertrude. 1969. 'Generation kinship nomenclature as an adaptation to endogamy'. *Southwestern Journal of Anthropology* 25(2): 105–23. doi.org/10.1086/soutjanth.25.2.3629197

———. 1984. 'The structure of Kuikuru marriage.' In *Marriage Practices in Lowland South America*, edited by Kenneth M. Kensinger, 45–62. Urbana and Chicago: University of Illinois Press.

Dumont, Louis. 1953. 'The Dravidian kinship terminology as an expression of marriage'. *Man* 53: 34–39. doi.org/10.2307/2794868

———. 1983. 'Nayar marriages as Indian facts'. In *Affinity as a Value: Marriage Alliance in South India, with Comparative Essays on Australia*, 105–44. Chicago, IL: University of Chicago Press, first published as 'Les mariages Nayars comme faits indiens', *L'Homme* 1(1) (1961): 11–36. doi.org/10.3406/hom.1961.366338

Elmendorf, William W. 1961. 'System change in Salish kinship terminologies'. *Southwestern Journal of Anthropology* 17(4): 365–82. doi.org/10.1086/soutjanth.17.4.3628948

Elwin, Verrier. 1947. *The Muria and their Ghotul*. Bombay: Oxford University Press.

Feng Han-yi. 1937. 'The Chinese kinship system'. *Harvard Journal of Asiatic Studies* 2(2): 139–275.

Forth, Gregory. 1985. 'Layia (FZS, ZH, m.s.): The evolutionary implications of some Sumbanese kin terms'. *Sociologus* 35(2): 120–41.

———. 1988. 'Prescription gained or retained? Analytical observations on the relationship terminology of Ndao, eastern Indonesia'. *Sociologus* 38(2): 166–83.

———. 1990. 'From symmetry to asymmetry: An evolutionary interpretation of eastern Sumbanese relationship terminology'. *Anthropos* 85(4–6): 373–92.

Fuller, C.J. 1976. *The Nayars Today*. Cambridge: Cambridge University Press.

Fuller, C.J. and Haripriya Narasimhan. 2008. 'Companionate marriage in India: The changing marriage system in a middle-class Brahman subcaste'. *Journal of the Royal Anthropological Institute* (n.s.) 14(4): 736–54. doi.org/10.1111/j.1467-9655.2008.00528.x

Glasse, Robert M. and Mervyn J. Meggitt (eds). 1969. *Pigs, Pearlshells, and Women: Marriage in the New Guinea Highlands*. Englewood Cliffs, NJ: Prentice Hall.

Godelier, Maurice, Thomas T. Trautmann and Franklin E. Tjon Sie Fat (eds). 1998. *Transformations of Kinship*. Washington: Smithsonian Institution Press.

Good, Anthony. 1980. 'Elder sister's daughter marriage in South Asia'. *Journal of Anthropological Research* 36(4): 474–500. doi.org/10.1086/jar.36.4.3629617

——. 1981. 'Prescription, preference and practice: Marriage patterns among the Kondaiyankottai Maravar of South India'. *Man* (n.s.) 16(1):108–29. doi.org/10.2307/2801978

Gough, Kathleen. 1959. 'The Nayars and the definition of marriage'. *Journal of the Royal Anthropological Institute of Great Britain and Ireland*, 89(1): 23–34. doi.org/10.2307/2844434

Graham, Penelope. 1987. 'East Flores revisited: A note on asymmetric alliance in Lebola and Wailolong, Indonesia'. *Sociologus* 37(1): 40–59.

Hart, Charles William Merton and Arnold R. Pilling. 1979. *The Tiwi of North Australia*. New York: Holt, Rinehart and Winston.

Henley, Paul. 1996. 'South Indian models in the Amazonian lowlands'. *Manchester Papers in Social Anthropology* 1.

Hiatt, Lester Richard and Chandana Jayawardena (eds). 1971. *Anthropology in Oceania: Essays Presented to Ian Hogbin*. Sydney: Angus and Robertson.

Hickerson, Harold. 1962. *The Southwestern Chippewa: An Ethnohistorical Study*. Washington: American Anthropological Association, Memoir 92.

Hicks, David. 1978. *Structural Analyses in Anthropology: Case Studies from Indonesia and Brazil*. St Augustin bei Bonn: Anthropos-Institut.

——. 1985. 'A transitional two-section system among the Mbae-speakers of Manggarai, eastern Indonesia'. *Sociologus* 35(1): 74–83.

——. 1990. *Kinship and Religion in Eastern Indonesia*. Gothenburg: Acta Universitatis Gothoburgensis.

Ives, John W. 1998. 'Developmental processes in the pre-contact history of Athapaskan, Algonquian, and Numic kin systems'. In *Transformations of Kinship*, edited by Maurice Godelier, Thomas T. Trautmann and Franklin E. Tjon Sie Fat, 94–139. Washington: Smithsonian Institution Press.

Kapadia, Karen. 1993. 'Marrying money: Changing preference and practice in Tamil marriage'. *Contributions to Indian Sociology* 27(1): 25–51. doi.org/10.1177/006996693027001002

——. 1995. *Shiva and her Sisters: Gender, Caste, and Class in Rural South India*. Boulder, CO: Westview Press.

Kensinger, Kenneth M. (ed.). 1984. *Marriage Practices in Lowland South America*. Urbana and Chicago: University of Illinois Press.

Krengel, Monika. 1989. *Sozialstruktur in Kumaon: Bergbauen im Himalaya*. Wiesbaden: Franz Steiner Verlag.

Kryukov, M.V. 1998. 'The synchro-diachronic method and the multidimensionality of kinship transformations'. In *Transformations of Kinship*, edited by Maurice Godelier, Thomas T. Trautmann and Franklin E. Tjon Sie Fat, 294–313. Washington: Smithsonian Institution Press.

Kuper, Adam. 1982. 'Lineage theory: a brief retrospect'. *Annual Review of Anthropology* 11: 71–95. doi.org/10.1146/annurev.an.11.100182.000443

Layton, Robert. 2008. 'What can ethnography tell us about human social evolution?' In *Early Human Kinship: From Sex to Social Reproduction*, edited by Nicholas J. Allen, Hilary Callan, Robin Dunbar and Wendy James, 113–27. Oxford: Blackwell. doi.org/10.1002/9781444302714.ch6

Leach, Edmund. 1960. 'The Sinhalese of the dry zone of northern Ceylon'. In *Social Structure in Southeast Asia*, edited by George P. Murdock, 116–26. Chicago: Quadrangle.

Lévi-Strauss, Claude. 1949. *Les structures élémentaires de la parenté*. Paris: Presses Universitaires Françaises.

Lindell, Kristina, Rolf Samuelsson and Damrong Tayanin. 1979. 'Kinship and marriage in northern Kammu villages: The kinship model'. *Sociologus* 29(1): 60–84.

Lounsbury, Floyd G. 1964. 'The structural analysis of kinship semantics'. In *Proceedings of the Ninth International Congress of Linguistics*, edited by Horace G. Lunt, 1073–93. The Hague: Mouton.

Lowie, Robert 1928. 'A note on relationship terminologies'. *American Anthropologist* 30: 263–68. doi.org/10.1525/aa.1928.30.2.02a00060

Lunt, Horace G. (ed.). 1964. *Proceedings of the Ninth International Congress of Linguistics*. The Hague: Mouton.

Mogey, John (ed.). 1963. *Family and Marriage*. Leiden: E.J. Brill.

Moore, Melinda A. 1985. 'A new look at the Nayar taravad'. *Man* (n.s.) 20(3): 523–41. doi.org/10.2307/2802444

Nakane, Chie. 1963. 'The Nayar family in a disintegrating matrilineal system'. In *Family and Marriage*, edited by John Mogey, 17–28. Leiden: E.J. Brill.

Needham, Rodney. 1958. 'A structural analysis of Purum society'. *American Anthropologist* 60(1): 75–101. doi.org/10.1525/aa.1958.60.1.02a00080

———. 1960. 'Alliance and classification among the Lamet'. *Sociologus* 10(2): 97–119.

———. 1966. 'Terminology and alliance, I—Garo, Manggarai'. *Sociologus* 16(2): 141–57.

———. 1967. 'Terminology and alliance, II—Mapuche; Conclusions'. *Sociologus* 17(1): 39–53.

———. 1971. 'Remarks on the analysis of kinship and marriage'. In *Rethinking Kinship and Marriage*, edited by Rodney Needham, 1–34. London: Tavistock.

———. 1973. 'Prescription'. *Oceania* 43(3): 166–81. doi.org/10.1002/j.1834-4461.1973.tb01207.x

———. 1974. 'The evolution of social classification: A commentary on the Warao case'. *Bijdragen tot de Land-, Taal, en Volkenkunde* 130(1): 16–43.

———. 1986. 'Alliance'. *Oceania* 56(3): 165–80. doi.org/10.1002/j.1834-4461.1986.tb02130.x

———. 1987. *Mamboru: History and Structure in a Domain of Northwestern Sumba*. Oxford: Clarendon Press.

Needham, Rodney (ed.). 1971. *Rethinking Kinship and Marriage*. London: Tavistock.

Oppitz, Michael. 1988. *Frau für Fron: die Dreierallianz bei den Magar West-Nepals*. Frankfurt am Main: Suhrkamp.

Parkin, David (ed.). 1982. *Semantic Anthropology*. London: Academic Press.

Parkin, Robert. 1992. *The Munda of Central India: An Account of their Social Organization*. Delhi: Oxford University Press.

———. 1996. 'Genealogy and category: An operational view'. *L'Homme* 36(139): 85–106. doi.org/10.3406/hom.1996.370119

———. 1998. 'Dravidian and Iroquois in South Asia'. In *Transformations of Kinship*, edited by Maurice Godelier, Thomas T. Trautmann and Franklin E. Tjon Sie Fat, 252–70. Washington: Smithsonian Institution Press.

———. 2009. 'What Shapiro and McKinnon are all about, and why kinship still needs anthropologists'. *Social Anthropology* 17(2): 158–70. doi.org/10.1111/j.1469-8676.2009.00067.x

———. 2013a. 'Relatedness as transcendence: On the renewed debate over the meaning of kinship'. *Journal of the Anthropological Society of Oxford* 5(1): 1–26.

———. 2013b. 'From tetradic society to dispersed alliance: notes arising from a chapter by N.J. Allen'. *Journal of the Anthropological Society of Oxford* 5(2): 194–206.

Parkin, Robert and Linda Stone (eds). 2004. *Kinship and Family: An Anthropological Reader*. Oxford: Blackwell.

Radcliffe-Brown, A.R. (Alfred Reginald). 1952. *Structure and Function in Primitive Society*, London: Cohen & West.

Reining, Priscilla (ed.). 1972. *Kinship Studies in the Morgan Centennial Year*. Washington DC: Anthropological Society of Washington.

Rivière, Peter. 1969. *Marriage Among the Trio: A Principle of Social Organization*. Oxford: Clarendon Press.

Scheffler, Harold W. 1965. *Choiseul Island Social Structure*. Berkeley: University of California Press.

———. 1966. 'Ancestor worship in anthropology: Or, observations on descent and descent groups'. *Current Anthropology* 7(5): 541–51. doi.org/10.1086/200770

———. 1971. 'Dravidian-Iroquois: The Melanesian evidence'. In *Anthropology in Oceania: Essays Presented to Ian Hogbin*, edited by Lester Richard Hiatt and Chandana Jayawardena, 231–54. Sydney: Angus and Robertson.

———. 1972. 'Kinship semantics'. *Annual Review of Anthropology* 1: 309–28. doi.org/10.1146/annurev.an.01.100172.001521

———. 1977. 'Review: Kinship and alliance in South India and Australia'. *American Anthropologist* 79(4): 869–82. doi.org/10.1525/aa.1977.79.4.02a00060

———. 1984. 'Markedness and extensions: The Tamil case'. *Man* (n.s.) 19(4): 557–74. doi.org/10.2307/2802326

———. 1985. 'Filiation and affiliation'. *Man* (n.s.) 20(1): 1–21. doi.org/10.2307/2802219

———. 2001. *Filiation and Affiliation*. Boulder, CO: Westview Press.

Scheffler, Harold W. and Floyd G. Lounsbury. 1971. *A Study in Structural Semantics: The Siriono Kinship System*. Englewood Cliffs, NJ: Prentice Hall.

Shapiro, Warren. 1968. 'Kinship and marriage in Siriono society: A re-examination'. *Bijdragen tot de Taal-, Land- en Volkenkunde* 124(1): 40–55. doi.org/10.1163/22134379-90002883

Smith, James G.E. 1974. 'Proscription of cross-cousin marriage among the southwestern Ojibwa'. *American Ethnologist* 1(4): 751–62. doi.org/10.1525/ae.1974.1.4.02a00090

Taylor, Anne-Christine. 1998. 'Jivaro kinship: "simple" and "complex" formulas: A Dravidian transformation group'. In *Transformations of Kinship*, edited by Maurice Godelier, Thomas T. Trautmann and Franklin E. Tjon Sie Fat, 187–213. Washington: Smithsonian Institution Press.

Trautmann, Thomas R. 1981. *Dravidian Kinship*. Cambridge: Cambridge University Press.

Walker, Harry. 2009. 'Transformations of Urarina kinship'. *Journal of the Anthropological Society of Oxford* 1(1): 52–69.

Wilkerson, James and Robert Parkin (eds). 2013. *Modalities of Change: The Interface of Tradition and Modernity in East Asia*. New York and Oxford: Berghahn Books.

Witowski, Stanley. 1971. 'A universalist account of kinship semantics'. PhD thesis. University of Iowa.

——. 1972. 'Guttman scaling of semantic distinctions'. In *Kinship Studies in the Morgan Centennial Year*, edited by Priscilla Reining, 167–88. Washington DC: Anthropological Society of Washington.

9

Toward Reinvigorating an Ethnolinguistic Approach to the Study of 'Kin Terms': A View from Nascent-based Zuni Relational Terminology

Linda K. Watts

Introduction

I welcome this opportunity to honour the work of Harold K. Scheffler by suggesting that his semantic extensionist approach to the cross-cultural study of kin terminology could be expanded to a broader linguistic field than the domain of lexical-referential, genealogically based relational terminology forms. A more holistic linguistic account of relational terminology is discussed with regard to the relational terminology system in use at Zuni Pueblo about which the author and other scholars have elsewhere made relevant contributions (Kroeber 1917; Ladd 1979; Schneider and Roberts 1956) or have analysed directly (Watts 1992, 2000).

In 1917, Alfred Kroeber asserted that the Zuni peoples' use of their own so-called kinship terminology system was 'utterly slovenly' and 'by rule of thumb' (76–77). In view of observational data he collected on 'errata' of kin-term applications according to the anthropological perspective that the Zuni kin-term system comprises a 'modified Crow' type—

that is, distinguishing mother's mother from father's mother as included in one sort of Crow system—Kroeber assumed that Zunis had been erratically affected by linguistic acculturation to a 'thoroughly bilateral' pattern (ibid.: 48). This resulted, he thought, in speakers often 'violating' their native principles of kin-term usage in favour of bilateral as versus matrilineal extensions.

The fact is, the Zuni cares remarkably little for system or theory. 'He is an opportunist. He has the broad, vague outlines of his kinship system well in mind; but he is not in the least interested in following out basic principles into consistent detail' (Kroeber 1917: 76).

Thus, for instance, Kroeber observed that speakers might address someone of a father's sister (Schneider and Roberts 1956: 3) or a father's older sister's daughter (Kroeber 1917: 54) kin type with possessively marked forms of the relational term *tsitda*, associated in an ethnogenealogically defined Crow system with M/MZ kin types. This so-called 'bilateral' principle of usage was, in 1917, neither pervasive nor was it systemically diagnostic— then or since—of the nature of Zuni kin-term usage 'errata'. Speakers in 1917 and since were often also addressing and referring to their maternal side genealogical +2 generation grandmothers as *tsitda*, a term culturally associated at Zuni with a senior generation, matricentric suprahousehold group- (or clan-) based, socially proximal female. An elder female sibling or even a friend's mother or grandmother who adopts, raises, or is highly supportive to a person may also be designated and addressed with appropriate possessive constructions as one's *Tsitda*.[1] In 1986, I spoke with a centenarian who had been called from a boarding school in Albuquerque around the turn of the century to assume the position of *Tsitda* to her mother's newborn son because her mother had died in childbirth. This woman remained *Tsitda* to her genealogical younger brother all her life, and he remained *Aktsek'i* ('young household-group boy') and later *Ts'awak'i* ('mature' or 'kiva-initiated household-group' 'teen' or 'older boy') to her. I asked if this woman had ever explained her genealogical relationship to her *Ts'awak'i*. After some confusion about why I was asking this, she answered simply: 'That's possible, I guess; but I will always be his *Tsitda*'.

Shift forward to 1979 with Edmund Ladd's reappraisal of Zuni kin-term usages from a native perspective. Ladd was a native, fluent Zuni-speaking linguistic and cultural anthropologist. Contrary to Kroeber's grim and

---

1   I shall from here on capitalise Zuni household-based role designations.

rather contemptuous-seeming assessment of Zuni peoples' 'slovenly, irrational' use of their own kin-term system—a vital component of Zuni language use altogether, even today—Ladd explained native cultural principles of alternation in Zuni kin-term usages that revealed how factors of relative social distance, relative familiarity, and degrees of relative household based and/or ceremonial seniority—that is pragmatic factors—trump genealogical factors in accounting for the systemic, situational use of so-called kin terms by Zuni speakers.

Ladd demonstrated how a speaker might indexically mark degrees of relative social—and not necessarily genealogical at all—proximity by using Zuni relational kin terms either inclusively or exclusively, often applying so-called kin terms to nongenealogical relatives who are socially proximal (see Watts 2000: 55), or applying them to indicate ceremonial affinity such as kiva group comembership or 'godparental' medicine society (or Catholic) sponsorship rather than as genealogical markers.

The Zuni relational particle stem form *hotda* has been ethnogenealogically associated with MM/MMZ. Yet informants from one household group have told me that in their extended household-group history they have chosen not to use any form of this particle for a specific maternal grand-aunt. This is due to a disagreement over land inheritance between their maternal grandmother (whom they address as *Tsitda*, not *Hotda*, and who owned the house they were raised in) and one of her sisters, who did not reside therein as an adult (Watts 2000: 129–32). Members from each side of the fission to this day no longer exchange or refer to one another with direct relational kin-particle forms at all, employing the Zuni relational terminology system principle of exclusion mentioned above that Ladd (1979) described.

Another Zuni informant described a long telephone conversation she had engaged in with her genitor. This man offered to give her so many sheep if only she would agree to address him as *datchu* (in Crow terms, referring to one's father/father's brother kin types) in public, especially at ceremonial settings. She refused because he had not been socially proximal with her since leaving her mother's household when she was young. She used situationally appropriate forms of *datchu* both in reference and in address to her mother's second (in-household living) husband, and she and her children utilised relational terminology appropriately with all of this in-married man's maternal and extended household-group members. Rather than regarding these usages as polysemic metaphorical extensions of focal genealogical referents, this woman stated emphatically about her genitor, 'He has never been a *Datchu* or *'hom* (1st sg. poss.) *datchu'* to me'. This same woman also explained to me that rather than using the direct Zuni relational expression *'hom oyemshi'* to refer to her first husband whom she had separated from, she would refer to him only indirectly using the teknonymous relational expression *'hom ts'awak'i 'an datchu'* (1st sg. poss. 'older boy-of-household' 3rd sg. poss. *Datchu*).

I found that English referential expressions such as 'my mother' were sometimes linguistically accommodated in place of the Zuni expression *hom tsitda*; for example, in reference to a woman who was the subject's genetrix but who had not served as an adequately socially-proximal *mater*. In these cases generally the subject would address and might refer to her maternal grandmother or to an older sister or aunt—whichever female had been her primary caregiver while growing up—as her possessively marked *Tsitda*.

So far then we find, in contrasting Kroeber's with Ladd's accounts of Zuni kin terminology, two at times apparently diametrically opposed interpretations of the facts with regard to both referential and address forms. Zunis are 'slovenly' and 'chaotic' in their application of their modified-Crow kin terms, or conversely, Zunis maintain a flexible, pragmatic, role-based system of social semiotic nomenclature which has allowed their traditional domestic and ceremonial household groups to persist and indeed to flourish despite stochastic variation in household-group membership composition for over seven centuries.

Still, there is a bigger canvas to be painted. What if the focus on describing a Zuni ethnogenealogically based kin-term system was culturally inappropriate from the start? As David Schneider (1984) arguably likewise demonstrated for the Trukese of Yap—and as he made observations about earlier himself regarding Zuni (Schneider and Roberts 1956)—it could well be that a kinship-based analysis deriving from Lewis Morgan's 1871 and W.H.R. Rivers' 1910 'genealogical method' is culturally inadequate as a semantic frame of reference for eliciting data about how people refer to and address one another at Zuni.

Several scholars—notably including Ellen Basso (1973), Schneider (1980, 1984), Hansjakob Seiler (1980, 1982), Anthony Wallace (1970), Susan Bean (1975, 1978), and Roger Keesing (1969, 1970)—have investigated the dimension of address-terminology systems as a sociolinguistic

9. REINVIGORATING AN ETHNOLINGUISTIC APPROACH TO THE STUDY OF 'KIN TERMS'

endeavour complementary with the analysis of referential kin term systems. Kinship terminology has since Rivers (1910)—notwithstanding contrary viewpoints associated with A.M. Hocart (1937), Rodney Needham (1962), and Edmund Leach (1958), among others (see Service 1985)—been based primarily upon the elicitation of referential usages of genealogical nomenclature (e.g. 'What do you call your [genealogical kin type]?'). Address-terminology usages, by contrast, comprise a range of indexical-symbolic shifter forms which might include morphosyntactic variants of kin-term forms but also exceed these, varying pragmatically in face-to-face encounters.

Bean (1978; also see 1975), a student of Harold Scheffler, conducted a sociolinguistic investigation of address terminology of Kannada speakers in South India, in addition to conducting an extensionist-based analysis of Kannada kin classification. Bean sees address terminology as comprising a pragmatic system of speech markers—an indexical-symbolic, deictic system. After focusing her study initially on 'pure referential' kin-term vocabulary, Bean analysed the full range of linguistic forms in use. Bean discovered culturally meaningful and socially relevant principles of usage in the Kannada address terminology system that, simply put, would elude a more narrow genealogical-referential approach to kin terms.

Bean (1978: 111) includes shortened forms of Kannada kin terms along with nonkinship related second person pronouns, personal names and status terms in the Kannada address terminology system. She accounts for semantically significant features of the address forms using situational criteria, including social distance, sex of addressee and seniority. Her separate treatment (1975) of a wide array of generalised and metaphorical applications of the Kannada term *amma* (M/MZ per a Dravidian genealogical translation) reveals pragmatic patterns of use in face-to-face discourse. Most often, Bean finds that Kannada speakers prefer to address social relatives with nomenclature other than kinship-based expressions altogether. Hence, her study arrives at a wider linguistic analysis of both kin-classification and address-based relational terminology than would a study of referential kin terms alone.

From a linguistics perspective, relational terminology comprises a higher-order, more-inclusive ethnolinguistic domain than either a genealogically based approach to referential kin classification or a sociolinguistic study of address usages. As early as 1923, Franz Boas, in his treatment of 'The relationship system of the Vandau' (in Mozambique), recognised that referential kin terms—if we should methodologically isolate such a vocabulary at all in an a priori manner—represent but one heuristically possible component of a broader, more genuinely universal linguistic field of relational terminology, available in all languages. Maurice Bloch's 'The moral and tactical meaning of kinship terms' (1971), Francis Conant's 'Jarawa kin systems of reference and address' (1961), Murray Leaf's (1971) analysis of the semantics of Punjabi kin terms, and Marc Swartz's emphasis on the situational use of kin terminology among the Trukese (1960: 397) also approached kin terms qua a broader system of relational terminology 'shifters'. For example:

> Sometimes, however, more than one role is called for and on Truk this is accomplished by being able to shift the kin category membership. Given the possibility of such shifting, the kin terms cannot be taken to mean only a certain genealogical relationship. The properties which people have that bring them to be classed together are not only sex, age, generation, and so on, but also their standing in various situations or contexts, and to understand the use of these terms the situational determinants must be analyzed (ibid.: 397).

Still, none of the studies cited above examines an entire relational terminology system from a comprehensive ethnolinguistic or social semiotic perspective. Linguistic analysis of a total relational terminology system, I will go so far as to assert, is what linguistics requires for an adequate investigation of how people utilise the full potentials of their linguistic system for purposes of social classification and pragmatic social interaction. From this vantage point, anthropology has been unnecessarily constrained by the misguided notion of genealogical kin-term elicitation as being a logical prerequisite or primary domain for the study of a relational terminology system and by the concept of kinship itself as a universally prototypical semantic domain for social classification. This approach limits empirical access to a full range of relational terminology forms utilised in the pragmatics of social interaction.

My point is that the entire field of so-called kinship studies in social anthropology has been based on incomplete linguistic data elicitation procedures resulting in, hence, artificially delimited ethnosemantic analyses (see Goodenough 1956; Wallace 1970; Wallace and Atkins 1960; also see Carsten 2000; Holland 2004). While this problematic is embedded implicitly within some of the challenges contained in Schneider's *A Critique of the Study of Kinship* (1984), Schneider has also not recognised the broader linguistic problem.

It is unfortunate, then, that linguistics has been appealed to and is often applied to the limited data of kin terms collected by ethnogenealogical and sociolinguistic methods as if such analyses would comprise an adequate linguistic-systemic account. Such a study requires collecting and observing a full range of linguistic forms-in-use employed to accomplish both referential-semantic social classification generally, as well as indexical-symbolic pragmatic social interaction. While the linguistic scope of relational terminology forms vary typologically from language to language, they are likely to include at least minimally: pronominal systems, personal names, nicknames, kin terms (or, wider relational particle forms where semantically relevant), household-based or land-holding-based role terminology, ceremonial-status terminology and usage protocols, occupational-status forms and principles of use, self- and other-introductive phraseology, 'Indian' or initiatory statuses and names, etc. See Linda Watts for a social semiotic account of the range of linguistic options available within the Zuni relational terminology system in 1986 (2000: 61–75).

A relational terminology system includes all lexical and grammatical forms—along with their morphosyntactic variants and context-appropriate reciprocals—of nomenclature and propositional expressions utilised within a particular linguistic and cultural system. The linguistic composition and native criteria for functional selection and syntactic typological expression of these forms (i.e. for referential, introductive, polite or impolite address functions, ceremonial formulaic use, etc.) all may be documented and analysed within a systemic framework of use in relation to whole-language typology in order to arrive at a comprehensive systemic analysis.

A nascent-based view of Zuni relational terminology

In *The Social Semiotics of Relational Terminology at Zuni Pueblo* (Watts 2000; also Watts 1997), I approach this sort of analytic purview regarding the Zuni relational terminology system from a social semiotics frame of reference (Fawcett 1984; Halliday 1978). This approach allows me to arrive at a revisionist account of Zuni social organisation, social classification and pragmatic address and reference as based on household group-related rather than essentially genealogical prototypicality and ethnosemantics.

Folk definitions, best exemplar focality data, and reported and observed usages and reciprocals of Zuni relational nomenclature that I collected at Zuni in 1986 analytically bear out this interpretation (Watts 1992, 1997, 2000).

Alfred L. Kroeber in 'Zuni kin and clan' (1917), went further than to mechanically apply Rivers's genealogical method. Kroeber elicited data from Zuni informants about referential Zuni kin terms. Yet, to his credit as an ethnographer, he also took note of direct observational and interview data involving actual usages of not only these elicited kin-term forms but also of usages pertaining to social classification and address that would not technically be included within the semantic domain of kinship vocabulary. As Stanley Newman aptly noted in his 'Zuni dictionary' (1958), Zuni language includes a broader-than-genealogically defined, lexically specialised domain pertaining to pragmatically significant social classification. This lexical-pragmatic domain of 'relational particle' forms incorporates but also notably supersedes kin-term forms.

Thus, Kroeber identified household-based relational nomenclature (see Figure 33), including *k'yakwen'ona*, people of one's mother's—or natal—household (*k'yakwenne*); *dak'inne*, mother's husband's or one's recognised *Datchu's* natal household; *a:ɬashhina:we*, 'elders' of a household, including deceased ancestral elders (along with *okkyana:we*, adult women of the household; and *ottsina:we*, adult men of the household); and *chawe*, children of the household). Kroeber also identified (Figure 33) relational particle forms referring to some specific household-related affines and their households, including: *ula:kwe*, wife's husband's household; *dala:kwe*, husband's wife's natal household; and *dala:k'i*, married-in daughter's husband. Kroeber (1917: 70–71) also noted reciprocal ceremonial exchanges of relational status forms (suffixed by +*mo*) that include some of the so-called kin-term derived forms along with some purely ceremonial lexemes.

Figure 33 shows Zuni relational terminology associated with members of an interlinked Zuni household group system comprised of one's natal or core household and interlinked affinal households of a *Tsitda*'s (maternal caregiver) husband's natal household and the natal household of a *Tsitda*'s brother's wife, representing much of the household-based nomenclature observed by Kroeber. Each of these households may further be associated with an extended, suprahousehold group, including usually matrilineally extended 'clan' households insofar as relations are socially maintained or recognised.

9. REINVIGORATING AN ETHNOLINGUISTIC APPROACH TO THE STUDY OF 'KIN TERMS'

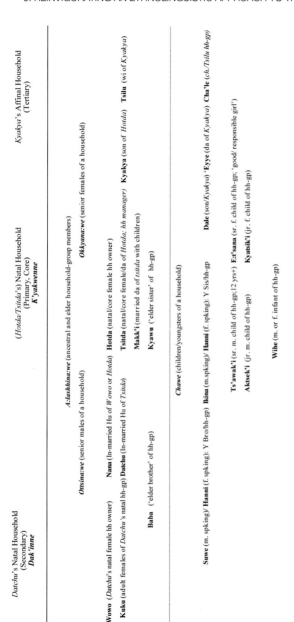

Figure 33. Zuni household-group roles

Note: m. = male, f. = female. Wi = wife, Hu = husband, da = daughter, ch. = child. Upper case relational terms are household-group role terms. Additional household-group (hh-gp) terms include *ula:kwe* (husband's natal household), *dala:kwe* or *dala:k'I* (wife's people or natal household), and *dak'i:kwe* or *dak'inne* (people of father's natal household).

Source: Created as original for this article by © Linda Watts.

311

Newman recognised in his 'Zuni dictionary' (1958) and later affirmed in *Zuni Grammar* (1965) that the so-called Zuni kin terms Kroeber had elicited via the genealogical method should be considered as not semantically distinct or privileged members of a wider inflectional class of 'relational particles' that function as 'active nouns'. Relational particles in Zuni comprise an inflectional class that behaves and is treated distinctively with regard to morphology and syntax. They are inflected for number as a distinctive class and they alternate in usage between possessively marked predicative (or relationship-establishing) and possessively unmarked (or labelling) stem or reduced forms.

Hence, the so-called kin terms Kroeber identified at Zuni are not simply 'nouns' as are English kin terms; rather, they alternate between stem or inflected shortened stem forms of relational particles and several degrees of more fully predicative expressions, depending on degrees of social proximity, kinds of settings and actual social relations.

Similarly as Seiler demonstrated for Cahuilla's labelling/absolutive versus descriptive relational expressions (1980, 1982), Zuni relational terminology forms are used according to cultural-pragmatic principles involving situationally indexical alternation involving labelling versus relationship-establishing relational particle forms. These relational particle variants are also systemically interconnected with pronominal forms (independent or affixed), personal names, 'Indian names', nicknames, slang forms and ceremonial status forms within a unified social semiotic system of 'meaning potential' (see Halliday 1978). That is, depending upon the cultural setting and the degree of actual social proximity obtaining between interlocutors or speakers, addressees and/or referents, a Zuni relational particle usage will be interpreted as situationally unmarked (i.e. neutral) or marked within that setting and for that immediate relation.

Thus, for example, the expression '*Lukkya hom Tsitda*' [This- [goal] (is) she-who-is-TSITDA-to-me] contrasts situationally as a relationship-establishing expression with the shortened address usage, '*Tsitd*', which is a nonpossessively marked, phonologically reduced relational particle stem form. The latter form is used most appropriately in direct address to a socially proximal addressee within a familiar (i.e. at home) setting (Watts 2000: 49).

9. REINVIGORATING AN ETHNOLINGUISTIC APPROACH TO THE STUDY OF 'KIN TERMS'

A case in point is the use of the Zuni form *homme* (<*hotda* [Eng. geneal. transl, mother's mother/mother's mother's sister] +*mme* [noun class sg. suffix]) used in address to an elderly female (Newman 1955: 62–63). This term may be used appropriately within one's familial household setting to address a socially proximal cohousehold group, elder-senior female. In this context it is a polite, familiar, intimate form of address. However, the same form used outside the home to address an elderly female with whom one has no close or familial social tie is an impolite, youth slang usage translating roughly as 'rigid, wooden old woman'. This is because the suffix +*mme* is associated with a noun class that includes semantic forms pertaining mainly to 'long, rigid objects' including desiccated wooden objects (Walker 1966: 220).

The primary issue with which I am concerned here has to do with what should be adopted as the broader linguistic frame of reference for an adequate ethnolinguistic investigation of so-called kin terms. As Michael Silverstein declared in 1976, abstracted, nominal referential kin term forms have little if any value for anthropological linguistic study except as part of—where relevant—a broader pragmatic, morphosyntactic and semantic analysis of relational terminology systems in toto. It is unfortunate that Kroeber allowed theoretical blinders to shield from his analytic purview the rich cultural significance of relational terminology usages he observed both within and beyond a kinship context at Zuni. The pertinent fact is that Kroeber's full range of observed Zuni relational nomenclature usages are both linguistically valid and culturally significant.

Rather than a narrowly defined set of genealogically-based referential, nominal kin terms, we find in pragmatic use at Zuni—in 1917 as yet today—a role-based system of relational nomenclature that accords with what Anthony Carter (1984) identifies as a *household-based* relational terminology system. Regarding actual usages in this way greatly expands a nativistic understanding of Zuni social organisation. As ethnographers have long noted (e.g. Cushing 1979; Dozier 1970; Eggan 1950; Mindeleff 1891; Titiev 1967), the Western Pueblo of Zuni is fundamentally—that is culturally—a social system organised around a network of interconnected household groups. Social interaction at Zuni involves role relations and relative seniority based statuses appropriate to this household-group structure (Cushing 1979; Kroeber 1917: 103–09). Zuni 'families' are organised as a system of interlinked households and socioceremonially interconnected household groups. Kroeber (1917) was astute enough to comment on this obvious ethnographic fact many times over in his study.

Yet, influenced by the anthropological canon of his time of applying the genealogical method in order to study the Zuni kinship system, Kroeber neglected to ground his analysis of the actual use of Zuni relational forms according to household group-based social relations. Almost all of the kin-term usage errata mentioned by Kroeber—as he himself notes—make sense in relation to factors of domestic and ceremonial household group relations (cf. also Eggan 1950: 188–90; Schneider and Roberts 1956: 18):

> The house is basic in Zuni life ...
>
> In daily life it is common residence, and known blood common to individuals, and even friendship and neighborliness, that count (Kroeber 1917: 48).

Allow me to close with some key ethnolinguistic facts—observed but not systemically accounted for by Kroeber—that serve to further corroborate what I classify as a 'nascent'-based—that is 'where one was raised, or from what household one has emerged'—as versus a 'descent'-based system of use of Zuni relational terminology.

First, one's 'family' may be referred to in Zuni as '(*Hom* [1st sg.poss.]) *a:willi kyak'wen'ona*'. Kroeber correctly noted that a direct translation for this expression is not (genealogically kin related) 'family' or even 'relatives' per se but rather, 'Those I grew up with in the same household'. Thus the question, '*Chuwap do' a:willi kyak'wen'ona?*' translated broadly by Kroeber from an English frame of reference as 'Who is your family?' really translates: 'Who are those you grew up/emerged together with in the same household/household-group?'

An appropriate answer to the above question might be '*Hom i:yanikina:we*'. Kroeber translated this expression into English as 'my (genealogical) relatives/kin'. However, Kroeber also correctly acknowledged that a more accurate translation of this Zuni relationship-establishing relational particle form in point of fact does not mean kin but rather, 'those one greets (with terms of relationship)'; or, lit., 'those whom are greeted by terms of relation to me (obj)'.

In 1986 I asked a man in his late nineties or early centenary years, 'Who are those who are *i:yanikina:we* to you?' His response was to explain that when he grew up in the Zuni farming village of Nutria, he was taught from an early age that, 'Everyone in your same village is your *i:yanikina:we*'.

Hence he was to greet anyone within his own village with Zuni relational terminology forms, applying the principles of relative seniority and relative social proximity appropriately as the situation called for.

In sum, a study of variation in referential kin-term forms in terms of their kinship context-based prototypicality and extensional semantics does not amount to a full linguistic or ethnosemantic account of a broader relational terminology system; or at least it does not do so for Zuni. Silverstein framed the problem well:

> Such lexical items as so-called kinship terms or personal names in any society can hardly be characterized by 'semantic' analysis. It is the pragmatic component that makes them lexical items to begin with … it is the pragmatic functions that make them anthropologically important … as Schneider, among others, have never ceased pointing out (Schneider 1965, 1968 [1976]). Further, so-called folk taxonomies of nominal lexical items, again 'semantically' analyzed by a procedure of ostensive reference, essentially ripped from the context of speech, give us no cultural insight (Silverstein 1976: 52).

Certainly there is nothing inherently objectionable with choosing to examine kin terminology as if it could be extracted and decontextualised linguistically from its broader social-semiotic field of relational terminology. Warren Shapiro notes (in Alés, Watts and Shapiro 2009; cf. Shapiro Chapter 1), indeed, that he 'learned to isolate the domain of kin term usage by locally pertinent questions' (Alés, Watts, and Shapiro 2009: 29), as is true for Bean with respect to her study of Kannada kin terminology (1975, 1978). I have no doubt that this could at least artificially be accomplished at Zuni, except that the assumptions thus imposed would be, I believe, culturally erroneous as traditional core praxis and belief. There are simply speaking no terms for 'true blood relatives' per se at Zuni. I was once told by a Zuni informant, when I asked about the value of tracing someone's 'blood relatives', that one should not count one's relations as it would be like counting sheep; accordingly, some might die.

The Zuni relational particle stem forms *tsitda* and *datchu,* for instance, simply are not focally or prototypically identified with nearest genealogical referents of genetrix and genitor. Folk definitions and focality data that I collected from a wide range of informants in 1986 revealed that these terms are focally associated with household-based or otherwise socially proximal relations—always—and that they shift in focal reference according to actual, 'on the ground' pragmatic relations, including nonkinship-based adoption into a household. Thus, for 10 key informants representing a range of age, gender and degrees of traditionality variables, only one claimed a genetrix as their focal member of the relational class '*tsitda*', whereas all 10 (including that same informant) claimed an elder, socially proximal female who had 'raised' the informant. This was true for all 'primary' relational terminology forms that informants mentioned in their relational histories which I collected prior to eliciting focality data (Watts 2000: 90). Folk definitions elicited for these core relational particle forms also emphasise roles and social proximity relations, rather than genealogical nearness, as primary (ibid.: 212–15).

Shapiro assumes (in Alés, Watts and Shapiro 2009: 29) that the fact that Zuni genealogically defined parents may be referred to by unmarked kin-term stem forms in contrast with in his view metaphorically 'extended', marked collateral forms associate genealogical focality semantically with the unmarked forms, but this misinterprets the Zuni data. The so-called marked, 'extended' relational forms attaching the independent particles *łashhi* (big/older) or *ts'ana* (little/younger) to *tsitda* and *datchu* or other relational particles do not indicate metaphorical extensions of genealogically nearest referent forms. Rather, these qualifying particles, when used at all, indicate relative seniority status within a role-based suprahousehold group cohort. If one's *Tsitda* (natal or core household-based, primary female manager/caregiver) is not the eldest female of her natal or adoptive household-based female cohort group, then she is not directly in line to assume, for instance, the important ceremonial role of a *Kuku* (i.e. a *Tsitda*'s husband's *Tsitda*'s suprahousehold-group female cohort senior) for the speaker's suprahousehold group once a *Datchu*'s (married-in husband of a *Tsitda*) natal *Tsitdas* have died. Someone needs to perform important ceremonial roles such as burials and naming ceremonies from the *Datchu*'s (one's secondary) matricentric household group. In similar fashion that a *Tsitd' łasshi* may assume the role of one's ceremonial *Kuku* after the decedence of the original *Kuku*'s immediate cohort set members, according to one informant a *Kya' łasshi* (<*kyakya* + *łashhi*, eldest *Kyaykya*) may be called in to mediate a family conflict within a suprahousehold-group context, in order to facilitate an impartial yet caring hearing about the dispute.

One is said to be 'born into' one's natal, core domestic household group, while one is 'born *for*' one's secondary, affinally interlinked *Datchu*'s natal household group (see Figure 33). One's *Kyakya*'s (*Tsitda*'s cohousehold group 'brother's) offspring from his wife's natal household are likewise 'born *for*' one's own core household group. Accordingly then, one has ceremonial obligations with respect to one's *Kyakya*'s wife's or tertiary household-group children.

Much of the semantic problem involved in anthropological misinterpretations of Zuni relational terminology arises from using English kin-type translations as assumed denotata for Zuni relational particle forms.

So long as the analyst is intent on isolating a narrowly defined, semantically nonfocal, morphosyntactically stripped subset of relational particle forms, ignoring wider pragmatic principles of alternation that would require including additional nomenclature and additional linguistic morphosyntactic elements in order to conduct a more holistic systemic analysis, then the cross-linguistic analysis of kin terminology can proceed—as indeed it has historically and often quite impressively—according to a controlled, cross-cultural comparative framework. However, such an approach to the study of genealogically derived referential kin-term applications need not, I believe, be undertaken a priori or in the absence of a wider ethnolinguistic or potentially even a wider extensionist semantic analysis of relational terminology forms.

Zunis—or at least those Zunis who have not been converted (as many by now have been) to Anglocentric assumptions about 'family', 'clanship', and 'kinship'—say that a genealogical approach is not what matters most to them; at least, it is not what matters first. Zunis are neither ignorant of nor blind to facts of blood relations or to the role of sexuality in producing offspring. Indeed, quite often, it may well be the case that blood ties are nearly congruent with role relations within a household-group system such that it is hardly necessary to distinguish between them. Nevertheless, the Zuni 'rule of thumb' that Kroeber acknowledged yet could not bring himself to represent as primary or core to the use of Zuni relational terminology is in fact a quite effective, flexible, culturally ingenious method for sustaining a traditional household-group and communal socioceremonial system over time (Cushing 1979). Principles of fission and fusion long acknowledged as vital in the ethnographic literature on Zuni and other western pueblos (Eggan 1950; Dozier, 1970) are performatively instantiated and indexicalised through utilising Zuni relational terminology according to degrees of actual social proximity, relative role-based seniority, and an inclusive/exclusive principle (Ladd 1979).

Finally, as I have suggested elsewhere (Watts 2000: 24–29; and in Alés, Watts and Shapiro 2009), semantic extension rules could be applied to supraclasses and subclasses of Zuni relational terminology forms based on culturally attributed focal and extended usages (cf. Sheffler and Lounsbury 1971). Hence, I believe that Scheffler's use of extensionist semantics can be applied to a much broader spectrum of relational terminology than that elicited through a genealogical frame of reference alone. For example, while the prototypical, focal referent of *i:yanikina:we* would likely include those one has grown up or emerged with in the same household group, this form is extended semantically to interlinked secondary and tertiary suprahousehold groups and to wider 'clan'-interconnected households, as well as to one's initiatory kiva group or medicine society group, to ceremonial godparents' household-groups, to one's village as a whole, and to the political government council. Whether such a broadening of analytic scope might serve to help resolve the longstanding theoretical debate over 'old' versus new' 'kinship studies' (Shapiro Chapter 1) is yet to be seen. Notwithstanding, from a linguistic standpoint, widening the scope of study to a complete relational terminology system is not only possible but it would fill a major gap in our scholarly understanding of how relationship classificational systems operate in their entirety.

Focality data, classes and supraclasses of relational terminology, and even equivalence reduction rules for the extension of Zuni relational particle categories could be analysed in such manner as to throw light on universals of relational terminology systems overall. Factors such as degrees of social proximity, kinds of settings and situations and features such as familiar versus nonfamiliar, formal versus casual, and polite versus impolite (cf. Brown and Levinson 1978) might turn out to have been involved with the evolution of human cognition and pragmatic social interaction. Hence, cultural principles of use applying to the 'meaning potential' of relational terminology usages (Halliday 1973: 54)—though heuristically varying according to types of sociocultural organisation—might be indexicalised according to pragmatic selection and alternation rules in the use of relational terminology everywhere. Yet, we cannot discover such higher-order, possibly universal features or their typologically significant modes of variation if we do not examine relational terminology systems in their broadest linguistic scope.

For Zuni, relational terminology usages focally refer to immediate household group-based and/or socially proximal social relations. Zuni relational particle variants can be metaphorically extended to members of the suprahousehold group that includes 'clan' relations, on one hand, and to members of one's *Datchu*'s (natal household married-in *pater*) and *Kyakya*'s (out-married adult male of natal household's) affinally interlinked household groups, on the other. Additionally, Zuni relational terms can be metaphorically extended to members of one's kiva group and medicine society. These are culturally conceptualised as ceremonial household groups (cf. Eggan 1950: 190–93), such that relational particles are used to frame role relations involving seniority and reciprocal role obligations within these groups as well as within familial household-group units.

I:yanikina:we (lit., those one greets by relational particle forms) also may include and be extended by appropriate relational terminology usages to 'godparental' relations and members of their household groups, also to all official political and religious leaders, or even to a close friend's (*kuwaye*) cohousehold-group members, and ultimately to members of one's entire neighbourhood, village, tribe, or historical alliance group (e.g. familially interrelated Hopi clan members). Principles involved in the pragmatic use of Zuni relational terminology—including the inclusive/exclusive principle, degrees of relative social proximity, ceremonial sponsorship and relative seniority within and beyond the immediate household—have facilitated an enduring flexibility in the traditional role-based organisation of molecular household-group units and their wide-reaching extensions for many centuries. They remain vital to maintaining traditional values at Zuni Pueblo today.

References

Alés, Catherine, Linda K. Watts and Warren Shapiro. 2009. 'Discussion of "A.L. Kroeber and the new kinship studies"'. *Anthropological Forum: A Journal of Social Anthropology and Comparative Sociology* 19(1): 21–31. doi.org/10.1080/00664670802695426

Basso, Ellen B. 1973. 'The use of Portuguese relationship terms in Kalapalo (Xingu Carib) encounters: Changes in a Central Brazilian communications network'. *Language in Society* 2(1): 1–21. doi.org/10.1017/S0047404500000038

Basso, Keith and Henry A. Selby (eds). 1976. *Meaning in Anthropology*. Albuquerque: University of New Mexico Press.

Bean, Susan S. 1975. 'Referential and indexical meanings of *amma* in Kannada: Mother, woman, goddess, pox, and help!' *Journal of Anthropological Research* 31(4): 313–30. doi.org/10.1086/jar.31.4.3629884

———. 1978. *Symbolic and Pragmatic Semantics: A Kannada System of Address*. Chicago: University of Chicago Press.

Bloch, Maurice. 1971. 'The moral and tactical meanings of kinship terms'. *Man* (n.s.) 6(1): 79–87. doi.org/10.2307/2798429

Boas, Franz. 1923. 'The relationship system of the Vandau'. In *Race, Language, and Culture*, edited by Franz Boas, 384–96. New York: Free Press.

Brown, Penelope and Stephen Levinson. 1978. 'Universals in language usage: Politeness phenomena'. In *Questions and Politeness: Strategies in Social Interaction*, edited by Esther N. Goody, 56–289. Cambridge Papers in Social Anthropology, no. 8. New York: Cambridge University.

Burling, Robbins. 1964. 'God's truth or hocus pocus?' In *Cognitive Anthropology*, edited by Stephen Tyler, 419–27. Prospect Heights, IL: Waveland Press.

Carsten, Janet. 2000. *Cultures of Relatedness: New Approaches to the Study of Kinship*. Cambridge: Cambridge University Press.

Carter, Anthony T. 1984. 'Household histories'. In *Households: Comparative and Historical Studies of the Domestic Group*, edited by Robert McC. Netting, Richard R. Wilk and Eric J. Arnould, 44–83. Berkeley: University of California Press.

Conant, Francis P. 1961. 'Jarawa kin systems of reference and address: A componential comparison'. *Anthropological Linguistics* 3(2): 19–33.

Cushing, Frank Hamilton. 1979. 'Outline of Zuni mytho-sociologic organization'. In *Zuni: Selected Writings of Frank Hamilton Cushing*, edited by Jesse Green, 185–93. Lincoln: University of Nebraska Press. First published in *Popular Science Monthly* (June 1882): 186–92.

Dozier, Edward P. 1970. *The Pueblo Indians of North America*. New York: Holt, Rinehart, and Winston.

Eggan, Fred. 1950. *The Social Organization of the Western Pueblos*. Chicago: University of Chicago Press.

Fawcett, Robin P. 1984. 'System networks, codes, and knowledge of the Universe'. In *The Semiotics of Culture and Language*, vol. 2, edited by Robin P. Fawcett, M.A.K. Halliday, Sydney M. Lamb and Adam Makkai, 135–179. London: Frances Pinter Publishers.

Fawcett, Robin P., M.A.K. Halliday, Sydney M. Lamb and Adam Makkai (eds). 1984. *The Semiotics of Culture and Language*, vol. 2. London: Frances Pinter Publishers.

Goodenough, Ward H. 1956. 'Componential analysis and the study of meaning'. *Language* 32(1): 195–216. doi.org/10.2307/410665

Goody, Esther N. (ed.). 1978. *Questions and Politeness: Strategies in Social Interaction*. Cambridge Papers in Social Anthropology, No. 8. New York: Cambridge University.

Goody, Jack (ed.). 1958. *The Developmental Cycle in Domestic Groups*. Cambridge: Cambridge University Press.

Green, Jesse (ed.). 1979. *Zuni: Selected Writings of Frank Hamilton Cushing*. Lincoln: University of Nebraska Press.

Halliday, Michael A.K. 1973. *Explorations in the Functions of Language*. London: Edward Arnold Publishers.

———. 1978. *Language as Social Semiotic*. Baltimore, MD: University Park Press.

Hocart, A.M. 1937. 'Kinship systems'. *Anthropos* 32: 545–51.

Holland, Maximilian. 2004. 'Social bonding and nurture kinship: Compatibility between cultural and biological approaches'. PhD thesis. London School of Economics.

Keesing, Roger M. 1969. 'On quibblings over squabblings of siblings: New perspectives on kin terms and role behavior'. *Southwestern Journal of Anthropology* 25(3): 207–27. doi.org/10.1086/soutjanth.25.3.3629275

———. 1970. 'Toward a model of role analysis'. *Handbook of Method And Theory in Cultural Anthropology*, edited by Raoul Naroll and Ronald Cohen, 423–53. New York: Columbia University Press.

Klar, Kathryn, Margaret Langdon and Shirley Silver (eds). 1970. 'Toward a model of role analysis'. In *Handbook of Method and Theory in Cultural Anthropology*, edited by Raoul Narroll and Ronald Cohen, 423–53. New York: Columbia University Press.

———. 1980. *American Indian and Indoeuropean Studies: Papers in Honor of Madison S. Beeler*. The Hague: Mouton. doi.org/10.1515/9783110808681

Kroeber, A.L. 1917. 'Zuni kin and clan'. *Anthropological Papers of the American Museum of Natural History* 18(2): 39–204.

Ladd, Edmund J. 1979. 'Zuni social and political organization'. In *Handbook of North American Indians, Volume 9: The Southwest*, edited by Alfonso Ortiz, 482–91. Washington, DC: Smithsonian Institution.

Leach, Edmund. 1958. 'Concerning Trobriand clans and the kinship category "*tabu*"'. In *The Developmental Cycle in Domestic Groups*, edited by Jack Goody, 120–45. Cambridge: Cambridge University Press.

Leaf, Murray J. 1971. 'The Punjabi kinship terminology as a semantic system'. *American Anthropologist* 73(3): 545–54. doi.org/10.1525/aa.1971.73.3.02a00020

Mindeleff, Cosmos. 1891. 'A study of Pueblo architecture in Tusayan and Cibola'. *Eighth Annual Report of the Bureau of American Ethnology for the Years 1886–1887*. Washington, DC: Government Printing Office, 3–228. Online: archive.org/details/tusayancibola00mindrich (accessed 9 June 2017).

Morgan, Lewis Henry. 1871. *Systems of Consanguinity and Affinity of the Human Family*. Washington, DC: Smithsonian Institution.

Murdock, George P. 1949. *Social Structure*. New York: Macmillan.

Narroll, Raoul and Ronald Cohen (eds). 1970. *Handbook of Method and Theory in Cultural Anthropology*. New York: Columbia University Press.

Needham, Rodney. 1962. 'Genealogy and category in Wikmunkan Society'. *Ethnology* 1(2): 223–64. doi.org/10.2307/3772877

Netting, Robert McC., Richard R. Wilk and Eric J. Arnould (eds).1984. *Households: Comparative and Historical Studies of the Domestic Group*. Berkeley: University of California Press.

Newman, Stanley. 1955. 'Vocabulary levels: Zuni sacred and slang usage'. *Southwest Journal of Anthropology* 11(4): 345–54. doi.org/10.1086/soutjanth.11.4.3628910

——. 1958. 'Zuni dictionary'. *International Journal of American Linguistics* 24(1): part II.

——. 1965. *Zuni Grammar*. University of New Mexico Publications in Anthropology no. 14. Albuquerque, NM: University of New Mexico Press.

Ortiz, Alfonso (ed.). 1979. *Handbook of North American Indians, Volume 9: The Southwest*. Washington, DC: Smithsonian Institution.

Rivers, William H.R. 1910. 'The genealogical method of anthropological enquiry'. *Sociological Review* 3(1): 1–12. doi.org/10.1111/j.1467-954X.1910.tb02078.x

Scheffler, Harold W. and Floyd G. Lounsbury. 1971. *A Study in Structural Semantics: The Siriono Kinship System*. Englewood Cliffs, NJ: Prentice Hall.

Schneider, David M. 1980. *American Kinship: A Cultural Account*. 2nd edition. Chicago: The University of Chicago Press.

——. 1984. *A Critique of the Study of Kinship*. Ann Arbor: University of Michigan Press. doi.org/10.3998/mpub.7203

Schneider, David M. and John Roberts. 1956. *Zuni Kin Terms*. Notebook no. 3, Laboratory of Anthropology. Lincoln, NB: University of Nebraska Press.

Seiler, Hansjakob. 1980. 'Two systems of Cahuilla kinship expressions: Labeling and descriptive'. In *American Indian and Indoeuropean Studies: Papers in Honor of Madison S. Beeler*, edited by Kathryn Klar, Margaret Langdon and Shirley Silver, 229–36. The Hague: Mouton. doi.org/10.1515/9783110808681.229

——. 1982. 'Inherent versus established relation, proximity versus obviation, and two types of Cahuilla kinship expressions'. *International Journal of American Linguistics* 48(2): 185–96. doi.org/10.1086/465727

Service, Elman. 1985. *A Century of Controversy: Ethnological Issues from 1860–1960*. New York: Academic Press.

Shapiro, Warren. 2009. 'A.L. Kroeber and the new kinship studies'. *Anthropological Forum* 19(1): 1–20. doi.org/10.1080/00664670802695418

Silverstein, Michael. 1976. 'Shifters, linguistic categories, and cultural description'. In *Meaning in Anthropology*, edited by Keith Basso and Henry A. Selby, 11–56. Albuquerque: University of New Mexico Press.

Smith, Watson and John Roberts. 1954. *Zuni Law: A Field of Values*. Papers of the Peabody Museum of American Archaeology and Ethnology, Harvard University 43(1). Reports of the Rimrock Project, Values Series 4. Cambridge, MA: Peabody Museum.

Swartz, Marc J. 1960. 'Situational determinants of kinship terminology'. *Southwestern Journal of Anthropology* 16(4): 393–97. doi.org/10.1086/soutjanth.16.4.3628884

Titiev, Mischa. 1967. 'The Hopi use of kinship terms for expressing sociocultural values'. *Anthropological Linguistics* 9(5): 44–49.

Walker, Willard. 1966. 'Inflectional class and taxonomic structure in Zuni'. *International Journal of American Linguistics* 32(3): 217–27. doi.org/10.1086/464906

Wallace, Anthony F.C. 1965. 'The problem of the psychological validity of componential analysis'. *American Anthropologist* 67(5): 229–48. doi.org/10.1525/aa.1965.67.5.02a00800

———. 1970. 'A relational analysis of American kinship terminology'. *American Anthropologist* (n.s.) 72(4): 841–45. doi.org/10.1525/aa.1970.72.4.02a00090

Wallace, Anthony F.C. and John Atkins. 1960. 'The meaning of kinship terms'. *American Anthropologist* 62(1): 58–80. doi.org/10.1525/aa.1960.62.1.02a00040

Watts, Linda K. 1992. 'Relational terminology at Zuni Pueblo: A social semiotic case study'. PhD dissertation, Arizona State University.

———. 1997. 'Zuni family ties and household group values: a revisionist cultural model of Zuni social organization'. *Journal of Anthropological Research* 53(1): 17–29. doi.org/10.1086/jar.53.1.3631113

———. 2000. *The Social Semiotics of Relational Terminology at Zuni Pueblo*. Mellen Studies in Anthropology, vol. 3. Lewiston, NY: Edwin Mellen Press.

Part VI. Extensionist Theory and Human Biology

10

Creeping Plants and Winding Belts: Cognition, Kinship, and Metaphor

Bojka Milicic

Introduction

Hal Scheffler's work has been fundamental in illuminating studies of human kinship and his perspective on kin terms lends itself to a cognitive approach. There is a growing body of research (e.g. Leaf and Read 2012) showing that the study of kinship has a great potential for gaining insight into cognitive processes. Thus studying metaphors that describe concepts from the domain of kinship are salient for the study of human cognition.

Advocates of culturalist or performative persuasion argue that native theories about biological procreation are purely culturally constructed and are only metaphors of social relations, while sociobiologists and evolutionary ecologists would have it the other way around: for the former, Darwinian fitness is just a metaphor of immortality; for the latter, immortality is just a metaphor of Darwinian fitness. Thus Marshall Sahlins, a culturalist, argues: 'Whereas it is commonly supposed that classificatory kin relations represent "metaphorical extensions" of the "primary" relations of birth, if anything it is the other way around: birth is the metaphor' (2012: 677). What lies at the heart of both positions are metaphors. Metaphorical thought plays an important role in the concepts of kinship. As Sahlins notes, kinship is often perceived through shared substances of blood, milk, semen, flesh, bone, spirit (2011a, 2011b).

A metaphorical expression provides a relation between a source concept and its target concept, which is essentially based on analogy (Pinker 2007: 253–55). Metaphors are extensions from one semantic domain to another. As kinship is by definition relational, I propose here that perhaps the very concept of kinship is the model for metaphorical thinking. Metaphors, probably unique to our species, are fundamental for human cognition. They are produced when a concept from one domain (target source) is related to another concept from another domain (Kronenfeld 1996; Lakoff and Johnson 1980). George Lakoff asserts that metaphors are not mere linguistic expressions, but conceptual mappings that physically exist in the brain structure. According to Lakoff, the neural theory of metaphor explains the 'neural computational mechanisms' involved in their production (2009: 4).

Social cognition is fundamental for the functioning of human society, beginning with the recognition of one's immediate caregivers, usually one's kin or those who are perceived as kin. Concepts of kinship are often expressed metaphorically. I argue here that metaphorical thought might have originated at the same time as the need for social recognition that required charting and navigating the space of kin. I will draw on recent research in psychology and neurology that provide the psychological and biological underpinnings of metaphorical thought. Further, I will analyse ethnographic examples of kinship metaphors from the Mediterranean region, within the domain of plants and the domain of clothing, to show that these two semantic domains are members of a more inclusive class of 'coiling things' finding their way to the domain of kinship through the analogy of relations. This is also exemplified in visual metaphors associated with kinship that Carl Schuster collected from a broad range of societies from prehistoric to living ethnographic examples (Schuster and Carpenter 1996). Finally, I will hypothesise that thinking about kinship as primarily a system of relations might have been the model for thinking about the world. Indeed, we might say that thinking about kinship is the mother of all thought.

In Scheffler's approach, metaphoric extensions of kinship terms from focal kin terms to nonfocal ones play a fundamental role (Scheffler 1972; Scheffler and Lounsbury 1971). Following Lounsbury, Scheffler writes:

[M]etaphor is often described as simile without the 'like', but we must consider the underlying semantic structure of such a comparison. It consists in suspending one or more of the defining features (criterial attributes) in the primary sense of the word and substituting in its place some feature of connotative meaning which is associated with the primary sense of the word. In the process connotative features become criterial. By this means words may be transferred from one semantic domain to another, for example from the domain of classification to the domain of classification on the basis of kinds of social or affective relationships (1972: 319).

Scheffler highlighted the very nature of metaphorical usage, namely metaphors necessarily only partially overlap with their referents' meanings. If the two sets of connotations were the same there would be no metaphor. For example, the American kinship term *mother* only in some of its criterial features corresponds to the criterial features of 'mother superior'. Although speakers might refer to the latter only as 'mother', they know she is only in some attributes like a biological mother. For Scheffler, the genealogical reference is primary and its many metaphoric extensions are secondary. Moreover, metaphors are not only a partial overlap of two concepts across semantic domains, but are based on the comparisons of relations between the concepts and other members within their respective domains, or between whole classes of objects and their relations.

Social cognition and metaphors of space

It has been suggested that our understanding and descriptions of the world are largely, and mostly unconsciously, structured by metaphors. Most conceptual metaphors are derived from human spatial orientation (Lakoff and Johnson 1980; Pinker 2007). Humans use concrete references to orientation in space to express the broad range of other more difficult and often abstract or ambiguous meanings. For example, up/down and in/out orientations supply metaphorical models for emotional states, such as in the expressions 'the mood was uplifting', 'it is all downhill after 40', and 'she is down and out on her luck'.

Giovanni Bennardo (2010) argues that the ability to think about space also allows for the observation of ideas as real objects from different perspectives. The conceptual use of space makes use of perspective-taking within a Frame of Reference (FOR). In the Basic FOR the viewer (speaker) is the central point from which she/he constructs the space within a set of three coordinates: sagittal, vertical and transversal. The Intrinsic FOR has at its centre another object separate from the viewer, and the Absolute FOR uses fixed orientation markers, such as cardinal points (2010: 382). In kinship systems this is evident in the position of ego as well as in the ability to put one's self in the position of alter. Orientation in space, as an ontological prime, is replicated in other domains, such as time, as well as kinship. Thus time is perceived as motion in the orientation space within a FOR and the concept of space is also used as a metaphorical referent to time (Lakoff and Johnson 1980; Pinker 2007). An example of time metaphorically expressed with a space referent comes from Croatian colloquial language when space is sometimes substituted with time prepositions, as in the expression '*iza rata*', literally 'behind the war' instead of after the war.

Ethnographic examples of time-as-space come from the Inca view of time clearly rooted in FOR. The Inca culture contemplated the past and future in reverse to western cultures, so the past is in front because it can be seen, the future is behind because it is invisible. The head is also associated with the beginning and the source, while the feet with chaos and the dead (Classen 1993: 111–12). One of the most important Inca concepts was *pachacuti*, the reversal of space and time. The reforms of the great Inca ruler Pachacutec were considered to have been groundbreaking reversals, but the catastrophe of Spanish conquest of the Inca Empire was also referred to as *pachacuti*. Likewise, the millenarian myth of Inkarri foretells the return of the metonymic figure of the Inca king and the reversal, the *pachacuti*, to the old Inca ways. It is a concept associated with *pacha*, 'mother earth', and her spatial as well as temporal attributes (Allen 2002; Classen 1993).

Bennardo proposed that the use of different FOR perspectives, ego-centred or alter-centred, generate kinship terminologies that focus on ego or other than ego (2010: 382). In English one's kin, as well as friends, are often referred to as 'close' or 'distant'. One of the most common spatial metaphors is the association between closeness and warmth derived from the close physical experience when in contact with other members of the social group, such as grooming, breast feeding or comforting a child, having sex, or just socialising (Ijzerman and Koole 2011). Research in developmental psychology shows the presence of spatial knowledge, as well as the ability to recognise faces in early infancy. Based on these findings the two seem connected—closeness/distance in physical space and known/unknown faces in social space. In other words, spatial orientation and social cognition are connected. According to social psychologists, communal sharing relationships that imply spatial proximity are grounded 'in innate and evolved mechanisms, or relational models that allow people to coordinate social interaction' (Fiske 1992: 701). This is conceptualised by crossing over from the domain of space to the domain of close kin as focal members and its extensions. To cite just a couple of ethnographic examples, among many kinship metaphors, when extended to nonrelatives, the *brother* metaphor suggests a horizontal egalitarian relationship such as in many 'brotherhoods' in the western tradition, while father/child indicates a hierarchical relationship (Rigney 2001). This confirms Mary Douglas's (1966) suggestion that the human body can stand for anything and vice versa, anything can stand for human body exemplified in English metaphors 'the head of state' and 'body politic' as well as in the Inca view quoted above where head is associated with life and order, and feet with death and chaos. The human body and its limbs can also represent kin-group segmentation, such as among some Bedouin groups (El Guindi 2010).

Neurological underpinnings for metaphorical thought

Although the exact underlying mechanisms involved in the production of metaphors are subject to current debates, metaphorical mappings involving neural pathways that cross various domains have been corroborated in neurological studies (Anderson 2010: 25). Metaphorical use from the domain of the bodily experiences, particularly the orientation in space, extends to referents in the social domain. How is this grounded in human neurology and the functioning of the brain? Lakoff studied the neural circuits involved in the production or understanding of metaphors:

> During learning, much of the abstract domain is structured by fixed projections from the embodied domain. When processing source domain words in the context of a target domain subject matter, the fixed connections result in co-activation of the two domains. Thus, source domain activations arising from inferences are projected onto the target domain via the preestablished mapping (2009: 18).

Neurological research has shown that traumatic injuries to the left peri-Sylvan region result in the impairment of relational knowledge. Cognitive disorders following stroke and associated with autism and schizophrenia, among others, involve the inability to produce or understand metaphors. Cognition seems to be grounded in sensory-motor terms such as visual, gustatory, olfactory or tactile. For example, thinking about an object recalls a particular physical experience with that object simulating it in the brain (Pecher, Boot and Van Dantzig 2011: 218). Metaphors based on different sensory-motor concepts may have different neural substrates. Metaphorical use of image schemata explain how abstract concepts can also be grounded in physical experience (Lakoff 2009; Pecher, Boot and Van Dantzig 2011: 219). Neuroimaging studies of the neural basis of metaphors show that conventional metaphors found in everyday language trigger the neural circuits in the right hemisphere, while unconventional ones, such as those found in poetry and literature, activate the left (Schmidt et al. 2010).

Kinship metaphors

A broadly defined metaphor is an extension of some attributes of the source term out of its domain to a target item in another domain (Kronenfeld 1996). Moreover, it is an applied analogy of relations (Pinker 2007). Research in psychology suggests that the conceptual metaphor is a unique cognitive mechanism that shapes social thought and attitudes (Landau, Meier and Kiefer 2010). As Scheffler has noted in his discussion of focality in kinship (1972), human kinship implies much more than primary kin recognition as well as genealogical relationships that might be real or fictional. It abounds with multiple symbolic meanings and metaphors that presuppose the cognitive abilities far beyond the capacity of nonhuman primates (Leaf and Read 2012; Milicic 2013). Understanding kinship through metaphors is common across cultures. Thus varied classification of kin often includes the denial of biological reproduction, as well as the metaphorical creation of kinship ties where there are none. However, that does not imply a lack of biological knowledge.

Scheffler's (1972) stance on metaphors, discussed above, has been amply corroborated by several authors (Shapiro 2012; Shapiro Chapter 1). According to Lakoff (1990), the English term *mother* is radially structured with respect to a number of its subcategories defined by a cluster of converging cognitive models—the birth model, the nurturance model, etc. In addition, there are 'noncentral extensions' such as *birth mother, adoptive mother, surrogate mother*, etc. that are variants acquired through learning. These latter terms are understood via their relationship to the central category of *mother* (ibid.: 91). The capacity for metaphorical thought

10. CREEPING PLANTS AND WINDING BELTS

implies partial overlap between two semantic domains (Kronenfeld 1996; Lakoff and Johnson 1980; Pinker 2007) and a 'blended space' (Lakoff 2009; Pecher, Boot and Van Dantzig 2011). Many cultures use metaphors of creeping plants such as 'grapevines' (Milicic 1998), or other winding objects, to think about kin groups. This metaphorical usage is based on image schemata—mental associations between two referents based on similarity and important for grounding abstract concepts (Lakoff 1990: 106). The relative similarity between the source and the target can be in shape (denotative), function (connotative), or based on the similarity of relation between the source and its larger framework (Kronenfeld 1996).

In the Croatian ethnographic example of the metaphoric use of grapevines in the domain of kinship the similarity is connotative: the kin group, referred to as a grapevine is based on what it *does* rather than what it *is*. In the village of B., located on the island of Hvar off the Croatian coast with about 150 permanent inhabitants, villagers are keenly aware of their kin ties as evidenced by frequent references and discussions about the membership in a particular kin group or *loza* (grapevine). If not entirely sure, they employ a kinship calculus tracing the relations, and relations of relations, to locate an individual mentally within the kin network. The most inclusive category of relatedness is the village itself in opposition to another village on the island, or the island in opposition to the entire mainland. When in need of favours the villagers refer to one another by the generic term *zermo* (relative). Within the village, individuals were most often identified at the level of the *loza* (grapevine) or kin group. A *loza* is a bilateral localised kin group with an apical ancestor, male or female, associated with a house. Its *loza* name is added to all individual names, since many have identical first and last names (Milicic 1998). There are about 15 'grapevines' with living members. Many of these individual 'grapevines' are actually branches of the same 'grapevine' that got detached from its 'stem' in some more or less distant past. Some of these original connections are forgotten, but many are remembered and often commented upon. The ideal of village endogamy and socioeconomic homogamy necessarily presented problems and overlapping of *lozas*, which was partially solved by splintering off.

In the denotative sense of what it *is*, a grapevine is a plant, while in the connotative sense, to what it *does*, it is a winding, coiling, creeping thing. An object not in the domain of plants, but with similar attributes, is the *zinari*, a long winding belt in Greek folk costume, also metaphorically used when thinking about kinship. It is wrapped several times around the waist, and it metaphorically represents degrees of blood relatedness. In the Greek folk model the contrasting metaphors of blood and oil refer to consanguineal and spiritual kinship respectively, the latter established through baptism as an extension of the degrees of blood kinship (du Boulay 1984; Just 2000). In the Pidhalion, the Greek Orthodox Church instructions, the first permissible marriage is between third cousins. In the local interpretation, it is permissible between ego and the child of a third cousin. In contrast, marriage is forbidden between affinal (in-law) kin of the relatives of prohibited degrees down to and including the sixth degree (ibid.: 101). The number of turns of the metaphorical belt explicitly describes the genealogical distance as an index of prohibited degrees of marriage. The *zinari* represents the winding path of blood that must always be directed in the same direction. 'The blood must not turn around' lest an act of incest is committed (du Boulay 1984: 548). Similarly, god parenthood, or ritual sponsorship, is always asymmetrical and collective because it binds not just individuals but two families who cannot sponsor each other's children. The oil, used in the ritual of baptism is the symbol of god parenthood and the spiritual counterpart of blood and kinship: 'the oil and the blood must not turn around' (Just 2000: 131–35). God parenthood, or fictive kinship, as a collective notion is practised asymmetrically in that ritual sponsorship cannot be directly exchanged between two families. It is an explicit comparison of the rules of marriage that should not take place between those families who are already in-laws. Marriage and blood kinship between relatives within the prohibited degrees are considered incestuous, as well as direct symmetrical exchange of spouses such as two brothers marrying each other's sisters. It is an extension of consanguinity to the prohibition of reciprocal god parenthood, itself being a kind of parenthood.

In order to show that a metaphor is structured by our experience, Lakoff (1987: 276) asks three questions: (1) What determines the choice of a possible well-structured source domain? (2) What determines the pairing of the source domain with the target domain? (3) What determines the details of the source-to-target mapping? To follow him:

- The blood is a life-giving substance.
- The oil gives spiritual life in the ritual of baptism.
- The grapevine is an easily observable model of a fast-reproducing form of life in the environment.
- Kin relationships are similar to the winding grapevine shoots as evidenced in the metaphorical use of *loza*.

10. CREEPING PLANTS AND WINDING BELTS

- Kin space is envisioned as the space often 'invaded' by the ever-expanding vines. Grapes are children to the grapevines.
- Kinship groups split when too large.
- Grapevine cuttings are used to plant new plants.
- New families that split off build new houses.
- New grapevines get new nicknames and old connections are broken.

Compared with the Greek example, we can see how both objects, one from the domain of plants, the other from the domain of clothing, are similar and comparable in terms of some of their attributes. The grapevine and the *zinari* kinship metaphors show how the two classes, plants and clothing, are merged into the same more inclusive class of 'coiling things' based on their shared winding, coiling image (Figure 34).

COILING THINGS	(image schema)	LIQUIDS
SHARED FUNCTION		SHARED SUBSTANCE
Connotative		**Denotative**
(what something DOES)		(what something IS)
GRAPEVINES (Domain of plants)		SHARED SOURCE of kin groups
ZINARI BELT (Domain of clothing)		BLOOD (biological)/OIL (spiritual kin)

Figure 34. Image schema of the domain of plants and the domain of clothing
Source: © Bojka Milicic.

Just as the coiling grapevine metaphor facilitates the understanding of kinship dynamics in the first case, the Greek example provides insight into the character of kinship through the attributes of the long and winding *zinari* belt. In the latter example the analogy is between the domain of 'blood' kin and fictive kin metaphorically associated with the domain of another liquid substance—the oil establishing a spiritual relation and modelled on the concrete physical relation of 'shared blood'. The degrees of kin distance/closeness is perceived in terms of the clothing domain, the *zinari* belt, referring to it both denotatively (what the *zinari* IS) and connotatively (what the *zinari* DOES), coiling around the waist in one prescribed direction. But this is not all. This particular element of clothing is also analogous to the blood that 'must not return' in the rules of marriage. Hence reference to an item that coils around the body only in one direction also alludes to the ritual oil as the metaphor of spiritual kinship that also must not return lest an act of spiritual incest be committed.

Visual metaphors of kinship

Carl Schuster (Schuster and Carpenter 1996) has compiled a collection of artefacts from numerous world cultures that depict various representations of kinship, from simple notches to elaborate figurative and abstract patterns in a broad range of media: clay, cloth, wood, and textiles. Etched, painted, carved, or woven objects and tattooed bodies carry motifs that represent ancestors expanding vertically or horizontally, and sometimes in both directions. Although it is hard to establish such meanings based on the archaeological record, many of the ethnographic examples in this work are explicitly associated with kinship, such as the motifs that repetitively evoke concatenation of stylised or realistically depicted human bodies. Alfred Gell (1993) has discussed numerous ethnographic examples of Polynesian tattooing patterns in the context of social structure and kinship. Thus in the Marquesas, the common tattoo motif of climbing, vine-like stylised human figures represents the *etua* (ancestors). Gell noted that one of the main attributes of Polynesian tattooing is its protective function of creating a second layer of skin, particularly in the use of the images of shell animals such as the tortoise. He also interprets the widely used Polynesian mythological motif of doubles in terms of its protective attributes. A Samoan tattoo pattern of the *pe'a*, the flying fox, illustrates the metaphorical connection between the domain of animals and the domain of kinship. The flying fox, a species of bat, hanging upside down envelops itself into its own wings creating a self-protective layer. The *pe'a* motif also occurs carved in the rafters and beams of a house that itself is a spatial and temporal representation of a kin group (ibid.: 96–99). Furthermore, Gell cites numerous examples of other Polynesian cultural practices, from many layers of tapa cloth to layers of fat, in terms of their protective functions metaphorically associated with kin groups as protective social layers (ibid.: 177–79).

The foregoing, very short selection out of numerous visual and verbal examples of kinship metaphors, shows the attributes of kinship expressed across the cognitive domains in terms of winding, coiling, layering or protective properties of various objects, as well as the analogy of relations and relations of relations within and between classes of objects. This makes plausible the hypothesis that metaphorical thought, fundamental to human cognition, at least originated simultaneously with or perhaps developed out of the social cognition and its fundamental field of kinship.

10. CREEPING PLANTS AND WINDING BELTS

Possible origin of metaphorical thought

How were metaphors produced in proto-human language and is it possible to hypothesise about an actual shift from the premetaphorical stage to the metaphor production stage? Steven Mithen (1996) has hypothesised that cognitive fluidity took place about 50,000 years ago through the opening of the connections between specialised cognitive modules and general intelligence, triggered by language bridging across the specialised cognitive modules. Using a metaphor from medieval sacral architecture, Mithen illustrates the architecture of the mind. In this model, language 'vandalised' the partitions between previously walled-off 'chapels', or modules, of social, natural and technical intelligence making possible the free flow of information between the four domains of intuitive knowledge (Figure 35). Thus, 'the mind acquires not only the ability but a positive passion for metaphor or analogy' (ibid.: 71). Of course, his theory is itself a metaphor: a concept or a set of ideas used to elucidate a more difficult concept or set of ideas across, in this case, the domains of sacral and cognitive architecture respectively.

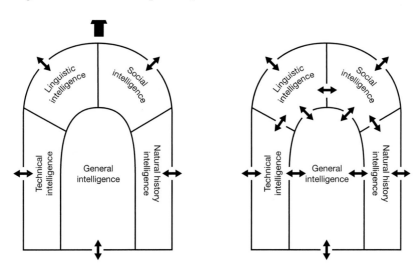

Figure 35. The mind as a chapel
Source: Adapted from Mithen (1996: 67) and used with the permission of © Steven Mithen and Thames and Hudson Ltd.

Mithen associates the transition itself with fully modern behaviour, the set of traits distinguishing our species from its predecessors as well as other primates, which is inferred from the archaeological record. There is a debate whether this transition actually took place as an abrupt behavioural change 40,000–50,000 years ago or more plausibly, considering the scale of changes, it evolved slowly over a longer period (Klein 2000). In a different approach, Murray Leaf and Dwight Read (2012) hypothesise the coevolution of thought and social organisation as evidenced in the archaeological record in the European Upper Paleolithic cave paintings within their new paradigm in the study of kinship. In this analysis the representations of various animals grouped together according to their respective species may be interpreted as the human capacity to understand the concept of class versus an individual as well as several more inclusive classes of classes. This is analogous to the ability to think about the individual selves, as well as classes of people and relations among them (ibid.: 68–88). I contend, then, that this is also the evidence of metaphorical thought founded not only on the similarity of objects, but on the analogy of relations within and between classes of objects. Concepts of kinship are the prime example of such thought associated with human behavioural modernity.

Conclusion

As Scheffler has proposed in his approach to kinship terminology, metaphorical thought is based not only on the similarity of objects, but also on analogical similarity of relation. This is one of the hallmarks of human cognition, but it is also the main attribute of kinship. I hypothesised here that concrete bodily experiences, rooted in the FOR and closely related to social cognition, triggered the metaphorical thought that was then used in other semantic domains. This is evident in the widespread metaphors of space that are used as concrete referents to the domain of kinship in terms of close/distant and transferred to the domain of emotions. The ethnographic examples of the referents across the domain of plants to the domain of kinship, as well as the metaphorical construction of fictive kinship, confirm that metaphorical thought is at the basis of human complex social cognition. The transition to cognitive fluidity between different semantic domains, probably fully in place by 40,000–50,000 years ago, perhaps included kinship terminologies providing cognitive building blocks for the linguistic production of metaphors.

References

Allen, Catherine. 2002. *The Hold Life has: Coca and Cultural Identity in an Andean Community*. Washington: Smithsonian Institution Press.

Anderson, Michael L. 2010. 'Neural reuse: A fundamental organizational principle of the brain'. *Behavioral and Brain Sciences* 33(4): 245–313. doi.org/10.1017/S0140525X10000853

Bennardo, Giovanni. 2010. 'Space, kinship, and mind'. *Behavioral and Brain Sciences* 33(5): 382–83. doi.org/10.1017/S0140525X10001925

Classen, Constance. 1993. *Inca Cosmology and the Human Body*. Salt Lake City: University of Utah Press.

Douglas, Mary. 1966. *Purity and Danger: An Analysis of Concepts of Pollution and Taboo*. London: Routledge & Kegan Paul. doi.org/10.4324/9780203361832

du Boulay, Juliet. 1984. 'The blood: Symbolic relationship between descent, marriage, spiritual prohibitions, and fictive kinship in Greece'. *Man* (n.s.) 19(4): 533–56. doi.org/10.2307/2802325

El Guindi, Fadwa. 2010. 'The cognitive path through kinship'. *Behavioral and Brain Sciences* 33(5): 384–85. doi.org/10.1017/S0140525X10002050

Fiske, Alan P. 1992. 'The four elementary forms of sociality: Framework for a unified theory of social relations'. *Psychological Review* 99(4): 689–723. doi.org/10.1037/0033-295X.99.4.689

Gell, Alfred. 1993. *Wrapping in Images: Tattooing in Polynesia*. Oxford: Clarendon.

Ijzerman, Hans and Sander L. Koole. 2011. 'From perceptual rags to metaphoric riches—bodily, social, and cultural constraints on sociocognitive metaphors: Comment on Landau, Meier, and Keefer (2010)'. *Psychological Bulletin* 137(2): 355–61. doi.org/10.1037/a0022373

Jones, Doug. 2010. 'Human kinship, from conceptual structure to grammar'. *Behavioral and Brain Sciences* 33(5): 367–416. doi.org/10.1017/S0140525X10000890

Just, Roger 2000. *A Greek Island Cosmos: Kinship & Community on Meganisi*. Santa Fe and Oxford: SAR Press.

Klein, Richard G. 2000. 'Archaeology and the evolution of human behavior'. *Evolutionary Anthropology* 9(1): 17–35. doi.org/10.1002/(SICI)1520-6505(2000)9:1<17::AID-EVAN3>3.0.CO;2-A

Kronenfeld, David B. 1996. *Plastic Glasses and Church Fathers: Semantic Extensions from the Ethnoscience Tradition*. New York: Oxford University Press.

Lakoff, George. 1987. *Women, Fire, and Dangerous Things*. Chicago: Chicago University Press. doi.org/10.7208/chicago/9780226471013.001.0001

———. 2009. 'The neural theory of metaphor'. *Social Science Research Network*. doi.org/10.2139/ssrn.1437794

Lakoff, George and Mark Johnson. 1980. *Metaphors We Live By*. Chicago: Chicago University Press.

Landau, Mark J., Brian Meier and Lucas Kiefer. 2010. 'A metaphor enriched social cognition'. *Psychological Bulletin* 136(6): 1045–67. doi.org/10.1037/a0020970

Leaf, Murray J. and Dwight Read. 2012. *The Conceptual Foundation of Human Society and Thought: Anthropology on a New Plane*. Lanham, MD: Lexington Books.

Milicic, Bojka. 1998. 'The grapevine forest: Kinship, status, and wealth in a Mediterranean community (selo, Croatia)'. In *Kinship, Networks, and Exchange*, edited by Thomas Schweizer and Douglas R. White, 15–35. Cambridge: Cambridge University Press. doi.org/10.1017/CBO9780511896620.004

———. 2013. 'Talk is not cheap: Kinship Terminologies and the Origins of Language'. *Structure and Dynamics: e-Journal of Anthropological and Related Sciences*. Online: escholarship.org/uc/item/6zw317jh (accessed 1 June 2017).

Mithen, Steven. 1996. *The Prehistory of the Mind: The Cognitive Origins of Art, Religion, and Science*. London: Thames and Hudson.

Pecher, Diane, Inge Boot and Saskia Van Dantzig. 2011. 'Abstract concepts: Sensory-motor grounding, metaphors, and beyond'. In *The Psychology of Learning and Motivation*, edited by Brian Ross, 217–48. Burlington: Academic Press. doi.org/10.1016/b978-0-12-385527-5.00007-3

Pinker, Steven. 2007. *The Stuff of Thought: Language as a Window into Human Nature*. New York: Viking.

Rigney, Daniel. 2001. *The Metaphorical Society: An Invitation to Social Theory*. Lanham, MD: Rowman and Littlefield.

Ross, Brian (ed.). 2011. *The Psychology of Learning and Motivation*. Burlington: Academic Press.

Sahlins, Marshall. 2011a. 'What kinship is (part one)'. *Journal of the Royal Anthropological Institute* (n.s.) 17(1): 2–19. doi.org/10.1111/j.1467-9655.2010.01666.x

———. 2011b. 'What kinship is (part two)'. *Journal of the Royal Anthropological Institute* (n.s.) 17(2): 227–42. doi.org/10.1111/j.1467-9655.2011.01677.x

———. 2012. 'Birth is the metaphor. Comment'. *Journal of the Royal Anthropological Institute* (n.s.) 18(3): 673–77. doi.org/10.1111/j.1467-9655.2012.01782.x

Scheffler, Harold W. 1970. '*The Elementary Structures of Kinship*, by Claude Lévi-Strauss: A review article'. *American Anthropologist* 72: 251–68. doi.org/10.1525/aa.1970.72.2.02a00020

———. 1972. 'Kinship semantics'. *Annual Reviews in Anthropology* 1: 309–28. doi.org/10.1146/annurev.an.01.100172.005121

Scheffler, Harold W. and Floyd Glenn Lounsbury. 1971. *A Study in Structural Semantics: The Siriono Kinship System*. Englewood Cliffs, NJ: Prentice Hall.

Schmidt, Gwenda L., Alexander Kranjec, Eileen R. Cardillo and Anjan Chatterjee. 2010. 'Beyond laterality: A critical assessment of research on the neural basis of metaphor'. *Journal of the International Neuropsychological Society* 16(1): 1–5. doi.org/10.1017/S1355617709990543

Schuster, Carl and Edmund Snow Carpenter. 1996. *Patterns that Connect: Social Symbolism in Ancient and Tribal Art*. New York: Harry N. Abrams.

Schweizer, Thomas and Douglas R. White (eds). 1998. *Kinship, Networks, and Exchange*. Cambridge: Cambridge University Press. doi.org/10.1017/CBO9780511896620

Shapiro, Warren. 2012. 'Extensionism and the nature of kinship. Comment'. *Journal of the Royal Anthropological Institute* (n.s.) 18(1): 191–93. doi.org/10.1111/j.1467-9655.2011.01738.x

11

Kinship in Mind: Three Approaches

Doug Jones

Social anthropologists mostly study kinship as a principle of social organisation. But there is also a psychological and cognitive side to human kinship, involving questions like: How do people recognise others as kin of one sort or another? What do kin categories mean and how are they related to one another? What, if anything, distinguishes thinking about kinship from other varieties of social cognition?

Different schools of anthropology offer very different answers to these questions. Here I review three approaches to the psychology of kinship. One has its roots in evolutionary theory and human/nonhuman comparisons. The second is concerned with symbolism, culture, and the natives' explicit theories of procreation and kinship. These approaches are likely to be familiar to students of evolution and human behaviour, and cultural anthropology, respectively. The third approach stems from recent developments in cognitive science, especially in the study of specialised domains of cognition. This approach is newest, and probably least familiar to most anthropologists and even to most cognitive scientists, so it receives most attention here. I argue that human beings have a specialised cognitive system—which can be called 'kinship core cognition' or 'kinship conceptual structure'—comprising a set of universal building blocks for organising knowledge of kin and kin categories in an abstract kinship space. Much of the success of formal methods in the study of kin categorisation, as carried out by authors like Floyd Lounsbury (1964), Ward Goodenough (1965), Harold Scheffler (1978), Dwight Read (2010), Murray Leaf (Leaf and Read 2012) and others, depends on these building blocks. They also turn out to play a role in generating social organisation—at least so I argue in a discussion of Aboriginal Australian kinship systems. In particular, Hal Scheffler's monumental work on Australian kin classification is a major influence on the last section of the paper, which proposes that the conceptual structure of kinship plays a role in generating not just kin terminologies but social organisation.

Kinship and attachment

For evolutionary biologists, kinship means genetic relatedness. This can be defined numerically, as the coefficient of relatedness of organism B to organism A; the expected number of copies of a gene in B that are identical by descent with a copy of that gene in A, over and above whatever gene copies B shares with A by virtue of being part of the same population. (The last part means that the coefficient of relatedness is defined relative to some background population.)

Natural selection is expected to build organisms that are sensitive to coefficients of relatedness, for several reasons. First, in most populations, the gene pool contains some fraction of deleterious recessive alleles, which are harmless in one dose (as heterozygotes), but harmful in a double dose (as homozygotes). Since the offspring of genetically related parents are more likely to be genetically identical—homozygous—at any given genetic locus, they are more likely to get a double dose of deleterious recessives, and to suffer reduced fitness. So, natural selection is expected to favour an inhibition on mating with close relatives. Second, an organism that behaves altruistically to a genetic relative, acting in a way that reduces its own fitness, while increasing the fitness of its relative, will end up leaving more copies of its genes in the next generation than a less altruistic one. So natural selection is expected to favour altruism toward genetic kin, depending on their coefficient of relatedness.

Such is the theory. But organisms cannot read one another's genotypes directly. Inbreeding avoidance and altruism based on kinship require some machinery for *kin recognition*, sensitive to phenotypic or other cues correlated with kinship. Two broad classes of mechanisms are known to biologists—phenotype matching and associational cues. Both have been demonstrated in a variety of nonhuman organisms (Hauber and Sherman 2001; Hepper (ed.) 1991; Chapais and Berman (eds) 2004; Parr and de Waal 1999;), and there is some evidence they operate in humans as well, summarised below.

Phenotype matching

Genetically similar individuals are likely to be phenotypically similar, so natural selection may favour rules of thumb that say 'Avoid mating with … be extra nice to … those who resemble you.' Human beings seem to be sensitive to olfactory cues in choosing mates, preferring the smell of those who differ at genetic loci in the major histocompatibility complex (MHC) (Porter and Moore 1981; the MHC controls much of the immune system in vertebrates). Friends tend to be more genetically similar than expected by chance at loci controlling olfaction (Christakis and Fowler 2014). People judge faces that have been morphed to resemble themselves as more trustworthy (DeBruine 2002), and (in the case of child faces) more appealing (DeBruine 2004). Behavioural similarity also may serve as a heuristic cue for kinship (Park and Schaller 2005).

Associational cues

Primates in general (Silk 2001; Pusey 2005), probably including humans, rely more on associational cues than on phenotypic similarity to recognise kin. An early proposal invoked associational cues as a proximate mechanism in inbreeding avoidance. Edward Westermarck (1903) argued that children raised together from a young age would later show a lack of erotic interest in one another. In most cases these individuals would be siblings, and the Westermarck effect would make inbreeding less likely. This effect is well-documented among nonhuman animals, under the label of *negative sexual imprinting* (Pusey 2005). In humans, test cases arise when nonsiblings are raised together but sexual relations are not discouraged, or are even encouraged. Several versions of this natural experiment have been studied, involving adolescents raised together in nursery groups in Israeli *kibbutzim* (Talmon 1964; Shepher 1971), married cousins raised in the same extended families in Lebanon (McCabe 1983), and Taiwanese couples where the girls were adopted at an early age into the families of their husbands-to-be (Wolf 1995). These all support Westermarck's hypothesis, which stands as the most plausible explanation for the near-universal avoidance of nuclear family incest. An amplified version of Westermarck's hypothesis has recently been proposed by Debra Lieberman, John Tooby and Leda Cosmides (2007; Lieberman 2009). They argue for two psychological mechanisms regulating kinship sentiments, childhood coresidence, and observing one's mother caring for a newborn. The evidence is that both sorts of cues affect both altruism and sexual indifference.

This research suggests some obvious extensions. If older siblings bond to an infant cared for by their mother, then men may bond to an infant cared for by a long-term sexual partner. And both sibling and paternal bonds may extend to an infant known to have been born to a woman even when she is not directly observed caring for the child.

Kinship and cultural models

In the documentary *Stories We Tell*, filmmaker Sarah Polley (2012) tells the story of her discovery that her late mother's husband is not her biological father. A crucial moment comes when she learns that a DNA test has assigned paternity to one of several potential genitors with 99+ percentage probability. She comes to know her biological paternity with much more certainty than if she relied just on an evolved modular kin-recognition system, which in this case could never support more than suspicions. But this only works because Polley accepts what she has been told about genes and genetic testing. Her theories about the biology of kinship, acquired as part of her culture, affect her beliefs about who her 'real' kin are and the strength of her attachment to them.

This clearly poses a puzzle, because formal theories and informal cultural models of kinship are not guaranteed to agree with the modern biologist's theories of genetic relatedness and genetic inheritance. Before the twentieth century even experts had some strange ideas. Charles Darwin, for example, made a considerable effort, mostly unsuccessful, to discover the nature of heredity. His investigations convinced him that traits acquired during the course of an organism's lifetime could be passed on to its offspring (1868: vol. II: 23–24). He was also convinced by reports of telegony in horses and pigs, in which offspring supposedly inherited traits from their mothers' previous mates (vol. I: 403–05, vol. II: 264). He tried to come up with a physiological mechanism that would make these unusual modes of inheritance possible.

Similar beliefs—in the inheritance of acquired traits and telegony (in the guise of partible paternity)—are recorded for many societies (e.g. Beckerman and Valentine (eds) 2002). And anthropologists have reported other exotic native statements about procreation. In some cases, the substance of a child is said to come only from its father, with the mother being just an incubator. Conversely, according to some anthropologists, paternity and even the necessity of intercourse in conception may be denied. (For the Trobriand Islands, see Malinowski 1987: 142–66; but cf. Weiner 1988: 53–58. For Aboriginal Australia, see review in Hiatt 1996: 120–41, and a sceptical take in Scheffler 1978: 5–13.)

Taken at face value, these accounts raise the possibility that kinship means something different in different cultures. Some anthropologists go so far as to propose that the western concept of 'kinship' does not translate everywhere. Perhaps anthropology needs to replace the study of kinship with the study of an open-ended fuzzy domain of 'relatedness.' Relatedness might result not just from intercourse or parturition, but from sharing a wet nurse or sharing meals, from being born at the same time or place, or working together (Sahlins 2013).

This approach is defended at some length by Janet Carsten in an ethnography of Malay kinship. According to Carsten, the Malay villagers she studied conceptualise kinship as shared blood. While this sounds close to prescientific western ideas of blood kinship, Carsten argues that her subjects saw blood as malleable. 'Blood changes through life – as does kinship' (1997: 107). Blood is manufactured from food, especially heated food, so people sharing food at the same hearth—including adopted children—come to have the same blood, and 'children's physical appearance and character are believed to be strongly influenced by the people they reside with' (ibid.: 60). Carsten herself was told that she was coming to resemble members of her host family. Also, blood is transformed into milk, so children who share a wet nurse come to be kin, and are covered by an incest taboo, even if they have different mothers and fathers.

These Malay beliefs about relatedness and inheritance have different sources. Concepts of 'milk kinship' and related incest taboos are apparently of Muslim origin. The idea that hereditary traits are not fixed at birth, but unsettled throughout life, up to death, is widespread in the Austronesian-speaking culture area, and may originate in a body of custom, or *adat*, going back to a founding population of farmers and mariners on Formosa (Bellwood, Fox and Tryon (eds) 2006). It is interesting to note that many of the strong claims about the cultural construction of kinship have come from anthropologists working with Austronesian-speaking populations. On Yap, in Micronesia, it has been claimed that natives denied the role of intercourse in conception and considered that a woman's children become kin to her husband because she works on his land (Schneider 1984). In Polynesia, adoption and coresidence were supposed to generate relatedness (Caroll (ed.) 1970; Brady (ed.) 1976). On Madagascar, it is said that inherited potential is flexible, and that membership in hereditary groups is fixed at death rather than birth (Astuti 2001).

These accounts seem hard to square with either the evolutionist's view that human behaviour toward kin is governed by evolved mechanisms of kin recognition, or the classic social anthropologist's view that genealogy is the universal underpinning of kinship. It is important to note, therefore, that there are good reasons to question whether the culturalist account is really the whole story about kinship. First, there are serious questions about whether the ethnographic evidence really supports the strong theoretical claims made for it. For Malaysia, Warren Shapiro (2011) cites ethnographies that seem to undermine Carsten's more extreme claims. For Yap, Adam Kuper (1999) is sceptical on a number of grounds. For example, based on David Labby's (1976) work, either Schneider's understanding of Yapese conception beliefs was seriously incomplete, or those beliefs changed radically in just 20 years. For Oceania, Joan Silk (1980) argues that adoption overwhelmingly involves closely related families, and is largely consistent with predictions from the theory of kin selection.

Second, research in cognitive science shows that what people say they believe, and how they think, are two different things. Explicitly avowed theories and models are an imperfect guide to the implicit concepts that may actually guide reasoning (Kahneman 2011). Consider religious beliefs, for example (Barrett 1999). Adherents of the major monotheistic religions explicitly avow that God is omnipotent, and can do any number of things at once, but when asked to reason about God's actions they imagine that God finds it easier to act sequentially rather than simultaneously. There may be a similar disconnect in the psychology of kinship. Some evidence comes from the Vezo of Madagascar (Astuti 2001; see also Bloch, Solomon and Carey 2001, for the Zafimaniry, another Madagascan group). Like many other Austronesian speakers, the Vezo profess that individuals take on the character of their surroundings. They claim, for example, that adoptees grow to resemble their adoptive parents, and that children who spend a lot of time associating with missionaries turn light skinned. Yet in psychological tests involving scenarios of infants switched at birth to a different family, Vezo adults clearly differentiate between physical traits resulting from biological parentage, and social traits influenced by adoptive parents—between nature and nurture. In short, at some level, Vezo do not reason in accordance with their professed beliefs. Rita Astuti (2001) argues that these beliefs constitute an ideology, which supports cultural practices like adoption and the symbolic demotion of nuclear family ties in favour of wider connections. However, this explicit ideology coexists with an implicit concept of kinship close to the western one.

Kinship and conceptual structure

Suppose we try to split the difference between the evolutionist and the culturalist account of kinship. Perhaps the evolutionists are right in thinking that people have emotional machinery that leads to the formation of attachments, the strength of which roughly correlates with genetic distance via some proximal cues. Perhaps the culturalists are right in thinking that there is wide variation in cultural models of how people come to be related one another, with less of a common core across cultures than one might expect. The evolutionist account might work best for behaviour toward close kin, while the culturalist account might work best for behaviour toward distant relatives (Rodseth and Wrangham 2004).

I think, however, that neither the standard evolutionist account, nor the culturalist account, nor a blend of the two offer a full theory of human kinship. Kinship also includes a special-purpose cognitive/conceptual side, evident in kin terminology and other areas of social interaction, where interacting individuals draw on their common knowledge of conceptual universals to construct shared codes for categorising and dealing with kin. Kin terminologies reveal the working of the kinship part of the mind with exceptional clarity. Across cultures, there are regularities in which kin types are terminologically merged and separated, or otherwise linguistically unmarked and marked, that implicate a common conceptual structure underlying local vagaries in theories of relatedness and procreation (Jones 2010). These regularities include:

1. *Kin terminologies form a closed system, a separate semantic domain.* Terms for kin—like *father* or *aunt* in English—are distinct from terms for other social relationships, like *boss* or *friend*. Words for kin are sometimes used for nonkin as well, but for core kin terms it can

be shown, sometimes by the evidence of marked linguistic forms like *godfather*, sometimes by patterns of usage, that these nonkin uses are secondary.

2. *Kin terminologies are systematically related to one another.* Kin terminologies form around a core set of terms, which can be combined to give terms for more distant relatives. For example, *father's sister* and *mother's sister* are both *aunt* in English. These mappings are highly structured. Thus *aunt* is a nondisjunctive category, built from the natural classes of parent and sister. Disjunctive categories—a single word for mother and father's sister, which excludes mother's sister—are logically possible, but rare or non-existent (Hage 1997).

3. *Kin categories map onto genealogical categories.* Words like father, mother and aunt can be assigned to positions on genealogical charts, and this is true of kin terms across cultures. That kin categories are genealogically structured is not a logically necessary truth, but one of the great empirical discoveries of anthropology.

4. *Kin terms are subject to formal analysis, using methods analogous—or even identical—to those in linguistics.* A large literature demonstrates the success of formal analysis of kin terms, although there are differences among scholars over preferred techniques. The parallels with formal linguistics have been noted by many authors (Greenberg 1966, 1990; Jones 2010; Kroeber 1909; Lévi-Strauss 1969).

I suggest that the best explanation for these findings is that kinship is governed not just by machinery for emotional attachment, but by a specialised panhuman conceptual system. In the rest of this section, I consider how this hypothesis fits within a larger universe of overlapping research programs in cognitive science, which go under the names of conceptual structure (Jackendoff 2002; Pinker 2007), domain specificity (Barkow, Cosmides and Tooby 1992; Hirschfeld and Gelman (eds) 1994) and core cognition (Carey 2009).

What these research programs have in common is the theory that the human mind comes equipped, from birth, not just with sensory, motor and motivational systems, but with a system of innate abstract ideas. In a sense, this amounts to trying to put Immanuel Kant's philosophy of knowledge on a scientific footing (Kant 2009; Kitcher 1990; Pinker 2007: 153–233). Kant argued that concepts of number, space, time, and causation could not be derived from experience, but had to be already present in the mind to organise the raw material of perception (2009). For example, in the absence of some preexisting conceptual structure relating to causation, nothing in experience implies a distinction between 'A happens, then B happens' and 'A causes B'. In the modern cognitive science reworking of this argument, innate conceptual structure is organised into a number of domains. These domains probably include interconnected concepts: of stuff and things in space; of processes and events in time; of quantity, including amount, number, and likelihood; of force and causation; of life, animacy and living kinds; of the minds of others; and of possession and other social relationships and responsibilities. On the account proposed here, the conceptual structure of kinship is a major subdivision of the last of these domains.

Below I review two domains of conceptual structure: the domains of objects in space and of kinship. The first is of interest here because the conceptual structure of objects in space seems to be a kind of master domain, from which derivative domains, including kinship, borrow much of their organisation. This means that when we review the conceptual structure of kinship, it will turn out to be organised around an abstract 'kinship space'.

A major source of evidence for conceptual structure comes from language, with different conceptual domains attaching themselves to different linguistic domains. In English, for example, the conceptual structure of space attaches particularly to spatial prepositions like *on, in, over, along*, and so on. Other languages use other word form classes (Levinson 2003; Levinson and Wilkins (eds) 2006). Languages vary not only in the form classes they recruit to express spatial conceptual structure, but in the range of spatial positions covered by a given construction. For example, English 'A is *on* B' requires that A and B be in contact ('The table lamp is *on* the table', but 'The hanging lamp is *over* [or *above*, but not *on*] the table'). However, English *on* does not require that A be above B ('The picture is *on* the wall'). By contrast, Japanese *ue* works differently, applying to the first two cases but not the third (Levinson and Wilkins 2006a: 554).

Underlying this variation are some common principles that suggest the language of space is built on a common foundation across cultures. A review of cross-cultural evidence suggests that the prototypical spatial scene involves 'a relatively small, manipulable, inanimate, movable and independent figure object ... in close contiguity with a relatively large, relatively stationary ... ground object—for example a cup on a table' (Levinson and Wilkins 2006b: 515). Normally the smaller object is the figure, or focus of attention, but exceptionally the figure/ground relationship is reversed. Spatial terms recognise variations from this and a few other prototypical scenes corresponding to a limited number of distinctive features—whether or not the figure is in contact with the ground, or above it, or enclosed by it, and so on. Across languages, the number of distinctive features organising the language of space is probably in the low tens, with some features very widely used, others less so.

The kind of information conveyed by the language of space is limited, implying that the representation of space in conceptual structure is pretty schematic compared to its representation in perception (Pinker 2007: 174–88). Scale is largely absent: 'The plane is *on* the tarmac' gets the same preposition as 'The fly is *on* the table'. Metric information ('10 metres', '30 degrees') is largely omitted from prepositions and other spatial terms, as is most information about shape, except for a few dimensional contrasts (0-D/point-like versus 1-D/elongated versus 2-D/flat), and much other important information, like the worth of the object on the table. Almost any such information can of course be conveyed by stringing words together into sentences ('The lamp is on the table, 18 inches from the edge.' Or 'Reno is 427 miles west by southwest of Salt Lake City.'), but this falls outside the scope of the language and conceptual structure of space, properly speaking.

The language of space, as encoded in prepositions or other closed-class forms, seems to be a window onto a particular representational system. This system does not register everything that might be of interest about a collection of objects in space, but rather generates a stripped-down sketch of figure/ground spatial relationships. It exists alongside other representational systems that allow for a richer representation of other aspects of a scene, as needed.

The cross-cultural commonalities in the language of space suggest panhuman psychology. Further evidence for this comes from cognitive psychology, especially developmental psychology. Contrary to William James claim that an infant's world is 'a blooming buzzing confusion', babies seem to come into the world primed to recognise and track objects. Much of the evidence for this comes from studies of habituation: babies (and other folk as well) will spend more time staring at unusual events, as when an object moving behind a barrier is absent when the barrier is removed. Susan Carey (2009: 67–116) summarises the extensive evidence for 'core cognition' of objects in space, for 'representation of objects …

created by modular, encapsulated, perceptual input analyzers that have a long evolutionary history [and] continue to articulate our representation of the world throughout life' (ibid.: 115).

An anthropologist familiar with kin terminology who learns about the conceptual structure of objects in space may experience a sense of recognition. The connection between the language of space and its inferred conceptual structure looks a lot like the connection between the language of kinship and *its* inferred conceptual structure. Consider some of the parallels. Kin terms form a closed semantic domain. Although kin terms are nouns in the syntax of most languages, semantically they are more preposition-like than noun-like. They are about 'where' (metaphorically speaking), not 'what'. They denote relationships, not individual qualities—one is only *aunt* in relation to somebody. Kin relationships situate a figure (conventionally *alter*) in relation to a ground (conventionally *ego*). Alter is normally foregrounded, so that, for example, sex-of-alter distinctions are more common than sex-of-ego distinctions (but see the discussion of Lapp and Aboriginal Australian kinship below for motivated exceptions). Some kin types are cognitively prototypical, especially father and mother, as shown by patterns of linguistic markedness (Greenberg 1966, 1990; Shapiro Chapter 1). Kin terms differ from one another in distinctive features, and across cultures the number of such features is limited—probably not many more than the eight proposed by Alfred Kroeber (1909). These features rarely include quantities like 'more than 10 years older' (but see Gould 2000: 138–42 for an exception in Samoan), or important information like 'richer'. Even some particulars of spatial representation carry over. Distance is one dimension of variation in kin terms, and there is a vertical dimension as well, including older/younger than ego, and ascending/descending generation. Of course, there are important differences too between kinship space and physical space; most notably kinship space is built up by compounding genealogical primitives, instead of being a preexisting background.

The parallels between physical space and kinship space are only one instance of a broader pattern in conceptual structure. Linguists have noted for some time that just about every domain of conceptual structure studied so far—including time, causation, change of state, and possession—seems to borrow some of its organisation from the conceptual structure of objects in space (Jackendoff 2002; Pinker 2007). In some ways, this puts theories of conceptual structure at odds with standard evolutionary psychology, which emphasises how different cognitive domains are specialised for the adaptive demands of different cognitive tasks, rather than how they share a common organisation (Barkow, Cosmides and Tooby 1992). However, these cross-domain similarities have a potential evolutionary explanation, in the principle of homology. Homology is familiar in the study of anatomy; human hands and feet differ from each other because they are specialised for walking and grasping, but they have important structural similarities because of a shared evolutionary history. By the same token, in the course of human evolution, the neurological machinery specialised for spatial cognition may have been duplicated and reassigned the task of representing more abstract domains. Very recently, neuroanatomical evidence has been collected that supports this theory (Parkinson, Liu and Wheatley 2014; Parkinson and Wheatley 2013).

On a purely adaptationist account, one might expect the evolved psychology of kinship to consist of a collection of mechanisms optimally engineered to assess coefficients of relatedness. But the conceptual structure of kinship on display in kin terminology looks more complicated than this, and may bear the marks of a deeper evolutionary history.

Aboriginal Australians in kinship space

The previous section argued that kin terminology provides an especially clear view of the conceptual structure of kinship. This section argues that the conceptual structure of kinship is involved not just in kin terminology but in kin categorisation and social organisation more generally. It traces a path from conceptual structure to social structure, from figure/ground distinctions in kin terminology to Aboriginal Australian marriage rules and sections.

As noted above, figure/ground relationships—with the figure being the focus of attention—are a major feature in the conceptual structure of both kinship and physical space. In physical space, the figure is syntactically privileged as head of a noun phrase ('*the lamp* on the table') or the subject of a sentence ('*The lamp* is on the table.'). Usually the smaller and more moveable of two objects is the figure, but exceptional circumstances lead to the reverse ('*The table* you're looking for is under that lamp.').

Kin terms are generally nouns, so figure/ground relationships in kinship space, involving alter, ego, and linking kin, do not show up in prepositional argument structure as they do for spatial prepositions. However, they may be evident in other ways, as markedness relationships involving the presence or absence of sex distinctions, for example. Typically, alter is the figure and ego is the ground. This is how English works: knowing that A is *granddaughter* to E, tells you the sex of A but not E. In English, both grandparent and grandchild terms mark the sex of alter, not ego, indicating that more attention is focused on alter. However, in some cases other factors dominate categorisation. Konkoma Lapp provides an example. Terms for grandparents handle sex distinctions as English does: parent's father is *aggja* and parent's mother is *akko*, giving sex of alter, not ego. But grandchild terms work the opposite way, giving sex of ego, not alter. Man's child's child is *aggjot* and woman's child's child is *akkot*, so knowing that A is *akkot* to E tells you the sex of E but not A (Gould 2000: 289–91). What's going on in this case is that giving the sex of the senior individual in a kin relationship (a grandparent) is more important than giving the sex of the junior (a grandchild), regardless of who is alter and who is ego.

Aggjot and *akkot* are *inverse* terms. A gloss on 'A's *aggjot*' is 'he/she to whom A is *aggja* (grandfather)', and a gloss on 'A's *akkot*' is 'he/she to whom A is *akko* (grandmother)'. Following Gould, these grandchild types might be labelled 'grandfatherling' and 'grandmotherling,' or Grandfather[-1] and Grandmother[-1] (ibid.: 28). With these terms, ego is figure, not ground, because he or she is more perceptually salient by virtue of being senior. Consistent with their inverse status, the two grandchild terms are obvious morphological derivatives of the two grandparent terms, coming close to merging with their reciprocals.

Inverse kin terms are analysed by Joseph Greenberg (1990), and shown by George Murdock (1970) to be widespread. They are an instance of a common situation in linguistics where multiple constraints may be active—in this case, roughly, 'Emphasise alter over ego' and 'Emphasise senior over junior'—but one or the other is given precedence in cases of conflict (Jones 2010). In the rest of this section I argue that how this semantic conflict is resolved can have consequences not just for what people call their kin, but for how they organise their social lives. I look at kinship systems in Aboriginal Australia, where opting for inverse kin terms and corresponding categorisations have far-reaching social structural effects.

Although there is some variation, Aboriginal Australian kinship systems tend to fit in the broad category that anthropologists label Dravidian (Godelier, Trautmann and Tjon Sie Fat (eds) 1998; Scheffler 1978;

Trautmann 1981). In a generic Dravidian system the suppression of lineal/collateral distinctions coexists with parallel/cross distinctions and cross/affine equations. The first two principles mean that parents are terminologically equated with same-sex siblings (parallel), but distinguished from opposite-sex siblings (cross). These mergers and distinctions also extend to more distant relations. Mother's sister's child is equated with mother's child and thus with sibling, and father's brother's child is equated with father's child and thus with sibling. These equations extend to reciprocals as well, so that man's brother's child and woman's sister's child are equated with own child. Cross/affine equations mean that cross-kin are systematically equated with affines: Mother's brother's child and father's sister's child with spouse or spouse's sibling, mother's brother with spouse's father, father's sister with spouse's mother, and man's sister's child and woman's brother's child with child's spouse. Cross/affine terminological equations are accompanied by marriage rule; opposite-sex cross-cousins are not just labelled husband and wife, but are preferred or prescribed spouses.

Most Aboriginal Australian systems depart from generic Dravidian in one important respect (Scheffler 1978; Shapiro 1970, 1979; Viveiros de Castro 1998). They start with inverse kin categories for children, so that the fundamental distinction among children is not between son and daughter but between man's child and woman's child—'fatherling' and 'motherling' in Gould's nomenclature (2000: 28)—although a secondary distinction between male and female children may be included as well. This distinction is combined with a parallel/cross distinction among siblings' children. A man's brother's child (who calls him their 'father'), along with his own child, is man's child, or 'fatherling'. A woman's sister's child (who calls her their 'mother'), along with her own child, is woman's child, or 'motherling'. The parallel/cross distinction means that the children of same-sex parents are not equated with the children of opposite-sex parents, leaving several options for labelling children of cross-siblings. In the most economical case, since a man has already used up 'fatherling' for his own and his brother's children, he uses 'motherling' for his sister's children, and a woman uses 'fatherling' for her brother's children. Other terminologies add additional terms for these cross-kin types.

On the surface it looks as if there are two kinds of crossness, Dravidian and Aboriginal Australian, that differ in how they classify own and siblings' children. However, I propose that, at a deeper level, what is involved is an interaction between: (1) a single parallel/cross distinction, operating in both standard Dravidian and Aboriginal Australian, and (2) a senior-focused sex distinction, operating in Australian, but not Dravidian, resulting, in G^{-1}, in an ego-focused inverse fatherling/motherling distinction. (In addition, Dravidian and sometimes Aboriginal Australian may include the more standard alter-focused son/daughter distinction.) As we have seen in the discussion of Lapp above, it is possible to have senior-focused kin terms, with sex-of-ego distinctions when ego is senior, without parallel/cross distinctions. Treating the Dravidian/Aboriginal Australian difference as the product of the interaction of constraints already observed in other contexts is more economical than inventing new varieties of crossness.

The Aboriginal Australian classification of G^{-1} relatives has further structural consequences, which have been spelled out by a number of authors (reviewed by Scheffler 1978). The division of G^{-1} relatives into 'fatherling' and 'motherling' classes (i.e. man's child/brother's child, and woman's child/sister's child) mirrors a division of G^{1} relatives into father and mother. To maintain the symmetry of descending and ascending generations, father's sister can be grouped with father and mother's brother with mother. The result is to partition G^{1} and G^{-1} relatives together into two superclasses: a father/fatherling class (father, father's sibling and their reciprocals), and a mother/motherling class (mother, mother's sibling and their reciprocals). And two more superclasses may be recognised as well. In G^{0} there is a category of siblings and parallel kin including father's fatherling and/or mother's motherling, plus a category of potential spouses and cross-kin, including father's motherling and mother's fatherling. This G^{0} bifurcation can be extended to the alternating generations, $G^{\pm2}$. In G^{2} the parallel class can be expanded to include father's father and mother's mother, and the cross-class to include father's mother and mother's father. In G^{-2} the parallel class can be expanded to include fatherling's fatherling and motherling's motherling, and the cross-class to include fatherling's motherling and motherling's fatherling.

This division into four superclasses is implicit in standard Aboriginal Australian kin categorisation. As long as people follow the rule of not marrying members of the three classes that stand to them as father, mother and sibling and marrying the fourth class that stands as cross-cousin, everyone will agree on where the lines between classes are drawn.

As a number of authors have recognised, this division of kin into implicit classes is probably the basis for the section systems seen in much of Aboriginal Australia (Scheffler 1978: 432–80). 'The categories and intercategory relations of section and subsection systems are derived from the highest-order superclasses of systems of kin classification' (ibid.: 432). Where sections exist, each section is related to two other sections as father/fatherling, and mother/motherling, and to one other section as cross-cousin/potential spouse/potential sibling-in-law. Membership in sections is normally transmitted according to the same logic of patrifiliation and matrifiliation as membership in superclasses, although section and super-class do not always coincide exactly and additional rules are needed to resolve inconsistencies when someone's parents have made a marriage that violates the rules. In the earlier literature, sections are sometimes called marriage classes, but this is often a misnomer. In many, not all (Shapiro 1979), Aboriginal Australian groups, membership in egocentric kin categories rather than section membership is used to settle marriage rights when the two are in conflict, and the chief importance of sections is religious and ritual (Scheffler 1978: 474). This and other lines of evidence led Scheffler and others to argue that egocentric genealogical categories are logically prior to sociocentric sections. They are probably historically prior as well, with section systems developing just a few times as a reification of genealogical superclasses, and then diffusing, in some cases to societies without the corresponding kin categories.[1]

To further demonstrate the importance of genealogically based categorisation to social structure, compare the rather different structural possibilities inherent in standard Dravidian. At first blush, the Dravidian categorisation of kin, like that in Aboriginal Australia, seems to allow a division of relatives into four superclasses. Among generation $G^{\pm 1}$ kin, Dravidian allows a division between parallel and cross-kin (in contrast to the patrifilial/matrifilial division in Australia). Parallel $G^{\pm 1}$ kin include parents and their same-sex siblings, plus reciprocals (own children and children of same-sex siblings). Cross $G^{\pm 1}$ includes parents' opposite-sex siblings, plus reciprocals (children of opposite-sex siblings). And a G^0

---

1   This argument could be extended further. For example, Aboriginal Australian subsection systems follow from Aranda kin categorisation, as spelled out in Scheffler (1978: 453–60). And the section systems found in scattered locations outside Aboriginal Australia (Viveiros de Castro 1998) may also derive from kin superclasses. Among Panoan-speaking groups in Western Amazonia, FZ is grouped with F rather than with MB ... different kinds of grandkin are distinguished from each other and equated with kin or affines at Ego's own generation. This Kariera-type terminology is in perfect agreement with their system of sociocentric, alternating generation marriage classes (Hornborg 1993: 104). One such group, the Sharanahua, lack named sections, but have just eight basic kin terms dividing Ego's kin into four Aboriginal Australian–style superclasses, further distinguished by sex or cross-sex (Siskind 1973: 47–66).

11. KINSHIP IN MIND

parallel/cross distinction operates as in Aboriginal Australia, distinguishing siblings and parallel cousins from cross-cousins, who are also potential spouses.

However, in contrast to the Aboriginal Australian case, this division cannot form the basis for a sociocentric four section system, because people will disagree on who belongs to what section. A man will consider a wife or potential wife, in his own generation, to belong to the cross category, while his father will belong to the parallel category. But the position of his mother will be ambiguous; parallel to him, but cross to his father. Ego and his kin will thus not be able to agree on a division of their kin into four sections. The best that can be managed by way of sectioning in a system of Dravidian categories is a two-fold division into moieties, patrilineal or matrilineal, with own moiety and opposite moiety standing as consanguines and affines.

Aboriginal Australian and Dravidian categorisations also have different consequences for marriage rules. In generation G^0, both systems are consistent with a rule of cross-cousin marriage, but they treat cross-generational marriages differently. Under Aboriginal Australian categorisation, kin in generations G^1 and G^{-1} fall into father/fatherling and mother/motherling superclasses, and are normally ineligible for marriage. Under Dravidian categorisation, by contrast, these relatives are merely members of the affine superclass, and may be possible or even preferred spouses (Good 1996; Trautmann 1981). Cross-generational marriages, especially between a man and his sister's daughter—an unmarriageable 'motherling' under Aboriginal Australian rules—are common in many Dravidian systems in southern India and Amazonia.

By way of summary, let us run through the argument backwards. Differences between Aboriginal Australian and Dravidian social organisation, including section systems and marriage rules, seem to derive from differences in kin categorisation: Scheffler (1978) and others make a strong case that the causal arrow runs from categorisation to social structure, rather than vice-versa.

And in turn, key differences in kin categorisation seem to derive from the possibilities inherent in the conceptual structure of kinship; in particular, from different ways of assigning figure and ground roles to 'objects' in kinship 'space'. So without denying the evidence that cosmology is enlisted as an ideological prop for Aboriginal Australian sections (von Brandenstein 1970), or the possibility that ecological factors are involved in the genesis of Aboriginal Australian–type systems in Australia and elsewhere, what stands out here is the way these systems seem to be exploring the combinatorial potential of conceptual structure.

Conclusion: Good to think

The study of kinship is one of the great success stories in social anthropology. Yet this empirical success is in some ways a theoretical embarrassment. Kinship rules in many societies seem to be more structured, and structured differently, than one would expect just from people helping— and not copulating with—other people according to inferred coefficients of relatedness. And the organisation of kinship categories around a set of underlying universals seems to go beyond what one would expect if kinship were just a poorly demarcated cultural domain at the intersection of social life and folk theories of heredity. Here I have made the case that kinship is also a domain of evolved conceptual structure. Sharing this conceptual structure makes it easier for people to converge on shared-kin categories and associated rules, while the permutations permitted by the structure can generate variation in kinship systems and kin-based social organisation, such as the difference between standard Dravidian and Aboriginal Australian systems. I suggest that kinship systems are as orderly as they are, and the study of kinship is as successful as it is, because human kinship is partly about what is 'good to think'.

References

Astuti, Rita. 2001. 'Are we all natural dualists? A cognitive developmental approach'. *Journal of the Royal Anthropological Institute* 7(3): 429–47. doi.org/10.1111/1467-9655.00071

Barkow, Jerome, Leda Cosmides and John Tooby. 1992. *The Adapted Mind: Evolutionary Psychology and the Generation of Culture*. Oxford University Press.

Barrett, Justin L. 1999. 'Theological correctness: Cognitive constraint and the study of religion'. *Method and Theory in the Study of Religion*. 11(4): 325–39. doi.org/10.1163/157006899X00078

Beckerman, Stephen and Paul Valentine (eds). 2002. *Cultures of Multiple Fathers: The Theory and Practice of Partible Paternity in Lowland South America*. Gainesville, FL: University Press of Florida.

Bellwood, Peter, James J. Fox and Darrell Tryon (eds). 2006. *The Austronesians: Comparative and Historical Perspectives*. Canberra: ANU E Press. Online: press-files.anu.edu.au/downloads/press/p69411/pdf/book.pdf?referer=106 (accessed 31 May 2017).

Bloch, Maurice, Gregg Solomon and Susan Carey. 2001. 'Zafimaniry: An understanding of what is passed on from parents to children: A cross-cultural investigation'. *Journal of Cognition and Culture* 1(1): 43–68. doi.org/10.1163/156853701300063570

Brady, Ivan (ed.). 1976. *Transactions in Kinship: Adoption and Fosterage in Oceania*. Honolulu: University of Hawaii Press.

Carey, Susan. 2009. *The Origin of Concepts*. Oxford: Oxford University Press. doi.org/10.1093/acprof:oso/9780195367638.001.0001

Caroll, Vern (ed.). 1970. *Adoption in Eastern Oceania*. Honolulu: University of Hawaii Press.

Carsten, Janet. 1997. *The Heat of the Hearth: The Process of Kinship in a Malay Fishing Community*. Oxford: Clarendon Press.

Chapais, Bernard and Carol M. Berman (eds). 2004. *Kinship and Behavior in Primates*. Oxford: Oxford University Press.

Christakis, Nicholas and James H. Fowler. 2014. 'Friendship and natural selection'. *Proceedings of the National Academy of Sciences* 111: 10796–801. doi.org/10.1073/pnas.1400825111

Darwin, Charles. 1868. *The Variation of Plants and Animals under Domestication*, vols I and II. London: John Murray.

DeBruine, Lisa M. 2002. 'Facial resemblance enhances trust'. *Proceedings of the Royal Society* 269(1498): 1307–12. doi.org/10.1098/rspb.2002.2034

——. 2004. 'Resemblance to self increases the appeal of child faces to both men and women'. *Evolution and Human Behavior* 25(3): 142–154. doi.org/10.1016/j.evolhumbehav.2004.03.003

Denning, Keith and Suzanne Kemmer (eds). 1990. *On Language: Selected Writings of Joseph Greenberg*. Stanford, CA: Stanford University Press.

Godelier, Maurice, Thomas R. Trautmann and Franklin E. Tjon Sie Fat (eds). 1998. *Transformations of Kinship*. Washington DC: Smithsonian Institution Press.

Good, Anthony. 1996. *On the Non-Existence of 'Dravidian Kinship'*. Edinburgh Papers in South Asian Studies, No. 6.

Goodenough, Ward H. 1965. 'Yankee kinship terminology: A problem in componential analysis'. *American Anthropologist* 67(5): 259–87. doi.org/10.1525/aa.1965.67.5.02a00820

Gould, Sydney Henry. 2000. *A New System for the Formal Analysis of Kinship*. Lantham, Maryland: University Press of America.

Greenberg, Joseph H. 1966. *Language Universals, with Special Reference to Feature Hierarchies*. The Hague: Mouton de Gruyter.

———. 1990. 'Universals of kinship terminology: Their nature and the problem of their explanation'. In *On Language: Selected Writings of Joseph Greenberg*, edited by Keith Denning and Suzanne Kemmer, 310–27. Stanford, CA: Stanford University Press.

Hage, Per. 1997. 'Unthinkable categories and the fundamental laws of kinship'. *American Ethnologist* 24(3): 652–67. doi.org/10.1525/ae.1997.24.3.652

Hauber, M.E. and Paul W. Sherman. 2001. 'Self-referent phenotype matching: theoretical considerations and empirical evidence'. *Trends in Neuroscience* 24: 609–16. doi.org/10.1016/S0166-2236(00)01916-0

Hepper, Peter G. (ed.). 1991. *Kin Recognition*. Cambridge: Cambridge University Press.

Hiatt, L.R. 1996. *Arguments about Aborigines: Australia and the Evolution of Social Anthropology*. Cambridge: Cambridge University Press.

Hirschfeld, Lawrence A. and Susan Gelman (eds). 1994. *Mapping the Mind: Domain Specificity in Cognition and Culture*. Cambridge: Cambridge University Press.

Hornborg, Alf. 1993. 'Panoan marriage sections: A comparative perspective'. *Ethnology* 32(1): 101–08. doi.org/10.2307/3773548

Jackendoff, Ray. 2002. *Foundations of Language: Brain, Meaning, Grammar, Evolution*. Oxford: Oxford University Press. doi.org/10.1093/acprof: oso/9780198270126.001.0001

Jones, Doug. 2010. 'Human kinship, from conceptual structure to grammar'. *Behavioral and Brain Sciences* 33(5): 367–416. doi.org/10.1017/S0140525X10000890

Jones, Doug and Bojka Milicic (eds). 2010. *Kinship, Language, and Prehistory: Per Hage and the Renaissance in Kinship Studies*. Salt Lake City: University of Utah Press.

Kahneman, Daniel. 2011. *Thinking, Fast and Slow*. New York: Farrar, Straus and Giroux.

Kant, Immanuel. 1781. *Kritik der reinen Vernunft*; Marcus Weigelt, editor, translator, Introduction, Max Müller, translator. *The Critique of Pure Reason*. London: Penguin Press. 2009 (references are to the translated edition).

Keesing, Roger M. 1975. *Kin Groups and Social Structure*. New York: Holt, Rinehart and Winston.

Kitcher, Patricia. 1990. *Kant's Transcendental Psychology*. Oxford: Oxford University Press.

Kroeber, Alfred L. 1909. 'Classificatory systems of relationship'. *Journal of the Royal Anthropological Institute of Great Britain and Ireland* 39: 77–84. doi.org/10.2307/2843284

Kuper, Adam. 1999. *Culture: The Anthropologists' Account*. Cambridge, MA: Harvard University Press.

Labby, David. 1976. *The Demystification of Yap: Dialectics of Culture on a Micronesian Island*. Chicago: University of Chicago Press.

Leaf, Murray J. and Dwight Read. 2012. *Human Thought and Social Organization: Anthropology on a New Plane*. Lanham, MD: Lexington Books.

Levinson, Stephen C. 2003. *Space in Language and Cognition: Explorations in Cognitive Diversity*. Cambridge: Cambridge University Press. doi.org/10.1017/CBO9780511613609

Levinson, Stephen C. and David P. Wilkins. 2006a. 'Appendices'. In *Grammars of Space: Explorations in Cognitive Diversity*, edited by Steven C. Levinson and David P. Wilkins, 553–75. Cambridge: Cambridge University Press. doi.org/10.1017/CBO 9780511486753.016

———. 2006b. 'Patterns in the data: Towards a semantic typology of spatial description'. In *Grammars of Space: Explorations in Cognitive Diversity*, edited by Stephen C. Levinson and David P. Wilkins, 512–22. Cambridge: Cambridge University Press. doi.org/10.1017/CBO9780511486753.015

Levinson, Stephen and David Wilkins (eds). 2006. *Grammars of Space: Explorations in Cognitive Diversity*. Cambridge: Cambridge University Press. doi.org/10.1017/CBO9780511486753

Lévi-Strauss, Claude. 1949. *Les structures élémentaires de la parenté*. Paris: Presses Universitaires Françaises; rev. and trans. James Harle Bell and John Richard von Sturmer, ed. Rodney Needham as *The Elementary Structures of Kinship*. Boston: Beacon Press, 1969 (references are to the translated edition).

Lieberman, Debra. 2009. 'Rethinking the Taiwanese minor marriage data: Evidence the mind uses multiple kinship cues to regulate inbreeding avoidance'. *Evolution and Human Behavior* 30(3): 153–60. doi.org/10.1016/j.evolhumbehav.2008.11.003

Lieberman, Debra, John Tooby and Leda Cosmides. 2007. 'The architecture of human kin detection'. *Nature* 445: 727–31. doi.org/10.1038/nature05510

Lounsbury, Floyd G. 1964. 'The structural analysis of kinship semantics'. In *Proceedings of the Ninth International Congress of Linguistics*, edited by H.G. Lunt, 1073–93. The Hague: Mouton de Gruyter.

Lunt, H.G. (ed.). 1964. *Proceedings of the Ninth International Congress of Linguistics*. The Hague: Mouton de Gruyter.

Malinowski, Bronisław. 1929. *The Sexual Life of Savages in North-Western Melanesia: An Ethnographic Account of Courtship, Marriage, and Family Life among the Natives of the Trobriand Islands, British New Guinea.* London: Routledge and Kegan Paul; reprinted Boston: Beacon Press, 1987 (references are to the 1987 edition).

McCabe, Justine. 1983. 'FBD marriage: Further support for the Westermarck hypothesis of the incest taboo?' *American Anthropologist* 85(1): 50–69. doi.org/10.1525/aa.1983.85.1.02a00030

Murdock, George Peter. 1970. 'Kin term patterns and their distribution'. *Ethnology* 9(2): 165–207. doi.org/10.2307/3772782

Park, Justin H. and Mark Schaller. 2005. 'Does attitude similarity serve as a heuristic cue for kinship? Evidence of an implicit cognitive association'. *Evolution and Human Behavior* 26(2): 158–70. doi.org/10.1016/j.evolhumbehav.2004.08.013

Parkinson, Carolyn and Thalia Wheatley. 2013. 'Old cortex, new contexts: repurposing spatial perception for social cognition'. *Frontiers in Human Neuroscience* 7: 645. doi.org/10.3389/fnhum.2013.00645

Parkinson, Carolyn, Shari Liu and Thalia Wheatley. 2014. 'A common cortical metric for spatial, temporal, and social distance'. *Journal of Neuroscience* 34(5): 1979–87. doi.org/10.1523/JNEUROSCI.2159-13.2014

Parr, Lisa A. and Frans B.M. de Waal. 1999. 'Visual kin recognition in chimpanzees'. *Nature* 399: 647–48. doi.org/10.1038/21345

Pinker, Steven. 2007. *The Stuff of Thought: Language as a Window into Human Nature.* New York: Viking.

Polley, Sarah. 2012. *Stories We Tell* (documentary). Lionsgate.

Porter, Richard H. and John D. Moore. 1981. 'Human kin recognition by olfactory cues'. *Physiology and Behavior* 27(3): 493–95. doi.org/10.1016/0031-9384(81)90337-1

Pusey, Anne. 2005. 'Inbreeding avoidance in primates'. In *Inbreeding, Incest, and the Incest Taboo: The State of Knowledge at the Turn of the Century,* edited by Arthur P. Wolf and William H. Durham, 61–75. Stanford, CA: Stanford University Press.

Read, Dwight W. 2010. 'The logic and structure of kinship terminologies: Implications for theory and historical reconstruction'. In *Kinship, Language, and Prehistory: Per Hage and the Renaissance in Kinship Studies*, edited by Doug Jones and Bojka Milicic, 152–72. Salt Lake City: University of Utah Press.

Rodseth, Lars and Richard Wrangham. 2004. 'Human kinship: A continuation of politics by other means'. In *Kinship and Behavior in Primates*, edited by Bernard Chapais and Carol Berman, 389–419. Oxford: Oxford University Press.

Romney, A. Kimball and Phillip J. Epling. 1958. 'A simplified model of Kariera kinship'. *American Anthropologist* 60(1): 59–74. doi.org/10.1525/aa.1958.60.1.02a00070

Sahlins, Marshall. 2013. *What Kinship Is – And Is Not*. Chicago: University of Chicago Press. doi.org/10.7208/chicago/9780226925134.001.0001

Scheffler, Harold W. 1978. *Australian Kin Classification*. Cambridge: Cambridge University Press. doi.org/10.1017/CBO9780511557590

Schneider, David M. 1984. *A Critique of the Study of Kinship*. Ann Arbor: The University of Michigan Press. doi.org/10.3998/mpub.7203

Shapiro, Warren. 1970. 'The ethnography of two-section systems'. *Ethnology* 9(4): 380–88. doi.org/10.2307/3773044

———. 1977. 'Structure, variation, and change in 'Balamumu' social categorization'. *Journal of Anthropological Research* 33(1): 16–49. doi.org/10.1086/jar.33.1.3629484

———. 1979. *Social Organization in Aboriginal Australia*. New York: St. Martin's Press.

———. 2011. 'What is Malay kinship primarily about? Or the new kinship studies and the fabrication of an ethnographic fantasy'. In *Kinship, Language, and Prehistory: Per Hage and the Renaissance in Kinship Studies*, edited by Doug Jones and Bojka Milicic, 141–51. Salt Lake City: University of Utah Press.

Shepher, Joseph. 1971. 'Mate selection among second-generation kibbutz adolescents: Incest avoidance and negative imprinting'. *Archives of Sexual Behavior* 1(4): 293–307. doi.org/10.1007/BF01638058

Silk, Joan B. 1980. 'Adoption and kinship in Oceania'. *American Anthropologist* 82(4): 799–820. doi.org/10.1525/aa.1980.82.4.02a 00050

——. 2001. 'Ties that bond: The role of kinship in primate societies'. In *New Directions in the Anthropology of Kinship*, edited by Linda Stone, 71–92. Lanham, MD: Rowman and Littlefield Publishers.

Siskind, Janet. 1973. *To Hunt in the Morning*. Oxford: Oxford University Press.

Stone, Linda (ed.). 2001. *New Directions in the Anthropology of Kinship*. Lanham, MD: Rowman and Littlefield Publishers.

Talmon, Yonina. 1964. 'Mate selection in collective settlements'. *American Sociological Review* 29(4): 491–508. doi.org/10.2307/2091199

Trautmann, Thomas. 1981. *Dravidian Kinship*. Cambridge: Cambridge University Press.

Viveiros de Castro, Eduardo. 1998. 'Dravidian and related kinship systems'. In *Transformations of Kinship*, edited by Maurice Godelier, Thomas R. Trautmann and Franklin E. Tjon Sie Fat, 332–85. Washington DC: Smithsonian Institution Press.

von Brandenstein, Carl Georg. 1970. 'The meaning of section and section names'. *Oceania* 41(1): 39–49. doi.org/10.1002/j.1834-4461.1970.tb01114.x

Weiner, Annette B. 1988. *The Trobrianders of Papua New Guinea*. Belmont, CA: Wadsworth Publishing Co.

Westermarck, Edward. 1891. *A History of Human Marriage*. London and New York: Macmillan and Co; reprint 1903, London: Macmillan and Co. (page references are to the reprint edition).

Wolf, Arthur. 1995. *Sexual Attraction and Childhood Association: A Chinese Brief for Edward Westermarck*. Stanford: Stanford University Press.

Wolf, Arthur P. and William H. Durham (eds). 2005. *Inbreeding, Incest, and the Incest Taboo: The State of Knowledge at the Turn of the Century*. Stanford, CA: Stanford University Press.

12

Do Women Really Desire Casual Sex? Analysis of a Popular Adult Online Dating/Liaison Site

Michelle Escasa-Dorne and William Jankowiak

Introduction

Although Hal Scheffler never wrote on sexual behaviour per se, his overall approach in kinship studies lends itself readily to a Darwinian approach to the study of casual sex. To this end, we want to explore the sex differences in men's and women's willingness to seek out casual sexual liaisons. The incidence of casual sex promoted amongst straights appears to be a prominent feature in modern society (Grello, Welsh and Harper 2006; Hatfield, Forbes and Rapson 2011; Lambert, Kahn and Apple 2003; Paul, McManus and Hayes 2000) and has a number of colloquial terms, including 'hooking up' and 'no strings attached' sex. If 'hooking up' (i.e. casual sex with a stranger with no intention of meeting again) has become the preferred and most common form of sexual liaison, it would constitute a historic shift in female sexual behaviour. Moreover, the pervasiveness of popular 'dating' sex sites poses a potential challenge to evolutionary theory of human sexuality that has consistently documented sex differences in male and female erotic perception, imagination and behaviour (Baumeister, Catanese and Vohs 2001).

In this chapter, we investigate Adult Friend Finder, a large popular sex site—it claims to be the largest online sex and swinger personals community website in the world. It is consistently ranked between the 40th and 60th most visited website on the Internet with claims to over 20 million members. If there is a shift in sexual attitude amongst females in terms of their openness to casual sexual liaisons, their online profiles should be more explicit in stating a desire for entering into a casual sexual encounter.

Sex differences: An overview

A large body of evidence supports general expectations concerning sex differences in perceptions of sexual behaviour and psychology. An early compilation of various surveys, primarily from the United States (US), suggests that men prefer young, healthy and physically attractive partners, whereas women seek ambitious, generous and socially and economically successful partners when evaluating potential mates (Symons 1979). Related research finds males more than females utilise prostitutes, consume pornography, require less time before consenting to sex and sex with a stranger, and display higher rates of sex with farm animals (Gray and Garcia 2013; Mealey 2000). Differences are further manifested in men having more spontaneous thoughts about sex, a greater variety of sexual fantasies, greater frequency of wanting intercourse and with a larger number of partners, and higher participation in masturbation (even in societies that strongly discourage it) (Baumeister, Catanese and Vohs 2001: 242). In contrast, women give greater weight to cues of emotional intimacy with someone who is open to establishing an ongoing relationship (Buss 2003; Regan and Berscheid 1999; Schmitt, Shackelford and Buss 2001).

Sexual selection theory and data on sexuality suggest that heterosexual women's short-term sexual strategies may be motivated by accumulation of resources (Buss 2008; Hrdy 1999; Symons 1979; Townsend 1998), mate switching (Betzig 1989), or out of a desire to evaluate a prospective long-term mate (Buss 2008; Buss and Schmitt 1993; Greiling and Buss 2000; Meston and Buss 2007) rather than motivation to find momentary sexual pleasure. However, the emergent research on bisexual women finds they have on average more sexual partners than heterosexual or lesbian women. This research also finds that bisexual women often have higher testosterone levels than women in the general population (Lippa 2006). The higher testosterone levels may contribute to bisexual women having a stronger sex drive and thus desire to seek out more opportunities for short-term sexual encounters. Another exception is female swingers, or married women, who seek out sexual variety within spouse exchange contexts (Jankowiak and Mixson 2008). In this setting, women engage in casual sexual encounters that allow for the possibility of a physiological release, while also signalling to themselves and others that they are sexually attractive and therefore desirable (see Gangestad and Simpson 2000). Previous literature has also noted that extra-pair mating may be the stimulus necessary to activate women's short-term mating strategies (Pillsworth and Haselton 2006). Clearly, some women do engage in short-term mating encounters.

Although popular media has highlighted 'hooking up' as constituting a new trend whereby females avidly seek out casual sexual trysts, empirical research continues to find persistence sex differences, more men than women are seeking short-term sexual encounters (Garcia and Reiber 2008). Moreover, academic research regarding the 'hooking up' experience on college campuses finds young women overwhelmingly complaining that a 'one-night stand' is not emotionally satisfying (Bogle 2008; Campbell 2008; Garcia and Reiber 2008). College men seldom voiced a similar complaint (Townsend 1998). It is, thus, puzzling to find a proliferation of sexually oriented dating websites claiming that every locality has females eager to engage in casual sex encounters.

In the 1990s, due to the increased popularity of the web, there appeared numerous sex sites that advertised as being links for individuals who want to engage in nonmonetary 'no strings' casual sexual encounters. These websites were designed to provide a means for individuals interested in a short-term sexual tryst to more effectively 'hook up'. Moreover, these dating sites appear to be highly profitable. The ubiquity of the online sex sites raises an intriguing question: Are the participating women harbingers of an emerging shift in American female sexual behaviour? This raises other related questions: Who uses these sites? Is there a difference in the profiles of males and females? In what way, if any, do the well-documented sex differences continue to be manifested in profile ads or is there a striking transformation in females' public sexual persona? To this end, we hypothesised:

1. If a shift has occurred, straight and bisexual females' ads on the casual sex dating site will be more explicit in stating their desire for a casual, noncommittal sexual encounter.
2. If sex differences continue to be present, female profiles will have more qualifications and stipulations that seek to obtain evidence of a male's interest in forming an emotional attachment.
3. If sexual orientation and, thus, hormonal difference is a factor, there should be more bisexual women's ads compared to straight female profiles stating a preference for casual sexual encounters.
4. Because coitus is a favour women grant men, their ability to control the pace of a relationship ensured their profiles would be more explicit in stating their expectations and, thus, preference for a specific sex act or acts. Conversely, males' desire for some kind of sexual encounter contributes to the writing of a more flexible and, thus, less precise or demanding profile requesting a specific sex act or acts.

Methods

We assumed that people who advertise on casual dating sites were not representative of typical American males or females. However, cultural anthropologists have historically sought to identify emergent cultural patterns in the behaviours of what could be considered to be sociologically marginal individuals. It is something of a truism that what was once marginal often, in time, becomes a new mainstream cultural pattern. In this way, it is fruitful to investigate the possibility that online casual sex dating sites may represent the nascent presence of a new behavioural pattern within America's regional cultures.

Adult personal websites allow individuals to create a profile to advertise their availability and seek other individuals who may be interested in the same type of relationship or activities as themselves. Similar to other large-profile dating websites, such as Match.com or Chemistry.com, individual profiles include photographs, descriptive information from chosen categories and written information providing additional information about the individual and the type of person he or she is seeking. Unlike websites tailored to find a relationship (or, more directly, to 'find love', as one popular dating outlet states), adult online dating sites advertise themselves as websites to find sexual partners. While the layout of the adult dating site may be similar to other dating websites, the content, photographs and expectations are typically more sexually inclined and quite explicit in an individual's phrasing of what he or she is looking for in a partner. For example, 80 per cent of female profiles contain a photo(s) that had semi or full nudity, with 78 per cent of the ads containing sexually explicit words or phrases that would have been deleted had they been expressed on a mainstream media outlet. In this and many other ways, sex dating/liaison sites differ from eHarmony.com and Match.com.

Given the online sex sites' sexual explicitness, we assumed that men and women who placed an ad should have had a greater interest in short-term mating encounters compared to men and women who use more standard and socially respected dating sites (e.g. Match.com and eHarmony.com). Many other outlets for finding casual sexual encounters are available via websites. For this project, we focused on Adult Friend Finder for several reasons. While Craigslist offers a section for casual encounters, a large number of postings were found to be hinting towards prostitution. One new site, Ashley Madison, has gained recent popularity due to the specific nature of the website in offering an outlet for individuals who are already partnered or married and who are looking for an extra-partner affair. Because our intent was to focus on the mating preferences of females and males who are not currently partnered, we did not further analyse profiles in AshleyMadison.com. Given the commonality between these sites, we are confident that the adult dating we focused on is highly representative of other non–prostitution oriented, online sex dating services.

To test our hypotheses, the authors collected data from individuals' profiles on a large, casual sex dating website. The site is highly profitable and is found around the world (e.g. in Europe, Asia and Africa). The website defines itself as an 'adult personals' website where individuals can create a profile to advertise their availability and seek other individuals who may be interested in the same type of relationship or activities as themselves. The casual sex site offers two membership options: a 'silver' membership at approximately US$30 per month and a 'gold' membership at US$50 per month. A silver member has a limited amount of times they may contact other members, while a gold member has unlimited access to look at and respond to ads. Due to the initial uncertainty regarding individual or profile differences between gold and silver members, profiles were selected from each category equally. After an initial analysis, there were no differences between the gold and silver profiles in the prose, photo type, content or type of sexual encounter/relationship requested. We combined the two types of profiles for analysis.

Sample methods included a randomised selection of male and female profiles from a variety of geographical regions in continental US. The regions we sampled included the east, south, midwest and western US. We selected four states from each region. These states in alphabetical order are California, Florida, Georgia, Illinois, Indiana, Louisiana, Maine, Massachusetts, Minnesota, Mississippi, Montana, Nevada, New York, Ohio, Pennsylvania and Utah. Analyses showed no differences in sexual or relationship profile content by region. Certain cultural styles were evident in local areas. As an example, there were a larger number of beach photographs and surfer images in California and Florida profiles over the other states. In total, 50 ads (25 gold and 25 silver levels) per gender were selected by coding every third page on the website within the respected gold and silver categories. This provided an original sample of 1,508 profiles, which included an equal number of males and females.

The site asks individuals to list their age, height, body type, educational level, race and sexual orientation from a set selection of choices. In many cases, members are given the option to refuse disclosure of such information. Sexual orientation was by far the category most often checked as 'prefer not to say'. We treated these ads as a separate category unless we were able to determine their orientation from information in their profile. In most cases, we were able to determine a person's sexual orientation if they were seeking men, women or both. There were 13 incidences where a profile listed 'prefer not to say' concerning an individual's sexual orientation, yet had a profile statement that explicitly stated a preference for sex with males and females. In these instances the person was recoded as having a bisexual orientation.

There were four primary sexual orientations: heterosexual, homosexual, bisexual and bicurious (i.e. women who thought about but had not participated in a same-sex sexual encounter). We dropped from our sample the six homosexual profiles (i.e. profiles stating they were only interested in a same-sex partner) that had been erroneously included by the dating site in the heterosexual category. We kept the categories of bisexual, bicurious and heterosexual. Of these categories, 57 per cent of the females and 76 per cent of the males described themselves as heterosexual. The percentages of bicurious and bisexual females were modest (17.2 and 21.6 per cent, respectively), while males self-coded themselves in these categories to a lesser degree (6.9 and 6.6 per cent, respectively). A small number of males (10 per cent) and females (5 per cent) did not disclose sexual orientation nor were researchers able to classify their sexual orientation based on profile content. In these instances, we dropped the profiles from our sample.[1] Further details of the breakdown of our sample size categories can be seen in Table 3.

Table 3. Descriptives of the sample

	Females[a]	Males[a]
Age		
18–24	40 (7.3)	36 (5.3)
25–29	67 (12.3)	92 (13.6)
30–34	130 (23.8)	127 (18.8)
35–39	130 (23.8)	163 (24.1)
40–44	86 (15.8)	104 (15.4)
45+	93 (17)	155 (22.9)
Ethnicity		
Caucasian	404 (74)	537 (79.3)
Black	72 (13.2)	81 (12)
Hispanic	27 (4.9)	24 (3.5)
Asian	8 (1.5)	0 (0)
Other/No Data	35 (6.3)	35 (4.8)
Education		
High School	67 (12.3)	71 (10.5)
Associate's Degree	29 (5.3)	25 (3.7)
Some College	146 (26.7)	145 (21.4)
Bachelor's Degree	220 (40.3)	342 (50.5)
No Data	84 (15.4)	94 (13.9)
Sexual Orientation		
Heterosexual	309 (56.6)	515 (76.1)
Bicurious	94 (17.2)	47 (6.9)
Bisexual	118 (21.6)	45 (6.6)
No Data	25 (4.6)	70 (10.3)
Body Type		
Slim/Petite	8 (1.5)	1 (.1)
Athletic	99 (18.1)	379 (56)

---

1 Lisa Diamond (2008) argues that bisexuality (she prefers the term nonexclusive) is a deeply problematic category, as 'it is not clear if it refers to sexual identity, sexual behavior or sex orientation' (ibid.: 13).

	Females[a]	Males[a]
Average	173 (31.7)	227 (33.5)
Extra Padding	188 (34.4)	53 (7.8)
Ample	68 (12.5)	10 (1.5)
Not Determinable	10 (1.8)	7 (1)
TOTAL	546 (100)	677 (100.1)

a. Listed as *n* (% within gender)
Source: Collated from data collected by the authors. © Michelle Escasa-Dorne, 2014.

Research on the validity of online nonsexual dating sites finds a great deal of 'deception' with facts (Toma, Hancock and Ellison 2008; Hatfield, Forbes and Rapson 2011). For example, men tend to exaggerate their height, income and occupation, whereas women misrepresent their age, level of physical attraction and whether they have children. For the purposes of this study, we assumed that if and when individuals exaggerated the 'facts' in their profiles, it should be in the direction of what they truly value, prefer and want in a sexual encounter.

The researchers printed and then coded each profile by analysing the content of the profiles, as well as the listed relationship type and/or activities sought. Of our initial 1,508 profiles, there were 141 vague ads (e.g. had minimum or no information on what they wanted). These ads were dropped from our sample. Fourteen ads, all from females, were clearly about prostitution (i.e. ads acknowledging they would do ANYTHING in exchange for these special gifts). These ads were also dropped from the sample. We also identified (as stated in a person's ad) 130 swinger or spouse-exchange requests. The majority of swinger ads stated both partners were involved in creating the profile. Thus, we did not include swingers in the final analysis. However, we included men and women who claimed to be divorced, soon to be divorced or just married. After dropping the prostitution, swinger and vague ads, our original sample was reduced to 677 males and 546 females ($n = 1,223$). We did not conduct an in-depth survey of who actually used the site, thus we cannot be certain who actually engaged in casual sexual encounters. Our pilot survey, albeit large, is suggestive and not conclusive.

Five researchers served as coders of the individuals' profiles. We coded relationship type as 'casual', 'conflicted' or 'long-term/romantic' (LTR). Profiles were coded as LTR when individuals stated a preference for a continuous 'relationship' (e.g. going out on multiple dates, being friends first, emphasising having to know and trust a person, etc.). Moreover, individuals who were classified as having an LTR profile emphasised they were not looking for flings, promiscuous sex or one-night stands, but were more interested in developing a continuous, ongoing mutual relationship. Casual ads stressed a preference to meet numerous members of the preferred sex, did not mention a preference to establish an ongoing relationship and emphasised a desire for sexual satisfaction. Conflicted profiles included individuals seeking what the site refers to as a 'friends with benefits' relationship (these were identified from key phrases in profiles that highlighted a preference for establishing some type of emotional involvement). For women, this included a partner who would be available for a weekend of walks, talks, dinner, movies and sex; whereas for men, 'friends with benefits' usually meant wanting a sex partner who would meet at an appointed place for an allotted amount of time. Some of the ads contained mixed or conflicting messages in their profile statement. These mixed messages stressed different and, often contradictory, motives (e.g. a desire for a boyfriend and in a separate paragraph 'no strings attached' sex). Whenever a profile contained conflicting goals (i.e. wanting a casual sex encounter as well as a long-term relationship), the profile was coded as a conflicted profile.

All data were analysed using SPSS 16.0 for Windows. Except where stated, all analyses used a Chi-squared goodness of fit test and all tests assumed an alpha of 0.05.

Results

The motivation for being on the sex site significantly differs by gender (χ^2 = 125.01, df = 2, p < .001). Females' profiles were more likely to seek an LTR than males' profiles (see Table 4). Male profiles overwhelmingly (52 per cent, n = 350) emphasised a desire for casual sex compared to only 26 per cent (143) of female profiles. Conflicted profiles were fairly evenly distributed between males and females. These findings suggest that female profiles were less explicit in stating a desire for casual sex, while male profiles appeared more open to anonymous or casual sex.

Post-hoc tests reveal a pattern in women's profiles based on sexual orientation. When profiles of heterosexual women were separated from bisexual and bicurious women a significant pattern emerged—of the heterosexual women (n = 309), only 19.4 per cent (n = 60) sought a casual relationship. Comparatively, of the bicurious and bisexual women, 36 per cent (n = 77) sought a casual relationship. Forty per cent of straight women preferred a long-term romantic relationship, compared to an average of only 20 per cent for the bisexual and bicurious women (see Table 6). Further, bisexual profiles often expressed a preference to form an emotional monogamous relationship with one sex, while stating a preference for casual encounters with the other sex.

We also examined evidence of associations between individual physical characteristics and stated motives on the sex site. For these post-hoc analyses, we sought to see if there is a relationship between age, body type (e.g. thin, athletic, average and a few extra pounds) and degree of openness to casual sexual encounters. We found a positive statistical association between body type and relationship desired for females (χ^2 = 27.10, df = 10, p = .003) but not for males (χ^2 =6.70, df = 10, p = .753) (see Table 3). There was, however, an association between age of the subject and relationship desired for both males (χ^2 = 33.778, df = 15, n = 677, p = .004) and females (χ^2 = 40.700, df = 15, n = 546, p < .001) (see Table 4).

Of all the females who were between the ages of 18–24 (n = 40), 17 (43 per cent) expressed an interest in casual sex versus six (15 per cent) who were looking for an LTR relationship. Of the 93 females who were 45 and above, 46 were coded as seeking an LTR relationship (49.5 per cent) while only 11 (or 12 per cent) wanted variety or casual sex.

All profiles were coded to determine whether there was a difference between males and females seeking or offering specific services, sexual or nonsexual (e.g. conversation, hugs, or dinner dates), from potential partners (χ^2 = 109.568, df = 4, n = 546, p < .001). Only 7 per cent (n = 38) of females offered services, compared to 19 per cent (n = 131) of males. In the context of a potential first-time sexual encounter, males tended to be less demanding and were more willing to provide noncoitus sexual services. Based upon this evidence, hypothesis 4 is supported.

Table 4. Type of encounter sought by males and females

Motives	Males[a]	Females[a]	n	χ^2	df	p
LTR*	66 (9.7)	174 (31.9)	1223	130.915	3	< .001
Conflicted	165 (24.4)	120 (22)				
Friends with Benefits	96 (14.2)	109 (20)				
Casual/Variety	350 (51.7)	143 (26.2)				
TOTAL	677 (100)	546 (100)				

Motives by Body Type

	LTR*[b]	Conflicted[b]	FB**[b]	Casual[b]	n	χ^2	df	p
Males					677	11.535	15	.714
Small/Petite	0 (0)	0 (0)	0 (0)	1 (100)				
Average	21 (9.3)	59 (26)	42 (18.5)	105 (46.3)				
Athletic	37 (9.8)	88 (23.2)	47 (12.4)	207 (54.6)				
Ample	1 (10)	3 (30)	0 (0)	6 (60)				
Extra Padding	6 (11.3)	14 (26.4)	5 (9.4)	28 (52.8)				
No Data	1 (14.3)	1 (14.3)	2 (28.6)	3 (42.9)				
Females					546	30.813	15	.009
Small/Petite	5 (62.5)	1 (12.5)	0 (0)	2 (25)				
Average	65 (37.6)	37 (21.4)	27 (15.6)	44 (25.4)				
Athletic	29 (29.3)	20 (20.2)	13 (13.1)	37 (37.4)				
Ample	12 (17.6)	20 (29.4)	20 (29.4)	16 (23.5)				
Extra Padding	61 (32.4)	38 (20.2)	46 (24.5)	43 (22.9)				
No Data	2 (20)	4 (40)	3 (30)	1 (10)				

Motives by Age								
	LTR*c	Conflictc	FB**c	Casualc	n	χ^2	df	p
Males					677	33.778	15	.004
18–24	4 (11.1)	11 (30.6)	1 (2.8)	20 (55.6)	36			
25–29	5 (5.4)	18 (19.6)	10 (10.9)	59 (64.1)	92			
30–34	4 (3.1)	34 (26.8)	16 (12.6)	73 (57.5)	127			
35–39	16 (9.8)	39 (23.9)	19 (11.7)	89 (54.6)	163			
40–44	15 (14.4)	28 (26.9)	20 (19.2)	41 (39.4)	104			
45+	22 (14.2)	35 (22.6)	30 (19.4)	68 (43.9)	155			
Females					546	40.700	15	< .001
18–24	6 (15)	11 (27.5)	6 (15)	17 (42.5)	40			
25–29	12 (17.9)	21 (31.3)	17 (25.4)	17 (25.4)	67			
30–34	39 (30)	21 (16.2)	25 (19.2)	45 (34.6)	130			
35–39	43 (33.1)	31 (23.8)	26 (20)	30 (23.1)	130			
40–44	28 (32.6)	20 (23.3)	15 (17.4)	23 (26.7)	86			
45+	46 (49.5)	16 (17.2)	20 (21.5)	11 (11.8)	93			

* LTR: Long-term/romantic; ** FB: Friends with benefits/'fuck buddy'

a. listed as *n* (% within gender)

b. *n* (% within body type)

c. *n* (% within age)

Source: Collated from data collected by the authors. © Michelle Escasa-Dorne, 2014.

Additionally, profiles were coded for instances of listing specific traits desired of a partner. These traits included sexual characteristics or personality characteristics (e.g. wanting someone with certain types or standards of looks, intelligence, sexual openness to specific acts or behaviours, etc.). Profiles of individuals who expressed flexibility in traits or characteristics of a partner were coded as 'trait flexible' (see Table 5). Profiles that were trait flexible were those of females or males that stated they were open to all age groups, looks, backgrounds, etc. In our data, both sexes were overwhelmingly trait flexible. We suspect this was due to both sexes wanting to attract the largest number of responses possible. Trait flexibility was reported for 405 females (74 per cent), while 139 females (26 per cent) were coded as trait specific. Males followed a similar pattern: 556 men (82 per cent) were trait flexible, with 116 (17 per cent) of the men trait specific.

Table 5. Sexual content of profiles

Sexual Content By Age	Trait Flexible*	Trait Specific*	No Data*	Total (%)*	χ^2	df	p
Males	556 (82.1)	116 (17.1)	5 (0.7)		13.683	10	.188
18–24	34 (6.1)	1 (0.9)	1 (20)	36 (5.3)			
25–29	78 (14)	15.8 (12.1)	0 (0)	92 (13.6)			
30–34	106 (19.1)	21 (18.1)	0 (0)	127 (18.8)			
35–39	137 (24.6)	25 (21.6)	1 (20)	163 (24.1)			
40–44	79 (14.2)	24 (20.7)	1 (20)	104 (15.4)			
45+	122 (21.9)	31 (26.7)	2 (40)	155 (22.9)			
Females	405 (74.2)	139 (25.5)	2 (0.4)		9.183	10	.515
18–24	30 (7.4)	10 (1.8)	0 (0)	40 (7.3)			
25–29	54 (13.3)	13 (9.4)	0 (0)	67 (12.3)			
30–34	99 (24.4)	30 (21.6)	1 (50)	130 (23.8)			
35–39	95 (23.5)	35 (25.2)	0 (0)	130 (23.8)			
40–44	56 (13.8)	30 (21.6)	0 (0)	86 (15.8)			
45+	71 (17.5)	21 (15.1)	1 (50)	93 (17)			

* listed as n (% within sexual content)
Source: Collated from data collected by the authors. © Michelle Escasa-Dorne, 2014.

Twenty of the 60 heterosexual female profiles coded as seeking casual sex had profiles that explicitly stated the woman was coming out of a recent 'sexless' marriage and desiring a relationship that, in the words of a 38-year-old woman, would make her 'feel sexually desired once again'. This is consistent with research that found women prefer sexual validation instead of momentary physiological pleasure (Meana 2010).

Table 6. Females' motives listed by sexual orientation

Motives	Bicurious	Bisexual	Straight	No Data	Total
LTR					
Count	24	18	124	8	174
% within Motives	13.8	10.3	71.3	4.6	100.0
% within Sexual Orientation	25.5	15.3	40.1	32.0	31.9
Conflicted					
Count	21	26	67	6	120
% within Motives	17.5	21.7	55.8	5.0	100.0
% within Sexual Orientation	22.3	22.0	21.7	24.0	22.0
Friends with Benefits/'Fuck Buddy'					
Count	22	24	58	5	109
% within Motives	20.2	22.0	53.2	4.6	100.0
% within Sexual Orientation	23.4	20.3	18.8	20.0	20.0
Casual					
Count	27	50	60	6	143
% within Motives	18.9	35.0	42.0	4.2	100.0
% within Sexual Orientation	28.7	42.4	19.4	24.0	26.2
Total					
Count	94	118	25	309	546
% within Motives	17.2	21.6	4.6	56.6	100.0
% within Sexual Orientation	100.0	100.0	100.0	100.0	100.0

(χ^2 = 36.360, df = 9, p <. 001)
Source: Collated from data collected by the authors. © Michelle Escasa-Dorne, 2014.

Finally, there is little sex difference in ad content across all the US regions coded. If a state had a fluid or static migration pattern or high or low percentage of college graduates, male and female, the ads are strikingly similar.

Discussion

Camille Paglia points out that 'since the sexual revolution of the 1960s, American society has become increasingly secular, with the media environment drenched with sex' (2010: A23). The cultural shift away from sexual restraint to a greater openness and tolerance in public expression of sexual desire does not mean there has been a corresponding shift in women's sexual behaviour. Edward Laumann et al.'s (1994) extensive survey of sexual behaviour in the US did not find strong evidence for this nor did our online study of female sexual preferences. The majority of heterosexual women's profiles, regardless of the degree of sexual explicitness, overwhelmingly noted a preference for sex within some type of ongoing or imagined relationship. In this way, evidence for heterosexual women's preference for 'no strings attached' sex, or, sexual variety for its own sake, continues to be absent. This is consistent with other studies (Buss 2008; Jankowiak, Gray and Hatman 2008; Schmitt, Shackelford and Buss 2001; Symons 1979; Townsend 1998) that repeatedly found women to be the choosier sex, showing overwhelming preference for some form of a 'relationship partner' over an anonymous 'one-night stand' sexual encounter.

Kathleen Bogle's (2008) research on contemporary college 'dating' provides another correction to the media's assertion that there has been a fundamental shift in female sexual behaviour. Her research found female casual sexual encounters were confined to their college years. Upon graduation, men and women returned to more conventional forms of dating in an effort to find a long-term mate. Further, Bogle reports that college women who did engage in numerous casual sexual encounters showed disappointment, regret and remorse. For most American women a 'one-night stand' produced an acute negative emotional reaction (as opposed to a moral objection).

Russell Clark's (1990) research found that heterosexual women had no problem dating a stranger; however, they did have a problem immediately having sex with a stranger. John Townsend's (1998) ethnographic study of American women's 'one-night stand' dating behaviour found a similar negative reaction. In a different but related study, Townsend and Wasserman (1998) found American women required more information than men in order to make the decision to have sex with someone. In this way, women required some form of contextualisation, imaginary or real, before entering into a sexual encounter with a stranger. Highlighting the importance of communication and trusting a sex partner, when women could talk with their sex partner about their experience with him, they were able to personalise that experience and were thus less troubled with entering into a casual sexual encounter (Paul and Hayes 2002). Women's need to be able to, in some fashion, 'control' the way they participated in a sexual encounter was also evident among American female swingers who did not immediately select the first attractive male they saw, but, rather, preferred to wait and discuss things with their husband, meet with the desired individual(s), exchange small talk and then, and only then, decided to have or not have sex (Jankowiak and Mixson 2008).

In contrast, men, especially men in their 20s, remained keenly focused on seeking out a variety of sex partners. It is a motivation that makes young men more than any other age cohort attracted to finding 'no strings attached' sex opportunities. As men age, however, we found a shift in their use of language away from an exclusive emphasis on 'no strings attached' sex to one more open to the possibility of forming an ongoing relationship (Table 4). Is this shift in men's language representative of a shift in male sexual desire or evidence only of a shift among more mature or experienced males in their understanding of what females want? We suspect it may be a little of both. As men learn that women do not want 'no strings attached' sex, they also realise they too want some of the emotional benefits that can only be gained from being in an ongoing relationship. However, women's conflicted profiles may be nothing more than a by-product of a new cultural tolerance toward the acknowledgement, if not advertisement, of an interest in sexual pleasure.

It could be argued that these mixed signals found in the female profiles are the by-product of an individual female making a nod toward fitting into a cultural role of dampened sexual desire, while preferring to engage the newer ethos of sexual frankness, sexual exploration and sexual casualness. In this way, the conflicted profiles may represent nothing more than a partial presentation of a proper persona. If this interpretation is correct, how can we account for the low frequency of mixed messages among the bisexual profiles? After all, bisexual women who have been socialised within similar age cohorts and live across the US in similar communities should have internalised a similar sexual script concerning social propriety and sexual respectability. Why then, were their profiles more direct as to their interest in and desire for casual sex? In every way, bisexual women's profiles were closer to heterosexual men's profiles than they were to heterosexual women's profiles.

It is revealing that of the females who expressed the strongest preference for partner variety, the majority of the females are bisexual. It is significant that 54 per cent of females who stated or strongly hinted at wanting 'no strings attached' sex were bisexual/bicurious. This is a rather high percentage and requires further commentary.

We did not anticipate that bisexual females would be the most prominent users on the dating site. It is consistent, however, with studies that find a strong relationship between higher testosterone and enhanced sexual desire (van Anders, Hamilton and Watson 2007). There is also a relationship between testosterone and sexual activity itself—it has been noted postmenopausal women using testosterone patches reported an increase in sexual activity (Bergner 2009: 5). Other research has found that bisexual women tend to have higher levels of testosterone, which may contribute to their having a stronger sexual desire (Brizendine 2006). Lippa's (2006) survey research, which did not collect testosterone data, did find that women, but not men, who admitted to having a high sex drive also stated they had a greater sexual attraction to both sexes. Whatever the relationship between testosterone and heightened or diminished sex drive turns out to be, it cannot account in and of itself for a woman's sexual orientation. Lisa Diamond noted that prenatal testosterone exposure did not produce a lesbian or bisexual woman. Rather, it appeared to produce a more fluid sex orientation, whereby a woman may have a periodic same-sex attraction (or be bicurious), while also preferring a heterosexual relationship (Diamond 2008). Diamond did not discuss whether a high amount of prenatal testosterone could account for a woman having a stronger sex drive. However, research on polycystic ovary syndrome, characterised by higher than normal testosterone levels in women, suggests higher reports of bisexuality and changing sexual orientation than the control group of women (Manlove et al. 2008).[2]

Many bisexual women acknowledged that they were sexually attracted to one sex while being emotionally drawn to forming a relationship with the other sex. Moreover, the sex they were more emotionally attracted to was the sex they wanted to form a monogamous relationship with. In contrast, the sex they were physically attracted to was the one they preferred to have 'no strings attached' sex with. Typical of these women was the following ad written by a 43-year-old bisexual who desired an emotional connection more than straightforward sexual satisfaction. She wrote that 'Men capture my attention in an instant with their muscle, strength, cologne, deep voice, a 5 o-clock shadow, the feel, smell and taste

---

[2] Bisexual/bicurious interest may also be associated with childhood abuse. Laumann and colleagues' US sexual survey (1994) found a correlation between women who claimed to be bisexual and women who reported childhood sexual abuse. Perhaps a difficult parent–child relationship makes it more difficult to bond emotionally with one sex, contributing to a greater willingness to state a preference for both sexes.

of them. How they are different from me'. She added, however, 'women too hold a fascination for me: softness, unexplored yet familiar territory, physical knowing, and the emotional connection. How they are similar to me'. She concluded by noting she 'longs to give the same things that I seek in another ... friendship, passion, desire, comfort, humor, tenderness, mental stimulation, soulful nourishment and perhaps even love'. For her, the stronger subjective and emotional connection was with the female or, in her words, 'her soul mate', and not the male.

Our study found that, at least for women who constructed ads on the sex website, the 'new' heterosexual female sexual persona may be essentially something of a tease to attract a potential partner's interest with little genuine interest in having a casual sexual encounter. David Buss (2008) referred to this female strategy as an example of a 'bait and switch' marketing ploy whereby a female's dress, gestures or voice are sexually suggestive, while there is no serious intention of entering into an immediate sexual tryst. The straight female profile ads suggest a sexual openness and thus availability to any and all men, while continuing to be insistent on engaging in sex only within an established relationship.

A separate, albeit related, control study featured a middle-aged male's facial photo with a profile that stated: 'have an interest in hot pleasurable sex'. Over a two-month period, the profile attracted 15 female emails. Each email was sent the same sentence: 'I think you are hot, too, let's meet.' Only two of the 15 initial females responded to the message. One female acknowledged she was a swinger and invited the man to participate in a threesome with her husband. The other reply was from a 20-something female who sent a new set of pictures of herself wearing a bikini and asked if she 'was sexy'. A return email requesting a meeting did not receive a response. It is possible to interpret the females' correspondence with the man's profile as never being truly interested in meeting. Instead, they may have wanted to see if their overture email would invoke a reply that would mean, from their perspective, an unfamiliar man desired them. We are not alone in this interpretation: in our larger sample we would occasionally find a male ad that shouted in large bold print: 'DOES ANYONE ON THIS SITE RESPOND TO ADS AND EMAILS? COME ON LADIES!'. We did not find a single female profile wondering if anyone responds to these profiles. Nor did we find a single male profile asserting they were 'Not interested in a one-night stand' or 'No married women, please!'. More to our point, heterosexual women's (but not men's) profiles overwhelmingly and repeatedly asserted they were not interested in a 'ONE NIGHT STAND!'. For women who are not in a swinger relationship or identifying as bisexual, it seems that the urge to be desired is fulfilment enough.

Lisa Diamond (2008) suggested that for females there is a strong link between intimacy and sexual desirability. Women want, first and foremost, to be validated; thus, seeking casual sexual opportunities has less to do with sexual pleasure than it does with wanting to be desired. In concurrence, Marta Meana (2010) suggested that women's primary personal validation is based on a narcissistic need to be seen as sexually desirable more than it does with finding a physiological outlet for sexual fulfilment (Bergner 2009). In this way, it is significant that 20 of the 60 straight women who expressed a strong interest in 'no strings attached' sex also noted they were coming or just about to come out of 'dead marriages'. Rebound dating is often more about ego validation that one is still sexually desirable than it is about obtaining just sexual satisfaction. For example, a 24-year-old woman wrote:

> I'm on the prowl for athletic guys that take very good care of their bodies and have a great style. Finally ended a bad relationship and am ready for something totally new and different. I'm fun, athletic, blond and brown with crazy night and a very active day life. If you are fat or gross don't bother, yes you know who you are. My age limit is 26, if over that don't bother.

In time, however, rebound sex dating usually leads to the establishment of another relationship. For example, a 38-year-old straight woman who was preparing to leave a sexless marriage wrote:

> My situation is changing rapidly. I need something to get out of the rut. I'm not single yet, but I will be VERY soon. Looking for a guy that has his own things in life that he enjoys … I totally believe in family, and romance for that matter, and if I was with a man that I love you would be all mine and no one else's, that's just how I feel about it.

If the bisexual, bicurious or heterosexual women coming out of a 'dead marriage' are dropped from the sample, there are only 40 women, or 7 per cent of our entire sample population, who state they are interested only in a casual sexual encounter. Of the 40 women who expressed this interest, it is difficult to know if they truly wanted a series of anonymous sexual encounters or were only using a highly suggestive ad to see who responded as a means to validate their own desirability. For women who are not in a swinger relationship or identify as bisexual, the urge to be desired may be fulfilment enough.

At first, it may seem contradictory that females would use a sex site to find a relationship. However, as we thought more about this, it made some cultural sense. Females appear to be engaging in a form of intrasexual competition with other females. In a culture that has come to embrace sexual satisfaction as an important aspect of a satisfactory life, and where 30 per cent of the American female population reports having a low or nonexistent sex drive (Diamond 2008), it may be a good mating strategy to demonstrate the presence of a strong interest in sexual enjoyment.

Conclusion

Adult Friend Finder is the world's largest online dating site. Its home page advertises itself as being a site where men and women can find good opportunities to find like-minded people interested in casual sexual encounters. We found the site functions, however, more as a dating site in which heterosexual women, in spite of their sexually suggestive profiles, prefer to form some type of ongoing relationship.[3] Straight women often

---

3   Not every male in our sample advertised as wanting only a casual sexual encounter. Our sample found 66 males (10 per cent) who were straightforward in acknowledging they were more interested in finding a steady girlfriend than engaging in anonymous sex. This seems to be slightly correlated with age. A majority of males (>50%) from 18–39 listed casual sexual encounters as the desired motive; however, by 40 and above more men's ads stated an interest in multiple motives—that is, they continued to state a willingness for 'no strings attached' sex while also noting an openness to a long-term/romantic relationship (LTR). The correlation between men aging and desiring a LTR may not simply be an artefact of them becoming cleverer in the way they prepared their profile. For example, Mathes, King, Miller and Reed (2002) found a strong correlation between increasing age and men's desire to form stronger emotional bonds. Similarly, Del Giudice (2009) noted that, 'males throughout the world tend to shift from high mating effort in young adulthood to a phase of increased parental investment' (also see Winking et al. 2007). While our findings did see a trend for a majority of males on the website who were seeking casual sex, it is also important to note that men may not be solely seeking sex with no emotional implications. Men, too, have been noted to have romantic inclinations and fall in love just as women do. As sex and sexuality is an important facet of human evolutionary lineage, 'choosing mates carefully and establishing long-term mateship were adaptive problems faced by both sexes, not just females, throughout evolutionary history' (Salmon and Symons 2003: 68). For example, a 43-year-old wrote that his ideal person is:

> someone who is not interested in one night stands or likes to sleep around … if that's you, please pass me up … I'm worth more than that and wish for someone who feels the same. I know that lots of women won't make it this far [reading the ad] but I trust that if you have that you will give me some feedback … good or bad.

He added 'he would very much like to meet someone who was looking for a short term/long term lover or great friend with relationship benefits to enjoy'.

A 36-year-old man concurred and wrote, 'I am a good looking male that is currently looking for one and only one awesome lady to spend some one on one time with having fun in and out of the bed'. He added, 'There are a lot of game players out there but I am willing to wait to meet my special lady'.

tease an interest in a 'hook up' encounter or willingness to enter into a casual sexual tryst when most have no intention of doing so. With the exception of a few heterosexual women (who were not bicurious or bisexual), our study found most heterosexual women are not interested in short-term mating for the primary purpose of seeking sexual pleasure. What American women's profiles repeatedly emphasise is the desire to form some type of ongoing relationship. This raises the never-ending question: Is the qualified caution found in women's profiles the result of lingering cultural restraint, or is it further evidence of the presence of underlying evolutionary derived sex differences? Clearly, we need renewed scholarly effort.

Acknowledgements

We would like to thank Jocie Barlett, Daniel Bergner, Dan Benyshek, Carolyn Brewer, Don Brown, David Buss, Lisa Diamond, Justin Garcia, Peter Gray, Sara Hill, Marta Meana, Tom Gregor, John Townsend, Warren Shapiro, Jen Soket and Don Symons for their suggestions, encouragement and scholarship.

References

Baumeister, Roy F. and Dianne M. Tice. 2001. *The Social Dimension of Sex*. Boston: Allyn and Bacon.

Baumeister, Roy F., Kathleen R. Catanese and Kathleen D. Vohs. 2001. 'Is there a gender difference in strength of sex drive? Theoretical views, conceptual distinctions, and a review of relevant evidence'. *Personality and Social Psychology Review* 5(3): 242–73. doi.org/10.1207/S15327957PSPR0503_5

Men, more so than women, tended to use a broader sex strategy that suggests an openness to enter into any type of sexual encounter: 'no strings attached' sex, regular sex at a specific time or a long-term relationship. This does not mean, however, that the men did not also crave emotional intimacy. Research has documented that the desire to form a love attachment is as strong in males as it is in females (Ellison and Gray 2009; Fisher 2004; Jankowiak 1995, 2008). Other work has noted that some men try to establish an emotional relationship with prostitutes and strippers, which speaks loudly to the male need for emotional intimacy (Jankowiak and Paladino 2008). For men, the pull toward seeking sexual variety is impossible to satisfy and often undermines a man's ability to sustain his relationship based on emotional monogamy and sexual intimacy (Baumeister and Tice 2001).

Bergner, Daniel. 2009. 'What do women want?' *New York Times Magazine*, 22 January: 1–12. Online: www.nytimes.com/2009/01/25/magazine/25desire-t.html (accessed 1 June 2017).

Betzig, Laura. 1989. 'Causes of conjugal dissolution'. *Current Anthropology* 30(5): 654–76. doi.org/10.1086/203798

Bogle, Kathleen A. 2008. *Hooking Up: Sex, Dating and Relationships on Campus*. New York: New York University Press.

Brizendine, Louann. 2006. *The Female Brain*. London: Bantam Books.

Buss, David M. 2003. *The Evolution of Desire: Strategies of Human Mating*. New York: Basic Books.

——. 2008. *Evolutionary Psychology: The New Science of the Mind*. 3rd ed. Boston: Pearson.

Buss, David M. and David P. Schmitt. 1993. 'Sexual strategies theory: An evolutionary perspective on human mating'. *Psychological Review* 100(2): 204–32. doi.org/10.1037/0033-295X.100.2.204

Campbell, Anne. 2008. 'The morning after the night before: Affective reactions to one night stands among mated and unmated women and men'. *Human Nature* 19(2):157–73. doi.org/10.1007/s12110-008-9036-2

Clark, Russell D. 1990. 'The impact of AIDS on gender differences in the willingness to engage in casual sex'. *Journal of Applied Psychology* 20(9): 771–82. doi.org/10.1111/j.1559-1816.1990.tb00437.x

Del Giudice, Marco. 2009. 'Sex, attachment and the development of reproductive strategies'. *Behavorial and Brain Sciences* 32(1): 1–67. doi.org/10.1017/S0140525X09000016

Diamond, Lisa M. 2008. *Sexual Fluidity: Understanding Women's Love and Desire*. Cambridge: Harvard University Press.

Ellison, Peter T. and Peter B. Gray (eds). 2009. *Endocrinology of Social Relationships*. Cambridge: Harvard University Press.

Fisher, Helen. 2004. *Why We Love*. New York: Henry Holt.

Florida, Richard. 2009. *Who's Your City?: How the Creative Economy is Making Where to Live the Most Important Decision of your Life.* New York: Random House.

Gangestad, Stephen W. and Jeffry A. Simpson. 2000. 'The evolution of human mating: Trade-offs and strategic pluralism'. *Behavioral and Brain Sciences* 23(4): 573–87. doi.org/10.1017/S0140525X0000337X

Garcia, Justin R and Chris Reiber. 2008. 'Hook-up behavior: A biopsychosocial perspective'. *Journal of Social, Evolutionary, and Cultural Psychology* 2(4): 192–208. doi.org/10.1037/h0099345

Gray, Peter B. and Justin R. Garcia. 2013. *Evolution and Human Sexual Behavior.* Cambridge: Harvard University Press.

Greiling, Heidi and David M. Buss. 2000. 'Women's sexual strategies: The hidden dimension of short term extra-pair mating'. *Personality and Individual Differences* 28(5): 929–63. doi.org/10.1016/S0191-8869(99)00151-8

Grello, Catherine M., Deborah P. Welsh and Melinda S. Harper. 2006. 'No strings attached: The nature of casual sex in college students'. *The Journal of Sex Research* 43(4): 255–67. doi.org/10.1080/00224490609552324

Hatfield, Elaine, Megan Forbes and Richard L. Rapson. 2011. 'Marketing love and sex'. *Society* 49(6): 506–11. doi.org/10.1007/s12115-012-9593-1

Hatfield, Elaine, Elisabeth S. Hutchinson, Lisamarie Bensman, Danielle M. Young and Richard L. Rapson. 2012. 'Cultural, social and gender influence on casual sex: New developments'. In *Social Psychology: New Developments*, edited by Jan Turn and Andrew D. Mitchell, 1–38. New York: Nova Science.

Hrdy, Sarah Blaffer. 1999. *Mother Nature: A History of Mothers, Infants and Natural Selection.* New York: Pantheon.

Jankowiak, William R. 1995. *Romantic Passion: The Universal Experience?* New York: Columbia University Press.

——. 2008. *Intimacies: Sex and Love Across Cultures.* New York: Columbia University Press.

Jankowiak, William R. and Laura Mixson. 2008. "I have his heart, swinging is just sex": The ritualization of the love bond in an American spouse exchange community'. In *Intimacies: Love and Sex Across Cultures*, edited by Jankowiak, 245–66. New York: Columbia University Press.

Jankowiak, William R. and Thomas Paladino. 2008. 'Desiring sex, longing for love: a tripartite conundrum'. In *Intimacies: Love and Sex Across Cultures*, edited by Jankowiak, 1–36. New York: Columbia University Press.

Jankowiak, William, Peter Gray and Kelly Hatman. 2008. 'Globalization and perception of attractiveness'. *Journal of Cross-Cultural Research* 10(1–22): 248–69.

Kinsey, Alfred C., Wardell B. Pomeroy and Clyde E. Martin. 1948. *Sexual Behavior in the Human Male*. Bloomington: Indiana University Press.

———. 1953. *Sexual Behavior in the Human Female*. Bloomington: Indiana University Press.

Lambert, Tracy A., Arnold S. Kahn and Kevin J. Apple. 2003. 'Pluralistic ignorance and hooking up'. *The Journal of Sex Research* 40(2): 129–33. doi.org/10.1080/00224490309552174

Laumann, Edward O., John Gagnon, Robert T. Michael and Stewart Michaels. 1994. *The Social Organization of Sexuality: Sexual Practices in the United States*. Chicago: University of Chicago Press.

Lippa, Richard A. 2006. 'Is high sex drive associated with increased sexual attraction to both sexes? It depends on whether you are male or female'. *Psychological Science* 17(1): 46–52. doi.org/10.1111/j.1467-9280.2005.01663.x

Manlove, Heidi Ann, Christelbeth Guillermo and Peter B. Gray. 2008. 'Do women with polycystic ovary syndrome (PCOS) report differences in sex-typed behavior as children and adolescents? Results of a pilot study'. *Annals of Human Biology* 35(6): 584–95. doi.org/10.1080/03014460802337067

Mathes, Eugene.W., Christine A. King, Jonathan K. Miller and Ruth M. Reed. 2002. 'An evolutionary perspective on the interaction of age and sex differences in short-term sexual strategies'. *Psychological Reports* 90(3 pt 1): 949–56. doi.org/10.2466/pr0.2002.90.3.949

Mealey, Linda. 2000. *Sex Differences: Developmental and Evolutionary Strategies*. San Diego, CA: Academic Press.

Meana, Marta. 2010. 'Elucidating women's (hetero)sexual desire: Definitional challenges and content expansion'. *Journal of Sex Research* 47(2): 104–22. doi.org/10.1080/00224490903402546

Meston, Cindy and David Buss. 2007. 'Why humans have sex'. *Archives of Sexual Behavior* 36(4): 477–507. doi.org/10.1007/s10508-007-9175-2

Paglia, Camille. 2010. 'No sex please, we're middle class'. *New York Times*, 25 June, A23.

Paul, Elizabeth L. and Kristen A. Hayes. 2002. 'The casualties of 'casual' sex: A qualitative exploration of the phenomenology of college students' hookups'. *Journal of Social and Personal Relationships* 19(5): 639–61. doi.org/10.1177/0265407502195006

Paul, Elizabeth L., Brian McManus and Allison Hayes. 2000. "Hookups': Characteristics and correlates of college students' spontaneous and anonymous sexual experiences'. *The Journal of Sexual Research* 37(1): 76–88. doi.org/10.1080/00224490009552023

Pillsworth, E.G. and Martie E. Haselton. 2006. 'Women's sexual strategies: The evolution of long-term bonds and extrapair sex'. *Annual Review of Sex Research* 17: 59–100.

Regan, Pamela C. and Ellen Berscheid. 1999. *Lust: What we Know about Human Sexual Desire*. Sage Series on Close Relationships. Thousand Oaks, CA: Sage Publications.

Salmon, Catherine and Donald Symons. 2003. *Warrior Lovers: Erotic Fiction, Evolution and Female Sexuality*. New Haven: Yale University Press.

Schmitt, David P. 2005. 'Sociosexuality from Argentina to Zimbabwe: A 48-nation study of sex, culture, and strategies of human mating'. *Behavioral and Brain Sciences* 28(2): 247–75. doi.org/10.1017/S0140525X05000051

Schmitt, David P., Todd K. Shackelford and David M. Buss. 2001. 'Are men really more "oriented" toward short term mating than women?' *Psychology, Evolution and Gender* 3(3): 211–39. doi.org/10.1080/14616660110119331

Symons, Donald. 1979. *The Evolution of Human Sexuality*. Oxford: Oxford University Press.

Tolman, Deborah L. and Lisa M. Diamond. 2001. 'Female sexuality and sexual desire'. In *Encyclopedia of Women and Gender*, edited by Judith Worell. New York: Academic Press.

Toma, Catalina L., Jeffrey T. Hancock and Nicole B. Ellison. 2008. 'Separating fact from fiction: An examination of deceptive self-presentation in online dating profiles'. *Personality and Social Psychology Bulletin* 34(8): 1022–36. doi.org/10.1177/0146167208318067

Townsend, John Marshall. 1998. *What Women Want – What Men Want: Why the Sexes Still See Love and Commitment so Differently*. Oxford: Oxford University Press.

Townsend, John Marshall and Timothy Wasserman. 1998. 'Sexual attractiveness: Sex differences in assessment and criteria'. *Evolution and Human Behavior* 19(3): 171–91. doi.org/10.1016/S1090-5138(98)00008-7

van Anders, Sari M., Lisa Dawn Hamilton and Neil V. Watson. 2007. 'Multiple partners are associated with higher testosterone in North American men and women'. *Hormones and Behavior* 51(3): 454–59. doi.org/10.1016/j.yhbeh.2007.01.002

Winking, Jeffrey, Hillard Kaplan, Michael Gurven and Stacy Rucas. 2007. 'Why do men marry and why do they stay?' *Proceedings of the Royal Society of London. B.* 274(1618): 1643–49. doi.org/10.1098/rspb.2006.0437

Index

Note: Page numbers in **bold** refer to figures.

Aboriginal Australia, 10, 34, 42n10, 205, 213, 227, 347, 355, 357–58, 358n1, 359
Aboriginal Australian(s), 10–11, 78, 356–57, 358n1, 359
   cultures, 10
   groups, 358
   kin categorisation, 357, 359
   kinship, 254, 354
   kinship systems, 230, 344, 355–56
   kinship terminologies, 9–11, 121, 227, 230–31, 241, 246, 254, 344, 353, 354, 355–56
   language(s), 249, 252
   marriage rules. *See* marriage, rules
   patrifilial groups, 39
   rules, 359
   social life, 10–11, 359
   superclasses, 357–58
Abu-Zeid, Ahmad, 185
action, 119–29, 213, 216
address terminology, 306–07
adoption, 6, 8, 13, 15, 16, 35, 85n17, 121, 122, 177–95, 203–18, 250, 316, 348, 349
affinal, 89, 95–97, 107, 156, 231, 239–40, 245, 246, 264, 266–72, 276, 279, 281, 283, 284n24, 286, 310–11, 316
   kin, 95, 107, 156, 194, 240, 334

affinity, 113, 265–67, 269, 283, 284n25, 305
Africa(n), 14n5, 67, 74, 78, 291n35, 373
algebra(ic), 68, 70n9, 72, 80, 96
Algonquian, 281
Allen, Catherine, 330
Allen, Nicholas J., 263–64, 272, 273n12, 275
alliance theory, 16–17. *See also* prescriptive alliance
alloparental care (alloparenting), 209–10
Alor, 282n20
altercentricity, 238, 249, 252, 254
alternate generation, 231–32, **232**, 232n4
Aluridja, 231, 242–43, **243**, **245**
Amazon, 7, 279, 290n32, 358n1, 359
Amazonian
   Peru, 74
   societies, 15
   type, 279
American terminology, 80, 80n15, 81, **81**, 89–90, 90n22, 92, 94, 96–98, 329
Americas, 279, 291
analysis, total structural, 271n11
Anderson, Michael L., 331
Apachean, 242
Ardener, Edwin, 290, 290n33
ascending terms. *See* terms, ascending

395

Asch, Michael, 282
Asia(n), 291, 373
  South, 283n23, 291, 291n34
asymmetry, 238, 270n9, 271
Athapaskan, 242, 281
Australia, 210, 214n5, 227, 230, 232–34, 237–39, 239n7, 242, 246–47, 247n14, 248, 251–53, 254, 254n16, 270, 278, 291n35, 358
  Central, 212
  South, 252
  Western, 73, 93, 113, 246, 247
Australian
  Aboriginal. *See* Aboriginal Australian
  community, 204
  context, 254
  kin classification, 344
  kinship, 227, 241, 246, 353. *See also* Aboriginal Australian, kinship, kinship systems, kinship terminologies
  sex distinction, 357
Australian Kin Classification (Scheffler), 9–10, 121, 227, 230
Australian kinship systems. *See* Australian Aboriginal, kinship systems
Australian kinship terms (language). *See* Aboriginal Australian, kinship terminologies
Australian Western Desert. *See* Western Desert
avoidance, 40n7, 155–56, 180, 188–94, 246, 253, 344–45

Bandjalangic, 242n11, 252
Baniata, 9
Barnard, Alan, 74, 275
Barnes, Robert H., 266n5, 279, 282n20
Basso, Ellen, 274, 275n16, 283, 283n22, 306

Bean, Susan, 306–07, 315
behaviour, 13, 18, 65, 67, 84, 85, 85n17, 85n18, 89, 122, 133–34, 136–37, 144, 145, 152, 161, 180, 191–92, 205–06, 208, 213, 217, 270, 273–74, 290, 338, 343, 345, 348–49, 369–72, 380, 383
behavioural ecology, 136
Behrens, Clifford, 68, 74, 80n15, 83, 98
Bengali, 292
Bennardo, Giovanni, 68, 93, 94n24, 98, 102, 329–30
Berlin, Brent, 289–90
Bihar, 274n15
bilateral
  cross-cousin marriage, 271–73, 275, 280–82, 282n20, 283–84, 286n28, 291
  kin/kinship, 15, 133–55, 155n1, 156–61, 273, 304, 333
bilocal residence/bilocality, 135, 138, 148, 152, 161
binary operator/operation, 80, 91
biological, 12, 36, 63, 77n14, 78, 79, 85n17, 85n18, 107, 122, 133–34, 161, 217, 285, 238, 332, 335
  birth, 85
  child(ren), 211
  kin, 134, 142, 161
  maternity (mother), 77n14, 85, 85n18, 87, 89, 142, 143, 203, 207, 329
  parents (parentage), 209–10, 264, 349
  paternity (father), 8, 41, 77n14, 89, 142, 346
  procreation (reproduction), 78, 84–86, 107, 121–22, 264, 327, 332
  relations, 78n14, 79, 89
biology, 42, 77n14, 78n14, 134, 161, 192, 206, 264n2, 346
birth, 6, 12, 38–39, 44, 78n14, 85, 85n17, 86, 138–39, 142–43,

147–48, 155, 178–79, 185–86, 191, 193–95, 205, 207n1, 210, 269, 286, 304, 327, 332, 347–50
kin, 178–79, 179n3, 179n4, 184–85, 194
bisexual, 370–72, 374–75, 378, 382, 384–85, 385n2, 387, 389
Blackman, Margaret B., 6
Bloch, Maurice, 10, 206–07, 212, 308, 348
Boas, Franz, 307
Bolivia, 7, 271
Boot, Inge, 332–33
Borroloola, 212
Brahmans, Nambudiri, 284n24
Brahmans, Vattima, 285
bride price, 289
British, 264, 284, 287
brother, 3, 5, 7, 9, 13, 63–64, 64n5, 65–66, 66n6, 77, 79, 87, 99–103, 125, 138, 143, 154–55, 155n1, 160, 182–84, 186–87, 190–93, 203–07, 207n1, 208, 215, 229, 230, 236–37, 246–47, 247n13, 248, 249–54, 282, 284, 288, 304–05, 310–11, 316, 331, 334, 356–57
Brown, Cecil, 289, 290

Canada, 85n18, 279
Cardillo, Eileen R., 332
Carpenter, Edmund S., 328, 336
Carsten, Janet, 32–33, 36, 45, 181, 308, 347–48
Cassidy, Jude, 15
casual sex, 369–89
category, 9–10, 12, 34, 66, 91–92, 92n23, 93, 103, 105, 119–22, 147, 264, 264n3, 265, 265n4, 266–67, 270n9, 273n14, 276–77, 278n17, 279, 290, 308, 332–33, 350, 355, 357–59, 373–75
Chagnon, Napoleon, 280
Chapman, Cynthia, 15
Chatterjee, Anjan, 332

Chettiar, Vellan, 287
child/children, 5–6, 9, 11–12, 14n5, 15, 34–39, 43–44, 44n13, 45, 45n14, 63, 65, 67n7, 71, 73–75, 77–78, 78n14, 79–82, 84–85, 85n18, 86, 86n19, 86n20, 87, 87n21, 88–90, 94–100, 100n25, 102, 121–22, 125, 139, 142–43, 145, 148, 150, 153, 155, 155n1, 156–57, 160, 182–84, 192–93, 203, 205–07, 207n1, 208–09, 209n3, 210, 210n4, 211–13, 215–17, 228n1, 230, 237, 240–41, 245, 247, 247n14, 248–50, 254, 254n16, 268, 270, 277, 281, 286, 304–05, 310–11, 317, 330–31, 334–35, 345–48, 355–58, 376, 385n2
childbirth, 304
China, 86n20, 278n17, 284n25, 291
Choiseul Island, 4–5, 16, 130
Clark-Decès, Isabelle, 287–88
Classen, Constance, 330
classes, marriage, 277, 358, 358n1. *See also* marriage
classification, Linnaean, 290
classificatory, 64–66, 74, 99, 102, 120, 124, 207–08, 217, 228n1, 231, 242, 267–69, 273, 276–77, 287, 290, 292, 327
classificatory terminology (terms), 62, 62n4, 63–66, 66n6, 67, 69, 93, 99, 100–07, 120
coefficient of relatedness, 79, 205, 207, 209–10, 213, 215, 217, 344, 354
cognition, 14, 318, 327–38, 343, 350, 352, 354
social, 328, 329, 330, 336, 338, 343
collateral terminology, 283
colour terms, 289, 290
comparison, 39, 71, 71n10, 72, 72n11, 73, 135–36, 152, 156, 158, 161, 235, 238, 283, 329, 334, 343

competition, 215, 217, 388
compound kin terms. *See* kin terms, compound
computational logic, 63, 77, 105
conception, 8, 36–37, 39, 41, 45, 269, 347–48
conceptual structure, 343–44, 349–54, 359–60
concubinage, 284
conjunctivist, 228
connexion, 32
consanguineal, 7–8, 95, 231, 246, 267–69, 272, 334
consanguines, 283, 288, 289n29, 359
consanguinity, 113, 265, 267, 269, 334
context, 33n2, 85n17, 88, 107, 119–20, 124, 126–28, 146, 156, 185, 188, 211, 214n5, 236, 238, 239, 239n8, 250, 254, 264, 278n17, 280, 288, 308–09, 313, 315–16, 331, 336, 357, 371, 378
contextual variation, 238
cooperation, 120, 136–38, 144, 161, 213, 215, 280
core cognition, 343, 350, 352
cores, sibling. *See* sibling, cores
coresidence, 13, 211, 215–17, 346, 348
counting numbers, 83–84
cousin(s), 45, 64n5, 75–76, 79, **81**, 138, 142–43, 154, 183, 186, 191, 204–05, 213–17, 231–33, 264n3, 287, 288, 292, 334, 345, 359
Cree, 279
Croation ethnography, 333
  colloquial language, 330
  informants, 18, 330
cross cousin(s), 231, 233, 237, 239, 240, **240**, **241**, 241–42, 265n4, 270, 272, 273n14, 275–78, 281, 283–84, 286–87, 292, 306, 359
  marriage, 247, 265–67, 269–82, 282n20, 283–84, 284n24,
285–86, 286n28, 287–89, 291–92, 359
cross-cultural studies, 135, 152, 161, 191, 303
cross-parallel distinctions, 241–42, 272, 292. *See also* parallel/cross
Crow skewing, 229, 234–36
Crow-type, 43–44, **229**, **230**, 235–36, 271, 303
crying, 203, 205, 206, 213
cultural models of kinship, 346
culturally salient, 60, 70, 72, 76, 80, 83, 98–99, 105–06
culture(s), 5, 10, 63, 67, 72, 75, 77, 83, 120, 143–44, 179, 192, 204, 206, 211, 235, 330, 332–33, 336, 343, 346–47, 349–51, 353, 372, 388
  bearers, 84–85, 85n17, 91–92, 98

D'Andrade, Roy G., 8, 69, 204
Dakota group, 235
Dakota–Iroquois, 142
Darwinian approach to casual sex, 369
Darwinian fitness, 327
dating sites, 18, 371–73, 376
descending terms, 95, 101
descent, 99, 119, 121, 134, 142, 152, 161, 185, 234, 263, 269, 270, 270n9, 271, 285, 314, 344
descriptive terminologies, 62, 66, 82, 102
developmental psychology, 330, 352
diachrony, 235
dispersal, 134, 136–37, 147–49, 151–52, 276–77, 282n20
Dole, Gertrude, 241, 274–75, 275n16, 282, 282n20, 283, 283n22
Dousset, Laurent, 74, 238, 242
dowry, 286–88, 289n29
Dravidian, 73, 142, 241n9, 266n6, 272, 279–81, 282n20, 283–84, 291, 291n34, 307, 355–60

Dravidian terminology, 100n26, 102, 269, 271–72
du Boulay, Juliet, 334
Dumont, Louis, 264, 266, 269, 284, 284n24, 288
Duna, 119

education, 285, 287–88, 374–75
Elmendorf, William, 283
employment, 14, 281, 285, 287–88
enangar, 284n24
encroaching spread, 242
endogamy, 280–82, 282n20, 333
English language, 121, 123
environment(al), 133–36, 139, 144–45, 157–58, 160–61, 180, 206–07, 214, 216–17, 334, 382
equivalence rules, 60, 66–67, 67n7, 67n8, 68–71, 76, 82, 106–07, 228, 230–31, 233, 267
ethnolinguistic, 303, 307–08, 311, 314, 317
Europe, 15, 183, 291, 373
Evans-Pritchard, E.E., 65
evolutionary theory, 206, 213, 343, 369
evolutionists
    lexical, 289
    universalist, 289
exogamous marriage, 136, 151, 153–55, 155n1, 156
exogamy, 214, 280, 282, 282n20
extension(s)/extensionism/extensionist, 3, 5, 7, 9, 13–18, 33, 33n2, 44–45, 45n14, 63, 64, 65–69, 89, 99, 103, 106, 119–20, 123–24, 126, 128–29, 134, 142, 179, 193–94, 204–05, 214, 227–28, 228n1, 228n2, 229–33, 235–41, 244–45, 247–48, 250, 254, 264, 266–69, 270n9, 303–05, 307, 315–19, 327–29, 331–32, 334, 346

extension problem, 59–61, 61n2, 62–64, 65–67, 67n8, 70–71, 73, 79, 82–83, 89, 93, 102
    resolution, 59, 103, 106
extensionist semantics, 318

family
    relations, 3, 63, 71, 77, 85
    space, 13–14, 83–85, 85n17, 87–89, 91, 99–100, 100n25, 106
Fanti, 67, 70–71, 73, 228, 236–37
    terminology, 68, 71
father, 3, 5, 9–13, 18, 35, 39, 41–43, 43n11, 44, 44n12, 44n13, 45, 62, 64, 64n5, 65–66, 66n6, 67n7, 75, 77, 77n14, 78, 78n14, 79, 80n15, 85–86, 86n19, 87–89, 90n22, 91, 92n23, 93–94, 99–100, 100n25, 101–06, 124–26, 142–43, 154, 187, 188–91, 193, 205, 207n1, 208–09, 213–16, 229–30, 232, 237, 240, 246, 249–50, 254n16, 277, 304–05, 311, 331, 346–47, 349–50, 353, 355–56, 358–59
Feinberg, Richard, 74
Feng, Han-yi, 291
fictive kinship, 334, 338
figure/ground, 352, 354
Fiji(an), 73–74, 99, 113, 115
filiation, 121, 270, 270n9
filiocentricity, 238, 249–51, 254, 254n16
Fischer, Michael D., 13, 72, 84, 89
fishing, 140–41, 158
Fison, Lorimer, 9, 241, 241n9
focal, 42, 105, 122, 124, 205, 228, 267, 268, 318
    denotata, 268
    gender class, 13
    genealogical referents, 305–06
    kin type (terms), 228, 235, 267–68, 272, 328
    meaning(s), 124–28, 228, 267

member(ship), 3, 5–7, 11, 34–35, 43, 45, 105, 316, 331
referent(s), 236, 318
status, 6, 15–16
focality, i, iii, 15–16, 32, 33n2, 124, 205, 214, 310, 316, 332
data, 310, 315–16, 318
and prototypicality, 310
Fogelson, Raymond D., 11
food, 45, 87, 121–22, 127, 137, 139–41, 153, 156–58, 160–61, 213, 217, 280–81, 347
foragers, 135–40, 144–47, 152, 155–59, 161
formal analysis, 7, 9, 60, 350
formal representation, 68, 94
fosterage, 13, 26, 182, 205, 209
fostering, 182, 209–11
frame of reference, 306, 309, 313–14, 318, 329
Fuller, Christopher, 283, 285–86

Garde, Murray, 227, 249, 251, 252
Garo, 283n23
gender (engender), 12–13, 16, 18, 44n13, 66, 100n25, 123, 125, 153, 178, 186, 236, 245–46, 278, 278n17, 316, 374, 376–77, 380
genealogical space, 67n7, 68, 71
genealogical ties, 120, 269
genealogy, 35, 68, 77n14, 79, 89, 100n25, 120–22, 181, 185, 264, 264n2, 264n3, 266, 292, 348
generative logic, 61, 61n2, 80n15, 93–94, 98, 105–07
genetic differentiation, 214n5
genetic relatedness, 161, 344, 346
genetrix, 5–6, 13, 43, 192–93, 306, 315–16
genitor, 5–6, 10, 10n4, 12–13, 13n5, 43, 78n14, 192–93, 305–06, 315, 346
ghotul, 278n17
Godelier, Maurice, 128, 355

Good, Anthony, 73, 75, 273n14, 287, 289, 359
Goodale, Jane, 21, 105
Goodenough, Ward H., 15, 192, 308, 344
Gough, E. Kathleen, 12
Graham, Penelope, 266n5
groin, 184–85, 190–92
Guggenheim, Stephen, 10n4, 19
Gujarati, 292
Gumbaynggir, 232n5, 239n8, 252–53
Guyana, 266n5

Hadza, 157–60
Hamilton, William, 205, 210, 213, 215
Hawaiian, 241, 275n16, 276
Hawaiianisation, 281, 283
Heath, Jeffrey, 207, 207n1, 252
Henley, Paul, 279
Herdt, Gilbert, 12
heterosexual(ity), 183, 370, 374–75, 378, 381, 383–84, 386–89
Hickerson, Harold, 281
Hicks, David, 266n5, 276
Himalayas (Himalayan), 274n15, 283n23
Hindi, 292
history (prehistory), 46, 64n5, 133–34, 149–50, 153, 160, 190, 204, 207, 209, 233, 235, 240, 246, 267–68, 270n9, 272, 275, 280, 337, 240, 353–54, 388n3
Holmberg, Allan R., 7
homosexual, 374
household-based, 304n1, 309–10, 313, 315–16
Howitt, Alfred William, 9, 241, 241n9
hunter-gatherer(s), 7, 15, 73, 93, 133, 134–39, 144, 146, 152–53, 155, 157–59
hunting, 135, 140, 142, 158, 160, 280–81

i:yanikina:we, 314, 318–19
ignorance of physiological paternity, 8, 10, 36, 36n5, 38, 40n8, 41n9
Ijzerman, Hans, 330
illocution(ary), 126–27
image schemata, 332–33
inbreeding, 87n21, 285–86, 344–45
Inca, 330–31
incest, 40, 155, 178, 190–91, 191n10, 194, 334, 345
  avoidance, 155, **189**, **190**
  spiritual, 335
  taboo(s), 86, 87n21, 179–80, 188–90, 192–94, 277, 347
inclusive fitness, 205–06, 211, 213
India(n), 272, 274n15, 276, 278n17, 282n20, 285–86, 287–88, 292, 309, 312
  South(ern), 73, 272, 273n14, 279, 283–84, 284n24, 286n28, 307, 359
Indo–European, 282n20, 291, 291n34
Indonesia(n), 139, 266n5, 279, 282n20
infant(s), 145, 179, 182–83, 184n6, 186–87, 193, 210, 212–13, 217, 311, 346, 349, 352
intension, 228n2
intergenerational mismatch, 237
intermarriage, 17, 181. *See also* marriage
Iroquois, 62, 79, 82, 104, 142, 234–35, 266n6, 271–72, 276, 280–81
Istirda', 182, 184
Ives, John, 242, 280–82

Jivaroan, 141, 280
Johnson, Mark, 215, 328–30, 333
Ju/'hoansi, 159–60
juniority–seniority, 249
Just, Roger, 334

!Kung, 74, 78, 160
Kachin, 271
Kalapalo, 283
Kannada, 307, 315
kanya dan, 285–86
Kapadia, Karen, 279, 283, 286–88
Kariera, 73, 93, 100n26, 102, 230–31, 245, 247, 273
  terminology, 107, 358n1
Kay, Paul, 289–90
Kelly, Robert L., 135, 157
Kerala, 284–85
Kham Magar, 283n23
Khatib-Chahidi, Jane, 15, 178
Kiefer, Lucas, 332
Kimberley, 246
kin
  recognition, 207, 332, 344, 346, 348
  selection, 205–07, 438
  terminologies, 128, 235, 344, 349–50
kin term(s), 7, 14, 16–17, 43, 59–62, 62n3, 62n4, 63–67, 67n8, 69–72, 72n11, 73–75, 75n12, **76**, 76–77, 79–80, 80n15, 82–83, 87, 90–92, 92n23, 93–97, **97**, 98–100, 100n25, 101, 102n27, 103–04, 104n28, 105, 105n29, 106–07, 119–24, 120, 121, 126–27, 142–43, 178–79, 179n3, 210, 216–17, 249, 252, 265, 268–69, 289, 291, 303, 305–10, 312–13, 315, 327–28, 349–50, 353–55, 357, 358n1
  calculations (computations), 73, 75n12, 77
  compound, 100, 102
  extensions, 65, 67
  forms, 307, 310, 315
  meaning, 228, 238
  product(s), 9, 14, 71–72, 75, 75n12, 76, **76**, 76n13, 77–83, 89–91, 91n23, 92, 92n23,

93, 95–96, 98, 100n25, 101, 102n27, 103–04, 104n28, 106
reciprocity, 82, 83, 107
relation(s), 83–84, 87, 89, 91–92, 96, 99, 100n25, 101
structure(s), 66, 90, **90**, 94, 107, 120
system(s), 303, 305–06
usage, 18, 63, 268, 304–05, 314
kin-relational expressions, 85n17
Kin Term Space (KTS), 68, 71–72, 100n25
kin types, 68, 72n11, 79, 83, 90–92, 92n23, 93–94, 103–04, 119–20, 126, 240, 267–68, 272, 304–05, 349, 353, 356
kindred, 34, 210, 214, 216
kinship
   and metaphor, 15, 18, 119, 268, 327–28, 331, 332, 334–36
   milk, 15, 177n1, 178, 180, 182, 182n5, 184, 238, 347
   semantics, 6, 115, 177, 254
   structure(s), 120, 177–78, 180, 182, 193
   studies, 11–12, 17, 32–33, 34n3, 46, 119–21, 127–28, 136, 181, 204, 227, 263, 308, 318, 369
   terminology, 7, 14, 17, 43, 59, 60, 61n2, 63–64, 67, 67n7, 67n8, 68–69, 70–72, 75, 77–84, 89, 93–98, 100n25, 102, 104–07, 142, 177n1, 207, 227–28, 236, 238, 252, 264, 267, 273, 289, 303, 307, 338
   tetradic, 272, 278
Klein, Richard G., 338
Koole, Sander L., 330
Kranjec, Alexander, 332
Kroeber, Alfred L., 64, 303–04, 306, 310, 312–14, 317, 350, 353
Kronenfeld, David, 67–68, 70–72, 228, 229–30, 235–38, 328, 332–33
Kuikuru, 282
Kumaon, 274n15
Kuper, Adam, 190, 348
Kurnai, 241–42

labelling/absolutive versus descriptive relational expressions, 312
Ladd, Edmund, 303–06, 317
Lakoff, George, 215, 328–34
Lamaholot, 279, 282n20
Lamet, 270n10, 271n11
Landau, Mark J., 332
Lang, Andrew, 10
Layton, Robert, 157, 275
Leach, Edmund, 39, 41, 60, 266, 278, 307
Leaf, Murray J., 14, 68, 72, 76n13, 80n15, 83, 89, 93–94, 98, 102, 107, 308, 327, 332, 338, 344
learning, 65, 79, 268, 331–32
Lehman, Kris, 13, 68–70, 72, 84, 89
lesbian, 370, 385
Lévi-Strauss, Claude, 6, 16, 136, 190, 266, 271n11, 275–77, 350
lexical universalists, 289
Lieberman, Debra, 207, 211, 215, 346
lineality, 138, 180
longitudinal study/data, 134–37, 144, 146, 148, 152, 156, 161
Lounsbury, Floyd, 5, 7–9, 11, 13, 35, 35n4, 45n14, 60–61, 66–70, 77, 79, 82, 103, 105, 120–21, 177, 228, 229, 229n3, 233, 254, 263, 265–66, 267–72, 318, 328, 344
love, romantic, 278
Lowie, Robert H., 15, 33, 143, 282
Lubbock, John, 9

Madagascar, 348
maharim, 188–89, 191–92
Makka, 184, 184n6, 191
Malay, 32, 45, 347
Malinowski, Bronisław, 10, 34, 36–38, 38n6, 39–40, 40n7, 41, 41n9, 42, 43–44, 44n12, 45n14, 65, 192, 228n1, 347
Malpahariya, 274n15
Mamboru, 266n5, 299
Manggarai, 276
Manitoba, 279
Mariana Trench, 290n32
Maric, 252
marital kin(ship), 178–79, 179n3
markedness, 353, 355
marriage, 13, 14n5, 15, 17, 26, 34, 59, 61, 63, 65–66, 71, 77, 82, 86, 86n20, 88, 120, 123, 135–36, 139, 144–55, 155n1, 156, 177, 179, 179n3, 179n4, 180–82, 184, 186–95, 209–10, 214, 240, 242, 246–47, 247n13, 253, 263–65, 265n4, 266–68, 270–78, 278n17, 279–82, 282n20, 283–84, 284n24, 284n25, 285–86, 286n28, 287–93, 334–35, 358n1, 359, 381, 387
  arranged, 284–85
  companionate, 285
  cross cousin, 247, 263–92, 359
    asymmetric, 271
    bilateral, 271–73, 275, 280–82, 284, 286, 291
  dowry, 287
  exogamous, 136, 151, 154–55, 155n1, 156
  group, 26, 120
  love, 285
  natolocal, 136, 140, 147–48, 150–55, 155n1, 156–59, 161
  neolocal, 147, 150, 154
  polygynous (polygyny), 148–49, 155, 214, 278

prohibitions, 276
rule(s), 71, 135, 240, 246, 270, 273–75, 282, 292, 334–35, 354, 356, 358–59
sexless (dead), 381, 387
sister's daughter, 286, 286n28, 287–88, 359
maternity, 185
matrilineal, 34, 34n3, 39–44, 121, 138, 142, 235, 269, 284, 284n25, 284n26, 304, 310, 359
matrilocal residence/matrilocality, 134, 137, 139, 143–44, 152–53
Mauss, Marcel, 138
Mbae, 276
Meier, Brian, 332
Melpa, 14, 105n29, 122, 124–26
merging rule, 229–30, 233
Merlan, Francesca, 227, 249, 252
metaphor(s), 10, 15, 18, 31, 44n13, 78n14, 119–20, 123, 127, 215, 246, 268, 305, 307, 316, 318–19, 327–38, 353
  of space, 329–30
  visual, 328, 336
metaphorical analogy, 10, 335, 337, **337**
Miao, 278n17
milk kinship. *See* kinship, milk
mobility, 133, 136, 144, 146, 155, 157, 159
Moore, Melinda, 284
Morgan, Lewis Henry, 9, 59, 61–62, 62n4, 63–64, 64n5, 65, 82, 102, 107, 235, 292, 306
morphology, social, 265–66, 269, 289
Mosuo, 26, 86n20, 284n25
mother(s), 3, 5, 8–9, 11, 15, 18, 34, 34n3, 35–36, 39, 42n10, 43, 44n13, 45, 62, 62n3, 64n5, 65–66, 67n7, 73, 75, 77, 80n15, 85, 85n17, 85n18, 86–87, 89, 90n22, 91, 92n23, 93, 100, 100n25, 104–06, 142–43, 154, 178, 181, 183, 187–90, 193–94,

203–07, 207n1, 208–12, 214–17,
  228n1, 229, 229n3, 230–31,
  242, 246, 249, 251–52, 277, 288,
  304, 306, 310, 313, 328–30, 332,
  346–47, 350, 353, 356–59
  adoptive, 15, 332
  biological, 77n14, 85n18, 87, 89,
    142–43, 203, 207, 329
  birth, 194, 210, 332
  foster, 35, 182, 184, 210
  genealogical, 88–89
  suckling, 183, 190
  surrogate, 85n18, 332
mother-in-law, 210n4, 246
Mount Hagen, 122, 124, 127
multilocal residence, 135, 157, **159**
Munda, 276, 288
Murdock, George Peter, 65, 134–35,
  153, 234, 355
Muria, 278n17

Nakane, Chie, 285
Narasimhan, Haripriya, 283, 285–86
nascent-based relational terminology,
  303, 309
natolocal marriage. *See* marriage,
  natolocal
natolocal residence/natolocality, 136,
  140, 147–48, 150–54, 156–59,
  161
Nayar, 284, 284n26, 285
Needham, Rodney, 143, 264, 264n1,
  265, 265n4, 266, 266n5, 268,
  268n8, 270, 270n10, 271,
  271n11, 272–73, 273n14, 275,
  277, 280, 282n20, 282n21, 283,
  289–93, 307
neglect, 210, 212–13, 314
neolocal marriage. *See* marriage,
  neolocal
neolocal residence/neolocality, 147,
  150, 151–52
nerve (*'asab*), 184–85

networks, 18, 133–34, 136, 138,
  143–44, 154, 157, 160–61,
  178, 285
neurology, 328, 331
New Hebrides, 6
new kinship, 204
  relations, 91
  studies, 32, 181, 227
Newman, Stanley, 310–13
Ngarinyin, 231
nonreciprocal address (terms),
  236–37
nuclear family, 3, 5, 9, 14, 33–34,
  45–46, 84, 217, 266–67, 272,
  345, 349
Nuer, 14n5
Numan, 281
Numbulwar, 16, 203, 205, 207–10,
  212–14, 214n5, 215, 215n6,
  216–17

Oceania, 26, 192, 204, 291n35, 348
Ojibwa, 279–81
Omaha, 234–35
  skewing, 207, 231–35, 238, **239**,
    239–40, 242, 271
Omaha-type kinship, 231
  terminologies, 235, 269, 271,
    276, 291n34
Ontario, 279
Orinoco, 74, 140, 280
orphan, 148, 154, 203, 212
overlay, 107, 233, 235, 238–39,
  239n8, 242, 252, 254
Oxford, 263

Paman, 246, 251
Pama–Nyungan family, 232, 239,
  239n7, 240, 243, 246–47, 251
Panoan (Western Amazonian), 358n1
Pantar, 282n20
parallel/cross, 231, 356–57, 359. *See
  also* cross-parallel distinctions
Parkes, Peter, 15, 178, 182

partible paternity. *See* paternity, partible
paternity, 8, 38, 185, 208, 346
  biological, 8, 346
  ignorance of physiological, 38, 10, 36, 36n5, 40n8, 41n9
  partible, 78n12, 347
  physiological, 8, 36, 36n5, 38, 40
  social, 8
patrilineal, 34n3, 138, 142, 160, 235, 269, 285, 359
patrilocal, 152
  band(s), 15, 134
  residence/patrilocality, 136–37
Pecher, Diane, 332–33
Penutian, 234, 234n6
performative effects, 126
performative kinship, 33, 46
Pericliev, Vladimir, 228n1
perinatal association, 211, 215–17
Peru, 74, 280
phenotypic matching, 207
Pilbara, 243, 247, 251
Pinker, Steven, 206, 328–30, 332–33, 350, 351–53
Pintupi, 212, 251
poddy boys/girls, 212
polygyny. *See* marriage, polygynous (polygyny)
Polynesia, 74, 348
Polynesian tattooing, 336
polysemy, 7, 205, 227, 232, 245–46, 248, 254, 266–68
postmarital residence, 133–37, 139–40, 144–48, **150, 151**, 152–55, **153**, 161
pragmatic(s), 16, 119, 123, 127, 227, 249–54, 305–10, 312–13, 315, 317–19
prescriptive alliance, 265, 265n4, 266, 266n4, 267, 269, 270n10, 271
  terminology, 269–70, 272–73, 273n14, 274, 280, 282n20, 283, 290n32
prestations, 270–71, 286

Primary Genealogical Space (PGS), 68, 71–72, 100n25
primary generating term, 100, 100n25, 102
primary relation(s), 63, 67n7, 83, 90n22, 106, 316, 327
procreative kin(ship), 15–17, 32–33, 33n2, 45, 127–79, 179n4, 185, 188, 194
Purum, 270n10, 271n11, 283n23

Radcliffe-Brown, A.R., 10, 65, 73, 93, 134, 136, 230, 269
reduction rules, 228–29, 238, 318
relatedness, 77n14, 79, 133, 144–45, 156, 161, 194, 203, 205–07, 209, 211, 213–17, 267, 333–34, 344, 346–49, 354
relational, 18, 252–53, 305–06, 310, 312–14, 316, 328, 331
  density, 210
  particle(s), 304–05, 309–10, 312, 314–19
  terminology, 17, 303–05, 307–18
relations, 5, 14, 17, 62, 62n4, 63, 67n7, 71–73, 77–78, 78n14, 79, 83–85, 87, 90, 95, 100, 103, 105–06, 120–21, 126, 183, 185, 188–89, 189n9, 193, 195, 208, 214, 242, 277, 280–81, 284n24, 310, 313–17, 319, 327–29, 333, 336, 338, 356, 358
  genealogical, 10, 59, 61–62, 62n4, 63–70, 72n11, 73, 75, 75n12, 76–78, 78n14, 79, 82–83, 89–91, 92n23, 93–95, 99, 100n25, 103–06, 185, 269
  kin(ship), 59, 61–63, 65–67, 70, 72, 74, 77–79, 82–83, 90–91, 93–94, 106, 122, 128, 145, 178, 185, 195, 327
  kin term, 83–85, 87, 89, 99, 100n25, 101

parental, 44n13
sexual (coital), 34, 145, 191, 284, 345
social, 42, 124, 178, 269, 312, 314, 318, 327
remarriage, 13, 154, 160
renaissance of kinship, 227
residence, 133–39, 141, 143, 145–47, 150, 152–54, 156–58, 160–61, 234, 281–82, 314
   bilocal. *See* bilocal residence
   matrilocal. *See* matrilocal residence
   multilocal. *See* multilocal residence
   natolocal. *See* natolocal residence
   postmarital. *See* postmarital residence
Rida'a, 179, 181–82
Rigney, Daniel, 331
River Pumé, 142, 146
Rivers, William H.R., 6, 8, 33, 60–61, 192, 306–10
Rivière, Peter, 266n5
role-based, 306, 313, 316–17, 319
romantic love. *See* love, romantic
Roscoe, Will, 12
rules, 3, 7, 9, 14, 67, 67n8, 68–70, 82, 139, 191, 228–30, 233, 236, 242, 254, 268, 271, 273–74, 282, 290–91, 318, 345, 358–60
   equivalence, 60, 66–67, 67n7, 67n8, 68–71, 76, 82, 106–07, 228, 230–31, 233
   expansion, 228
   extension, 45, 120, 230, **233**, 236, 245, 318
   marriage. *See* marriage, rules
   reduction, 228–29, 238, 318
   social, 236
   structural, 97, 135
Ryder, James W., 6

Sahlins, Marshall, 32, 36, 42, 45, 73, 181, 204, 327–28, 347
Salish, 283
sambandham, 284
Sapir, Edward, 7
Savanna Pumé, 138, 140–42, 144–46, 148, 153, 155–59, 161
Scheffler, Harold K., 3–10, 10n3, 11–19, 31–32, 32n1, 33, 33n2, 35, 36n5, 46, 60–61, 64, 66–67, 69–70, 77, 78n14, 79, 82, 87, 101, 103, 105, 107, 119, 121–22, 128, 133, 142–43, 177, 179, 181, 192, 205, 227–28, 228n1, 230–31, 233, 238–39, 241, 245, 248, 250, 254, 263–64, 265–66, 267–68, 269–70, 271–74, 277, 292–93, 303, 307, 318, 327–29, 332, 338, 344, 347, 355–58, 359, 369. *See also Australian Kin Classification*
   on Aboriginal kin(ship) terminologies, 9–12, 16, 205, 227, 254
   on focality, 15–16, 18, 205
   on genealogy, 266
   on metaphoric extension, 328–29
Schmidt, Gwenda L., 332
Schneider, David, 4, 8, 11–12, 14, 31–32, 33, 33n2, 36, 42n10, 46, 82–83, 89, 107, 121–22, 134, 192, 204, 303–04, 306, 314–15, 348
Schuster, Carl, 328, 336
sections, marriage, 354, 359
Seiler, Hansjacob, 306, 312
semantic(s), 6–7, 10, 16, 32, 64, 66–67, 107, 122–24, 128, 177, 188, 227–28, 228n1, 228n2, 231, 238, 246, 251, 254, 263, 265–66, 266n6, 268, 272, 290, 303, 306, 308, 310, 313, 315, 317–18, 329, 355
   domain, 18, 121, 328–29, 333, 338, 349, 353

Seneca–Iroquois, 62, 82, 271. *See also* Iroquois
Seneca terminology, 62–63, 271–72
sensory-motor terms, 332, 350
Service, Elman R., 15, 26, 134, 136, 307
sex difference(s), 369–72, 382, 389
sexual, 11, 34, 36–40, 40n8, 41n9, 42n10, 86n19, 121–22, 134, 144–45, 147, 183, 191, 346, 369, 370–78, 380–85, 385n2, 386–88, 388n3, 389, 389n3
   behaviour, 18, 369, 370–71, 383
   imprinting, 345
   orientation, 372, 374–75, 378, 382, 385
   relations, 34, 191, 284, 345
Sexual Life of Savages, The, 34, 36, 44n12, 191
sexuality, 26, 317, 369–71, 388n3
Shadid, Anthony, 180–81
sharing, 16, 32, 122, 133, 136–37, 139, 153–54, 156, 160, 191, 205, 214, 216, 281, 331, 347
Sharp, Lauriston, 9
Shaver, Phillip R., 15
Shipibo, 74, 80–81
short-term mating, 371, 373, 389
sibling(s), 5, 11, 12, 45, 63, 65, 66, 66n6, 72n11, 73, 77, 82, 84, 86–87, 87n21, 88, 95–96, 98–100, 100n25, 101–02, 106–07, 125–26, 128, 142–43, 145, 154, 183, 186–88, 191–92, 203, 205, 207, 207n1, 208, 211–13, 215–16, 230–33, 239–42, 242n10, 245, 247, 249, 275–76, 278–79, 282, 288, 292, 304, 345, 346, 356–59
   cores, 281–82
   coresidence, 211, 215
   relation(ship), definition, 99, 100n25, 106–07
   rivalry, 216–17
Silk, Joan, 16, 26, 192, 204–05, 211, 216, 345, 348
Simpson, Jane, 371, 391
Sinhalese, 278, 291n34
Siriono, 7–8, 15, 105, 121, 266, 266n6, 271, 282n21
sister(s), 3–6, 13, 44, 44n12, 63, 66n6, 74, 77–78, 87, 100, 125, 138, 143, 155n1, 178, 183, 189–90, 203–07, 213, 215–17, 228–29, 229n3, 230, 236, 240–41, 246, 281–82, 284, 286n28, 287–88, 304–06, 311, 313, 334, 350, 356–57, 359
skewing, 138, 229–31, 233–36, 238–39, 239n8, 240, 245, 248, 254n16, 271. *See also* Crow skewing; Omaha, skewing
skirting (upstream) spread, 242
Slavey, Wrigley, 282
Smith, James G.E., 280–81
Smith, Mary, 4n1
Smith, William Robertson, 181–84
Sobo, Elisa J., 12
social
   morphology. *See* morphology, social
   organisation, 62, 133, 135–37, 144, 152, 161, 190, 192, 282n20, 309, 313, 338, 343–44, 354, 359–60
   paternity, 8
   semiotics, 309
societies
   complex, 275, 338
   semi-complex, 275
solidarity, 121–22, 124–25, 129, 214
sons by groin, 185, 190
South Asia. *See* Asia, South
spatial cognition, 354
Sperber, Dan, 206–07, 212
Spiro, Melford E., 204
spouse-equation, 239
Sri Lanka, 278
Stacey, Judith, 12
Stanner, William E.H., 39
stratification, 283

structural comparison, 72
structural equation(s), 72, 72n11, 80, 93–98, 101–04, 106
　reciprocal, 97, 101–02
structuralism/structuralists, 263–64, 264n2, 265–66, 266n5, 267–69, 271, 274, 276, 291
structure, 4, 10, 14, 32, 61, 61n2, 64n5, 66n6, 67, 67n7, 68–69 72, 77, 79–82, 86, 90, 90n22, 94, 94n24, 95, **97**, 97–98, 100n26, 101, 107, 120, 124, 133–34, 136, 139, 145, 177–78, 180, 182, 186, 193–95, 268–69, 271n11, 288, 313, 328–39, 331–32, 334, 336, 343–44, 349–54, 358–60
subsistence, 44n13, 133, 135, 139–41, 144, 146, 156–57, 160–61
suckling, 15, 177, 177n1, 178–79, 179n4, 180–14, 184n6, 185–91, 193–95
Sumba, 266n5
symbolism, 37–38, 45
symmetry, 270n10, 271, 357
syncretism, 228, 254n16

tahrim, 188–89
tali, 284n24
Tamil(s), 264, 269, 273n14, 285, 285n27, 286–88
taravad(s), 284, 284n26, 285
Taylor, Anne-Christine, 280
teenager, 215–16
teknonyms, 142
terminology
　bifurcate collateral, 275n16, 283
　bifurcate generation(al), 62n4, 241, 275n16, 283
　cognatic, 282n20, 283
　Crow–Omaha, 271, 276, 291n34
　English, 62, 64, 64n5, 66, 80n15, 89–90, 90n22, 92, 94, 94n24, 96–98
　kinship. *See* kinship, terminology

　lineal, 62n4, 103, 106
　prescriptive, 268–70, 272–73, 273n13, 273n14, 274, 280, 282n21, 283, 290n32
　relational, 17. *See also* Zuni, relational terminology system
　Seneca. *See* Seneca terminology
term(s)
　ascending, 93, 94, 94n24, 95
　descending 95, 101
tetradic kinship. *See* kinship, tetradic
tetradic theory, 275
Tevar castes, 287
Thomas, Northcote, W., 10
Thomas, Wesley, 12
Timor, 266n5
Tiwi, 105, 278
Tongan terminology, 66n6, 93–94, 94n24
total structural analysis. *See* analysis, total structural
Trager, George, 7
transition to modern behaviour, 338
transitional polysemy, 227, 232, **232**, 245–46, 248, 254
transitivity, 270n10
Trautmann, Thomas, 34, 268, 272, 283–84, 291, 355, 356, 359
Trio, 266
trirelational, 252–53
Trobriand(s), 40, 40n7, 41, 41n9, 42, 42n10, 43, 44–45
　Islands (Trobrianders), 8, 13, 34, 34n3, 35, 36–38, 40n8, 41, 43, 60, 121, 347
　kinship, 31, 34, 35n4, 36n5, 45
　men, 39–41
　mythology, 37, 41
　terminology, 43, 70, 100n26
　women, 38–39, 42n10
tsitda, 304–06, 310–12, 315–16
Tyler, Stephen A., 8

Upper Paleolithic, 338
Urarina, 280
urimai, 288
uxorilocality, 150, 153

Venezuela, 134, 136, 140, 141–42, 144, 145, 156, 158, 272
Vezo (of Madagascar), 348–49
virgin birth, 41–42. *See also* birth
virilocality, 150, 153–54
viscous population, 214, 217
vivification, 8

Waka-Kabi, 251
Walker, Harry, 280
Wallace, Anthony F.C., 8, 306, 308
wangulu, 212–13
Warao, 272, 280, 289
websites, 371–73
West, Stuart, 213
Westermarck (effect), 87n21, 345–46
Western Australia. *See* Australia, Western
Western Desert, 213, 242–43, 243n12, 247, 244, 247n14, 250–51, 254
wet-nursing, 15, 182, 184, 184n6
Whistler, Kenneth, 233–34, **233**, **234**
Witowski, Stanley, 289
womb, 39, 44n13, 45, 184–85, 187, 207
women, 12, 14n5, 18–19, 38–40, 40n10, 74, 136, 140, 143–45, 148–49, 151–55, 158, 160, 179, 182–84, 184n6, 186, 191, 191n10, 207–08, 209n3, 210, 212, 253, 278, 284–86, 288, 310, 369–74, 376–78, 381, 383–85, 385n2, 386–88, 388n3, 389, 389n3

Yanomamo, 280
Yap, 121, 306, 348
yapunta, 212
Yolngu, 232, 239, 239n7, 240, 247, 247n14
Yuendumu, 208

Zuni, 17, 303–04, 304n1, 305–06, 310–17
houshold-group roles, **311**
kin and clan, 310
kin-term usage, 304–05
relational terminology system, 303, 305–06, 309–10, 312–15, 317–19
social organisation, 309, 313
Zuni Pueblo, 303, 309, 319